The Comprehensive Guide to
Shipwrecks of
the East Coast

Volume One (1766-1917)

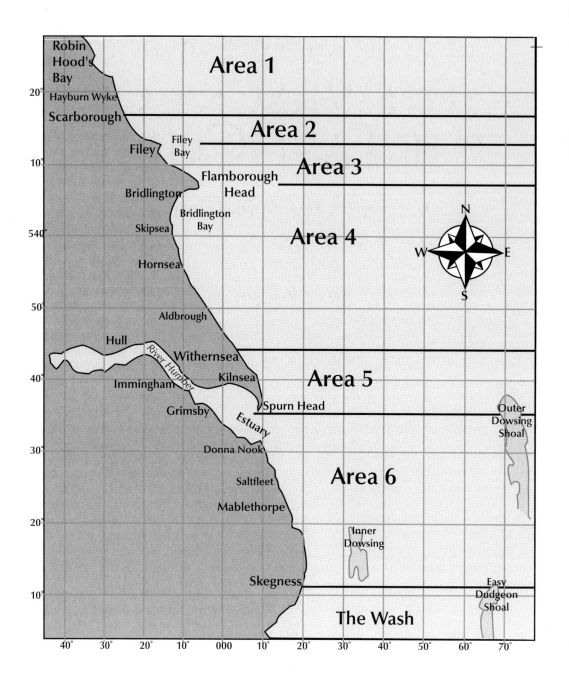

THE COMPREHENSIVE GUIDE TO
SHIPWRECKS OF THE EAST COAST

VOLUME ONE (1766-1917)

RON YOUNG

TEMPUS

The 295-ton Hull-registered steam trawler (H862) *Golden Sceptre* was wrecked on Kettleness Steel on 15 January 1912. (Courtesy of Jonathan Grobler)

First published 2003

PUBLISHED IN THE UNITED KINGDOM BY:
Tempus Publishing Ltd
The Mill, Brimscombe Port
Stroud, Gloucestershire GL5 2QG

PUBLISHED IN THE UNITED STATES OF AMERICA BY:
Tempus Publishing Inc.
2 Cumberland Street
Charleston, SC 29401

British Library Cataloguing in Publication Data.
A catalogue record for this book is available from the British Library.

ISBN 0 7524 2764 4

Typesetting and origination by Tempus Publishing.
Printed in Great Britain by Midway Colour Print, Wiltshire

Contents

Acknowledgements

The amount of information I have received from some people has been mind-boggling and it is something for which I am truly grateful. However, writing this type of book would not have been at all possible without the massive amount of help I have received from the following people and in particular, the Wreck's Officer, Nelson McEachan and his hard-working staff at the Hydrographic Department, especially June Dillon. It is really appreciated and I sincerely hope that we have been able to put a name to quite a number of 'unknown' wrecks over the past year or so.

I know from personal experience how long one can spend in libraries and museum record departments, searching for the details of just one vessel, let alone many dozens. Paul de Keijzer in Holland, known as 'wreckhound' on the internet, is one of those people that devotes this time. Paul, who runs an auto-parts business, has been invaluable in researching the ex-names and companies of ships lost off the English East Coast for me. I know he has spent many hours delving through the Rotterdam Maritime Museum archives. He began diving seventeen years ago and now spends all of his spare time searching for new wrecks. Paul and his diving buddies travel as far as fifty miles out in the North Sea from Holland (weather permitting), between April and November. With his colleagues, he found and identified the wreck of the *Elbe*. When details of their discovery appeared on television and newspapers around the world, including CNN, it brought his group some international fame. Paul is also an author; having written one book. He is in the process of writing two more, when time permits. One of the books is all about the *Elbe* and her fabulous cargo, while the other is describing the most beautiful shipwrecks he has seen.

A massive thank you must go to Michael Lowery of Charlotte, North Carolina, USA. Michael supplied me with most of the information about First World War U-boat patrols and the boat commanders, and he wrote a large section of the introduction to this book. Michael is an economist, writer and U-boat researcher and has taught at the Charlotte University of North Carolina and other area colleges. His writings have appeared in over a hundred papers, including the *Christian Science Monitor*, the *Charlotte Observer* and the (Raleigh) *News and Observer*. He may be contacted by email at: mlowery@infi.net.

Bill Butland of Lingwood, Norwich, has been a huge source of information and helped me with my two previous books on shipwrecks: *The Comprehensive Guide to Shipwrecks of the North East Coast*, Volumes 1 & 2. Bill and I first corresponded with each other when I wrote articles for the monthly *Sub Aqua Scene* and *Underwater World* magazines in the mid-1980s. At the time he was involved in writing and documenting the British Sub Aqua Club's Wreck Register. We have been long-term pen friends since then and yet we have never met, but I cannot emphasise how much I have appreciated his help, advice and assistance. Bill was a retired Chartered Civil Engineer and a keen sport diver in his younger days, having taken his first dive in Brittany in 1953. He was so hooked on the underwater environment that he went out and bought a mask, fins and snorkel there and then. In 1956 he joined the British Sub Aqua Club and eventually went on to become the National Equipment Officer on the General Committee. Whilst working in North Wales around 1964, Bill became extremely interested in shipwrecks and began recording information on a card-index system and had probably one of the biggest collections of wreck information in the U.K. As well as his other pastime, photography, he spent much of his retirement assisting a number of authors and answering questions about shipwrecks over the Internet. Sadly, on Tuesday 30 April 2002, while waiting to go into hospital for a major operation on his stomach, the dreaded cancer got the better of him and Bill passed away.

My wife Rose also deserves a big heart-felt thank you for spending so many hours proof reading, which I know is a long and tedious job. She has also had to put up with piles of paper, letters, and clusters of books and information which have lain strewn around my study-room for many months, without ever so much as a mention.

A big thank you goes to Graham Garner, an enthusiastic wreck diver from Garforth, Leeds. Graham has been a major help in supplying me with details of many of the wrecks off the Bridlington and Humber area, which he and his friends have dived on.

An appreciation also applies to Mike Radley, a sport and wreck diver who resides in Bridlington. Mike supplied me with a lot of details about the wrecks in Bridlington Bay.

Ian Spokes of Gateshead deserves a large thank you for his assistance in researching a number of vessels through Newcastle-upon-Tyne's museum archives for me. Ian spent many months researching the 'Great Storm of 1901', with the help of a Lottery grant and Gateshead Council. He and his colleagues searched for and discovered two of the vessels lost off the North East Coast during the storm; the iron 1,335-ton French, full-rigged ship *Quillota*, wrecked off Sunderland, and the iron 1,101-ton Norwegian barque *Inga*, wrecked off Cullercoats, North Tyneside.

Craig Wilson, an enthusiastic local sport diver for sixteen years and a determined wreck-hunter and researcher, deserves a special mention for his help with wrecks off the Dogger Bank.

Many thanks go to Jan Olov Hendig from Sweden for all the information about ships that he has supplied me with. Jan Olov is thirty-seven years old and has a daytime job working as a developer for a Swedish online brokerage company. He has a degree in Computer Science from the Royal Institute of Technology in Stockholm and has been interested in history most of his life, especially the war at sea, and U-boats in particular.

Many thanks to Jonathan Grobler for allowing me to use his photographs of steam trawlers.

For their help and information about shipwrecks, ships, trawlers and U-boats mentioned in this book, I would also like to express my deepest appreciation to the following people: my two buddies Trevor Corner and Joe Fletcher; Steve Lascoe of Fife and crew member of the St Andrews University Archaeological Diving Unit; Jim Porter and his Bosun's Watch web-site, www.fleetwood-trawlers.connectfree.co.uk; Forbes Wilson of the Royal Navy Reserve trawler web-site, www.royal-naval-reserve.co.uk; Siri Holm Lawson of the Second World War Norwegian War-sailors/ships web-site, www.warsailors.com; Barry Wilkinson, (ships of the Royal Navy) and owner/manager of the Navilis Press in Romania; Theodor Dorgeist; Axel Van Eesbreeck; Rainer Kolbicz; Nick Clark; Phil Day of Manchester, a diver and part-owner of ex-naval fleet tender *Sultan Venturer* and ex Ms *Meavy*; Bob Birmingham; Yves Dufeil of Martigues, France; Øistein Thomas Berge; Roger W. Jordan, international author and specialist in maritime history; Vince Edwards (Australia); Breda Wall; Ian Ellison; Dave Evans; Barry Flemming; John Griffiths; Colin Brittain of Whitby and his diver's web-site, www.eskside1.freeserve.co.uk; Steve Carmichael-Timpson, www.divetheworld.org.uk; Klaus-Peter Pohland of Gaillon, France; Ray Richardson of Grimsby and his trawler web-site 'Side Winder' www.gytrawlers.co.uk; Richard Spicer; Richard Driver of the USA for kindly allowing me to use his excellent photographs of pre-First World War warships and submarines; Harry Jaaskelainan; Keith Haywood; John Liddiad and his web-site of underwater photos at www.liddiard.demon.co.uk; David MacBrayne of Scotships; Dave Sowdon; Rob Steventon; Michael Weise of the German-language First World War U-boat web-site, www.u-boot-net.de/index.htm, and Gundhundur Helgason who runs the English Second World War version, www.uboat.net; John Edwards the Keeper of Science & Museum History at Aberdeen Museum; Ron Mapplebeck; local sport diver Rob Steventon; Ken Jackson and his Hull photo-graph web-site, www.hullheritageprints.co.uk; The World Ship Society, worldshipsociety.org; Ned Middleton; Harry Jääskeläinen of Finland; Darren Boardman; Nick Clark of the Royal Navy Patrol Service web-site, www.harry-tates.org.uk/trawlers.htm; Dirk Ludwig; Simon Schnetzke, a U-boat researcher whose home town is Potsdam in Germany; Arthur G. Credland, Keeper of Hull Maritime Museum; Jacco Goossens of Cedex AB, Sweden, for his translations.

There are also a number of other people who have been most helpful, but for reasons of their own, don't want an acknowledgement. However, I am still very grateful for their help.

Introduction

Although in the very early stages of the First World War, surface ships of the Imperial German Navy, (Kaiserliche Deutsche Marine) accounted for many Allied vessels sunk, especially by mines. SMS *Konigin Louise* carried out the first mine-laying operation during this period, on 5 August 1914 in the Thames Estuary. She was also the first ship of the Kaiserliche Deutsche Marine lost, but her mines sank the first British warship, the light cruiser HMS *Amphion*. The minelayers SMS *Nautilus* and SMS *Albatros* also laid mines along the East Coast during the month of August and they too accounted for quite a number of Allied vessels being sunk.

While the broad outlines of the First World War at sea are well known, the specifics of U-boat operations off the East Coast warrant a few words. Germany, like all naval powers, entered the First World War without any real appreciation of the potential of submarines. Germany, however, was soon effectively blockaded by the Royal Navy in a manner it had not foreseen and it regarded it as illegal. The obvious solution was a blockade of its own, using the only weapon available – submarines. In March 1915 U-boats first engaged (temporarily) in 'unrestricted' submarine warfare (attacking without warning, often while submerged) in an attempt to force Britain out of the war. The policy became a permanent one from October 1916 onwards, when Germany became willing to pay the inevitable price of this policy – the involvement of America in the war – for a chance at victory. Such a U-boat-based campaign could not be won off the English East Coast and a German victory at sea using the submarine, depended upon starving Britain out. This meant first and foremost, reducing the number of vessels reaching Channel and Irish Sea ports from America, and from the Mediterranean through the Bay of Biscay. However, operations off the East Coast were an important element of German strategy. Relatively simple to conduct, such patrols could significantly cut into the Scandinavian trade, coastal shipments, as well as trade for distant destinations from the Humber and Tyne ports in particular. Unrestricted warfare also contained an element of terror – it created a perception of a high risk of sinking, the hope was to scare ship owners and captains into avoiding British ports entirely.

The Early Years

Until mid–1916, the effects of U-boats off the East Coast were limited. German policy see-sawed widely until late 1916, from periods of unrestricted submarine warfare, to a restricted campaign operating according to Cruiser (Prize) Rules, to periods of avoiding action almost entirely. At times sinking British and neutral merchant ships was a priority, at other times, it was at best a secondary aim.

Even if U-boats had aggressively pursued unrestricted submarine warfare throughout the period, Germany lacked sufficient numbers of boats to mount a sustained threat to shipping, until well into 1916. They had only twenty-nine boats in commission as of 1 August 1914 and by 1 January 1915, the figure had only climbed to thirty-four. Germany's modern boats were all large, ocean-going vessels; concentrating them against the East Coast would have been a serious misallocation of resources.

German submarines were also frequently called on to support surface-ship operations. While these operations did provide the very occasional spectacular success, such as sinking the light-cruisers HMS *Nottingham* and *Falmouth* on 19 August 1916, for the most part they were unproductive. Of course, a U-boat standing watch for Royal Navy movements was a U-boat that was not out hunting for merchant ships.

This is not to say that U-boats did not operate off the English East Coast in 1915 or the first half of 1916, because on occasion they did. U 12, for example sank the steamer *Tangistan* off Flamborough Head on 9 March 1915 and U 10, U 23, U 25 and U 57, among others, made their presence felt as well. However, the losses inflicted by the boats were just more of a nuisance than anything else.

The Onslaught Begins

The pace of sinking vessels rapidly picked up from September 1916 onwards, as the restraints were removed. Of particular importance was the introduction of more powerful boats in the Flanders Flotilla. Since mid-1915, the Imperial Germany Navy had based small torpedo-attack UBI type U-boats, barely over 100 tons, and mine-laying UCI type boats, out of the occupied Belgian ports of Ostende and Zeebrugge. These vessels, though something of a pest in the Thames Estuary, off Folkestone and in the Downs areas, lacked the range, speed, and reliability to operate very far from home – although a very few mine-laying sorties did venture as north as the Humber.

The UBII, UCII and UBIII classes addressed the shortcomings of earlier boats; the UBII class UB 18-47, first introduced in January 1916, allowed Flanders-based boats to effectively operate off the British East Coast and in the Channel, though speed and armament of these boats was still somewhat limited. They only had two torpedo tubes and carried four, then later, six torpedoes. The UCII class UC 16-UC 79, came into service from September 1916 onwards and added a new dimension to the German offensive. In addition to having three torpedo tubes and seven torpedoes, they also carried eighteen mines. The UB III class, UB 48 and upwards, was in service from August 1917. They didn't carry mines, but were faster and carried five torpedo tubes, plus ten torpedoes. All three classes carried a deck-gun of between 5cm and 10.5cm (1.97in and 4.13in) but usually an 8.8cm (3.46in). Boats of these classes were also used by the Germany-based submarine flotillas, which also employed them along the East Coast. In the hands of aggressive commanders such as Otto Steinbrinck, Paul Hundius and Johannes Lohs, such craft were capable of inflicting a tremendous toll amongst Allied shipping.

U-boats spent the majority of their time on the surface during the First World War, although attacks were generally made while submerged. Later in the war, an increasing number of attacks were made at night, while surfaced. The deck-gun was the preferred manner for sinking smaller vessels of a few hundred tons and under, though this can be taken only as a general rule, because they also used scuttling charges or opened sea-valves when sinking fishing boats.

However, on occasion, even vessels under one hundred tons would be sunk by torpedo and a bold U-boat commander would sometimes even attempt to sink a decent sized steamer with his deck-gun.

The Royal Navy Responds

By May 1917, it was quite clear that without significant changes Britain would lose the war. U-boats in all theatres combined to sink over 800,000 tons of shipping in April, the highest monthly total of either world war. Existing anti-submarine measures had proven to be utterly ineffective.

The Royal Navy's answer was to introduce convoys from May 1917 onwards. By concentrating ships in a smaller area, U-boats soon had a more difficult time finding targets. Merely locating a convoy did not guarantee success; quite often U-boats failed to score even after discovering a large convoy. Germany soon realized the power of convoys, and attempted to exploit the weaknesses of the system. U-boat operations, for example, shifted closer to shore from August 1917, hoping to catch merchant ships before they joined or after they had left convoys. The introduction of coastal-convoys from June 1918, however, eliminated whatever hope had remained for the U-boats. Of the 16,000 plus ships that sailed in East Coast convoys in 1918, only thirty-five were lost due to U-boat attacks.

Another important development also occurred in 1918, when an effective combination of mines and patrol-craft was finally put into place in the Strait of Dover. Flanders-based U-boats could no longer reach their preferred hunting grounds in the western English Channel, the Bay of Biscay and the Irish Sea via the Dover Straits; they would have had to sail around the British Isles to the north of Scotland to reach these areas. While some boats did make these long treks, many were reassigned to waters that could be reached more easily. The number of boats operating off the East Coast increased substantially, although this did not translate into additional Allied losses.

How to use this book

This book is a form of dictionary, detailing practically every known vessel lost up to the end of 1917. It is about wrecks within a reasonable distance from land, but ones that can still be seen on the seabed, from Robin Hood's Bay down to the area off Skegness, south from the Humber Estuary.

Many thousands of vessels, just in the last 100 years or so, have foundered or been wrecked off this part of the East Coast of England. Vessels were lost for a variety of reasons, but a great many of them came to grief due to U-boat attacks. In the early years before the First World War, many ships and boats were built of wood, which meant they usually disintegrated within hours of coming to grief. However, even many hundreds of the iron or steel vessels that were driven into shallow water for whatever reason, have now disappeared, especially after being left to the natural elements. Some of their stories make interesting reading, but these days, there is nothing actually left of them for anyone to see. This book is about those wrecks, which can still be found today in various conditions. With many others the elements have taken their toll and, because some were classed as navigational hazards, the authorities dispersed them, often by demolition. Very little is left of many wrecks, just the last bare remnants of what used to be a proud ship. However, many dozens of others are partially or completely intact, just as they were on the day they went down to a watery grave. To help in differentiating between the various conditions of the wrecks and as a quick reference guide, a 'star-rated' system has been devised, using one star (★) to five stars (★★★★★). One star represents a wreck-site where very little remains, except perhaps the boilers, engine, or a few pieces of iron or steel debris. A wreck with five stars indicates one that is still completely intact, with lots of interesting things to see when diving on it. The star-ratings between the extremes of one and five are wrecks in varying sizes and states of preservation or decay. In some cases, the surrounding scenery has also been given a star-rated system. Here one star indicates a rather flat and featureless sea-bed surrounding the wreck-site, with little or nothing of interest. At the other extreme, five star scenery indicates an area around the wreck-site where there are interesting reefs, maybe covered in an abundance of soft corals or possibly caves, and marine life such as fish and crustaceans.

Depth

The depth shown, will be one of two things: 1. What was actually registered by the diver or boat's echo-sounder at the time the wreck-site was visited, and the information received from the person giving the report.

2. In the majority of cases, the lowest astronomical depth will be shown, which is usually the same as that shown on the Admiralty chart. This represents the very lowest depth that will ever be encountered on the lowest spring tide. It will also mean that on average, there may be up to another five metres or so in depth over the wreck-site, depending of course, on what time and date the site is visited. However, where it is an astronomical depth reading, the reader will be informed of this in the last paragraph on the 'Wreck-site'. The reference co-ordinates (latitude and longitude) supplied for each wreck is mostly WGS84 (GPS) but in some cases OAGB and Decca conversions have been used; they should all be reasonably accurate. Most of the positions have been surveyed for the Hydrographic Dept; so they are very accurate. Others have been supplied in good faith by individual divers, sub aqua clubs, diving club officers,

charter-boat operators, survey-boat personnel, fishermen, and so on. Each one has been doubly checked on the Admiralty charts and cross referenced to ensure they are as accurate as possible. However, users of this guide should bear in mind that: a) some areas of the seabed have not been reliably surveyed for many years, which means that there may not be a wreck marked down on the Admiralty chart in the position offered and b) GPS and/or Decca navigators all vary slightly from one unit to another and the accuracy of the position usually depends on factors such as how many satellites the unit picks up and, in the case of Decca, weather conditions at the time when the position was plotted. Therefore the exact position of a wreck-site cannot be completely guaranteed. It may require a few minutes of your time searching the immediate vicinity to locate the wreck.

Reference

Two sets of co-ordinates may have been suggested for the position of some shipwrecks. Where '**Also:**' is given below 'Reference:' the co-ordinate is for the same wreck, but a different part of it. Where '**Also given:**' is used it indicates that two completely different sets of co-ordinates have been offered or suggested for that particular wreck and, because the author was unsure which of them are correct, both sets have been supplied; in this way the interested reader can check both of them.

Location

The location of the wreck, and its distance from a certain point or place, should be fairly accurate, according to the Meridian Raster Chart Display System and A.R.C.S, but it cannot be totally guaranteed.

A quick perusal of this book shows that an extraordinary number of vessels were lost to German submarines (U-boats), especially during the First World War. On reading the majority of reference books relating to shipwrecks where a vessel was lost due to a U-boat, most, if not all books make no mention as to what eventually happened to the U-boats. The author, like many other people, was curious and often wondered what eventually did happen to the various German submarines mentioned. So, for the benefit of the readers, information is included in an additional chapter.

Equivalent Ranks

Owing to the fact that there is a lot of information about Royal Navy vessels, U-boats and their patrols and commanders, etc., the following is a list of the equivalent officer ranks and abbreviations for them, in the Imperial German Navy and Royal Navy during the First World War:

Imperial German Navy		Royal Navy	
Kapitan	(Kap.)	Captain	(Capt.)
Korvettenkapitan	(KvKpt.)	Commander	(Cdr)
Kapitanleutnant	(Kplt.)	Lieutenant Commander	(Lt Cdr)
Oberleutnant zur See	(Oblt.z.S.)	Lieutenant	(Lt)
Leutnant zur See	(Lt)	Sub-Lieutenant	(S-Lt)
		Skipper (RNR)	(Skpr)

CHAPTER 1

Robin Hood's Bay to Scarborough

Area 1 (N54 29' to N54 18')

MODEMI
Wreck: ****
Depth: 50m
Reference: N54 29' 244 W000 28 636
Location: 3 miles NE of North Cheek at Robin Hood's Bay

The *Modemi* was a steel 1,481-ton Norwegian steamship that was registered at the port of Christiania. She had dimensions of 74.06m in length, an 11.58m beam and a draught of 4.77m. Antwerp Engineering Co. built her as the *Modemi* at Antwerp in 1912 and I.A. Christensen owned her at the time of loss. Her single iron screw propeller was powered by a 3-cylinder triple expansion steam engine that developed 156hp using one boiler. Her cylinders measured 48.26cm, 78.74cm and 129.54cm. MacColl & Pollock Ltd at Sunderland built her centrally-positioned machinery and she had one deck.

On 17 November 1917, the *Modemi* was torpedoed and sunk by the Imperial German U-boat, SM UC 48. The steamer was in ballast on passage from Rouen for the Tyne, under the command of Captain L.M. Jensen. It is understood that all of her crew were lost. On 15 March 1919, UC 48 was supposed to be transferred to Brest, but instead, the crew scuttled the boat.

Wreck-site
The wreck, believed to be that of the steamer *Modemi*, is orientated in an almost north to south direction. She lies on a seabed of dirty sand, shell, mud and gravel in a general depth of 50m, the lowest astronomical depth. She is said to be partially buried with the highest 6m section situated amidships where her collapsed bridge structure once stood. She is now well broken up and decayed, with her boiler, condenser and engine exposed. There is reported to be broken machinery, twisted, flattened and bent copper pipes and steel plates jumbled together around the engine area where part of a derrick or lifeboat-davit stands out of the pile. Few fish have been observed around the wreck-site, but she may have large congers or ling hiding amongst the pipes.

The wreck-site is dark and gloomy and a good torch is essential. Tidal streams are very strong and underwater visibility is pretty grim most of the year, but improves during the summer.

EAGLESCLIFFE No.2
Wreck: ***
Depth: 49m
Reference: N54 29 011 W000 27 803
Location: 3.21 miles NE of North Cheek at Robin Hood's Bay
Also suggested: N54 17 160 W000 07 730
Location: 9.05 miles E from Scarborough Rock

The *Eaglescliffe* No.2 was a 101-ton iron British steamer registered at the port of Middlesbrough. She was 32.61m long with a beam of 6.25m. The vessel was launched as the *Eaglescliffe* No.2 at Stockton in 1870 for J. Smith of Middlesbrough, who was the owner at the time of loss. Her single iron screw propeller was powered by a 2-cylinder compound steam engine that used one boiler (being an early steamship, she would probably have also been fitted with masts and auxiliary sails). On 6 January 1873 the vessel, under the command of Capt. Postgate, was on passage from Middlesbrough for Dunkirk when she disappeared somewhere off Scarborough. She was carrying a crew of ten and what was referred to as a 'dead-weight cargo', 240 tons of cast pig iron ingots.

Wreck-site

The *Eaglescliffe* was last reported somewhere off Scarborough, but then she was never seen or heard of again. However, the author has suggested two possible sites.

At the first coordinates, the wreck of an old iron-hulled vessel is orientated in a west-north-west to east-south-east direction. She lies on a seabed of sand, shells, mud and gravel, in a general depth of 49m, the lowest astronomical depth. The wreck is totally collapsed, badly decayed and broken up, with her centrally-positioned boiler and compound engine being the highest point at 5m. Both of these are now visibly exposed and surrounded by a mound of iron debris and flattened, twisted lengths of copper piping. Her propeller stands upright, just forward of the boiler and held in place by her own shaft on the starboard side. Her aft and foreword holds, which have collapsed, are filled with large piles of cast pig iron ingots. The wreck-site is very dark and coated in thick sediment. Little else is known about the wreck and it is not known if the ship's bell has been recovered to proclaim officially if she is the long-lost *Eaglescliffe*.

The second coordinates are for the remains of an old wreck lying nine miles east of Scarborough Rock. She is marked on the Admiralty charts as 'foul' ground, which means nothing stands more than 2m high. The surrounding seabed is mud, sand, gravel, black shells and rock, lying in a general depth of 49m. What remains is partially buried, totally collapsed and well dispersed, but there is evidence of a cargo of iron ingots scattered around the site. Tidal streams are very brisk and underwater visibility is very poor most of the time.

GRANIT, ex SOUTH MOOR

Wreck: ***
Depth: 50m
Reference: N54 28 694 W000 26 286
Location: 3.68 miles NE of North Cheek at Robin Hood's Bay

The *Granit* (signal letters JSKV) was a schooner-rigged iron 927-ton (747 under-deck tons and 540 net tons) Swedish-registered steamship with dimensions of 63.70m in length, a 9.15m beam and a draught of 5.01m. Palmers of Newcastle-upon-Tyne built her as the *South Moor* under special survey over eleven months in 1877 for T.P. Wood of London, her original master being Captain Noal. Her single iron screw propeller was powered by a 2-cylinder compound steam engine that developed 113hp using one single-ended boiler working at a pressure of 5.2 bar. There were four plain furnaces, with a grate surface of 152.4cm. A new donkey boiler was fitted in 1906. Palmers of Newcastle-upon-Tyne built her machinery. Her cylinders measured 68.58cm and 129.54cm with an 83.82cm stroke.

The vessel appears on the 1912-1913 Lloyd's register for the first time as the *Granit*. She was classified as 100A1 under special survey at an inspection in April 1912 at Rotterdam, where her boiler and tail shaft were also surveyed. Presumably this was for new owners when she changed ownership and name. Her boilers and machinery were surveyed by Lloyd's in March 1911, as well as a No.2 survey at Shields. A new boiler was installed under special survey in September 1901 and she also had her second No.3 survey carried out at Shields in September 1901.

She had one deck, two tiers of beams, four bulkheads cemented, a 7.01m quarterdeck, 10.97m bridgedeck and an 8.23m forecastle. The *Granit* also had a 20.32cm bar-keel, a moulded depth of 5.36m, a summer freeboard of 68.58cm amidships, water ballast in double bottoms 17.68m aft and 14.94m forward.

Trading Steamship Co. Ltd owned her from 1886 until 1887-1888, with Captain E. George her master. In 1902-1903 the Lloyd's register gives the master as Captain F. Koster from 1892 and says Trading Steamship Co. Ltd was in liquidation. The register in 1907-1908 gives her owners as Trading Steamship Co., with Falconer Ross & Co. as managers, with Captain F. Thompson from 1903. In 1911-1912 Falconer Ross and Co. owned her and she was registered at the port of London, with Captain J. Thompson the master from 1910. Ångf. Aktien Bohuslän, who owned the vessel at the time of loss, purchased her in 1911 and renamed her *Granit*. J.E. Lindbom managed her, the master being Captain O.A. Olsson and she was registered at Lysekil in Sweden.

On 14 July 1912, the *Granit* foundered and was lost following a collision with the Newcastle-upon-Tyne-registered steamship *Saxon Prince* off North Cheek at Robin Hood's Bay. The *Granit* was in ballast on passage from Rotterdam for Warkworth.

Wreck-site

This wreck, which is orientated in an almost north-east to south-west direction, could possibly be that of the steamship *Granit*. She lies on a seabed of sand, broken shell, mud and gravel, in a general depth of 50m, the lowest astronomical depth. She is well broken up, decayed and totally collapsed, with the highest point at 4m being where her boiler, donkey-engine condenser and engine are located and all visibly exposed. Most of the wreck is a mound of iron debris, broken machinery, bits of hollow mast, iron bollards, etc., which are intermingled with bent and flattened copper pipes and various iron or brass cogs/wheels, brass flanges and valves. All of the wreck remains are coated in hard white marine worm casings and soft corals, while the seabed has masses of brittle starfish slithering about. Tidal streams are very strong and the underwater visibility is fairly grim much of the time.

GARTHWAITE

Wreck: ★★★★
Depth: 47m
Reference: N54 28 561 W000 29 269
Location: 2.34 miles NE of North Cheek at Robin Hood's Bay

The *Garthwaite* was a steel 5,659-ton British steamship that was registered at the port of London. She had dimensions of 121.92m in length, a 15.84m beam and a draught of 10.05m. W. Dobson & Co. built her at Newcastle-upon-Tyne in 1917 for Sir William Garthwaite of Glasgow, who owned her at the time of loss. Her single iron screw propeller was powered by a 3-cylinder triple expansion steam engine that developed 465hp using three 3SB 9CF boilers, giving her a maximum speed of 11 knots. Her cylinders measured 66.04cm, 109.22cm and 182.88cm-121.92cm. The ship was also armed with three guns: one 11.94cm (4.7in) quick-firing and two 19.05cm (7.5in) howitzers.

At 9.50 on the morning of 13 December 1917, the *Garthwaite* was torpedoed by SM UB 22, an Imperial German U-boat, and she sank three miles north-east of North Cheek at Robin Hood's Bay. The merchantman was in ballast on passage from the Tyne for New York with a crew of forty-three. The torpedo detonated between No.3 and No.4 holds, which caused so much damage that she went down in just four minutes. A ship's gunner, however, still managed to fire one round off from one of the howitzers, at the position he thought the submerged submarine was lurking in. Fourteen of the crew, including the captain, lost their lives; the survivors, who got away in the ship's boats, were picked up by patrol vessels and landed at Whitby.

SM UB 22 was proceeding through one of the 'safe' channels through the German minefields in the Heligoland Bight when the escort, torpedo boat S16, detonated a British mine. The boat sank with all hands, north-west of Heligoland. SM UB 22, which was following close behind, also struck a mine and sank with the loss of her crew of twenty-two, in position N54 40 W06

32.
Wreck-site
The wreck, believed to be that of the large steamer *Garthwaite*, is orientated in a south–south-east to north–north-west direction. She lies on a seabed of dirty sand, mud, shells and gravel in a general depth of 47m, the lowest astronomical depth. The wreck is extremely large and stands 6.5m high around the amidships section, where her engine, condenser and boilers are located. However, the wreck has mostly collapsed, is very decayed and well broken up. Her boilers are visibly exposed through the mountain of collapsed steel plates, ribs, bollards, broken machinery, flattened copper pipes, brass valves, wheels and cogs, etc. Dead man's fingers and colourful anemones adorn much of the upper structures. Her large howitzer guns are still on the wreck and it was from these and her boiler/engine details that the wreck was eventually identified. There are reported to be masses of fish over this wreck so she will be a worthwhile boat-angling venue. The surrounding seabed is reported as being carpeted with thousands of brittle-starfish. Tidal streams are very strong and underwater visibility, like in the rest of this area, is extremely poor to grim much of the time.

CORSICAN PRINCE, ex BRIARDALE
Wreck: ★★★★★
Depth: 46m
Reference: N54 28 478 W000 28 619
Location: 2.5 miles NE of North Cheek at Robin Hood's Bay

The *Corsican Prince* was a steel-hulled 2,776-ton British steamship that was registered at the port of Newcastle-upon-Tyne. She had dimensions of 96.31m in length, a 12.85m beam and a draught of 5.18m. Short Brothers built her as Yard No.289 and launched her as the *Briardale* at Sunderland in 1900 for G.H. Elder & Co. (in liquidation) of Newcastle-upon-Tyne in 1907.

Her single iron screw propeller was powered by a 3-cylinder triple expansion steam engine that developed 265hp using two 2SB 6CF boilers. Her cylinder sizes were 58.42cm, 96.52cm and 157.48cm-106.68cm. North Eastern Marine Engineering Co. Ltd at Sunderland built her centrally-positioned machinery. She had one deck, a 9.45m poop deck, a 24.99m bridge deck and a 9.45m forecastle. In 1907-1908 the vessel was in liquidation. The Prince Line Ltd of Newcastle-upon-Tyne, which was the owner at the time of loss, then purchased her, while J. Knott managed the ship.

At ten o'clock on the morning of 7 February 1917, the submerged Imperial German submarine, SM UB 34, torpedoed the *Corsican Prince*. Captain J.R. Gray was in command of the vessel, which was on passage from Dundee for Dunkirk with an unspecified cargo of timber. The crew of thirty and a pilot on board abandoned ship, some going into the water where a fireman drowned. However, most of the men got safely away in the ship's lifeboats. The U-boat surfaced shortly afterwards and then it submerged again, just prior to the arrival of the steamship *Saint Ninian*. One of the *Saint Ninian*'s boats was sent over to pick up survivors, but her captain did not see the U-boat's periscope or his crewmen in the ship's boat who were waving frantically to warn him of the submarine's presence. At 10.15 a.m. a torpedo was fired at nearly point-blank range and the *Saint Ninian* too was sent to the bottom, along with fourteen of her crew and the pilot. Most of the *Corsican Prince*'s confidential papers went down with the ship, while the survivors from both vessels were picked up by a minesweeper and landed at Whitby later that day. SM UB 34 surrendered to the Allies at the end of the First World War and became British war reparation. She was scrapped at Canning Town in 1922.

Wreck-site
This wreck, believed to be that of the *Corsican Prince*, is orientated almost north to south. She lies on a seabed of dirty sand, mud, shells and gravel, in a general depth of 46m, the lowest astro-

nomical depth. The wreck is quite substantial, standing around 6m from the seabed, but upside down and well broken up, with sections of double bottom lying over her engine and boilers. Her bows and stern-end are totally collapsed and badly broken up with lots of scattered debris, including what appear to be the lifeboat davits and steel bollards. It is not known if the ship's bell has been recovered, but access beneath her hull will be very difficult and dangerous. It is not known how many divers have visited the wreck, but she is reported as being an excellent dive. Soft corals encrust most of the exposed upper parts and the hull is coated in hard white marine worm casings. Cod and some very large ling have been seen around the wreck, which has a number of fishing lures and monofilament fishing lines tangled up in the top of it, so it must be well known to local boatmen as an angling venue. Tidal streams are very strong and underwater visibility is grim much of the time, making a good torch essential. The best time to visit the site is at low slack water on a neap tide after a spell of settled weather, during the summer months.

SAINT NINIAN
Wreck: *****
Depth: 49m
Reference: N54 28 461 W000 28 103
Location: 2.65 miles NE of North Cheek at Robin Hood's Bay

The *Saint Ninian* was a steel 3,026-ton British steamship registered at the port of Glasgow. She had dimensions of 97.53m in length, a 12.8m beam and a draught of 7.16m. D.&W. Henderson & Co. built her at Glasgow in 1894. She was managed by A. Mackay & Co. of Glasgow and owned by the Saint Ninian Steamship Co. Ltd at the time of loss. Her single iron screw propeller was powered by a 3-cylinder triple expansion steam engine that developed 258hp using two 2SB 6PF boilers. Her cylinders measured 60.96cm, 96.52cm and 157.48cm-106.68cm. Hendersons & Co. built her machinery at Glasgow. She had two decks and a superstructure consisting of a 13.72m poop deck, a 19.51m bridge deck and a 9.75m forecastle. The vessel was also armed with a large stern-mounted deck-gun that weighed 610kg and fired 5.44kg shells (12 pounders).

Under the command of Captain J. Muckart on 7 February 1917, the *Saint Ninian* came upon the torpedoed steamship *Corsican Prince*, which was gradually sinking, north-east of Robin Hood's Bay. The *Saint Ninian* was on a voyage from Port Kelah for the Tees with a cargo of pyrites, one passenger (a pilot) and a crew of twenty-seven. The crew had abandoned the sinking vessel after having been attacked by the Imperial German U-boat SM UB 34. The *Saint Ninian* stopped close alongside and one of her lifeboats was sent over to rescue survivors from the freezing sea. Unknown to Captain Muckart, the U-boat had not gone away, but was lying submerged close by. The men in the lifeboat suddenly observed the U-boat's periscope, which was turning towards their ship. They waved and yelled frantically trying to warn Captain Muckart of the imminent danger, but it was too late. At 10.15 a.m. a torpedo was fired at point-blank range and detonated on the *Saint Ninian* between the No.3 hold and the engine room. A huge explosion followed and the steamer sank in just five minutes, taking sixteen men down with her, including Captain Muckart and the pilot. The survivors managed to swim to an upturned lifeboat and clung onto its keel, until they were rescued by a minesweeper and landed at Whitby later that day.

Wreck-site
The wreck is orientated in a north to south direction, with her bows towards the south. She lies on a dirty seabed of sand, mud, shells and gravel, in a general depth of 49m, the lowest astronomical depth. The wreck is said to be huge, lying level on the seabed, but the amidships and stern section to the north are still reasonably intact, standing 11m high and listing to the port side. Lots of brass shell cases are strewn around at the stern end with a mass of other broken, decaying debris. The wreck has been positively identified by the ship's bell, but it is not known how many divers have visited the wreck or whether her bridge equipment and navigational

instruments, etc. are still around. She is reported as being an excellent dive site that will obviously take a number of dives to explore the whole wreck. Soft corals and anemones adorn the upper structures, but it is very possible that trawl nets may be entangled with it also. Large cod and ling of 10-15kg have been observed on and around the site and a number of enormous lobsters have been seen. This wreck will be a very notable boat-angling venue when weather conditions permit. Tidal streams are very strong and underwater visibility is nearly always very poor to grim, but improves during the summer months. Best time to dive the wreck-site is at low slack water on a neap tide and after a spell of settled dry weather and westerly winds.

BALLATER
Wreck: ★★★
Depth: 50m
Reference: N54 28 444 W000 27 320
Location: 3 miles NE of North Cheek at Robin Hood's Bay

The *Ballater* was an iron 741-ton British steamship that was registered at the port of Aberdeen. She had dimensions of 61.2m in length, an 8.3m beam and a draught of 4.7m. G. Hall, Russell & Co. built her in 1876 for J.A. Davidson of Aberdeen. Her single iron screw propeller was powered by a 2-cylinder compound steam engine that used one boiler. Adams Brothers at Newcastle-upon-Tyne, who were the owners at the time of loss, purchased her in 1885.

On 20 August 1886, the *Ballater* was on passage from the Tyne for Malta when she foundered four miles east from Whitby High Light after a collision with the London-registered steamship *Ceto*. The *Ballater*, which was under the command of Captain A. Wood, was carrying a cargo of coal and a crew of fifteen. With a very light variable wind blowing at the time, weather conditions were calm, but the Yorkshire coast was blanketed in a dense fog. The crew, none of whom were injured or lost, are believed to have taken to the ship's boat, while the other steamer, *Ceto*, which was in ballast, carried on with her voyage. The offending vessel, *Ceto*, foundered just a few hours later following a collision with the London-registered steamship *Lebanon*.

Note: There is also a possible chance that this wreck could also be that of the *Kathleen Lily*.

KATHLEEN LILY. Ex-EIDSVAAG, ex-ALBAN, ex-ADELAER, ex-BJORN, ex-JEMTLAND, ex-BRAGE
The *Kathleen Lily* was a wooden 521-ton British-registered schooner that had dimensions of 49.68m in length and an 8.22m beam. W. Haggesund at Sundswall built her as the *Brage* in 1872. F.A. Hobbs owned her at the time of loss, although another report says Hobbs, Linsley & Co. of Grimsby (Bargate Steamship Co. Ltd). She was equipped with schooner-rigged sails and an iron screw propeller, powered by a 3-cylinder triple expansion steam engine that used one boiler.

On 29 March 1917, the vessel was under the command of a Captain Woods, when she was rocked by a violent explosion at 2.45 p.m. The steamer was on passage from the Tyne for Boulogne, carrying a cargo of coke and a crew of fourteen. The chief officer, who was below decks at the time, rushed up to find the ship's boats being cleared away by the captain and crew. Unfortunately however, the davits and boats just fell away overboard still tied together, the bolts and sockets holding them having been loosened through the force of the blast. The ship was rapidly sinking and within a matter of minutes she was submerged to the mainmast. Her crew had to abandon ship by going into the sea, with Captain Wood being the last to leave. Just ten minutes after the explosion, the *Kathleen Lily* went down to the bottom. Very soon, a number of minesweepers were at the scene and picked up her crew. Captain Wood and four other crewmen had unfortunately drowned, but the Chief Officer and five men were picked up, along with the dead, and landed at Whitby. Another four men were landed at Scarborough. SM UC 31 laid the mines.

Wreck-site

The wreck, believed to be that of the steamer *Ballater*, or possibly the *Kathleen Lily*, is orientated in an east, north-east to west, south-west direction. She lies on a seabed of sand, mud and broken shells, in a general depth of 50m, the lowest astronomical depth. The wreck is said to be completely collapsed, decayed, well broken up and partially buried, covering an area of about 40m by 12m. The highest section of just under 4m is most likely the position where her engine and boiler are located and are at the western end of the wreck. Tidal streams are very strong and the underwater visibility in this region is usually very poor to dismal. Extra care will be needed, just in case there are nets entangled with the wreckage. Being a small wreck-site, there will be very few fish around so she will be of little value to boat-anglers.

QUAGGY, ex GLENPARK

Wreck: ★★★★★
Depth: 50 m
Reference: N 54 28 194 W 000 26 020
Location: 3.49 miles NE of North Cheek at Robin Hood's Bay

The *Quaggy* was a steel 993-ton British steamship registered at the port of London. She was 67.66m in length, with a 9.6m beam and a draught of 3.75m. G. Brown & Co. built her at Greenock as the *Glenpark* in 1904. The South Metropolitan Gas Co. Ltd owned her at the time of loss. Her single iron screw propeller was powered by a 3-cylinder triple expansion steam engine that developed 99hp using one 1SB 3CF boiler. Her cylinders measured 40.64cm, 66.04cm and 111.76cm. The centrally-positioned machinery was built by Ross & Duncan at Glasgow. She had one deck, a well deck and a superstructure consisting of a 46.94m quarterdeck and a 9.14m forecastle. She was armed with a stern-mounted deck-gun that fired 2.72kg shells (6 pounders).

On 11 April 1917, the *Quaggy* was on passage from London for the Tyne, under the command of a Captain MacFarlane, when she was rocked by a massive explosion between the bridge and foremast at 11.15 a.m. Two crewmen, who were up on the fore part of the deck, died instantly while the rest of the crew, seventeen in all including the captain, abandoned ship in the boats. The steamer went down in just seven minutes, taking all of the vessel's confidential papers with her. The survivors were picked up by a trawler and later transferred to a Royal Navy torpedo boat destroyer, which landed them at Hartlepool later that day. SM UC 31 had laid the mines.

Wreck-site

The wreck is reported as orientated in a north-east to south-west direction. She lies on a dirty sand, mud, pebble and gravel seabed in a general depth of 50m, the lowest astronomical depth. Her remains are said to be still fairly substantial, lying in two sections about 10m apart. The largest section to the south-west is about 65m in length and nearly 8m high at the area where she broke in two parts. The smaller section is in the region of 30m long. The superstructure has now collapsed, but her propeller is still in place at the stern end. The highest parts of the wreck have lots of dead man's fingers adorning them and large cod and a number of ling are in evidence, sheltering beneath the overhanging debris. It is very likely the ship's bell has now gone, which would probably be inscribed '*Glenpark*' and '1904', the date she was built. The wreck is said to be an excellent wreck-dive and should make an interesting boat-angling venue. Tidal streams are strong and the underwater visibility is usually poor to grim, making a powerful torch essential. Visibility improves significantly during the summer months, with the best time to dive on her being during a neap tide after a spell of settled dry weather and light westerly winds.

HARROW
Wreck: ★★★★
Depth: 42m
Reference: N54 28 128 W 000 30 469
Location 1.66 miles NE of North Cheek at Robin Hood's Bay

The *Harrow* was a steel 1,777-ton British steamship, registered at the port of London. She measured 81.78m in length with an 11.45m beam and a draught of 5.18m. S.P. Austin & Son built her at Sunderland in 1900 and Cory Colliers Ltd owned her at the time of loss. Her single iron screw propeller was powered by a 3-cylinder triple expansion steam engine that developed 194hp using two 2SB 6CF boilers. Her cylinders measured: 50.80cm, 83.82cm and 137.16cm. The centrally-positioned machinery was built at Sunderland by W. Allan & Co. Ltd. She had one deck, a well deck and a superstructure consisting of an 8.23m poop deck, a 22.56m quarterdeck, a 15.24m bridgedeck and an 8.84m forecastle. She was also armed with a large stern-mounted deck-gun that fired 5.90kg shells.

On 8 September 1917, the *Harrow* was in convoy, on passage from Granton for London with a cargo of coal, when she was torpedoed by SM UB 41. The torpedo detonated on the ship's port quarter at 6.45 p.m., instantly killing the chief officer and one gunner and leaving another gunner seriously injured. Captain B.R. Davison was injured when the force of the blast threw him out of his cabin. The ship's stern end was shattered and her propeller and rudder were blown completely away. The surviving crewmen abandoned ship at 7 p.m. and were picked up by an escort vessel and taken to Whitby, about the same time as the *Harrow* went to the bottom.

SM UB 41 disappeared and may have been lost in the extensive British minefield laid in September 1917, or in the minefield laid by SM UC 55 on 9 July. There is also the possibility that she was lost through navigational or equipment failure, or perhaps even through a drill procedure that went fatally wrong.

Wreck-site
The wreck, which has always been thought to be that of the *Harrow*, is lying on a seabed of mud, sand, gravel and pebbles in a general depth of 42m, the lowest astronomical depth. She is reported to be very substantial, partially buried, standing intact and upright from stern to bridge. Her bows are partly broken off the main wreck, standing 7m proud of the seabed and covered in an array of soft corals. The highest section is amidships, where her engine, boiler and machinery are located, and these are also covered in soft corals. Her large stern-mounted gun is said to be still in place in the poop deck area. A wave of sand comes up the hull side and covers part of the vessel's forward hold; however, her overall shape can still be made out. It will take a number of dives to explore this wreck and to observe all the most interesting areas where they have collapsed. The wreck-site is reported to be a very dark and eerie dive requiring the use of a powerful torch/lamp and visibility is seldom more than a metre or so, however it significantly improves during the middle summer months on neap tides and a spell of settled dry weather. On descending to the wreck-site, shoals of large pollack and pout whiting are to be seen hovering over the highest sections, while cod have been observed under the wreckage, making this a good boat-angling venue. Tidal streams are strong, making this a low slack water dive.

Note: This wreck was always believed to be that of the steamship *Harrow*, but the vessel used two boilers and it has been reported that there is only one boiler on this wreck. There appears to have been no positive identification of the wreck, so it is possible that she may be something else.

AIGBURTH
Wreck: ★★★★
Depth: 46m
Reference: N54 26 708 W 000 27 919
Location: 2.03 miles E of North Cheek at Robin Hood's Bay

The *Aigburth* was a steel 824-ton British-registered steamship that measured 59.43m in length, with a 9.44m beam and a draught of 3.65m. John Fullerton & Co. Ltd built her at Paisley in 1917 and A. Rowland & Co. owned her at the time of loss. Her single iron screw propeller was powered by a 3-cylinder triple expansion steam engine that used one 1SB 3PF boiler and gave her a maximum speed of 9 knots. Her cylinders measured 38.74cm, and 104.14cm-76.20cm. Ross & Duncan built her aft-positioned machinery at Glasgow. She was also armed with one stern-mounted HA gun that fired 2.72kg shells (6 pounders).

At 3.15 p.m. on 5 December 1917, the *Aigburth* was torpedoed by SM UB 75, two miles east of North Cheek at Robin Hood's Bay. The steamer was on passage from the Tyne for Treport with an unspecified cargo of coal when the torpedo detonated amidships, killing the captain and ten of her crew. The second engineer and second mate found themselves in the sea, clinging to floating wreckage, and were picked up by a patrol vessel. The only other survivor, a ship's gunner, managed to swim to the patrol boat and the three men were landed at North Shields later that day. SM UB 75 was listed as missing, presumed lost off Flamborough Head, about 13 December 1917, in an area that had extensive British minefields.

Wreck-site
The wreck lies on a dirty seabed of sand, mud and shells in a general depth of 46m, the lowest astronomical depth. She lies in two sections: the part to the north is orientated in a nearly north to south direction and is some 35m long and nearly 6m high. The highest part is where her aft-positioned engine and boiler are located. The other, longer, part, is 45m in length and well broken up, it lies south-east to north-west. She should be interesting to explore, and a large number of lobsters have been reported around the wreck-site. She was positively identified when the ship's bell was recovered. This wreck may be worth marking down as a boat-angling venue, because there are a fair number of fish to be seen around it. Tidal streams are fairly strong and the visibility is usually rather grim, but she is still well worth a visit. The best time to dive is on a neap tide, at slack low water and after a spell of settled dry weather during the summer months.

HIGHGATE
Wreck: ★★★★
Depth: 47m
Reference: N54 26 345 W000 26 586
Location: 2.81 miles ESE of North Cheek at Robin Hood's Bay

The *Highgate* was a steel 1,780-ton British steamship registered at the port of London. She was 81.73m long, with an 11.45m beam and a draught of 5.18m. She was built by S.P. Austin & Son at Sunderland in 1899 and Cory Colliers Ltd of London owned her at the time of loss. Her single iron screw propeller was powered by a 195hp 3-cylinder triple expansion steam engine that used two 2SB 6PF boilers. Her cylinders measured 52.07cm, 83.82cm and 137.16cm-99.06cm. George Clark Ltd at Sunderland built her machinery. She had one deck, a well deck and a centrally-positioned superstructure consisting of an 8.23m poop deck, a 22.56m quarterdeck, a 15.24m bridge deck and an 8.84m forecastle. She was also armed with a stern-mounted deck-gun that fired 1.36kg shells (3 pounders).

On 7 December 1917, the *Highgate* was torpedoed and sunk by the submerged Imperial German submarine, SM UB 75, at 3.15 p.m. Under the command of Captain A Wanless, the steamship was travelling at a steady 8 knots when the torpedo detonated just in front of the bridge. The crew, three of whom were injured in the blast, managed to get away in one of the ship's boats. They watched their ship go down, just three minutes later. Almost at once, two motor-launches picked up the crew and landed them at nearby Whitby town. The *Highgate* was carrying a 2,400-ton cargo of coal and a crew of twenty on passage from the Tyne for London.

SM UB 75 was listed as missing, presumed lost off Flamborough Head, about 13 December 1917, in an area that had extensive British minefields.

Wreck-site

The wreck of the *Highgate* is very close to the wreck of the *Amulet*. The *Highgate* is orientated in a north, north-east to south, south-west direction. She lies on a seabed of sand, mud and broken shells, in a general depth of 47m, the lowest astronomical depth. In 1980, the wreck was reported as standing upright 8m high, with the stern to bridge section complete and reasonably intact, while the two forward holds and bows are collapsed onto the seabed. Her large stern-mounted gun is still in position and lots of brass shell casings litter the poop deck area. Lots of brass valves, bent and flattened copper pipes and even the odd porthole can still be seen on this wreck, while myriads of soft corals bloom like spring flowers on the highest and most exposed sections. The wreck has been dived on a number of times and is reckoned to be a first-class dive site where shoals of pout whiting and large pollack can be seen at certain times of the year. Scarborough Sub Aqua Club was reported as having identified the wreck by such items as the crockery, bearing the 'Cory' house flag insignia, along with her engine details and date on the steering helm pedestal. However, it is not known whether the ship's bell has been recovered. This is a very dark dive and a powerful torch is required at all times. Sediment usually lies in a cloud all the way down until the last few metres near the seabed and then it seems to clear, but this keeps the light from penetrating to the bottom. Tidal streams are very strong.

FERRUCCIO, ex CICERONE, ex MARIA HERMINE, ex TEUTONIA

Wreck: ★★★★
Depth: 47m
Reference: N54 26 145 W000 25 370
Location: 3.55 miles ESE of North Cheek at Robin Hood's Bay

The *Ferruccio* was a steel 2,192-ton Italian steamship that measured 88.4m in length, with an 11.3m beam and a draught of 7.6m. Schlesinger, Davis & Co. built her as the *Teutonia* in 1881 for Teutonia Steamship Co. and Ward & Holzapfel managed her from 1881 to 1885. In 1885 she was sold to J. Hay & Sons. Elder Dempster & Co. purchased her in 1889. The Teutonia Steamship Co. bought her back in 1890 and T.R. Willing of Liverpool managed her. In 1897, she was sold to Fratelli Cosulich of Trieste, Austria-Hungary, and renamed *Hermine*. In 1900-1901, she was sold to Fratelli Grasso Cicerone of Via del Campo 10, Genoa, who kept her until 1914-1915 when she was sold to V. Bonavena Crasso Cicerone and renamed *Cicerone*. She was later sold to another Italian company, who was the owner at the time of loss and renamed her *Ferruccio*. Her single iron screw propeller was powered by a 2-cylinder compound steam engine that used two boilers.

On 6 February 1917, the *Ferruccio* was on passage from Sunderland for Savona with a cargo of coal, when she was torpedoed and sunk by the Imperial German submarine SM UB 34.

SM UB 34 surrendered to the Allies at the end of the First World War and became British war reparation. She was scrapped at Canning Town in 1922.

Wreck-site

The wreck, believed to be that of the Italian steamship *Ferruccio*, is orientated in a south-south-east to north-north-west direction, lying on a hard seabed of sand, mud, stone and black shells, in a general depth of 47m, the lowest astronomical depth. The wreck is in one piece, but totally collapsed, well broken up and rather decayed, with the highest 4.5m section being around her two boilers, condenser and engine, amidships. Most of the site is a mound of iron and steel debris, decayed and broken machinery, intermingled with copper pipes, brass valves and flanges. A number of complete, loose portholes could be seen, but no one seems to know if her bell has been recovered, which would provide definite proof of her identity. The bell would almost certainly be inscribed 'Teutonia' and the date she was built, '1881'. Very few fish or crustaceans have been observed on or around the wreck. A number of dead man's fingers have attached themselves to the boilers. The wreck-site is very dark and gloomy and requires a good torch to see anything, even in the best of conditions, and tidal streams are fairly strong.

SUNTRAP, ex SHERWOOD
Wreck: ★★★★
Depth: 44m
Reference: N54 25 311 W000 25 686
Location: 3.45 miles ENE of South Cheek at Robin Hood's Bay

The *Suntrap* (Official No-118369) was a steel 1,353-ton (1,049 under deck tons) schooner-rigged British steamship registered at the port of London. She was 70.1m long with a 10.99 beam and a draught of 4.57m. Sunderland Ship Building Co. Ltd at Sunderland built her in one month as the *Sherwood* in 1904 for the Gas Light & Coke Co. Ltd of London. The single iron screw propeller was powered by a 3-cylinder triple expansion steam engine that developed 159hp using one single-ended boiler, four corrugated furnaces, with grate-surface of 21.95m (a new boiler was fitted in July 1910). North East Marine Engineering Co. Ltd at Sunderland built her machinery. Her cylinder sizes measured: 48.26cm, 78.74cm and 129.54cm-91.44cm stroke, (19in, 31in and 51in-36in stroke). She had a flat keel, one steel deck and deep framing, a well deck, four cemented bulkheads, plus a superstructure consisting of an 8.84m poopdeck, a 20.42m quarterdeck, a 15.24m bridgedeck and a 6.71m forecastle. Her moulded depth measured 5.25m, with 43.18cm freeboard amidships in summer. She had 21.64m of water ballast cellular double bottom aft, 8.23m under engines and boilers and 28.04m forward giving 320 tons, fore-peak tank 52 tons and aft-peak tank of 53 tons. This vessel was also armed with a large stern-mounted deck gun that fired 8.16 kilo shells (18-pounders). Her signal letters were: VMHC. France, W. Fenwick & Co. Ltd, who renamed the ship *Suntrap* and owned her at the time of loss, later purchased her.

On 7 November 1917, the *Suntrap* was steaming south, under the command of Captain W. Clayburn, when she was torpedoed at 4.30 p.m. by the Imperial German submarine SM UB 22. The steamer was on passage from Newcastle for London with a cargo of coal and a crew of nineteen. Some of the crewmen saw the wake of the torpedo heading towards the ship, but before anyone could take evasive action it detonated against her port-quarter, about 11m from the stern. Her crew were able to abandon ship in the two boats without any serious casualties and were picked up by patrol vessels, then transferred to fishing drifters and landed at Scarborough.

On 19 January 1918, SM UB 22 was proceeding along one of the 'safe' channels through the German minefields in the Heligoland Bight when the escort, torpedo boat S16, detonated a British mine. The boat sank with all hands, north-west of Heligoland. SM UB 22, which was following close behind, also struck a mine and sank with the loss of her crew of twenty-two, in position N54 40 W06 32.

Wreck-site
The wreck, believed to be that of this steamer, lies orientated in a north-north-east to south-south-west direction. She lies on a hard seabed of dirty sand, mud and black shells in a general depth of 44m, the lowest astronomical depth. The wreck is on her starboard side and has now

collapsed onto the seabed, with the highest section of 5m being around amidships. Her exposed boiler, engine and condenser are located here. She is in one piece, but very broken up and decayed, covering an area of about 75m by 12m. The wreck is still quite large and will take more than one dive to explore properly. Lots of non-ferrous metal can be seen, along with recognisable pieces of her derricks, gunwales and hollow masts, and it is quite possible that her main bridge equipment is still around, although it is understood that the ship's bell has been recovered in recent years. There have been no reports as to how much marine life lives on and around the wreck, but it would be most unusual if there were not a variety of fish and crustaceans, especially cod, conger, ling and lobsters, because all wrecks collect a few residents. Being a fairly large wreck she may be worth noting as a boat-angling venue, when conditions allow. Tidal streams are very strong and visibility is not very spectacular, in fact it is usually grim, so a good torch is essential.

OAKWELL
Wreck: ★★★
Depth: 45m
Reference: N54 25 278 W000 25 170
Location: 2.72 miles ENE of South Cheek at Robin Hood's Bay

The *Oakwell* was a small iron 248-ton British steamship that was registered at the port of Stockton-on-Tees. She measured 38.1m in length, with a 6.73m beam and a draught of 3.14m. Craig, Taylor & Co. Ltd built her at Stockton-on-Tees in 1887 and United Glass Bottle Manufacturers Ltd owned her at the time of loss. Her single iron screw propeller was powered by a 2-cylinder compound steam engine that developed 50hp using one 1SB 2PF boiler. Her cylinders measured 45.72cm and 91.44cm-60.96cm. Westgarth, English & Co. at Middlesbrough built her aft-positioned machinery. She had one deck, a well deck and a super-structure consisting of a 12.80m quarterdeck, a 2.44m bridge deck and a 5.49m poop deck.

    Under the command of Captain W. Chilvers, this little merchant vessel was on passage from Seaham for London with a cargo of empty bottles and a crew of nine when at 11.40 a.m. on 28 March 1917 the Imperial German submarine SM UB 22 torpedoed her, nearly three miles east-north-east of the North Cheek, at Robin Hood's Bay. The *Oakwell* foundered almost immediately, taking four crewmen down with her. The others, including the captain, clung to floating wreckage until they were picked up sometime later by a Royal Navy destroyer and taken to North Shields. SM UB 22 was lost with her crew of twenty-two, in a 'safe channel' of the Heligoland Bight, after she detonated a mine on 19 January 1918.

Wreck-site
The wreck is orientated in an east-north-east to west-south-west direction. She lies on a hard seabed of dirty sand, mud and black shells, in a general depth of 45m, the lowest astronomical depth. She is reported as being totally collapsed, decayed and broken up with her boiler and engine visibly exposed and the condenser burst open. The highest point is around her boiler/engine, which stands about 3-4m high at the stern end, while the rest of the wreck is just a mound of broken machinery, bent pipes and flattened iron plates, standing no more than a metre high. Occasionally, part of her cargo of empty bottles can be found amongst the pile of debris, but otherwise there are not many interesting things to be seen. However, portholes are still being discovered. Local divers have recovered the ship's bell along with some other artefacts. The wreck is reported to be a reasonable dive site and still worth a visit. Fair numbers of cod have been observed on and around the wreck-site and large lobsters are not an uncommon sight. This is a fairly dark dive with usually very poor visibility, which requires a good torch to see anything. Tidal streams are strong and the best time to dive her is on a neap tide after a spell of settled dry weather and light south westerly winds.

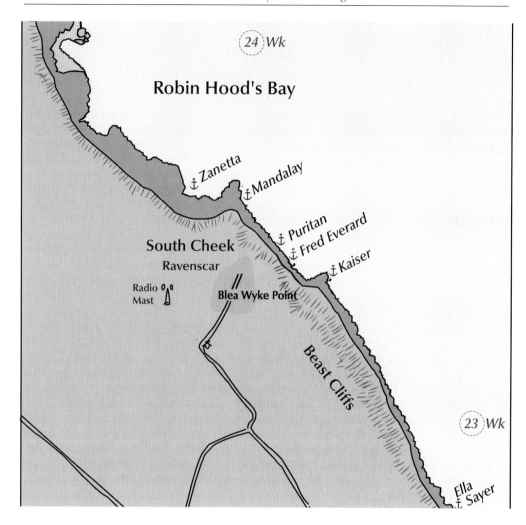

ZANETTA
Wreck: ★
Scenery: ★★★
Depth: 4m
Reference: N54 24 768 W000 29 882
Location: South Cheek at Robin Hood's Bay

The *Zanetta* was an iron 1,334-ton British steamship that was registered at the port of London. She measured 73.96m in length, with a 10.1m beam and a 6.09m draught. Palmers & Co. Ltd built her at Newcastle-upon-Tyne in 1878 and J.F. Fenwick of London owned her at the time of loss. Her single iron screw propeller was powered by a 2-cylinder compound steam engine that developed 155hp using one boiler. She had one deck and a superstructure consisting of an 8.23m poop deck and a 4.27m bridge deck.

On 13 November 1901, the steamer was in ballast on passage from London for Tyne Dock when she encountered winds blowing force ten, off Robin Hood's Bay. Under the command of Captain J. Gibson with a crew of fifteen, she was forced to anchor at South Cheek, but her anchors dragged. The force of the wind was so great that she was pushed into shallow water where she was wrecked on the rocks. While abandoning ship, one of her crew was lost.

Wreck-site

The wreck, believed to be that of the *Zanetta*, is now totally collapsed, well broken up and quite dispersed. She lies under the weed, in amongst the sand, rocks and boulders in a general depth of 4m, the lowest astronomical depth. Very little remains except a few broken iron spars and plates spread out underneath the carpet of bladder wrack and kelp. Tidal streams are quite reasonable, but underwater visibility is usually poor most of the year.

MANDALAY

Wreck: *
Scenery: **
Depth: 4m
Reference: N54 24 632 W00 29 331
Location: South Cheek, Ravenscar

The *Mandalay* (Official No.95845) was an iron 148-ton British steam fishing trawler that was 31.4m long with a 6.1m beam. Cook, Welton & Gemmell built her as Yard No.53 at Hull and launched her in 1890. She was registered on 27 August 1890 as trawler No.H105 for her new owners, George Beeching & Thomas Kelsall of Hull. Her single iron screw propeller was powered by a 3-cylinder triple expansion steam engine that developed 50hp using one boiler that gave the vessel a registered speed of 10 knots. Charles D. Holmes at Hull built her machinery. On 8 January 1897, she was transferred to Fleetwood as trawler No.FD146, then returned to Hull and registered as H77 by Kelsall Bros & Beeching on 1 January 1904.

On 22 October 1904, the *Mandalay* was fishing over the Dogger Bank with other vessels of the Hull trawler fleet, when the Russian Navy's Baltic Fleet, which was en route to the Pacific, attacked them. It was said that the Russians, who were at war with Japan, mistook the trawlers for Japanese torpedo boats and opened fire on the fleet, damaging many, including the *Mandalay*.

On 14 February 1908, the *Mandalay* was on a return fishing voyage from her home port of Hull when she ran aground in thick fog and became a total wreck; all her crew were rescued.

H77 *Mandalay*, ex H105, ex FD 146. Built C.W. & G., Hull, 1890. Yard no.53. Length: 103ft 2in. Gross Tonnage: 148. Wrecked after stranding at Ravenscar in thick fog, 14 February 1908. *(Courtesy Jonathan Grobler Collection)*

Wreck-site

The wreck is now totally collapsed, decayed and smashed to pieces, lying amongst the dense kelp, reefs and boulders in a general depth about 4m. All that remains are a few bent iron plates, a propeller, an anchor and a length of rusting chain that leads away from the anchor and disappears under the long strands of bladder wrack and kelp. The surrounding reefs and boulders make an excellent forage dive for crustaceans during the early summer months, when the visibility signif-icantly improves and lots of small saithe can be seen. Tidal streams are reasonable, but can be fairly strong on a spring tide, especially a little further offshore.

GIMLE

Wreck: ★★★★
Depth: 42m
Reference: N54 24 550 W000 24 587
Location: 2.87 miles E of South Cheek at Robin Hood's Bay

The *Gimle* was a steel 1,131-ton Norwegian steamship registered at the port of Bergen. She was 69.64m long with an 11.04m beam and a draught of 4.8m. Laxevaags Maskin & Jernskibsbyggeri, Laksevag, Bergen built her in 1904 and A/S D/S Gimle owned her at the time of loss. Her single iron screw propeller was powered by a 3-cylinder triple expansion steam engine that developed 132hp using one boiler.

On 4 November 1917, the *Gimle* foundered and was lost when SM UB 35 torpedoed her, three miles east of South Cheek at Robin Hood's Bay. The steamer was under the command of Captain B.C. Pedersen, on passage from Blyth for Caen, with a cargo of coal. UB 35 was depth-charged and sunk by HMS *Leven* in the English Channel on 26 January 1917.

Wreck-site

The wreck lies in almost an east to west direction, lying on a seabed of black shells, sand and mud in a general depth of 42m, the lowest astronomical depth. In 1986 she was reported as being very substantial, almost intact and complete from her bows to the after hold, but her stern-end was badly damaged where the torpedo exploded. She is now beginning to break up but is still very large, standing some 6m high around the amidships section and makes a first class dive site. The wreck has been positively identified from the boss on the ship's wheel, but it is not known whether the ship's bell has been discovered. Interesting items are still being found, but it is very dark and a good torch is essential. One or two good cod have been observed amongst the wreckage, so this wreck should make an interesting boat-angling venue when conditions are right. Tidal streams are very strong and visibility usually poor to dismal.

PURITAN

Wreck: ★
Scenery: ★★
Depth: 5m
Reference: N54 24 194 W000 28 704
Location: Off Peak Point, Blea Wyke near Ravenscar

The *Puritan* (Official No.110786) was an iron 219-ton British steam fishing trawler registered H497 at the port of Hull. She was 36.6m long, with a 6.23m beam and a 3.35m draught. Cook, Welton & Gemmell built her as Yard No.254 in 1899/1900 and launched her as the *Puritan* on 3 February 1900 for the new owner, George Walton of Hull, who was also the owner at the time of loss. Her single iron screw propeller was powered by a 3-cylinder triple expansion steam engine that developed 60hp using one boiler. Charles D Holmes of Hull built her machinery.

On 4 May 1903, the *Puritan* was on a return voyage from the Icelandic fishing grounds for Hull when she ran aground and stranded in dense fog near to the Ravenscar Hotel off Peak Point, Blea Wyke at Ravenscar. The impact broke off the ship's propeller blades. The crew took to the ship's boat and were picked up after six hours by the Hull steam trawler *Hero* (H886) and safely landed at Scarborough. On hearing distress signals, the local lifeboat was summoned, but the lifeboatmen found the vessel broken in two, partially submerged, deserted and her cargo of cod spilling out through her side. On 3 May 1915, the *Hero* was on a fishing voyage 150 miles off Hornsea, Yorkshire, when she was captured by an Imperial German submarine and sunk by time bombs.

Wreck-site
The wreck of the *Puritan* can be reached by going to the wreck of the *Fred Everard* at co-ordinates N54 24 195 W000 28 819, then swimming due north from her broken stern. The remains of the wreck are totally collapsed, decayed and well dispersed amongst the dense kelp beds and rocks in a general depth of 5m. A few iron plates, broken pieces of machinery, an anchor and half a propeller are all that remain, but the surrounding reefs, rocks and battered iron plates provide shelter for numerous lobsters, edible crabs, green shore crabs, squat lobsters and velvet swimming crabs; shoals of saithe and pollack are commonplace during the summer months. Tidal streams are moderate, but the strength increases considerably on a spring tide. Visibility is usually poor, but improves on a neap tide and after a spell of dry settled weather and westerly winds.

KAISER
Wreck: ★
Scenery: ★★★
Depth: 3m
Reference: N54 23 984 W000 28 481
Location: South of Blea Wyke Point

The *Kaiser* was an iron 816-ton British steamship that was registered at West Hartlepool. She measured 61.4m in length, with a 9.26m beam and a 3.36m draught. William Gray & Co. built her at West Hartlepool in 1880 and the West Hartlepool Steam Navigation Co. owned her at the time of loss. Her single iron screw propeller was powered by a 3-cylinder triple expansion steam engine that used one boiler. Richardson at Hartlepool built her machinery. She had one deck and a small centrally-positioned bridge structure.

On 25 July 1904, the *Kaiser* was travelling at her full speed of 11 knots when, in thick fog and blasting her foghorn, she drove ashore on rocks at Blea Wyke Point, near Ravenscar. She was on her normal return route, from Hamburg for West Hartlepool, which often included Gothenburg. The steamer was carrying a number of passengers and general mixed cargo, including various fruits, strawberries, ironmongery and pianos, plus other goods. The crew heard the echo of the foghorn bouncing back off the high cliffs just before she grounded. Except for the dense fog, the weather was fairly reasonable and the passengers, including a number of wealthy men, were safely taken ashore in the vessel's own boats. The vessel was held fast on the rocks with a big hole in the bottom plates and soon became a total wreck. Rumours abound locally that the aroma of jam being made could be smelt around the village for days afterwards.

Wreck-site
The wreck is now totally collapsed, well broken up and dispersed amongst the rocks, boulders, gullies and seaweed. All that remains are some bits of iron ribs, small pieces of iron plate and the propeller shaft, lying in a general depth of 3m, the lowest astronomical depth. The easiest way to locate the wreck is to approach Blea Wyke from seaward on a very low tide and dive about 30m or so to the south side. The wreck is certainly nothing to write home about, but a few nice crustaceans can be found amongst the surrounding rocks and gullies.

NOVILLO, ex AMASIS
Wreck: ★★★
Depth: 44m
Reference: N54 23 137 W000 22 811
Location: 2.70 miles NE of Hayburn Wyke

The *Novillo* was a steel 2,336-ton Danish steamship registered at Copenhagen. She waas 95.25m long, with a 12.19m beam and a draught of 6.62m. Hawthorn Leslie & Co. built her at Newcastle-upon-Tyne in 1895 as the *Amasis* for the J. Moss Steamship Co. of Liverpool. Soc. Anon. De Nav. Sud Atlántica of Buenos Aires, Argentina, purchased her in 1912 and renamed her *Novillo*. In 1917 the Danish company AS Valberg of Copenhagen, which was the owner at the time of loss, purchased her and Rasmus Rasmussen managed the vessel. Her single iron screw propeller was powered by a 3-cylinder triple expansion steam engine that developed 276hp using two 2SB 6CF boilers. Her cylinders measured 57.15cm, 96.52cm and 158.75cm-106.68cm.

On 22 October 1917, the SS *Novillo* was torpedoed and sunk by the German submarine SM UB 57, north-east from Hayburn Wyke. The steamer was under the command of Captain Fragnul and she was on passage from the Tyne for Blaye with a 3,500-ton cargo of coal. SM UB57 detonated a mine and was lost off Zeebrugge on 14 August 1918.

Wreck-site
The wreck believed to be the SS *Novillo*, lies orientated in more or less a north-east to south-west direction, on a seabed of fine sand, mud, stones and rock, in a general depth of 44m, the lowest astronomical depth. She is totally collapsed and partially buried at the stern end, with the highest section of just over 3m being at amidships around her boilers and the debris-covered remains of her engine. The wreck is now little more than a heap of broken decayed debris, covered in lots of dirty sand and silt, but there are a number of large bent and flattened copper pipes and her brass condenser protruding out of it all. Most of her interesting equipment should still be around to see and her bell, if located, will probably be inscribed with '*Amasis*' and the date she was built, '1895'. Very little marine life has been reported on or around the wreck and she is not likely to make a very good boat-angling venue. Tidal streams are fairly strong and underwater visibility is usually poor to dismal, but improves during the summer months.

LADY HELEN
Wreck: ★★★★
Depth: 34m
Reference: N54 22 903 W000 24 645
Location: 1.8 miles NE of Hayburn Wyke.

The *Lady Helen* was a steel 811-ton British steamship registered at the port of Sunderland. She was 60.96m in length, with a 9.14m beam and a draught of 3.68m. S.P. Austin & Son built her at Sunderland in 1909 and the Marquis of Londonderry at Seaham owned her at the time of loss. Her single iron screw propeller was powered by a 138hp 3-cylinder triple expansion steam engine using one 1SB 3CF boiler, and the North East Marine Engineering Co. Ltd at Sunderland built her machinery. Her cylinders measured 43.18cm, 71.12cm and 116.84cm-76.20cm. She had one deck, a well deck and a superstructure consisting of a 6.40m poop deck, a 13.41m quarterdeck, a 14.02m bridge deck and a 6.40m forecastle.

At 9 a.m. on 27 October 1917, the *Lady Helen* was on passage from Great Yarmouth for Seaham Harbour when, it is believed, she detonated a German mine. She was under the command of Captain E.J. Roberts and carrying a crew of fourteen. The explosion took place just aft of the engine room, ripping the hull open, which caused her to go down by the stern almost immediately. The crew lowered the port lifeboat and climbed into it, but before they could clear the ship, it capsized, throwing the men into the sea. Seven of her crew were drowned, but the second officer and six seamen clung desperately to the upturned hull of the boat for thirty minutes until a patrol vessel rescued them. It picked up the lifeless body of the captain at the same time and landed them all at Scarborough. Since records were released after the war, it has been shown that the *Lady Helen* was actually torpedoed by the SM UB 34, a German U-boat. SM UC 55 laid six mines north-east of Scarborough on 7 July 1917 and on 3, 10 and 17 September 1917, the British Navy laid another 1,200 mines in this region, so it is no wonder people believed the steamer had detonated a mine! SM UB 34 surrendered to the Allies at the end of the First World War and became British war reparation. She was scrapped at Canning Town in 1922.

Wreck-site
The wreck lies north to south, on a seabed of fine sand, mud and rocks, in a general depth of 34m, the lowest astronomical depth. She is reported to be standing on an even keel, is upright and complete from her bows to the aft hold, but with a lot of damage around her port-quarter and stern section. The upper structures have collapsed and her hull has collapsed amidships on one side. She is still fairly large and makes a great dive. It is not known if the ship's bell and interesting bridge equipment are still in place, but she makes an interesting wreck to explore. The vessel was identified in the 1980s by the builder's plate and boiler/engine details. Fish of varying species have been observed, so she will make a good boat-angling venue. Visibility is very poor, even with a good torch, and tidal streams are fairly strong. The best time to dive the wreck is on a neap tide at low slack water and after a spell of dry settled weather, during the summer months. Snagged trawl nets hanging over the stern end can also be a problem in the murky light.

PHARE, ex GROVELEA, ex LADY FURNESS
Wreck: ★★★
Depth: 32m
Reference: N54 22 605 W000 23 856
Location: 1.9 miles ENE of Hayburn Wyke and north of Scarborough

The *Phare* (Official No.132808) was a steel 1,282-ton British steamship measuring 71.47m long, with a 10.49m beam and a 4.59m draught. She was built at Blyth in 1906 by Blyth Shipbuilding & Dry Docks Co. Ltd as Yard No.133 for A. Christensen of Copenhagen, Denmark, and was launched as *Lady Furness*. Her single iron screw propeller was powered by a 3-cylinder triple expansion steam engine that developed 166hp using one 1SB 4CF boiler and her cylinders measured 48.26cm, 78.74cm and 129.54cm. North Eastern Marine Engineering Co. at Newcastle-upon-Tyne built her machinery. She had one deck, a well deck and a superstructure consisting of a 36.88m quarterdeck, a 3.05m bridge deck and 7.32m forecastle. The vessel was armed with a stern-mounted deck-gun that fired 6.80kg shells (15 pounders). In 1909 the owners became Internationalt Dampskib og Bjerrgnings Co. and A. og H. Christensen in Copenhagen managed her. In 1911 the British Maritime Trust Ltd bought her and Furness Withy & Co. Ltd of London managed her. In 1912 she was sold to Rederiaktlebolag 'Groveland', renamed *Grovelea* and managed by J.P. Johnson of Landskrona in Sweden. The Gas Light & Coke Co. purchased her on 8 March 1915 and owned her at the time of loss. They renamed her *Phare*.

On 31 October 1917, the SS *Phare* was on passage from the Tyne for London when she was torpedoed by SM UB 35. The steamer was carrying an unspecified cargo of coal and a crew of eighteen, under the command of Captain A. Smith. She was making around 8.5 knots when some of the crew witnessed the track of the torpedo just before it detonated level with the engine room after bulkhead on the port side at 3 p.m. The order was given to abandon ship, but as the crew were attempting to lower the starboard boat, the *Phare* rolled over to port and went down. The captain and surviving crew were thrown or jumped into the sea and stayed afloat as best they could by clinging to floating wreckage until a patrol boat picked them up two hours later. Thirteen men were killed in the explosion or drowned. The remaining survivors landed at Scarborough but one man died aboard the rescue vessel before they could reach port. SM UB 35 was later depth-charged and sunk in the English Channel by HMS *Leven* on 26 January 1918.

Wreck-site

The official position for the wreck is at co-ordinates N54 19 00 W000 23 00, but no wreck has been located in that position. This wreck, which could well be that of the SS *Phare*, is known locally as the 'Punch-Up' wreck. She lies in a north-north-west to south-south-east direction, on a seabed of sand and stone in a general depth of 32m, the lowest astronomical depth. She is now totally collapsed, well broken up and rather decayed with her boiler and engine exposed, which are surrounded by a mound of broken steel debris. If her bell is located, it will almost certainly be inscribed '*Lady Furness*' and the date she was built '1906'. Edible crabs and a few lobsters can often be seen amongst the jumble of jagged metal and during the summer months nice bags of mackerel can be caught in the immediate vicinity of the wreck. Tidal streams are fairly strong, but it is possible to visit the site at most states of the tide. Visibility is usually poor but improves significantly after a spell of settled weather and westerly winds during the summer.

GLOW, ex MONKWOOD

Wreck: ★★★★
Depth: 43m
Reference: N54 22 510 W000 22 620
Location: 2.5 miles ENE of Hayburn Wyke and north of Scarborough

The *Glow* was a steel 1,141-ton British steamship registered at London. She was 71.7m long, with a 10.8m beam and a draught of 4.39m. J. Blumer & Co. Ltd at Sunderland built her as the *Monkwood* in 1900 for France, W. Fenwick & Co. Ltd. In 1917, the Gas Light & Coke Co. of London, which owned her at the time of loss, purchased and renamed her *Glow*, while S. Clarke & Co. of London managed the vessel. A 179hp 3-cylinder triple expansion steam engine that used two boilers, powered her single iron screw propeller. J. Dickinson & Sons Ltd at Sunderland built her machinery. She had one deck, a well deck and a superstructure consisting of a 5.79m poop deck, a 21.64m quarterdeck, 14.63m bridge deck and a 6.71m forecastle. The vessel was armed with a stern-mounted deck-gun that fired 5.90kg shells (13 pounders).

At 9.30 p.m. on 22 July 1917, the steamer was making a steady 10 knots on passage from the Tyne for London when, five miles east-south-east from Ravenscar, she was torpedoed and sunk by the Imperial German submarine, SM UB 21. Captain T.H. Baty, the skipper of the *Glow*, saw the torpedo approaching rapidly, some 100m away on the starboard side, but there was not enough time to take evasive action. The missile detonated about 3m above her sternpost, blowing off most of the vessel's stern section and killing the chief gunner instantly. The *Glow* immediately began to sink, however the sixteen surviving crew, including the steward who had been injured, scrambled into one of the boats that they had managed to lower. The boat had just cleared the stricken vessel when she turned over completely, and in three minutes, at 9.40 p.m., she slipped beneath the surface. A patrol boat picked up the survivors after about fifty minutes and landed them at Scarborough, where the injured steward received medical attention.

Following the armistice, SM UB 21 was surrendered to the French. She was sunk somewhere along the English East Coast in 1920, en route to being broken up.

Wreck-site

The wreck believed to be that of the *Glow* is reported as lying in a south to north direction, on a seabed of fine sand, shell, stone, mud and rocks in a general depth of 43m, the lowest astronomical depth. She is quite substantial, standing upright and 6m high amidships around her boilers and engine, however most of the wreck has collapsed, is well broken up and decayed, with the engine and boilers now exposed and surrounded by a mountain of debris, including pieces of broken hollow mast, steel bollards and lengths of flattened copper pipes with brass flanges still attached. The wreck-site is very dark and requires a good torch to see anything. Anyone discovering the ship's bell should remember that it will almost certainly be inscribed '*Monkwood*' and '1900', the date she was built. Tidal streams are rather strong and visibility is usually pretty grim, but the remains are certainly worth looking at, especially as the site has not been much dived. The best time to dive is at low slack water during a neap tide and following a spell of dry settled weather and light westerly winds. She may be also worth looking at as a boat-angling venue because there are almost certain to be a number of large fish lurking around amongst the wreckage.

ELLA SAYER

Wreck: ★
Scenery: ★★★
Depth: 3m
Reference: N54 22 415 W000 26 985
Location: Just north of Hayburn Wyke

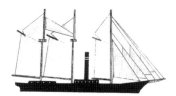

The *Ella Sayer* was an iron 1,744-ton British schooner-rigged steamship registered at Newcastle-upon-Tyne. She was 75.54m long, with an 11.27m beam and a 5.05m draught. Doxford & Sons built her at Sunderland in 1883 and Fisher, Renwick & Co. of Newcastle-upon-Tyne owned her at the time of loss. A 200hp 2-cylinder compound steam engine powered her single iron screw propeller that used two boilers.

On 31 August 1897, the *Ella Sayer* was making a steady 8 knots, on passage from Kotka, Finland, for Hull with a 2,100-ton cargo of pit props, when she drove hard ashore just after midnight near Hayburn Wyke. A number of factors were to blame for the stranding, including a major miscalculation by her master, who had underestimated the vessel's progress. During her voyage down the coast, she had had to change direction a number of times to avoid fishing vessels and her patent log was also giving erroneous readings. The crew, who had been unable to see Whitby light due to poor visibility caused by rain and a coastal fog, believed they were well offshore, so no sounding lead was employed, which would have forewarned them of the shallow depth. It appears that there was no forward lookout employed either. All attempts to salvage the vessel failed and she soon broke up and became a total wreck. Months after the incident, her cargo of pit props could be found jamming the crevices and inlets all along that part of the coastline.

Wreck-site

The wreck is now totally collapsed, well broken up and dispersed at the bottom of the high cliffs, under a carpet of fine purple seaweed, in a general depth of 3m, the lowest astronomical depth. Very little remains, except for a few battered iron plates and the occasional piece of flattened copper pipe, but the only way to reach the wreck-site is from the sea. Small crustaceans, like green shore crabs and squat lobsters can be found amongst the surrounding rocks. Tidal streams are very reasonable, but the underwater visibility is usually poor most of the year.

SNA-II, ex M.E. HARPER

Wreck: ★★★★
Depth: 43m
Reference: N54 22 310 W000 22 470
Location: 2.6 miles ENE of Hayburn Wyke and N of Scarborough

The *SNA-II* was a steel 2,294-ton French steamship registered at the port of Le Havre. She was 75.28m in length and had a beam of 10.05m. Great Lakes Engineering Works, in Michigan,

USA, built her as the *M.E. Harper* in 1911 for Harper Transportation Co. of Philadelphia. The Sawmut Steamship Co. of Philadelphia purchased her in 1915. Société Nationale D'Affètements (SNA) bought her a few months before she was lost in 1917 and renamed her *SNA-II*. Her single iron screw propeller was powered by a 3-cylinder triple expansion steam engine that used two boilers. Her cylinders measured 53.34cm, 87.63cm and 144.78cm-106.68cm.

On 6 June 1917, the *SNA-II* was on passage from the Tyne for Dunkirk with a cargo of coal when, five miles north by east of Scarborough, she was torpedoed and sunk by SM UB 21. UB 21 survived the First World War and was surrendered to the French following the armistice. She was sunk somewhere along the English East Coast in 1920, en route to being broken up.

Wreck-site

This wreck, believed to be *SNA-II*, lies in a south-south-east to north-north-west direction, on a dirty seabed of fine sand, mud, small broken shells and stone, in a general depth of 43m, the lowest astronomical depth. She is still very substantial, but broken into two sections, with her stern end standing upright about 5m high close to the break where her centrally-positioned bridge structure was located. The bow section lies on its side and is beginning to collapse. The ship's bell if recovered, will probably be inscribed '*M.E. Harper*' and the date she was built, '1911'. Her boilers, condenser and engine block are exposed and the upper and most exposed parts of her are covered in a colourful array of soft corals; the wreck-site also has quite a number of lobster creels entangled with it. When the light penetrates down through the eerie green murk on a sunny day, the wreck looks very bright, but reports say that the visibility is normally very poor and tidal streams very strong. Lots of cod and pout whiting can be seen around the boiler area, but the occasional ling has also been seen, so the wreck has prospects of making a good boat-angling venue when conditions are right. The surface boat cover requires a good lookout, because the wreck-site is close to the main shipping lanes.

VICTORIA

Wreck: ★★★★
Depth: 43m
Reference: N54 21 885 W000 20 589
Location: 4.95 miles ENE of Scarborough.

The *Victoria* was a steel 1,620-ton British steamship that measured 79.24m in length, with an 11.17m beam and a 5.02m draught. She was built in 1887 by A. Stephenson & Sons at Glasgow and owned at the time of loss by the SS Victoria Co. Ltd. Her single iron screw propeller was powered by a 3-cylinder triple expansion steam engine that developed 258hp using two 1DB 4CF boilers and her cylinders measured 45.72cm, 73.66cm and 116.84cm-99.06cm. She had one deck, a well deck, and a superstructure consisting of a 28.04m quarterdeck, a 20.73m bridge deck and a 9.45m forecastle.

On 29 April 1917, the SS *Victoria* was on passage from Jarrow-on-Tyne for Bayonne, under the command of Captain W.D. Falconer and carrying a crew of nineteen and an unspecified cargo of coal. At 4.07 p.m., a torpedo fired by SM UB 21, an Imperial German submarine, exploded amidships on her port side, killing one fireman instantly. The surviving crew immediately abandoned ship in the boats and managed to land at Scarborough later that day. The *Victoria* drifted for a while, before going down to the bottom, unobserved.

SM UB 21 survived the First World War and following the armistice she was surrendered to the French. She was sunk along the English East Coast in 1920, en route to being broken up.

Wreck-site

The wreck lies orientated in a south-east to north-west direction on a seabed of sand and stone in a general depth of 45m, the lowest astronomical depth. She is totally collapsed and well broken up with her double-ended boiler standing amidst the mound of twisted steel debris, broken pipes, bollards, valves and mangled rails. Tidal streams are rather strong and underwater visibility is usually very poor, but significantly improves after a spell of dry settled weather during the summer months. Large shoals of mackerel can be caught in the vicinity of the wreck around the months of July and August, but Lion's mane jellyfish can be rather a nuisance when diving during this period. As this wreck is a grave, she should be treated with respect.

MAGNETA

Wreck: *
Depth: 2m
Reference: N54 21 436 W000 26 326 (approximate)
Location: Off Creek Point, Burnston, near Hayburn Wyke

The *Magneta* (Official No.91421) was an iron 116-ton steam fishing trawler, registered as trawler No.H1447 at Hull on 18 June 1885. The vessel was built as Yard No.3 by Cook, Welton & Gemmell at Hull and was launched in May 1885. She was originally built as an iron 89-ton sailing smack for Francis & Thomas Ross Ltd of Hull, who was the owner at the time of loss. Her dimensions at the time of her sinking were 24.75m long and 6.16m beam. In October 1888, the boat was converted to a stream trawler and lengthened to 29.17m in length with the same beam. Her single iron screw propeller was powered by a 3-cylinder triple expansion steam engine that developed 40hp using one boiler. Charles D. Holmes at Hull built her machinery that gave her speed of 9.5 knots. She was re-registered as a steam trawler on 15 October 1888.

   On 24 January 1908, the *Magneta* was on a return fishing voyage from Hull when, in thick fog, she drove ashore and was wrecked off Creek Point, near Hayburn Wyke. It is understood that her crew got safely to shore without any loss of life.

H1447 *Magneta*, built by C.W. & G., Hull, 1885. Yard no.3. (Built as an iron-hulled sailing smack) Converted to a steam trawler in October 1888. Wrecked at Creek Point, Burniston, nr Hayburn Wyke (Yorkshire) 24 January 1908. *(Courtesy Jonathan Grobler Collection)*

Wreck-site
The wreck of the steam trawler is now totally collapsed, well broken up and quite dispersed. She lies scattered under the seaweed, amongst the rocks and boulders, in a general depth of 2m, the lowest astronomical depth, just off the Point. Very little of her remains to be seen these days, except for a few scattered bits of iron plate, a few spars and bits of broken unrecognisable pieces of machinery. A number of green shore crabs, velvet swimming crabs and squat lobsters can be found under the surrounding rocks and boulders, but very little else. Tidal streams are quite reasonable, but underwater visibility is usually poor most of the year.

SPRINGHILL, ex PORTHCAWL
Wreck: ★★★★
Depth: 38m
Reference: N54 21 298 W000 23 166
Location: 2.8 miles E of Hayburn Wyke and 3.98 miles N of Scarborough Rock

The *Springhill* was a steel 1,507-ton British steamship registered at Cardiff. She measured 77.16m in length, with an 11.12m beam and a draught of 5.3m. J. Crown & Sons Ltd built her at Sunderland as the *Porthcawl* in 1904 for the Porthcawl Steamship Co. Thomas, Stephens & Wilson of Cardiff managed her. Her single iron screw propeller was powered by a 3-cylinder triple expansion steam engine that developed 166hp using two 2SB 4PF boilers and her cylinders measured 48.26cm, 78.74cm and 129.54cm. North Eastern Marine Engineering Co. Ltd built her machinery at Sunderland. She had one deck and a superstructure consisting of an 18.29m bridge deck and 9.14m forecastle. In 1915, Fisher, Renwick & Co. of Newcastle-upon-Tyne, who was the owner at the time of loss, purchased her and renamed her *Springhill*. When the Porthcawl Steamship Co. sold her in 1915 they bought a new vessel of about 2,000 tons, which was built by Craig & Taylor, and called her *Porthcawl* again, to keep the name in their company.
    At 11.34 a.m. on 24 August 1917, the SS *Springhill* foundered and was lost north from Scarborough, after detonating a mine laid by the Imperial German submarine SM UB 21, which survived the First World War. Under the command of Captain W. Williams, the *Springhill* was on passage from West Hartlepool for London carrying a 2,200-ton cargo of coal. The explosion ripped a huge hole in her side amidships, instantly killing the chief engineer and a fireman, who were both in the engine room. The vessel went down in less than four minutes, drowning the second steward and an able seaman, while a fifth man died of his injuries later. The steamship *Eden* picked up most of the surviving crew soon after the incident, then the steam drifter *White Rose* rescued one other crewman and landed him at Scarborough.

Wreck-site
The wreck lies orientated in a north-north-west to south-south-east direction, on a seabed of gravel, stones and rock, in a general depth of 38m, the lowest astronomical depth. She is very substantial, but totally collapsed, lying on her port side, with her boilers exposed and surrounded by a jumble of twisted steel plates and broken machinery. A bollard, large winch and lots of flattened copper pipes, brass valves and wash/scupper valves lie intermingled with the mound of steel debris. Apparently the vessel has been identified by her boiler details and it is understood that her bell was also recovered some time ago. Some large crustaceans have been observed around the boilers/engine area and cod have also been seen, so she may make an interesting boat angling venue. The wreck-site is a fair way from the nearest launch site and well into the shipping lane, so a good lookout will be required. Tidal streams are fairly strong and underwater visibility usually rather grim, but improve significantly during the summer months.

SUMUS
Wreck: ★★
Depth: 37m
Reference: N54 21 171 W000 22 469
Location: 3.83 miles NNE from Scarborough Rock

The *Sumus* was an iron 223-ton British steamship that was registered at Middlesbrough and measured 38m in length, with a 6.8m beam and a 2.80m draught. Built by J. Hogg & W. Henderson at Middlesbrough in 1871, she had a single iron screw propeller, powered by a 2-cylinder compound steam engine that used one boiler and was not classed at Lloyd's.

The *Sumus* left the River Tees on 18 January 1906, on passage from Middlesbrough for Shoreham, when she foundered and was lost for reasons unknown. She was under the command of Captain T.W. Vickers, carrying a 250-ton cargo of rough slag and a crew of nine. Most of this coastline has sheer high cliffs, making the rocks below them almost inaccessible. However, a man out exploring these rocks discovered the bodies of four of the steamer's crew that had been washed ashore in a bay at Gristhorpe Wyke, just north of Filey.

Wreck-sites
The remains of the small steamer are believed to lie in the position suggested above, lying 3.83 miles north-north-east of Scarborough. She lies orientated north to south, on a seabed of sand and rock, in a general depth of 37m, the lowest astronomical depth. The wreck stands only 2.5m high, is now totally collapsed and well broken up, with her bow section collapsed onto the seabed. The remains of her cargo of rough slag have also been reported as being spread around the surrounding seabed. Local divers recovered one of the vessel's wrought-iron anchors in the 1980s.

NIKARD NORDRAAK
Wreck: ★★★★
Depth: 48m
Reference: N54 21 166 W000 19 282
Location: 4.49 miles NNE of Scarborough Rock

The *Nikard Nordraak* was a steel 1,123-ton Norwegian steamship that was registered at the port of Bergen. She measured 70.4m in length, with a 10.36m beam and draught of 4.08m. Jernsk Hasseldalens built her at Grimstad in 1901 and A/S D/K Rikard Nordraak in Bergen owned her at the time of loss. Her single screw, possibly bronze, was powered by a 3-cylinder triple expansion steam engine that developed 97hp using one boiler. Bergens Mek Vaeks in Bergen built her machinery and she had one deck.

On 2 February 1917, the vessel was on passage from Sunderland for Rouen with a cargo of coal, under the command of Captain H. Huun, when she was torpedoed and sunk by SM UB 21. It is not known if anyone died on this vessel.

Wreck-site
The wreck is said to be lying on a seabed of sand, stone and shells, in a general depth of 45m, the lowest astronomical depth. She is upright, with her top structures collapsed down almost to seabed level and standing around 6m high amidships where her single boiler and engine are located. Many of the vessel's interesting artefacts, e.g. her navigation and bridge/wheelhouse equipment and bell, are said to be missing, so she must be fairly well dived. Tidal streams are strong and underwater visibility usually very poor to dismal, improving slightly during the summer months. A fair number of fish, including very large cod, have been observed among the wreckage, so she should make an excellent boat-angling venue when conditions permit. The best time to visit is during a neap tide and after a spell of dry settled weather and westerly winds.

GOLDEN SUNRISE
Wreck: ★★★
Depth: 49m
Reference: N54 21 059 W000 14 482
Location: 6.38 miles NE of Scarborough Rock

The *Golden Sunrise* was a steel 224-ton British steam fishing trawler that was registered as H517 at Hull. She measured 38.10m in length and had a beam of 6.42m. Cochrane & Cooper built her at Beverley as Yard No.280 in 1901 for Hall, Leyman & Co. of Hull, which was the owner at the time of loss. Her single iron screw propeller was powered by a 3-cylinder triple expansion steam engine that developed 50hp using one boiler. It is understood that Amos & Smith Co. at Hull would have built her machinery. She had one deck and a 5.18m quarterdeck.

On 16 August 1908, the trawler was on a return fishing voyage from Hull when she foundered and was lost off Scarborough (the author is not sure of the reason, or whether any of her crew was lost, but it was probably caused by a collision).

Wreck-site
This wreck is probably that of the steam trawler. She lies on a seabed of sand, stone, black shells and mud, in a general depth of 49m, the lowest astronomical depth. The wreck is totally collapsed and well broken up, standing some 3m high at her bow and around amidships to stern, where her boiler and engine are now exposed. A shoal of small fish, probably pout-whiting, has been observed over the wreckage and a few crustaceans hide amongst the debris. However, apart from a number of bent copper pipes, there is very little else of interest to be seen. The wreck-site is very dark, with usually poor visibility and tidal streams fairly brisk.

LACONIA
Wreck: ★★
Depth: 43m
Reference: N54 20 915 W000 20 521
Location: 2.90 miles NNE of Scarborough Rock

The *Laconia* (Official No.113178) was an iron 195-ton steam fishing trawler measuring 33.95m long with a 6.55m beam. Cook, Welton & Gemmel built her as Yard No.258 at Hull and launched her as *Laconia* on 30 April 1900. She was registered as Grimsby trawler No.GY1173 on 2 June for Great Grimsby & East Coast Steam Fishing Co. Ltd. Her single iron screw propeller was powered by a 3-cylinder triple expansion steam engine that developed 55hp using one boiler, which gave the vessel a top speed of 10 knots. Amos Smith & Co. built her machinery at Hull.

On 17 May 1911 the SS *Laconia* was on a return fishing voyage when she foundered, following a collision with the 2,619-ton steamship *Loch Lomond*, three miles north-north-east of Scarborough. It is understood that the crew were taken on board the SS *Loch Lomond*.

Wreck-site
The wreck is upright, lying on a seabed of sand and stone, in a general depth of 43m, the lowest astronomical depth. She is now totally collapsed, well broken up, standing 3m high amidships, where her boiler, engine and donkey engine are exposed. Very little of interest is obvious, except some lengths of flattened copper pipe and a few small brass valves, intermingled with a mound of decayed, broken debris. She will nevertheless be an interesting wreck to explore, because her bell and most if not all of her bridge and steering equipment should still be around. Very few fish and little other marine life have been observed. Tidal streams are strong and with generally poor to grim visibility most of the time with the chance of nets being snagged on the wreck, she is one for experienced divers only. During the summer months, visibility significantly improves.

SAN ANTONIO
Wreck: *
Depth: 5m
Reference: N54 19 635 W000 24 700
Location: 0.41 miles SSE of Long Nab and N of Scarborough

The *San Antonio* was an iron 1,870-ton Spanish steamship registered at Bilbao measuring 83.75m long, with a 12.35m beam and a 5.60m draught. She was built in 1881 and owned at the time of loss by Compañía de Navigacion of La Blanca, Bilbao. Her single iron screw propeller was powered by a 3-cylinder triple expansion steam engine that used two boilers and she was classed at Lloyds as 100 A1. She was equipped with a brass pedestal-mounted steering helm and telegraph.

On 10 December 1900 the SS *San Antonio* was on passage from Bilbao for Newcastle-upon-Tyne when, during dense fog she was stranded on rocks, 150m out in Burniston Bay. She was carrying a cargo of cast iron ingots/pigs and a crew of twenty, under the command of Captain V. Berrojain.

Wreck-site
What remains of the wreck lies 150m towards the coastguard lookout station from the bottom of the cliff-steps. She is now totally collapsed, well broken up and scattered about on a seabed of rock, small reefs and boulders in a general depth of 5m, the lowest astronomical depth. The wreck is generally orientated in a north-north-west to south-south-east direction and subjected to rather moderate tidal streams but, except for the occasional edible crab and some shoals of small saithe, very little of interest remains. However the site is a nice beginner's dive during the summer months when conditions are good, but to shore-dive it requires a half mile trek, which is extremely tiring. Visibility is usually poor, but significantly improves after a dry spell of weather and westerly winds, especially during the summer months.

COGNAC
Wreck: *
Scenery: ***
Depth: 3-5m
Reference: N54 19 320 W000 24 740
Location: Off Cromer Point, Burniston Bay

The *Cognac* was a steel 1,200-ton French dumb barge that measured approximately 85m in length, with a 13m beam.

On 6 June 1917 she was on a voyage from Sunderland to Le Havre with a cargo of coal and a crew of ten when she went ashore in heavy seas and stranded, becoming a total wreck. Part of the vessel was later salvaged.

Wreck-site
The remains are now totally collapsed, well broken up and dispersed among the rocks and boulders just off the shore at low tide. It is quite possible to reach the wreck-site from land but it requires quite a considerable trek from the parking area, south from the nearby farm and coastguard station. There is not a lot of her to see, but the occasional crustacean can be found amongst the rocks, making the effort reasonably worthwhile. Tidal streams are very reasonable and underwater visibility usually poor, but can be in the region of 10m during periods in the summer months.

The remains can be found in Ordnance Survey position OS 929N.

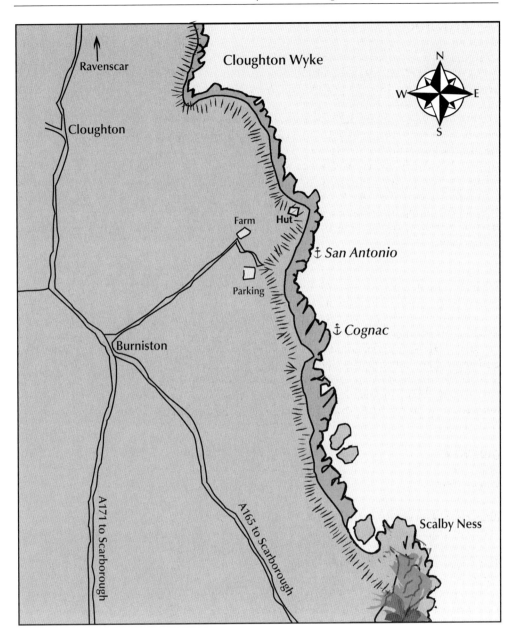

SIR FRANCIS
Wreck: ★★★★
Depth: 32m
Reference: N54 19 078 W000 20 795
Location: 2.2 miles NE of Scarborough Rock

The *Sir Francis* was a steel 1,991-ton British steamship that was registered at the port of London and measured 85.44m in length by 12.31m beam with a 5.61m draught. She was built in 1910 by S.P. Austin & Son at Sunderland and owned at the time of loss by Cory Colliers Ltd. Her single screw was powered by a 3-cylinder triple expansion steam engine that developed 208hp using two 2SB 6PF boilers, and cylinder sizes: 53.34cm, 86.36cm and 142.24cm-99.06cm.

G. Clark Ltd of Sunderland built the machinery. She had one deck and a superstructure consisting of a 7.62m poop deck, 16.46m bridge deck and an 8.84m forecastle. She was also armed with one stern-mounted Mk 4 deck-gun that fired 1.36kg shells.

On 7 June 1917, at 4.40 a.m., the SS *Sir Francis* was in ballast making 10 knots, on passage from London for the Tyne when she was struck under No.3 hold by a torpedo fired by the German U-boat SM UB 21. At no time was the U-boat sighted by the steamship's crew. The freighter, which was under the command of Captain R.G. Strickland and carrying a crew of twenty-two, started to sink by the stern. However, as her crew began to lower the ship's boats, another torpedo detonated under the bridge causing her to sink almost at once, taking with her the confidential papers. Ten of the crew were killed or drowned, including the captain, while the twelve survivors were picked up out of the sea by passing ships and landed at South Shields.

The steamship *Dryade* was in the vicinity and her captain later reported that he had seen the submarine that fired the first torpedo, but he said the second one was fired at his ship. It was either by his evasive actions or by sheer chance that it missed and struck the SS *Sir Francis* instead. The SS *Dryade*, which was seized from the Germans as a prize of war in 1914, was also lost six months after the SS *Sir Francis* when, on 8 December, she foundered following a collision with the London-registered steamship *Upminster*, some ten miles south-east of Flamborough Head. She was on passage from the Tyne for London, carrying an unspecified cargo of coal and a crew of twenty-three, none of whom were lost.

Following the armistice, SM UB 21 was surrendered to the French and was sunk somewhere along the English East Coast in 1920, en route to being broken up.

Wreck-site

The wreck believed to be the SS *Sir Francis* lies in a north-north-west to south-south-east direction on a seabed of fine sand, in a general depth of 32m, the lowest astronomical depth. She stands about 6m high and is substantial but collapsed, with the highest section amidships, around her boilers and engine. These are surrounded by a mass of debris, broken steel plates, valves and twisted pipes etc. Very little if any of the vessel's bridge equipment or navigational gear is likely to be left; a brass pedestal-mounted telegraph and pedestal-mounted steering helm have been recovered. There is also the possibility that her bell has also been recovered in recent years. Tidal streams are strong and underwater visibility is usually very poor at most times of the year. Lion's mane jellyfish can be a hazard when diving during the months of July and August too. The wreck is said to attract fair numbers of saithe, which often shoal over the top of her. Ten crew members died on the ship, the wreck should be treated with respect.

SM UB 41, Imperial German submarine

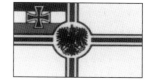

Wreck: ★★★★★
Depth: 48m
Reference: N54 18 005 W000 13 213
Location: 5.8 miles E of Scarborough Rock

SM UB 41 was a UB11-class attack boat of the SM U30-41 type, designed as a single-hulled boat for coastal patrol work. She was built by Blohm & Voss at Hamburg for the Imperial German Navy, launched on 6 May 1916 and commissioned for service on 25 August 1916. The boat had a surface displacement of 274 tons, 303 tons submerged, and was 36.9m long, 4.26m in beam and 3.7m draught. Two 135hp diesel/oil engines powered her two bronze screw propellers giving her a maximum speed of 9 knots. Rows of lead-acid batteries powered her two 140hp electric motors for running submerged and gave her a maximum speed of 5.7 knots. Her armament consisted of two bow torpedo tubes and one 88mm deck-gun, and she carried four torpedoes. Her normal complement was two officers and twenty-one crewmen, but she sometimes carried more on active service.

On her thirteenth patrol, under the command of Max Ploen and carrying a crew of twenty-four, SM UB 41 left her base at Bremerhaven on 30 September 1917. Her patrol took her to the stretch of coastline between Flamborough Head and Whitby. On 3 October 1917, UB 41 torpedoed and badly damaged the 502-ton steamship *Clyderbrae*, some three to five miles north-east of Scarborough. The U-boat was reported as missing on 5 October 1917. However, coastal watchers at Scarborough reported a massive explosion that same morning in the estimated position of: N54 18 W00 21. The explosion was believed to be that of UB 41 detonating a mine. However, it is not really clear what happened to her. She may have been lost in the extensive British minefield laid earlier in September that year, or in the minefield laid by SM UC 55 on 9 July. There is also the possibility that she was lost through a navigational or equipment failure, or perhaps even through a drill procedure that went fatally wrong.

Wreck-site
The wreck of UB 41 has never been located and previous suggested positions have turned out a blank. However, there is an unknown wreck of similar proportions to that of the U-boat, in position N54 18 005 W000 13 213, and the author believes that it could possibly be her. The wreck is lying in a north-north-west to south-south-east direction, on a seabed of fine sand and small stones, in a general depth of 48m, the lowest astronomical depth. She is upright, intact, well defined and covers an area of 35m long by 7m across and 4m high. The length and height are about right for the UB 41, though the width is a little too big, but there could be a number of explanations for this. It is very unlikely that the wreck has been dived, so she will be an interesting one to explore, even if it turns out not to be the U-boat. Tidal streams are very strong around this area and underwater visibility is poor to grim, but will improve during the summer months.

ELFRIDA
Wreck: ★★★★
Depth: 30m
Reference: N54 17 863 W000 19 282
Also: N54 17 863 W000 19 409
Location: 2.27 miles E by N of Scarborough Rock

The *Elfrida* was a steel 2,624-ton British steamship that was registered at Newcastle-upon-Tyne and measured 95.4m long by 13.71m beam and a draught of 6.4m. Wood Skinner & Co. built her at Billquay-on-Tyne in 1907 and the Brewis Line Ltd of Newcastle-upon-Tyne owned her at the time of loss. Her single iron screw propeller was powered by a 3-cylinder triple expansion steam engine that developed 260hp using two 2SB 6CF boilers and her cylinders measured 58.42cm, 95.25cm and 156.21cm-99.06cm. North Eastern Marine Engineering Co. built her machinery. Her bridge/wheelhouse equipment also included a brass pedestal-mounted telegraph and pedestal-mounted steering helm.

At 12.40 a.m. on 7 January 1915, the SS *Elfrida* was preparing to anchor off Scarborough and was taking lead and line soundings when she detonated a German mine. She was in the middle of her voyage at the time, on passage from the Tyne for London with a 4,150-ton cargo of coal and a crew of twenty-one. The crew took to the boats just before she foundered twenty minutes after the explosion. At 3.40 a.m., thirteen of the crew, including the captain, were picked up by the steamship *Glenesk* and landed at West Hartlepool, while a minesweeper picked up the remaining eight and took them to Scarborough.

SMS *Kolberg*, a German Navy light cruiser, had laid the mine, one of 100 she had put down between Filey and Scarborough. Within ten days, those mines sent eight allied steamships to the bottom and left several more seriously damaged. From 19 December, a fleet of Royal Navy minesweeping trawlers were employed to clear the area, but four of the trawlers and eighteen sailors were lost in the operation. The mines caused in total the loss of over twenty vessels and killed more than 100 personnel over a period of a few months.

Just four months after Britain declared war on Germany on 4 August 1914, the realities of war were brought home to England. SMS *Kolberg*, which was part of a battle-cruiser squadron consisting of three warships, came close inshore and bombarded the coastal towns of Scarborough, Whitby and Hartlepool. Scarborough alone was pounded with over 200 heavy shells for twenty minutes on 16 December. This resulted in the death of eighteen civilians and at least 100 more were left badly injured. Considerable damage was also done to 200 homes and business properties. Britain was enraged and Royal Navy warships were immediately deployed to intercept the squadron of enemy ships, but a coastal fog brought visibility down to 1,000 yards and the two opposing fleets never actually engaged. One theory was that the German bombardment was a ploy to lure the British fleet into the minefield, which, if it had been successful, would have had devastating results for the pride of the Royal Navy.

Many of Imperial Germany's surface raiders were destroyed during the First World War, but the 4,350-ton SMS *Kolberg*, which had a complement of 379 crew, survived and in 1920 became the French *Colmar*. Schichau built *Kolberg* at the Kiel yard and her keel was laid in March 1907, with the launch taking place in December 1909. Steam turbines built by Melms & Pfenningean powered her four bronze screw propellers. She developed 19,600hp and used fifteen boilers built by Schulz-Thornycroft, and was designed to travel at a maximum of 25 knots. She was 130.4m long (130m at the waterline) and had a beam of 14.02m and a draught of 5.41m. She normally carried 400 tons of fuel coal, with a maximum of 900 tons. SMS *Kolberg* had an armament of six 14.99cm (5.9in) guns, two 9.98kg guns (22 pounders), two machine guns and two submerged 44.96cm (17.7in) torpedo tubes. She also carried 120 mines. The *Kolberg*'s sister ship SMS *Augsburg* also survived the war and surrendered at the end of it. Both vessels were then disarmed.

Wreck-site
The wreck, probably that of the SS *Elfrida*, lies in a north–north-west to south–south-east direction on a seabed of fine sand, in a general depth of 30m, the lowest astronomical depth. She stands some 8m high at amidships, is collapsed and broken up with the upper structures covered in an array of soft corals. The majority of her interesting artefacts (e.g. navigation equipment, portholes etc.) are no longer around and it is very likely that the ship's bell has been recovered. The wreck is dived quite regularly and is said to be still worth a visit for diving and as a boat-angling venue. Tidal streams are rather strong and underwater visibility usually very poor, but it significantly improves following a dry spell of weather, westerly winds and neap tides during the summer months.

ELTERWATER
Wreck: ★★★★
Depth: 47m
Reference: N54 17 495 W000 13 693
Location: 5.53 miles E of Scarborough

The *Elterwater* was a steel 1,228-ton British steamship that was registered at Newcastle-upon-Tyne, and measured 71.62m in length, with a 10.18m beam and a 4.40m draught. Blyth Shipbuilding Co. built her in 1907 and the Elterwater Steamship Co. Ltd of Milburn House, Newcastle-upon-Tyne owned her at the time of loss (although other sources quote the Sharp Steamship Co.) Her single iron screw propeller was powered by a 3-cylinder triple expansion steam engine that used one 1SB 4CF boiler. Her cylinders measured 48.26cm, 78.74cm and 129.54cm-91.44cm. North Eastern Marine Engineering Co. built her machinery at Sunderland.

On 16 December 1914, the SS *Elterwater* detonated a mine placed by the Imperial German Navy light cruiser SMS *Kolberg*. The steamer was under the command of Captain David Gillan and on passage from the Tyne for London with a 1,750-ton cargo of coal and a crew of eighteen. She struck the mine at 6.13 p.m., heeled over and sank by the stern in just three minutes, leaving no time to launch the boats and the seventeen crewmen had no other option but to go into the water. However, Captain Gillan was actually washed off the bridge as the ship went down. The resulting explosion had blown out the port side of the ship, near the engine room. To avoid being sucked down, the men swam for their lives to get clear of the ship and then just swam around, clinging onto what floating wreckage they could find. The steamship *City*, which had left the Tyne with coal only an hour or two after the *Elterwater*, heard the explosion and saw the ship's lights disappear in the darkness. She hurried over to the spot and her master ordered a boat to be launched to assist, but the blackness of night and floating wreckage hampered the search for survivors. Eventually they reached the men who had managed to stay close together after having been in the freezing water for over an hour. Unfortunately five of the men had already perished and were missing. The second mate, John Tapping, aged thirty-five, who was lifted into the boat unconscious with a serious head injury, also died later from the injuries he had received in the explosion. The five crewmen missing were the second engineer, Thomas Digman of South Shields, the mess room steward, Thomas Hoop also from South Shields, and three Arab seamen.

The *City* returned to the Tyne with the twelve survivors, including Captain Daniel Gillan, the following day and an inquest on the incident was held six days later.

Wreck-site
The wreck, possibly that of the steamship *Elterwater*, lies in an east-south-east to west-north-west direction, on a hard seabed of fine sand and stone, in a general depth of 47m, the lowest astronomical depth. She is intact, upright and partially buried, but standing some 7m high with her superstructure collapsed. The wreck is very impressive and substantial, covering an area of around 85m by 20m. The upper structures are covered in a fine array of soft corals and numerous fish have been observed, so she should make an excellent boat-angling venue when weather conditions permit. It is not known how often divers have visited the site, but she will be a nice one to explore. However a large trawl net is reported as snagged up with the stern section, so great care will be warranted. Tidal streams are very brisk and underwater visibility usually poor but improve during the summer months. The wreck should also be respected as the final resting place of those seamen who perished with their ship.

PRINCESS OLGA
Wreck: ★★★★
Depth: 46m
Reference: N54 17 762 W000 15 676
Location: 4.34 miles E by N of Scarborough Rock

The *Princess Olga* was a steel 998-ton British steamship that was registered at the port of Glasgow, and measured 72.17m in length, with a 9.8m beam and a draught of 4.72m. She was built at Port Glasgow in 1901 and owned at the time of loss by M. Langlands & Sons of Liverpool and Glasgow. Her single iron screw propeller was powered by a 3-cylinder triple expansion steam engine that developed 125hp using one boiler.

On 16 December 1914 the SS *Princess Olga* was on passage from Liverpool for Aberdeen with a 1,000-ton general cargo, when she detonated a German mine and foundered. The explosion occurred at 7.30 p.m. and her crew of nineteen were ordered to abandon ship immediately. The two boats were lowered, one with the captain in and the other with the mate in charge, then they lay off until the vessel sank two hours later. At 9 p.m., the party in the captain's boat were picked up by the steamship *Glenrose* and landed at Scarborough at 10 a.m. the next day. The crew in the second boat containing the mate, made their way back to

Scarborough under their own steam, arriving at the port at 1.30 a.m. on 17 December.

The SS *Princess Olga* was one of three casualties to detonate mines laid by the Imperial German Navy light cruiser SMS *Kolberg* on 16 December 1914. The others were the *Elterwater*, which had left the Tyne for London with a cargo of coal, and the Norwegian steamship *Vaaren,* on passage to Palermo with a cargo of coal. Following the sinking of these vessels, the Admiralty instructed the Hull fishing fleet to suspend its operations in the area until the minefield had been swept clear. Then, on 19 December, a fleet of Royal Navy minesweepers were employed to clear the minefield. The operation lasted until 23 April 1915, but at a cost of eighteen sailors and four RN trawlers, which were lost as a result of detonating mines.

Wreck-site

The wreck, probably that of the steamship *Princess Olga,* lies north–north–west to south–south–east on a seabed of fine sand and stone, in a general depth of 46m, the lowest astronomical depth. She covers an area of seabed some 60m by 16 or 17m, stands upright around 5m high, and is fairly intact, but now collapsed and broken up with her boiler and engine exposed and surrounded by a mass of twisted steel and broken debris. A number of portholes are said to be visible on the now corroding steel hull plates, along with brass valves, lengths of copper piping, bollards and winches. The upper structures have a coating of soft corals and numerous fish, including some large cod, shoal around the boiler/engine area. Tidal streams are very strong and underwater visibility usually rather dismal, but improves during the mid summer months. A bonus is that a number of great scallops and queen scallops ('queenies') can be found on the seabed in the vicinity of the wreck-site. A good lookout is required by anyone visiting the wreck, because she is in the main shipping lanes.

Chapter 2

Scarborough to Filey

Area 2 (N54 18′ to N54 13′)

LADY ANN
Wreck: ★★★★
Depth: 29m
Reference: N54 16 967 W000 18 685
Location: 2.62 miles E by S of Scarborough Rock

The *Lady Ann* was an iron 1,016-ton British steamship registered at the port of Sunderland and measured 68.65m in length, with a 10.05m beam and a 4.95m draught. She was built by Austin & Son at Sunderland in 1882 and owned at the time of loss by Lambton & Hetton Collieries Ltd. Her single iron propeller was powered by a 2-cylinder compound steam engine that developed 99hp using one 1SB boiler, which was replaced in 1906. North Eastern Marine Engineering Co. Ltd at Sunderland built her machinery.

At 2.40 p.m. on 16 February 1917, the SS *Lady Ann* was carrying an unspecified cargo of coal and a crew of sixteen, under the command of Captain R.M. Blakeburn. She was on passage from Sunderland for Rochester when a tremendous explosion suddenly rocked the ship beneath her bridge. The whole ship was lifted upwards, throwing the helmsman and chief officer off their feet, while the complete bow section of the vessel broke off, rolled over and sank immediately. As the captain, chief officer, helmsman, chief engineer and two seamen scrambled to launch the port lifeboat, the SS *Lady Ann* slipped beneath the waves, taking her captain and ten men down with her. The helmsman and four surviving crew clung to floating wreckage and were picked up by a local fishing coble, which landed them at Scarborough.

Official records do not say what caused the explosion, but it is believed that the vessel detonated a mine.

Wreck-site
The wreck lies in a north-east to south-west direction, on a seabed of sand and mud, in a general depth of 29m, the lowest astronomical depth. She is collapsed, although the stern-end is, or was, reported to be fairly intact. The broken-off bow section is upturned and pointing back towards the stern, with the boiler and engine standing upright and lying abreast of it. The wreck stands some 3m high and covers an area of seabed measuring about 60m by 20m. She has been well dived in recent years so very little of interest will remain of her navigation and steering equipment etc. However she is a pleasant dive and well worth a visit. Members of the Scarborough Sub Aqua Club recovered what remained of the huge emergency steering wheel. Tidal streams are reasonably strong and underwater visibility usually very poor, although it improves significantly during the summer months after a spell of dry weather and westerly winds. A number of large cod and saithe have been reported on and around the wreck-site, so she may be worth a visit as a boat-angling venue.

The wreck should be given the respect of a war grave by visiting divers.

H675 *Sapphire*, built 1912, Cochranes, Selby. Yard No.553. Length: 133ft 5in, Gross Tonnage: 289.2. Sunk by mine off Filey, 1 March 1915, with one man lost. *(Courtesy Jonathan Grobler Collection)*

SAPPHIRE
Wreck: ★★★
Depth: 46m
Reference: N54 16 945 W000 14 117
Location: 5.13 miles E by S of Scarborough Rock

The *Sapphire* was a steel 289-ton steam fishing trawler that was registered at Hull, and measured 40.66m in length, with a 7.01m beam and a 3.7m draught. Cochrane & Sons Ltd built her as Yard No.553 at Selby in 1912 and Kingston Steam Trawling Co. Ltd owned her at the time of loss. Her single iron screw propeller was powered by a 3-cylinder triple expansion steam engine that developed 83hp using one 1SB 4PF boiler and her cylinders measured 33.02cm, 55.88cm and 93.98cm. C.D. Holmes & Co. Ltd built her machinery at Hull. She had one deck, four bulkheads and a superstructure consisting of a 22.25m quarterdeck and 6.10m forecastle.

On 1 March 1915, the steam trawler was on a return fishing voyage from Iceland to Hull under the command of Captain G. Leighton, when she detonated a German mine and sank 4.12 miles north-north-east of Filey Brigg. One of her crew was lost with the vessel. The Imperial German Cruiser SMS *Kolberg* laid the mine.

Wreck-site
The wreck believed to be the steam trawler lies orientated in a south-east to north-west direction, on a seabed of fine sand and shell, in a general depth of 46m, the lowest astronomical depth. She is intact, totally collapsed, broken up and partially buried, standing 2m high amidships, with her boiler/engine exposed. The wreck-site has a covering of sediment, but soft corals are established on the upper parts of the wreckage. One or two crustaceans were observed but there were no signs of any fish around her. Tidal streams are very strong and underwater visibility is usually very poor, but improves significantly during the summer months.

VILLE D'ORAN, ex FLINK, ex SIPAN, ex ISLANDER

Wreck: ★★★
Depth: 48m
Reference: N54 16 837 W000 11 080
Location: 7 miles ESE of Scarborough Rock

The *Ville d'Oran* was a steel 399-ton French steamship that was registered at the port of Oran in Algeria. She measured 45.72m in length, with a 7.34m beam and a 3.25m draught. R. Thompson & Sons built her as the *Islander* at Sunderland in 1896 for the Steamship Islander Co. and managed by M. Whitwall & Son. She was later sold to Navigation à Vapeur Ragusa, managed by M. Marinovic and registered at Ragusa in Austria-Hungary and her name changed to *Sipan*. Later she was renamed *Flink* when purchased by her new owner C. Martinolich e Figlio of Trieste in Austria-Hungary. The French company, Scotto, Ambrosino & Pugliese of Oran, which was the owner at the time of loss, then purchased her and changed her name to *Ville d'Oran*. Her single iron screw propeller was powered by a 2-cylinder compound steam engine that developed 78hp using one boiler and her cylinders measured 48.26cm and 101.60cm-68.58cm. Jameson & MacColl built her machinery at South Shields. She had one deck, a well deck, four bulkheads, and a superstructure consisting of a 25.30m quarterdeck, 4.88m bridge deck and 4.57m forecastle.

On 5 September 1916 the vessel was on passage from North Shields for Dunkirk when she detonated a German mine and foundered. She was under the command of Captain Cantarelli and carrying a cargo of coal. It is not known if anyone was lost with this vessel.

Wreck-site

The wreck, possibly that of the small French vessel, lies in a south-east to north-west direction, on a seabed of sand and stone, in a general depth of 48m, the lowest astronomical depth. She is mostly collapsed, standing some 5m high amidships to stern and covers, an area of seabed measuring 50m by 15m. The upper bridge structures have collapsed and at least one large trawl net is entangled with the broken superstructure. Pieces of debris lie strewn around the site and large lengths of flattened and bent copper pipes protrude from the wreck near to the stern end, where her steel screw is in place and visible. If the ship's bell is recovered, it will almost certainly be inscribed '*Islander*' and the date she was built, '1896'. A number of large cod have been observed under the wreckage too. Tidal streams are very strong and underwater visibility is usually poor, but improves during the summer months, although the site always appears dark and eerie. A bonus to the area where this wreck lies is the occasional scallop that can be found on the seabed.

LEANDER

Wreck: ★★★★★
Depth: 45m
Reference: N54 16 768 W000 14 607
Location: 4.98 miles E by S of Scarborough Rock

The *Leander* was a steel 2,968-ton Norwegian steamship that was registered at the port of Arendal and measured 96.01m in length, by a 12.31m beam and a draught of 6.42m. Tyne Iron Shipbuilding Co. Ltd built her at Newcastle-upon-Tyne in 1892, although another report has her built by Wallsend Slipway Co. Kallevig & Measles in Norway owned her at the time of loss. Her single screw, possibly bronze, was powered by a 3-cylinder triple expansion steam engine that developed 267hp using two boilers. She had cylinders measuring 58.42cm, 96.52cm and 154 94cm. Her bridge and wheelhouse equipment included a brass pedestal-mounted steering helm and telegraph, plus an emergency pedestal-mounted steering helm on her deck.

On 20 October 1917 the SS *Leander* was on passage from Hartlepool for Savona with a cargo of coal, under the command of Captain K. Pettersen, when she was torpedoed and sunk by the Imperial German submarine SM UB 57. The author is not sure if anyone perished on the vessel when she went down. SM UB 57 was later mined off Zeebrugge on 14 August 1918.

Wreck-site
The wreck lies in a north-east to south-west direction, on a seabed of fine sand and stone, in a general depth of 45m. She is quite substantial, standing some 6m high and covering an area of seabed measuring 110m by 18m. She is broken into three parts, with her bows upright, but listing to port. The amidships section is partially collapsed, lying over to port, and part of her boiler is protruding through the side of the hull. The stern section lists over to starboard and is the highest part of the wreck with a lovely array of soft corals established over the upper reaches. It is believed that her bell and much of her interesting navigation equipment has long since gone, but the wreck is said to be a nice one to visit when conditions permit. Large shoals of fish can be observed all around her, including cod, pout whiting and saithe, so she will make an excellent boat-angling venue. Tidal streams are very strong and the underwater visibility is usually very poor to grim at most times of the year, but improves during mid-summer. Trawl nets and fishing lures are an additional hazard, so great care will be required, especially as the wreck is in rather deep water.

JERV
Wreck: ★★★★★
Depth: 50m
Reference: N54 16 747 W000 04 498
Location: 11.19 miles E by S from Scarborough Rock

The *Jerv* was a steel 1,112-ton Norwegian steamship registered at the port of Risor and measured 69.8m in length, with a 10.71m beam and a draught of 4.8m. She was built in 1906 by Bergens M.V. at Bergen and owned at the time of loss by A/S Bjorn of Risor. Her single screw propeller, possibly bronze, was powered by a 3-cylinder triple expansion steam engine that developed 106hp using one boiler and she had one deck.

On 1 February 1917, the SS *Jerv* was in ballast on passage from Rouen for Middlesbrough, under the command of Captain H. Madsen, when SM UC 32, an Imperial German submarine, torpedoed her. Other sources believe she detonated a mine laid by SM UC 32, which was later lost off Sunderland on 23 February 1916 when she detonated one of her own mines.

Wreck-site
The wreck of the *Jerv* lies orientated in a north-west to south-east direction, on a seabed of sand and stone, in a general depth of 50m, the lowest astronomical depth. She is now mostly rather collapsed and broken up, standing some 6m high with her boiler/engine around amidships both exposed. However, the stern-end, which is said to be reasonably intact, is covered in an array of soft corals and has a large shoal of pout whiting swarming around it. Tidal streams are rather strong and underwater visibility usually very poor. The wreck of the *Jerv* should make an interesting boat angling venue when weather conditions permit. Added bonuses to this site are the scallops and 'queenies' that can be found on the seabed in this area.

HOUGHTON
Wreck: ★
Depth: 47m
Reference: N54 16 662 W000 13 631
Location: 5.41 miles ESE of Scarborough Rock

The *Houghton* was an iron 763-ton British schooner rigged steamship that was registered at Sunderland, and measured 59.73m in length, with an 8.86m beam and a draught of 4.98m. H.T. Morton built her at Sunderland in 1870 and H.T. Morton of Biddick Hall, Durham, owned her at the time of loss. Her single iron screw propeller was powered by a 2-cylinder compound steam engine that used one boiler.

On 18 August 1886, the old schooner-rigged vessel was on passage from Sunderland for Dieppe when she foundered off Scarborough, following a collision with the London-registered steamer *J.M. Strachan*. She was under the command of Captain H. Swinson and carrying an unspecified cargo of coal and a crew of sixteen.

Wreck-site
The wreck, possibly that of SS *Houghton*, lies in a south-south-east to north-north-west direction, on a seabed of fine sand and stone, in a general depth of 47m, the lowest astronomical depth. If these are her remains, she is now totally collapsed, partially buried and well broken up, with the highest section standing no more than 1.5m. Tidal streams are fairly brisk and underwater visibility is usually very poor, but improves during the summer months. Very little else is known about this wreck-site, but it may well be worth investigating, although not as a boat-angling venue.

HORNSUND
Wreck: ★★★★★
Depth: 22m
Reference: N54 16 520 W000 18 920
Also: N54 16 533 W000 18 929
Location: 2.55 miles ESE of Scarborough Rock

13 pdr MI/2I Vickers Pattern stern gun was lifted by Scarboro' Sub Aqua Club in 1982 – now mounted next to Lighthouse in harbour.

The *Hornsund* was a steel 3,646-ton British steamship that was registered at the port of London. She measured 114.75m in length, with a 15.41m beam and a draught of 6.5m. Schiffsw. V. Henry Koch built her at Lübeck, Germany, in 1913 for German owners. However, at the time of her loss she was managed by Everett, but owned by the Admiralty. Her single screw was powered by a 3-cylinder triple expansion steam engine, with cylinder sizes: 68.58cm, 107.95cm and 173.99cm-109.22cm, which developed 310hp using two boilers. Ottensener Masch. Fabrik built her machinery in Lübeck. Her top structures were one deck, a shelter-deck and a 13.11m forecastle. The vessel was also armed with one stern-mounted deck-gun that fired 5.90kg shells (13 pounders). The vessel's bridge-wheelhouse equipment included a brass pedestal-mounted steering helm and telegraph, plus one large pedestal-mounted iron steering helm, positioned at the stern on her deck.

At the outbreak of the First World War, the SS *Hornsund* was taken over as a prize of war and the Admiralty requisitioned her as a collier.

On 23 September 1917, she was making 8.5 knots on passage from the Tyne for London, when she was torpedoed and sunk by SM UC 71, an Imperial German U-boat. At no time was the submarine sighted by the steamship's crew. She was under the command of Captain M.B. Walker, carrying a crew of thirty-two and a cargo of coal. The torpedo detonated in the engine room at 1.10 p.m., killing one seaman outright and leaving the third engineer badly injured. The ship immediately started to sink, going down in ten minutes, leaving just sufficient time for the crew to abandon ship in the boats and get clear of the vessel. Only one man was lost and the thirty-one survivors, including the third engineer, were picked up by a torpedo boat destroyer and landed at Scarborough. Only after the First World War ended and U-boat records were released was it known how the SS *Hornsund* was sunk. SM UC 71 went on to survive the First World War, but sank en route to being surrendered on 2 February 1919 in position N54 10 E07 54.

Wreck-site
The wreck, probably that of the SS *Hornsund*, lies orientated in a south-east to north-west direction, on a seabed of sand, in a general depth of 22m, the lowest astronomical depth. She is now totally collapsed and well broken up, lying in three sections, with the engine block being the highest part of the wreck at 3m and stands by itself, the hull plates having collapsed. These are surrounded by a mass of broken twisted debris covering a large area of the silty seabed. The occasional crustacean can be found amongst the cluttered steel debris and shoals of saithe and pout whiting (a small colourful member of the cod family), are sometimes seen during the summer. Tidal streams are fairly strong and underwater visibility usually poor to dismal, but improve after a spell of settled dry weather and westerly winds during the summer months. The best time to visit the site is during neap tides at slack water, which occurs 1 ½ to 2 hours after low tide on the shore.

BUR, ex A.J. HOCKEN
Wreck: ★★★★
Depth: 27m
Reference: N54 16 502 W000 18 133
Location: 2.98 miles ESE of Scarborough Rock

The *Bur* (Official No.4471) was a steel 1,942-ton Swedish steamship that was registered at the port of Stockholm, Sweden. She measured 82.3m in length, with a 12.5m beam and a draught of 5.5m. Grangemouth & Greenock Dockyard built her as the *A.J. Hocken* in 1901 for Rederi Aktieb Union and G.O. Wallenberg managed her. Rederiaktieb AB 'Bur' of Stockholm, which was the owner at the time of loss, later purchased her and renamed the vessel *Bur*. The manager was then Olof Brodin of Stockholm, Sweden. Her single iron screw propeller was powered by a 3-cylinder triple expansion steam engine that developed 181hp using two 2SB 4CF boilers. S.H. Morton & Co. of Leith built her machinery. Her cylinders measured 50.80cm, 82.55cm and 134.62cm-91.44cm.

The SS *Bur* left Gothenburg on Tuesday 18 October 1917, under the command of Captain G. Perssen. The ship was in a fully seaworthy condition and well manned with a crew of twenty-two. She was on passage for London with a 2,839-ton general cargo, which included iron, steel, 363 bundles of sawn wood and wood-pulp. The *Bur* stayed in Swedish and Norwegian home waters until she reached Bergen, where she joined up with a convoy. From there the convoy made its way to Lerwick, which it reached on the evening of 30 October without any incidents. The next day, Wednesday 31 October, the *Bur* joined a different convoy at 2 p.m. in the afternoon, to continue her voyage to London. The journey was without incident until 3.45 p.m. on Friday 2 November, when the convoy was about 3 degrees magnetic from Scarborough.

The weather was fine and clear with good visibility and the steamer sailed at top speed, which was about 9.5 knots, in agreement with an order, to reach another steamship in the convoy. Suddenly the vessel was shaken violently and an explosion was heard from the stern. The whole aft section of the ship exploded into pieces and the *Bur* immediately began to sink. The ship's steward, Victor Nilsson, who was cleaning inside a cabin below deck, and the young mate F. Jansson (possibly a cabin-boy) who was assigned to buff the copper of the rudder, were both probably killed by the explosion, since nothing was ever found of them. The boats were put out during the whole voyage, so that in the event that she was hit, they could be lowered down very quickly. The crew abandoned ship quickly, but the lifeboat the captain was in sailed very near to the stern of the *Bur*, but no trace of the casualties could be found. An escorting trawler rescued the surviving crewmen within minutes. The escorting vessels stayed fairly close to the wrecked and sinking steamship, but when nothing was found of the missing men, they set course for the convoy again. Ten minutes after the explosion, the *Bur* was so low in the water that just 4.5m of the bows of the vessel could be seen above water and soon after that, she went down very fast. Nobody on the ship had seen anything of a torpedo or a submarine's periscope, but everyone on board was of the firm belief that the explosion was caused by a torpedo from a U-boat and not by a mine. The crew left the sinking vessel in such a hurry that the ship's confidential papers and the crew's personal effects were all lost when she went down. Near Spurn Head, a trawler was given the assignment of landing the survivors at Grimsby, which they did at 2 a.m. on 3 November.

The two men that perished were Bror Melker Douglas Jansson, young mate, born on 4 July 1898, who lived in Gothenburg and was not married, and Viktor Nilsson, who was the steward, born on 4th August 1892, and who lived in Gammalstorp (Blekinge). The SS *Bur* was actually torpedoed by SM UB 35, a German Navy U-boat. The U-boat was depth-charged and sunk by HMS *Leven* in the English Channel on 26 January 1917.

Wreck-site
The wreck lies in a north-north-east to west-south-west direction, on a seabed of fine sand, in a general depth of 27m, the lowest astronomical depth. She is upright and generally intact, standing some 6m high amidships, but her superstructure and hull has now collapsed, with her holds all silted up. The cargo of timber slats was reported to be still visible in the forward holds. Her stern end has substantial damage, possibly where the torpedo detonated, tearing a massive hole in the ship. The wreck-site covers an area measuring some 76m by 14m and there is no visible scour around it. Her boilers and engine are now said to be both exposed and surrounded by a mound of broken steel debris, intermingled with lengths of copper piping, much of which is bent and flattened. The vessel was equipped with a brass pedestal-mounted telegraph and steering helm making her an interesting one to explore and possibly photograph. Her bell if discovered, will almost certainly be inscribed '*A.J. Hocken*' and the date she was built, '1901'. Tidal streams are very strong and underwater visibility is rather poor most of the year. The occasional shoal of small fish has been observed over the wreck and one or two big cod have been seen hiding under the steel structures.

NIGHT HAWK, HM Trawler
Wreck: ★★★
Depth: 47m
Reference: N54 16 573W000 12 574
Location: 6.18 miles E by S of Scarborough Rock

The *Night Hawk* (Official No.132107) was a steel 287-ton steam fishing trawler and measured 39.6m in length with a beam of 7m. Cook, Welton & Gemmel built her as Yard No.216 at Beverley and she was launched on 29 April 1911. She was registered as trawler No.GY643 for Pioneer Steam Fishing Co. Ltd at Grimsby on 21 June 1911. Her single iron screw propeller was powered by a 3-cylinder triple expansion steam engine that developed 88hp using one boiler, which gave the vessel a maximum speed of 10.5 knots. In August 1914, the *Night Hawk* was requisitioned by the Admiralty and converted to Royal Navy minesweeper No.FY57.

On Christmas Day 1914, HMT *Night Hawk* was under the command of Lt W.E. Senior RN when she detonated a German mine and foundered, with the loss of six of her crew of thirteen.

H389 *Hawk*. Built 1898 by C.W. & G., Hull. Yard no.1. Length: 110ft, Gross Tonnage: 181.4. Sank following collision with Brazilian SS *Corcovado* five miles NE of Spurn LT/UL whilst outward bound from Hull to Iceland. *(Courtesy Jonathan Grobler Collection)*

She was part of a fleet of Royal Navy minesweepers attempting to clear up the 100 mines laid between Filey and Scarborough by SMS *Kolberg*, the German light cruiser, earlier that month. When HMT *Night Hawk* went down, weather conditions were utterly foul, with freezing temperatures and a strong icy wind blowing. However, Lt Senior managed to scramble onto a life raft, then sculled around to rescue his six surviving crewmen from the numbing water. Those six men owe their lives to this act of bravery.

Two other vessels were lost as a result of detonating the *Kolberg's* mines on that same fateful Christmas Day. They were the 1,107-ton Norwegian steamship, *Eli*, bound for Rouen from Blyth and the SS *Gem*, a British steamship of 464 tons en route to the Tyne from Mostyn.

The minesweeping operation lasted from 19 December until 23 April 1915, when a total of sixty-nine mines had been disposed of, but at the cost of four RN trawlers and eighteen sailors. During the First World War, no fewer than 214 minesweepers were lost, one for each week of the war.

Wreck-site
The wreck believed to be that of HM Trawler *Night Hawk* lies orientated in a north–north-east to south–south-west direction, on a seabed of sand and stone in a general depth of 47m, the lowest astronomical depth. She is now partially buried, totally collapsed and well broken up, standing no more than 1.6m around her upright boiler and engine, which are surrounded by a scattered mound of broken steel debris, intermingled with bent and flattened pieces of copper pipe. Her bows face to the south-west and the stern end of the vessel is broken off. The whole wreck-site covers an area of seabed measuring some 40m by 7m. Tidal streams are rather strong and under-water visibility usually utterly grim, but improve during the summer months following a spell of dry settled weather. Very little marine life has been observed on and around the wreck-site. The remains should be treated as a war grave because Royal Navy personnel died on the vessel.

NORHILDA

Wreck: ★★★★
Depth: 32m
Reference: N54 16 385 W000 17 105
Location: 3.57 miles ESE of Scarborough Rock

The *Norhilda* was a steel 1,175-ton British steamship registered at the port of Bristol. She measured 70.1m in length, with a 1.09m beam and a 4.9m draught. Swan Hunter & Wigham Richardson Ltd built her in 1910 at Newcastle-upon-Tyne. The owners at the time of loss were J. Cory & Sons and C. Tennant & Co. Her single iron screw propeller was powered by a 3-cylinder triple expansion steam engine that developed 145hp using two boilers. Her machinery was built by North East Marine Engineering Co. at Newcastle-upon-Tyne. She had one deck and a superstructure consisting of a 4.88m poop deck, an 18.29m bridge deck and an 8.23m forecastle. The vessel was also armed with one stern-mounted deck-gun that fired 5.90kg shells (13 pounders).

On 21 August 1917, the SS *Norhilda* was on passage from Harwich for the Tyne when the Imperial German submarine SM UC 17, which survived the First World War, torpedoed her. At no time was the U-boat sighted by any of the steamer's crew. At 4.15 p.m., the *Norhilda* was in ballast, carrying a crew of twenty-three, under the command of Captain J.J. Murphy, when the unmistakable wake of the torpedo was seen just before it struck the ship. A huge explosion occurred abreast the after-part of the bridge-deck, sending up a massive deluge of water. She then immediately began to sink by the stern so the crew boarded the port lifeboat, however it capsized before it was clear of the ship. Just five minutes after the explosion, the SS *Norhilda* sank beneath the waves, taking the upturned boat and the confidential papers down with her. Unfortunately the second engineer was missing, believed killed in the engine room, but the surviving twenty-two crewmen jumped into the water and floated around by clinging onto flotsam until they were picked up about thirty minutes later, by the steamship *Mergerison No.2*. Soon after, they were all transferred to a patrol vessel and landed at Scarborough.

Wreck-site

The wreck lies east-north-east to west-south-west, on a seabed of fine sand, in a general depth of 32m, the lowest astronomical depth. She is upright, reasonably intact and still very substantial, covering an area of seabed measuring 75m by 12m. The highest 4m sections are her bows, stern-end and part of the poop deck, which are still intact, but much of the wreck is now collapsed down, almost to seabed level, especially around the amidships section. Her two boilers and engine are now exposed, which are surrounded by lots of twisted, broken steel bulkhead and pipes, etc. The wreck was eventually identified by the name on her wheel-boss. Tidal streams are fairly strong and underwater visibility is usually dreadful, but it significantly improves during neap tides, westerly winds and dry settled weather in the summer months. Saithe, cod and pout whiting can often be seen around the wreck, so she may make an interesting boat-angling venue. Someone died and went down with this vessel so her remains should be treated with respect.

VAAREN
Wreck: ★★★
Depth: 45m
Reference: N54 16 365 W000 14 107
Also: N54 16 364 W000 14 125
Location: 3.53 miles NNE of Filey Brigg

The *Vaagen* was a steel 1,090-ton Norwegian steamship registered at Bergen. She was 68.88m in length, with a beam of 11.27m and draught of 4.9m. Howaldtswereke of Bergen built her in 1904 (another source has Bergen Mek Verksted in 1914) and B. Perderson owned her at the time of loss. Her single iron screw propeller was powered by a 3-cylinder triple expansion steam engine that used two boilers. Her cylinders measured 43.18cm, 66.04cm and 116.84cm-76.20cm.

On 16 December 1914, the newly built *Vaaren* was on a voyage from the Tyne to Palermo, Sicily, with an unspecified cargo of coal and coke when she sank 5.34 miles east-south-east of Scarborough Rock. She foundered after detonating one of the 100 mines laid by the Imperial German Navy light cruiser SMS *Kolberg*. The 988-ton Glasgow-registered steamer *Princess Olga* also succumbed to one of the mines and Hull trawlers were instructed by the Admiralty to suspend all fishing in that area until the minefield had been swept clear. From 19 December a fleet of Royal Navy minesweepers were employed to clear the minefield, under the command of Lt Godfrey Parsons RN.

Wreck-site
The wreck, possibly that of the steamship *Vaaren*, lies north-north-east to south-south-west, on a seabed of fine-sand and stone, in a general depth of 45m, the lowest astronomical depth. She is upright, intact, but partially buried in places, especially towards the bow section, which face to the north-east. Most of her superstructure is now collapsed down with lots of broken debris about, although the highest section stands 6m proud of the seabed. Her engine and two boilers are exposed and surrounded by a mass of twisted broken steel debris and lengths of bent and flattened copper piping. Tidal streams are very strong and underwater visibility poor to grim and with the wreck covered in nets, a lot of care is required when diving on her. The author is unsure whether anyone was lost with this vessel.

DEPTFORD
Wreck: ★★★★
Depth: 43m
Reference: N54 16 150 W000 14 617
Also: N54 16 148 W000 14 647
Location: 3.26 miles NNE of Filey Brigg

The *Deptford* (Official No.123662) was a steel 1,208-ton British steamship registered at the port of London. She measured 70.1m in length, with a 10.74m beam and a draught of 4.34m. Blyth Shipbuilding & Dry Dock Co. Ltd built her at Blyth in 1912 and William Cory & Son Ltd owned her at the time of loss. G. Clark built her machinery at Sunderland. Her single iron screw propeller was powered by a 2-cylinder compound steam engine that developed 170hp using two 1SB 4PF boilers. Her cylinders measured 48.26cm, 78.74cm and 129.54cm-91.44cm.

On 24 February 1915, the SS *Deptford* was on passage from Granton for Chatham with a cargo of Naval coal when she foundered after striking what was thought to have been an underwater obstacle. The steamship *Fulgens* picked up the survivors and landed them at North Shields.

A Board of Trade inquiry held on 5 May 1915 found that the vessel had been destroyed through enemy action, but were unable to decide if she had detonated a mine or had been torpedoed, and her captain was completely exonerated of any blame. In recent years it has been established that the Imperial German Navy light cruiser SMS *Kolberg* laid the mine that sank her.

Wreck-site
This wreck just may be that of the steamer *Deptford*, but only a few dives on her will tell. She is of roughly the same dimension, orientated north-east to south-west, on a seabed of sand and shell, in a general depth of 43m, the lowest astronomical depth. The wreck is upright and intact, standing some 6m high amidships to stern, with her upper structures collapsed and bows facing south-west. Tidal streams around this area are rather brisk and underwater visibility very poor on average, but it improves during the summer months. There is also the possibility that trawl nets could be snagged up in the wreckage so great care is required. Being so large, this wreck should make an excellent boat-angling venue when conditions permit.

LINARIA
Wreck: ★★★★★
Depth: 44m
Reference: N54 15 972 W000 13 608
Location: 3.29 miles NNE of Filey Brigg

The *Linaria* (Official No.127121) was a steel 3,081-ton British steamship that was registered at North Shields. She measured 100.96m in length, by 14.63m beam and a draught of 6.75m. W. Dobson Shipbuilding Co. built her in 1911 at Newcastle-upon-Tyne at a cost of £32,778 and Stag Line Ltd owned her at the time of loss. Her single iron screw propeller was powered by a 3-cylinder triple expansion steam engine that used three boilers. She had cylinders measuring 57.15cm, 92.71cm and 157.48cm-106.68cm. North Eastern Marine Engineering Co. built her machinery at Sunderland.

At 4.45 p.m. on Boxing Day 1914, the *Linaria* was in ballast, on passage from London for the Tyne with a crew of twenty-eight when she detonated a mine. The vessel was abandoned immediately, sinking soon after and the crew got safely away in the boats, without loss of life. Within a very short time, the Swedish steamship *Victoria* arrived on the scene and rescued the twenty-eight men, landing them at Sunderland early the following morning. The mine was one of the 100 laid by SMS *Kolberg* between Filey and Scarborough earlier that month and she was one of at least thirteen vessels to fall foul of them.

Wreck-site
The wreck believed to be that of the *Linaria* lies east-north-east to west-south-west, on a hard seabed of sand and stone in a general depth of 44m, the lowest astronomical depth. She is very substantial, upright and intact, standing some 4m high amidships, with some broken, collapsed superstructure visible. Much of her is now collapsed, with the lower hull partially buried. The bow section appears to be missing and her boilers and engine are exposed to the rather strong tides, which sweep over her. The wreck-site covers an area of seabed measuring 97m by 20m and scattered debris surrounds the site. Visibility is unfortunately usually poor to grim, being very typical for this part of the British East Coast, but improves during the summer months following a spell of dry settled weather. The wreck-site should also make a good boat-angling venue, especially during the summer months when large shoals of mackerel are also present in the area.

M.C. HOLM
Wreck: ★★★★
Depth: 31m
Reference: N54 15 843 W000 16 503
Location: 2.80 miles N of Filey Brigg

The *M.C. Holm* was a steel 2,458-ton Danish steamship that measured 94.50m in length, by 13.43m beam with a 6.20m draught. Richardson Duck & Co. built her in 1894 and M.C. Holm of Copenhagen were the owners at the time of loss. (Incidentally, the company M.C. Holm still existed in Copenhagen in the 1980s.) The vessel's single iron screw propeller was powered by a 3-cylinder triple expansion steam engine that used two boilers. This vessel's bridge-wheelhouse included a brass pedestal-mounted telegraph and steering helm.

On New Year's Eve 1914, the SS *M.C. Holm* detonated one of the 100 mines laid by the light cruiser SMS *Kolberg*. The steamship was carrying an unspecified cargo of raw cotton and phosphate on passage from Boca Grande, Savannah, for Copenhagen.

A fleet of minesweepers had been engaged in clearing the mines, laid between Filey and Scarborough, since 19 December. Within one month of beginning the formidable and dangerous task, they had cleared fifty-three of them.

Wreck-site
The wreck of SS *M.C. Holm* lies west-south-west to east-north-east. She lies on a seabed of sand and shell, in a general depth of 31m, the lowest astronomical depth. The wreck is upright, intact, standing around 4m high amidships, but collapsed and well broken up, with her boilers and engine exposed. The wreck is still very substantial, covering an area of seabed measuring around 93m by 15m, with a 1.5m scour around it. A mass of broken steel debris, flattened and bent lengths of copper pipe, brass valves and broken machinery litter the wreck-site. Divers from Scarborough first discovered the wreck in 1982 and identified her from the name on the ship's steering wheel boss. Tidal streams are very strong and underwater visibility usually rather poor to grim. Extra care should be taken by anyone visiting the site, because trawl nets have become entangled in the wreckage. A number of crustaceans have been observed on the wreck and she should make an excellent boat-angling venue when conditions permit.

BYWELL
Wreck: ★★★★
Depth: 47m
Reference N54 15 760 W000 11 082
Location: 4.03 miles NE of Filey Brigg

The *Bywell* was a steel 1,522-ton British steamship registered at Newcastle-upon-Tyne. She measured 74.67m in length, with an 11.35m beam and a 4.97m draught. Blyth Shipbuilding & Dry Dock Co. Ltd built her at Blyth in 1913 and Screw Collier Co. Ltd owned her at the time of loss. Her single iron screw propeller was powered by a 3-cylinder triple expansion steam engine that developed 224hp using two 2SB 6PF boilers. Her cylinders measured 55.88cm, 83.82cm and 137.16cm. North East Marine Engineering Co. Ltd at Sunderland built her machinery. She had one deck, a well deck and a superstructure consisting of a 37.49m quarterdeck, a 3.96m bridge deck and a 7.32m forecastle. The vessel was also armed with a stern-mounted deck-gun that fired 2.72kg shells (6 pounders).

On 29 March 1917 the SS *Bywell* was making around 8 knots, on passage from the Tyne for Rouen with an unspecified cargo of coal and a crew of twenty, under the command of Captain W.J. Chipchase, when at 1.40 p.m. she was torpedoed without warning by the U-boat SM UB 21. The crew took to the boats, the ship going down in just six minutes, and it was only then that the submarine's conning tower and periscope were seen circling around the spot where she had been. At 3.15 p.m. an armed trawler arrived on the scene and fired at the U-boat which dived to safety. The trawler kept the submarine busy while she rescued the crew of the SS *Bywell* and later landed them at Scarborough.

Wreck-site

The wreck lies orientated in almost a north to south direction, on a seabed of sand and shells in a general depth of 47m, the lowest astronomical depth. She is upright and intact, standing some 6m high amidships, with some broken collapsed superstructure visible. She is now much collapsed, with the lower hull partially buried. Her boilers and engine are exposed to the rather strong tides which sweep over her, and the wreck-site covers an area of 70m by 8m of seabed. There is quite a lot of scattered steel debris surrounding the wreck. The upper structures are covered in an array of soft corals and numerous fish have been observed on and around the wreck. It is doubtful if her bell was ever recovered. Visibility is usually poor to grim, being very typical for this part of the British East Coast, but improves during the summer months following a spell of dry settled weather. The wreck-site should also make a good boat-angling venue, especially during the summer months when large shoals of mackerel are also present in the area.

GEM

Wreck: ★★★★★
Depth: 36m (both sections)
Reference: N54 15 702 W000 15 368 (bow-section)
Also: N54 15 603 W000 15 282 (stern-section)
Location: 3.5 miles SE of Scarborough

The *Gem* was a steel 464-ton British steamship that was registered at Glasgow. She measured 53.3m in length, with a 7.6m beam and a 3m draught. J. Fullerton & Co. built her at Paisley, Scotland, in 1887 and William Robertson of Glasgow owned her at the time of loss. Her single screw was powered by a 3-cylinder triple expansion steam engine that developed 80hp using one 1SB 3CF boiler. Her cylinders measured 38.10cm, 60.96cm and 101.60cm-83.82cm, which gave her a maximum speed of 8 knots. W. King & Co. of Glasgow built her machinery.

At 6.15 p.m. on Christmas Day 1914, the steamship *Gem* was on passage from Mostyn for the Tyne when she detonated a mine laid by SMS *Kolberg*, which was part of a battle-cruiser squadron. The SS *Gem* was carrying a crew of twelve and a 460-ton cargo of salt cake. The massive explosion blew the vessel clean in two, killing her master and nine of the crew, but the mate and one ordinary seaman were picked up by the steamer *Alert* and taken to Wisbech.

Wreck-sites

The bow section lies almost north to south, on a dirty silted seabed, in a general depth of 36m, the lowest astronomical depth. She stands 3m high, is upright, with the whole section intact and broken off clean aft of the bridge. The wreck covers an area of seabed measuring about 37m by 6m and has a 1m scour surrounding it.

The stern section is located about 150m away from the bows, lying east-south-east to west-north-west on a dirty silted seabed, in a general depth of 36m, the lowest astronomical depth. The stern section, complete with the machinery, engine/boiler etc., stands 3.5m high, and is also largely intact, but lying over to port, in a 3m scour; however her boiler and engine are now somewhat exposed. Tidal streams are fairly brisk and underwater visibility usually very poor to grim, but improve slightly following a dry spell of weather and westerly winds during the summer months. Fair numbers of fish have been observed on and around the wreck, so she will make an interesting boat angling venue, when conditions are right. Divers should give both sections of the wreck the utmost respect, because quite a number of her crew went down with the ship.

TANGISTAN

Wreck: ★★★★Depth: 50m
Reference: N54 15 697 W000 05 132
Other section: N54 16 166 W000 05 265
Location: 8.76 miles N of Flamborough Head
Author's suggested position: N 54 46 215 W 000 53 531
Location: 12 miles ENE of The Heugh, Hartlepool

The *Tangistan* was a steel 3,738-ton British steamship registered at the port of London. She was 106.68m long, with a 14.93m beam and a draught of 4.87m. She was built in 1906 as Yard No.736 by William Gray & Co. at Hartlepool and owned at the time of loss by Frank C. Strick & Co. of London. Central Marine Engineering Co. built her machinery. Her single steel iron propeller was powered by a 3-cylinder triple expansion steam engine that used three 2SB 6PF boilers. Her cylinders measured 60.96cm, 101.60cm and 165.10cm.

On 9 March 1915, the SS *Tangistan* was on passage from Benisaf for Middlesbrough with a 6,000-ton cargo of iron ore when she was torpedoed by SM U 12. No warning was given and the submarine was not seen by any of the steamer's crew. The sole survivor of a crew of thirty-nine was a Mr J. O'Toole. In his statement he said the steamer arrived off Middlesbrough too early to enter for the tide and was going very slowly. At 12.30 a.m. she was brought up in a huge shock and explosion. The lights went out and the crew rushed onto the deck, but before they could launch the lifeboats the ship went down with a rush on a perfectly even keel. Mr O'Toole said he was sucked down with the ship, but came up to the surface again and swam around for two hours or so, drifting with the tide, before being picked up by the steamship *Woodville* and landed at West Hartlepool. SM U 12 was sunk by gunfire off Fife Ness on 9 March 1915.

Wreck-site

The first co-ordinates are given as the position where the SS *Tangistan* was reported to lie broken into two sections, on a seabed of sand, stone and black shells, in a general depth of 50m, the lowest astronomical depth. She is collapsed and well broken up but still very substantial. There has been no record of any diving being carried out on this site, so it will be interesting to see what information comes up from the wreck. Tidal streams are very strong and underwater visibility usually poor, but vastly improve during the summer months.

Author's suggested position:
The question remains: why would the SS *Tangistan*, after having arrived too early for the tide at Middlesbrough, go all the way back to Flamborough Head, doubly risking the menace of U boats. The most logical thing to do was to stay close to the Tees, but to keep moving. That is why I believe that this large wreck is that of the *Tangistan*. The wreck is very broken up and scattered over an area of 105m by 30m, twelve miles east-north-east of the Heugh at Hartlepool. She stands some 6m high, in a north-west to south-east direction, on a seabed of mud, fine sand and black shells in a general depth of 55m, the lowest astronomical depth, with no scour. The wreck is very substantial, although the hull and superstructure have totally collapsed, leaving the three boilers, condenser and engine exposed, with broken machinery, huge bent and twisted copper pipes and brass fittings sticking out of the debris in every direction. The highest point is reported to be the north-western end of the wreck, which is probably the bow section and a number of portholes can be seen within easy reach. Much of the debris is now starting to concrete into the seabed.

A number of large cod, in the region of 10kg, were observed in the proximity of the boilers and a small shoal of golden striped pout whiting hovered around the top of the wreck-site, although the wreck is a long way from land, so surface conditions would have to be fairly smooth for anyone contemplating fishing over her. The tidal streams are very strong and visibility usually poor to grim, but after a neap tide and spell of settled westerly winds and dry weather, this should vastly improve during the summer months.

MAY QUEEN
Wreck: ★★★
Depth: 52m
Reference: N54 15 658 W000 01 444
Location: 8.7 miles NNE of Flamborough Head

The *May Queen* was an iron 478-ton three-masted British steamship that was registered at the port of London. She measured 53.0m in length, by a 7.55m beam and a 4.72m draught. General Iron Screw Collier Co. of London built her in 1864 and Lungley of London managed her. The Screw Collier Co. of London owned her at the time of loss. A 4-cylinder compound inverted engine that developed 80hp using one boiler powered her single iron screw propeller. She had one deck, four bulkheads and was classed as A1 at Lloyd's.

On 7 February 1878, the SS *May Queen* was on passage from Rouen for Middlesbrough when she foundered following a collision with the London-registered steamer *Annie Anslie*. She was in ballast, under the command of Captain G.A. Clarke and carrying a crew of seventeen.

Wreck-site
The wreck lies north-west to south-east, on a hard seabed of stone, sand and gravel, in a general depth of 52m, the lowest astronomical depth. She is totally collapsed and well broken up, with her boiler and engine standing 3m high, being the highest section of the wreck. Her propeller, some bollards and an anchor are visible among the mound of partially buried and decaying debris. A number of twisted copper and large lead pipes also protrude out of it all. It is quite possible that the vessel's bell will still be around, too. Tidal streams are rather brisk, while underwater visibility is quite reasonable, especially during the summer months, however it is very dark all of the time. The wreck-site is a fair way from shore and in the main shipping lanes, so a good sharp lookout is required.

ORIANDA, HM Trawler
Wreck: ★★
Depth: 16m
Reference: N54 15 312 W000 18 553
Location: 2.69 miles NW from Filey Brigg

The *Orianda* (Official No.136999) was a steel 273-ton steam fishing trawler that measured 39.72m in length, with a 6.71m beam and a 3.81m draught. Cochrane & Sons built her as Yard No.610 at Selby and launched her as *Orianda* on 11 July 1914 for Dolphin Steam Fishing Co. Ltd of Grimsby. She was then registered as Grimsby fishing trawler No.GY291 in September 1914. Her single screw was powered by a 3-cylinder triple expansion steam engine that used one boiler. She had one deck and a superstructure consisting of a 21.95m quarterdeck and a 6.40m forecastle. The Admiralty, who was the owner at the time of loss, hired the vessel in 1914 and converted her to minesweeper No.99.

On 19 December 1914, HM Trawler *Orianda* was on minesweeping duties, under the command of Herbert B. Boothby, Lt RNR (Royal Naval Reserve), when she detonated a mine and foundered. Lt Boothby successfully got all his crew to safety, except deck hand J. Wilson who was killed, but several crewmen were injured. Boothby was blown up again on 8 January 1915 in trawler No.450. He was awarded the DSO, now Acting Lieutenant Commander.

The Imperial German light cruiser SMS *Kolberg* had laid the mines, 100 of them between Scarborough and Filey. HMT *Orianda* was one of a fleet of minesweepers sent to clear the minefield, with a retired naval officer, Lt Godfrey C. Parsons RN as SNO in HM Trawler *Passing* in overall charge of the fleet. (On 19 February 1915, the following quotation appeared in the *London Gazette*: 'Lt Parsons displayed great skill and devotion to duty in continuing to command his group after having been mined in trawler No.58 on 19 December. On this day his group exploded eight mines and brought to the surface six more, trawler No.99 being blown up and Nos 58 and 465 damaged, all in the space of about six minutes. Awarded the Distinguished Service Cross in recognition of his consistently gallant behaviour whilst engaged in minesweeping operations, and particularly on 4 September 1915, when the vessel on which he was serving having struck a mine and Lt Parsons himself having been crippled by severe wounds, he nevertheless crawled from the bridge to the boat-deck to obtain assistance for another officer who was lying unconscious on the bridge'.

Three more vessels, HMS *Skipjack*, *Jason* and *Gossamer*, all torpedo gunboats that had been converted to fleet minesweepers in 1909, were in the company with one of the new paddle minesweepers, HMS *Brighton Queen*, and being in the vicinity, were able to render assistance. These ships were in transit from Lowestoft to Scapa and were independently tasked to make a single sweep from Flamborough Head to Hartlepool, when this particular group got into difficulties. The mines were anchored to the seabed and close to the surface at low tide, so the minesweepers were limited in when they could work by the times of the tide. Around 8.30 a.m. and two hours after low tide, operations recommenced, the fleet having no idea how many mines had been laid. Eighteen mines were accounted for and dealt with in a very short time, but minesweeping is and was a very dangerous business. Many mines were cut from their anchor lines to float free and these were disposed of by gunfire, while others exploded underwater. However with such a large number and many of the lines getting snagged up with each other, it wasn't long before the inevitable catastrophe struck. HMT *Orianda* was working flat out and was steaming full speed ahead when she detonated one of the mines. Her bows were completely blown to pieces and deck hand J. Wilson died instantly. She was said to have been unable to stop and just steamed on under the surface until nothing remained but her masthead, which resembled that of a moving submarine periscope. Although another report said that she went down in ten minutes.

Lt Godfrey Parsons' vessel, HM Trawler *Passing*, also detonated a mine that same day and one man was killed, but the vessel was towed back to Scarborough.

Lt Boothby and the survivors of the *Orianda* were given a second minesweeper, HM Trawler *Banyers*. Unfortunately she also detonated one of the mines in Cayton Bay and she went to the bottom on 6 January 1915 with the loss of six of her crew.

Wreck-site
The wreck lies on a seabed of sand, in a general depth of 16m, the lowest astronomical depth. She is reported as standing upright and in intact, but totally collapsed and well covered in dirty sand. Only the top parts of her boiler and engine are visible, standing 2m above the seabed. Tidal streams are reasonably strong, but it is possible to visit the site at most states of the tide. Visibility is also usually rather poor and very little marine life is to be found on or over the wreck. This wreck-site is an official war grave and should be respected as such.

ELI
Wreck: ★★★
Depth: 16m
Reference: N54 15 312 W00018 595
Location: 2.70 miles NW of Filey Brigg

The *Eli* was a steel 1,107-ton Norwegian steamship that was registered at the port of Bergen. She measured 69.8m in length, with a 10.66m beam and draught of 4.77m. Bergens Mek Voerks at Bergen built her and the machinery in 1908 and Peter Lindoe of Haugesund owned her at the time of loss. Her single iron screw propeller was powered by a 3-cylinder triple expansion steam engine that developed 106hp using one boiler. She had cylinders measuring 38.10cm, 66.04cm and 111.76cm-76.20cm.

On Christmas Day 1914, the SS *Eli* was on passage from Blyth for Rouen with an unspecified cargo of coal and a crew of eight, when she detonated a contact mine and foundered in just three minutes. The mine was believed to have been one laid earlier by SMS *Kolberg*. She was responsible, along with two other German warships, for bombarding the coastal towns of Hartlepool, Whitby and Scarborough for twenty minutes on 16 December 1914.

Two other vessels, the 464-ton steamship *Gem* and 287-ton HMT *Night Hawk*, came to grief in the same vicinity on Christmas Day. At least twenty vessels were lost and many more damaged as a result of the *Kolberg*'s mines, including four Royal Navy trawlers attempting to clear the mines. The *Eli* was insured as a Norwegian war risk for 280,000 kroner at the time.

Wreck-site

This wreck, which was found by divers in 1971, lies close to the wreck of the *Orianda*. She lies north-north-east to south-south-west on a seabed of sand and stone in a general depth of 16m, the lowest astronomical depth. The wreck is reported as lying on her port side, with most of her starboard plates missing. Except for her bow section, which is reasonably intact but partially buried, the wreck is now totally collapsed and well broken up. Her donkey engine lies close to the boiler and behind this is her engine now lying flat on the seabed, all covered in the hard white casings of marine worms. Occasionally, lobster and edible crabs can sometimes be found sheltering in the openings around the boiler, or the overhanging sections of what is left of her once proud steam engine. Various species of fish can also be seen, especially during the months of July and August. Tidal streams are reasonably strong and she is best visited during a neap tide, while visibility underwater is pretty grim most of the time, but improves significantly during the summer months following a spell of dry settled weather and westerly winds.

BANYERS, HM Trawler

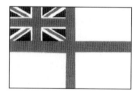

Wreck: ★★★★
Depth: 30m
Reference: N54 15 212 W000 15 503
Location: 2.8 miles N by E of Filey Brigg

The *Banyers* (Official No.136009) was a steel 448-ton steam fishing trawler measuring 48.76m in length with a 7.6m beam. She was built as Yard 296 by Cook, Welton & Gemmel at Beverley, launched on 9 April 1914 and registered as trawler No.GY128 for the South Western Fishing Co. at Grimsby on 9 June 1914. Her single iron screw propeller was powered by a 3-cylinder triple expansion steam engine that developed 89hp using one boiler, which gave her a maximum speed of 11 knots. Charles D. Holmes built her machinery at Hull. In December 1914 the vessel was requisitioned by the Royal Navy and converted to HM Trawler minesweeper No.FY 450.

On 6 January 1915, the *Banyers* was on minesweeping duties in Cayton Bay, under the command of H.B. Boothby, Lt RNR, when she detonated a mine laid by SMS *Kolberg*. Six of her crew died in the explosion and she went down in a few minutes. Captain Boothby managed to save himself by escaping through the wheelhouse window. Boothby was also in command of HMT *Orianda* when she detonated a mine and foundered less than one month earlier on 19 December. Sometime after the war Lt Boothby wrote a book, *Spunyarn,* about his experiences.

Wreck-site

This site is a war grave and should be treated as such. The wreck lies north-east to south-west on a seabed of sand and shell, in a general depth of 30m, this the lowest astronomical depth. She is upright, but collapsed and now broken up, standing some 4m high. Her engine and boiler are exposed and surrounded by a mound of twisted steel plates and machinery etc. A few nice crustaceans can sometimes be found under the debris during the summer months and small saithe and pout whiting shoal over the top of her. Tidal streams are fairly brisk and under-water visibility very poor to grim most of the time. However, it usually improves during the summer months. The best time to visit the site is on a neap tide after a spell of dry settled weather.

USS BONHOMME RICHARD, ex LE DUC DE DURAS

Wreck: *****
Depth: 70m?
Reference: N54 02E
Location: 35-50 miles off Filey Bay

The *Bonhomme Richard* was a wooden 900-ton American man-of-war sailing vessel. She was built in France as the *Le Duc de Duras* in 1766 and registered for the French Crown. With a length of some 44.19m, she was a rather cumbersome type of vessel, mainly built to carry bulk cargoes to the Indies. La Compagnie des Indes (French East India Co.) bought her from the Crown and made two round voyages to China. Then later, she made two voyages for the French Crown to Mauritius, before being sold on to private owners for the equivalent of $30,000 in 1771. The Frenchman M. Berard of Lorient then purchased her, with the intention of fitting her out as a privateer. He obtained six 8.16kg guns from the French Navy, but before she was ready for sea, the Minister of Marine, M. de Sartine, bought her.

John Paul Jones, a vain, highly-strung person, was a Scottish-born merchant captain, who fled to America after a fight with a Tobagan seaman, whom he killed. The war raging between Great Britain and America had created an ideal opportunity for him to move on. He took up service as a captain in the newly formed US Continental Navy and soon distinguished himself by capturing a Royal Navy sloop. Jones knew that if he was ever captured, he would be certainly hanged as a traitor, but he craved action and there was no going back. He arrived at Brest on 8 May 1778, in command of the American warship *Ranger*, having just made a daring raid on Whitehaven in Cumberland on 23 April. In Brest he relinquished his command of the *Ranger* and went in search of another vessel to command. His enquiries soon led him to the ex-French East Indiaman lying at anchor at Lorient. Hearing about Jones, the Minister of Marine, M. de Sartine, had bought the ship for the equivalent of $44,000 and the King of France agreed to pay for all of the ship's fitting out. The King of France then offered her as a gift to the rebellious Americans. Of course the main purpose was that she should be used to attack, plunder or sink Great Britain's merchant fleet. Jones was also given the job of fitting her out whichever way he wished and the first thing he did was to build a roundhouse on her deck to accommodate Lafayette. (Lafayette was an officer who had first planned to come with him on an amphibious assault on Liverpool, but the idea fell through.) He increased the ship's armament by placing six 4.08kg guns on her forecastle and quarterdeck. However, his main armament consisted of the twenty-eight 5.44kg cannon he placed on the gun-deck. Another six old 8.16kg guns were also put in the junior officer's mess room. He renamed her *Bonhomme Richard*, which was meant as a complement to Benjamin Franklin, who at that time was US Congress Ambassador to the Court of France. Franklin published a book in France titled *Poor Richard's Almanac* and *Bonhomme Richard* was the translation of the name. Jones formed a squadron of fighting vessels with *Bonhomme Richard* as the flagship and he took the courtesy rank of Commodore. His ship carried 380 officers and men from eleven different nationalities.

A Frenchman, Pierre Landaise of the US Navy, captained *Alliance*, a new American-built frigate that carried 215 officers and men. She had an armament of twenty-six 5.44kg guns and eight 4.08kg guns.

Capitaine de Brulot Denis-Nicolas Cottineau, a captain of the US Navy, commanded *La Pallas*, a French privateer built in 1778. *La Pallas* carried 253 officers and men and had an armament of twenty-six 4.08kg guns and six 1.81kg guns.

Lt de Vaisseau Philippe-Nicolas Ricot, a captain of the US Navy, commanded *La Vengeance*, a corvette. She carried 66 officers and men and an armament of twelve 1.81kg guns (4 pounders).

Le Cerf, ex HMS *Stag*, was a captured King's cutter, commanded by Ensigne de Vaisseau Joseph Varage, a temporary captain of the US Navy. She carried sixteen 2.72kg guns, two 3.63kg guns and 157 officers and men.

Monsieur, a French privateer of thirty-eight guns, was commanded by Capitaine Guidloop, and finally, *Granville*, another French privateer that carried ten guns, was commanded by Capitaine Dumaurier.

The vessels *Bonhomme Richard*, *Alliance*, *La Pallas* and *Monsieur* all had three masts and were square-rigged vessels, while *Le Vengeance* and *Le Cerf* were brigantines. To make everything official, Benjamin Franklin, then the American Ambassador in Paris, furnished Cottineau, Ricot and Varage with US Navy commissions. However, Landais, who had brought Lafayette over from America to France, was an honorary citizen of Massachusetts.

John Paul Jones commenced his trail of havoc on 14 August 1779, when his squadron slipped out of Groix Roads, Lorient, in a north-west direction, bound for Mizen Head, Ireland. On 18 August and approximately due west of Land's End, one of the French privateers, *Monsieur*, took a prize of war. However, Capitaine Guidloop refused to let Jones put a prize crew on board and the following day Guidloop parted company with the squadron. On 21 August, they captured the brigantine *Mayflower*, forty-five miles south of Cape Clear. A prize crew was placed on board the vessel, which was on passage from Liverpool for London with provisions and she was sailed back to Lorient. In becalmed weather on 23 August, while abeam of Mizen Head, the boats of *Bonhomme Richard* captured the brig *Fortune*, which was on passage from Newfoundland for Bristol with whale oil and staves. The *Fortune* soon set sail for Nantes or St Malo, with a prize crew and one of the officers of *Granville* on board. That same day, seven Irish seamen deserted the squadron in one of the ship's boats followed by a party of two officers and nine men pursuing them. The chasing band landed at Ballinskelligs Bay in thick fog, but they were taken prisoner by the Kerry Rangers. Although Jones' band of warships was reaping rewards, all was not well among the men. Morale was very low, desertion was rife and to top it all, the number of prisoners they had collected was becoming unmanageable. By this time, over 200 merchant seamen were held prisoner in the after-hold of the *Bonhomme Richard* and these required food and water, as well as a constant guard.

On 24 August, John Paul Jones and Captain Landaise of the *Alliance* had a major argument when Landaise refused to obey orders and grossly insulted the Commodore. At the beginning of the voyage, Landaise had already refused to give way to the *Bonhomme Richard*, resulting in a collision that delayed the venture. The eccentric Frenchman, who honestly believed he was the only American amongst them, disappeared with *Alliance* later that day and they were not seen again until 1 September.

The squadron headed northwards for 180 miles, then north-east past the Flannan Islands off the Outer Hebrides, where they captured the Letter-of-Marque ship *Union*, some fifty miles north-north-west of Cape Wrath. She was on passage from London for Québec with uniforms for the British Army. *Alliance* then returned to the fold with a captured prize, the *Betsy*. Landaise manned both prizes they had just captured and, against Jones' wishes, sent them to Bergen. The next vessel to fall foul of the squadron was an Irish brigantine on passage from Norway for Ireland. Landaise in *Alliance* took another two small vessels before parting company again. From there, the ships rounded the top of Scotland and went down the East Coast, reaching Dunbar on 14 September where the *Friendship* of Kirkcaldy, on passage from Leith for Riga, and an escort vessel were taken. Reaching the Firth of Forth, John Paul Jones sailed up towards Leith, with the intention of holding the town to ransom, but a sudden squall prevented him from doing so. Further down the coast, he prepared to attack Newcastle-upon-Tyne with his French marines, but decided against it at the last moment when his French captains showed they had no stomach for such a major venture. However, such was the havoc caused by this band of colonial rebels and Frenchmen around the coast of Britain, that it caused outrage and humiliated the Royal Navy. Off Whitby, two more prizes-of-war were taken, the sloop *Speedwell* and a collier in ballast. The collier was scuttled off Scarborough, but Captain Cottineau ransomed the *Speedwell*. The squadron chased after some vessels off Scarborough, captured a collier and drove another vessel ashore south of Flamborough Head. On 22 September, an English brigantine, on passage from Rotterdam, was captured near Spurn Head at 2 a.m. and by evening, Jones had turned north, towards Flamborough Head. When the squadron was a few miles from Bridlington on the 23rd, they sent a ship's boat into the Smithic Shoal to burn a merchant ship that had taken shelter there. It was here that Jones learnt from a captured Humber pilot that a valuable Baltic convoy was due in at any time. The war had made Britain dependent on the supplies of Baltic timber and tar for shipbuilding. By 5.30 a.m. the following day, *Alliance* and *La Pallas* had returned from their forages and rejoined the squadron. At 2 p.m. a brig was seen on the horizon, then an hour later the convoy came into view: forty-one vessels, escorted by the British warships HMS *Serapis* with fifty guns and HMS *Countess of Scarborough* carrying twenty guns. John Paul Jones and his piratical American/French squadron now had their ultimate prize in view and set off in pursuit at full sail. The convoy moved to the protection of Scarborough, while the two British escorts moved between Jones and the convoy. Captain Richard Pearson of the *Serapis* watched the squared-rigged *Bonhomme Richard*, which looked like a Line of Battle ship, bearing down on them. Little did he know then that all but six of her lower deck-gun-ports were empty. HMS *Serapis* was a match for any of the enemy vessels, but the *Countess of Scarborough*, having been built as a merchant vessel and being rather slow and cumbersome, was probably only a match for the brig. Captain Pearson feared the worst and sent the convoy racing for shelter beneath the guns of Scarborough Castle, where they would be safe. At 6 p.m. John Paul Jones gave orders to form a line of battle, but none of his 'brave' captains would obey him. Just over an hour later, HMS *Serapis* and *Bonhomme Richard* commenced a series of broadsides at each other at 300m range. Pearson's cannon fire from *Serapis* caused heavy casualties aboard the American ship. However, during the first broadside, one of Jones' old larger cannon in the gunroom added to the turmoil, when it burst open and exploded. It dismantled the next gun and killed or seriously wounded many of the men, who were packed in like sardines. *La Pallas* moved in to engage the smaller gunned *Countess of Scarborough*. However, except for a few long shots at the *Countess*, Captain Landaise of the *Alliance* made no attempt to join the action. *Countess* made no bones about it and fired at Landaise, hitting the ship three times; one shot stuck in the hull, but the other two bounced off. Jones was in deep trouble, because not only had his brave band deserted him but HMS *Serapis* was running rings round the *Bonhomme Richard*. The old East Indiaman was taking a real pounding, as *Serapis* outmanoeuvred and systematically demolished her. Captain Pearson prepared to finish her off and moved to cross her stern, but Jones turned his ship across her bow and the two ships collided. The bowsprit of *Serapis* ripped into the mizzen rigging of *Bonhomme Richard*, leaving her jib-stay, which was severed, trailing across Jones' quarterdeck. This was the last chance Jones was going to get to turn the tables. He screamed across to Stacey, his helmsman who was swearing his head off above the awful din, to stop swearing and help him. The two of them then set about binding the two ships together with fallen ropes and cordage. Captain Pearson saw what was happening and tried desperately to break free by letting go of the port anchor, hoping that the elements of wind and tide would pull them apart, but all was in vain. Meanwhile, while the two ships were lying almost broadside to each other, gun crews of both sides kept blasting away. By now both ships were very badly damaged, with fires raging around the men embroiled in hand to hand fighting with swords, knives and muskets. It was like Dante's *Inferno*, as cannon shot tore huge lumps of timber from the hulls and sent it tearing through tightly packed bodies of men. Jones' marines had fought hand-to-hand in the rigging to clear the British sharpshooters and now they concentrated their muskets on the decks below, killing at will. Soon the upper-guns fell silent as their crews were killed off and the few surviving officers sought shelter beneath the quarterdeck. Both vessels were lit up like a bonfire in the night-sky and it was at this point that Landaise decided to enter the fight. He brought

Alliance across the bows of *Serapis* and ordered his men to rake the British ship with grape and round-shot. Many tried to protest that they would hit their own colleagues, but Landaise was captain and his orders had to be obeyed, or it meant instant death. They opened fire as the ship passed by and the murderous volley brought down everyone in its path, Briton, American and French alike. The *Bonhomme Richard* was sinking fast, yet in the after hold, the seamen, captured from the merchant vessels, were trapped in darkness with water rising about them. The master-at-arms, who was in charge, heard the carpenter saying that the ship was going down and he prepared to release them as the carnage above continued. One of Jones' warrant officers ran screaming for quarter and tried to lower the American flag, but Jones clubbed him down with a pistol. Captain Pearson shouted to ask if they called for quarter, but Jones cried back 'I have not yet begun to fight' and the guns boomed out again. Down below, the master-at-arms had released the prisoners and they stumbled up onto the lower gun-deck, dazed by the carnage, raging fires and bombardment about them. One of the American officers set them to work at the pumps, but a Scottish captain refused, insisting that he would not help traitors and that they should let the treacherous pirate ship sink. John Paul Jones' orderly, a Frenchman, immediately shot him dead so the rest of the terrified men went and manned the pumps. William Hamilton of the Congress Service, another Scot, immortalised his name when he crawled out along the mainyard and dropped a grenade into the middle of the *Serapis*. It was the deciding factor in the battle, because as the gunners had been all killed, charges already to use had accumulated there. There was an enormous explosion when the grenade instantly detonated them. The blast tore through the frigate's lower gun-deck, killing all the crew and silenced the main battery. Landaise then brought *Alliance* round again, but Captain Pearson, who was sheltering from the hail of musket-fire under the quarterdeck, had no idea that gunfire from the *Alliance* was indiscriminate. All he knew was that if he defeated the *Bonhomme Richard*, he still had to contend with two more warships, standing off in the darkness. His main concern was the convoy, which had miraculously escaped unharmed. With arms held high at 10.30 p.m. on 23 September, Pearson walked out into the hail of fire and pulled down the White Ensign. *La Pallas* under Cottineau, had already succeeded in capturing HMS *Countess of Scarborough* at 10 p.m., but *La Vengeance* took no part in the action. Gradually the cannons ceased firing, just as *Serapis'* mainmast swung out and crashed down into the sea. The fighting was over and Captain Pearson was taken on board the *Bonhomme Richard*. As he was led aft, he was amazed at her shattered condition. Later he wrote, 'I found her to be in the greatest distress, with her counters and quarter entirely drove in and the whole of her lower deck-guns dismounted. She was also on fire in two places, and six or seven feet of water in her hold.'

John Paul Jones had a major nightmare on his hands with fires raging and water flooding the hull. He had restored what was left of his battered ship and got her away from the coast, before the Royal Navy arrived to finish his squadron off. However, everyone on the ship was in imminent danger from one fire, which was burning fiercely next to the powder magazine. Both sides had to work together to move the barrels of gunpowder. Carpenters plugged as many of the ball-shot holes below the waterline as they could, but it was an impossible task, because many were beyond reach. Of the 322 officers and seamen on board Jones' ship, 150 lay dead or dying and a similar number lay aboard *Serapis*. The ship's surgeon and his assistants were kept constantly busy attending to the wounded, many of who were screaming from unimaginable injuries, dreadful burns and severed limbs. Jones did his utmost to save his vessel and drafted in men to man the three remaining pumps from the other ships in the squadron. They toiled throughout the night, while the dead, with scant ceremony, were slid overboard, along with the six large old cannons. Her sails and rigging were hastily fixed and by 10 a.m. the squadron turned east towards safety. Meanwhile on the shore, messengers had already been dispatched to the Admiralty, as hundreds of people lining the shore had watched the battle raging, just a few miles offshore.

Despite the frantic efforts put in by the men on the *Bonhomme Richard*, she was doomed. At 7 p.m. on Friday 24 September, Jones ordered his crew to remove the wounded. Then at 4 a.m. on the 25th, orders were given to stop pumping. Seven hours later, Jones transferred his flag to the *Serapis* and the rebel warship slipped below the surface of the North Sea, about fifty miles east of Flamborough Head. On 25 September, *Serapis* reached Texel in Holland with 504 prisoners on board, including twenty-six Royal Navy officers. John Paul Jones later left Texel for France, where his victory received much acclaim. Jones continued his colourful career after his Flamborough battle, transferring to the Russian Fleet as an Admiral in the Black Sea operations against the Turks, after the US rebels' victory meant that a navy was no longer an American priority. However when he returned to America some time later, he found very little recognition for his famous exploits, at the time. In later years, he was credited with founding the Annapolis Naval Academy, being the American equivalent of Dartmouth in Britain.

There are two stories associated with the death of John Paul Jones. One said he died in poverty in 1792 at the age of forty-five and was buried in a pauper's grave. It was not for quite some time that he was recognised as an American hero. In 1905 his remains were reburied at the United States Naval Museum at Annapolis, where there is a sort of shrine to him. The other story says he died in Paris, but was taken back to America 100 years later, after his body had been discovered covered in alcohol in a lead-lined coffin (paupers would certainly not have had a lead-lined coffin). It was after that, that he was reburied in the US Naval Museum at Annapolis. The 'sailing navy' of the United States lasted less than 100 years, but Jones' reputation was never to be eclipsed. Quotations from John Paul Jones are still used in US Navy training manuals today and his determination to succeed, when he shouted to Captain Pearson, 'I have not yet begun to fight', encapsulates the spirit of the United States Navy.

Wreck-site

The wreck of *Bonhomme Richard* has never been found to date, although there have been numerous extensive searches and expeditions looking for her. However, it would have been a shame not to include the history of such an important vessel in these chapters. A French musket, probably belonging to one of Jones' marines, was dragged up in a trawl-net about six miles off Flamborough Head some time ago and the wreck of a wooden sailing vessel was discovered in Filey Bay during 1975. She is largely buried, broken into three sections, with one part of the hull measuring 36.59m in length and 6.10m wide. The vessel had at least two decks and the wood showed signs of fire damage; radiocarbon dating placed the date of the wood around 1776 to 1800, a similar date to that of the *Bonhomme Richard*. However there were no cannons or anchors to be found around the site and there has been no positive evidence that this is the wreck.

Rumours also abound that the wreck lies in position N54 11 564 W000 00 099, five miles north-east of Flamborough Head and lying beneath the wreck of the steamship *Commonwealth*, but again, there is no proof of this.

However, on 19 July 2002, an immediate protection order was placed on the barnacled remains of a warship thought to be that of the *Bonhomme Richard* off Flamborough Head. The Arts Minister, Lady Blackstone, issued the emergency order barring any approach to the wreck when the Department of Culture, Media and Sport was tipped off earlier in the week that a diving team, believed to American, was about to make a serious attempt to raise artefacts from the forty-gun converted French East Indiaman. Lady Blackstone said she understood the wreck had caught the eye of salvors and that there were concerns that the remains, which include cannon, French ironwork, and part of the oak hull, might have been stripped within days. She said it was vital to protect what is believed to be this historical wreck, while further investigations by experts take place. It will be interesting to see what the outcome is and if the wreck is that of the infamous US warship, it will certainly attract a lot of attention from the United States Government.

GARMO, HM Trawler

Wreck: ★★
Depth: 18m
Reference: N54 15 055 W000 18 146
Location: 0.97 mile N by E of Old Horse Rocks, near Filey

The *Garmo* was a steel 203-ton steam fishing trawler that was originally registered at Grimsby. She measured 34.1m in length and had a 6.7m beam. The vessel was built by Earle's Co. Ltd at Hull in 1900 for Ocean Steam Fishing Co. Earle's also built the machinery. Her single screw propeller, possibly bronze, was powered by a 3-cylinder triple expansion steam engine that used one 1SB 2PF boiler. She had cylinders measuring 27.94cm, 50.80cm and 81.28cm-58.42cm. In 1914 the Admiralty requisitioned her as an armed patrol vessel and later converted her to a minesweeper.

On 20 December 1914, HMT *Garmo* was on minesweeping duties in Cayton Bay, Scarborough, under the command of Captain T. Gilbert and carrying a crew of fourteen, when she detonated one of the 100 mines laid by SMS *Kolberg* between Filey and Scarborough. Six of her crew, including Captain Gilbert, lost their lives in the incident, but the drifter *Principal* picked up nine survivors. That same day, the armed yacht HMY *Valiant* accidentally detonated one of the mines, but she was safely taken into Scarborough Harbour.

Wreck-site

The wreck lies orientated in a south-east to north-west direction, on a seabed of sand and shingle, in a general depth of 18m, the lowest astronomical depth. She is now totally collapsed, well broken up and partially buried, with her boiler and engine exposed and coated in hard white marine worm casings. Tidal streams are reasonably strong, but it is possible to visit the site at most states of the tide, however underwater visibility is usually very poor to grim. Very little marine life is to be found on or around the wreck-site.

Being a Royal Navy vessel the wreck will probably be officially classed as a war grave and should be respected as such.

SALIENT

Wreck: ★
Scenery: ★★
Depth: 1-2m
Reference: N54 14 420 W000 19 683 (approximate)
Location: Castle Rocks, Gristhorpe and two miles N from Filey

The *Salient* was an iron 1,432-ton British schooner-rigged steamship that was registered at the port of Sunderland. She measured 76.2m in length, with a beam of 10.36m and a 5.48m draught. Bartram, Haswell & Co. built her at Sunderland for James Westoll of Sunderland who owned her at the time of loss. Her single iron screw propeller was powered by a 2-cylinder compound steam engine that developed 140hp using one boiler.

On 8 March 1891, the *Salient* was off Robin Hood's Bay when her propeller shaft broke in heavy weather. She was in ballast on passage from Rotterdam for the Tyne, under the command of Captain J. Blakey and carrying a crew of twenty. The captain instructed the crew to set her sails and run before the wind, heading for the safety of Bridlington Bay. On seeing their plight, the steamship *Walker* took her in tow, but the towline parted while off Scarborough. In a driving snowstorm and a strong south-westerly wind she proved unmanageable and some two hours before low water she was blown ashore, where she became stranded and a total loss. The crew were able to lower the ship's boats on the lee-side of her and made the shore in safety. Then Crawford Ltd, a salvage company from Scarborough, bought the rights to salvage her and after building a small explosives store half way up the cliffs, they worked the wreck from the shore. Unfortunately for James Westoll, the *Salient* was also not insured.

Wreck-site

The wreck is very close inshore and at low spring tide it is possible to walk to within a few metres of her boiler, which lies on the Castle Rocks near Gristhorpe. The area is covered in a thick blanket of kelp and although difficult, it is said that you can even visit the site by snorkelling from the shore. Obviously what remains of the once proud ship is now well broken up and dispersed, but still quite a bit of her remains, including some iron bottom plates, her rudder and the boiler, which shows at low water. A good rake around in the kelp may also uncover some of the artefacts lost when she went aground, plus the occasional crustacean amongst the boulders. Tidal streams are very moderate, but care should be taken when there is any surface swell.

JOHN RAY

Wreck: *
Scenery: ***
Depth 1-2m
Reference: N54 14 147 W000 18 462
Location: Gristhorpe Reefs, off Old Horse Rocks, near Filey

The *John Ray* was an iron 493-ton British steamship that was registered at the port of London. She measured 32.18m in length, with a 10.97m beam and a 3.81m draught. W.B. Thompson built her at Dundee in 1881 and Edwin R. Ray of 15 Fish Street in Hull owned her at the time of loss, although other sources quote M.A. Ray & Sons Ltd of London, owned her. The single iron screw propeller was powered by a 3-cylinder triple expansion steam engine that developed 90hp using one boiler. She was described as being a queer-shaped vessel, being very broad in the beam, but extremely sea-worthy, being seen in the Yarmouth Roads in a north-easterly gale when dozens of much larger ships would run for shelter. It was rumoured that the following short poem was written on the vessel's bridge:

The old *John Ray*,
She sails today,
She cares for neither wind nor weather,
The harder it blows,
The slower she goes,
The old *John Ray* forever.

During her thirty years of service, the *John Ray* ran aground at least twice and possibly more, along different parts of the Yorkshire coast. However, at 6.30 p.m. on 11 January 1912 she went aground once too often. The old vessel was on passage from Yarmouth for the Tyne, when she drove ashore near Old Horse Rocks, during dense fog. Carrying a cargo of coal and a crew of thirteen, she was under the command of her skipper, a Mr Cook. Her crew abandoned ship in their boat and were picked up by a passing steamship. The *John Ray* became a total wreck and is reported to have broken up within one week of striking the rocks, with wreckage being washed on shore soon after her striking the reef.

Wreck-site

The wreck is now totally collapsed, well broken up, with the largest piece left being the bow section, the rest of her mostly dispersed under the dense 2-3m long kelp, amongst the rocks and boulders. Very little remains of her except a few twisted decaying pieces of iron, standing no more than a metre high and intermingled with those of the 607-ton steamer *Volunteer*. She was wrecked in the same location on 1 February 1865, However, a ship's bell, believed to be that of the *John Ray* was recovered in recent years. Tidal streams are very reasonable, but visibility is usually poor, but improves during the summer months, when you can expect to see a few metres. There is also the possibility for those with a good eye of catching the occasional crustacean in this area too.

VOLUNTEER

Wreck: ★
Scenery: ★★★
Depth: 5m
Reference: N54 14 149 W000 18 467
Location: Off Old Horse Rocks near Filey

The *Volunteer* was an iron brig-rigged 607-ton British steamship that was registered at Leith. She measured 55.4m in length, with a 9.08m beam and a draught of 3.65m. Morton & Co. built her at Leith in 1861 and Donald McGregor & Co. of Leith owned her at the time of loss. (The owner had been a lieutenant-colonel in the 1st Midlothian Rifle Volunteers, hence probably her name.) Her single iron screw propeller was powered by a 2-cylinder compound steam engine that used two boilers and Lloyd's classed her as A1.

On 1 February 1865, the *Volunteer* was on passage from Leith for Rotterdam, carrying a crew of twenty-three and a cargo of cast-iron pigs, under the command of Captain J. Cairus. In a light southerly wind at 2.30 a.m., with the coastline shrouded in fog, she had steamed past Scarborough with her foresails set, at a steady 8 knots. The treacherous reefs were hidden from view as she ploughed on past Yons Nab and Filey Brigg, then at 2.45 a.m., a lookout reported broken water ahead. The warning had come too late to save the vessel, as she shuddered to a halt on the outside of the reef, with her bottom plates torn open. As water poured through the gaping hole, distress rockets were fired, but there was no response in the foggy dimness of the icy winter morning. Captain Cairus and crew abandoned ship and took to the boats, landing safely at Filey by 9 a.m. Within a few days, the 'sailing' steamer quickly broke up and became a total loss.

Beale, a 225-ton wooden snow, also came to grief in this position on 20 December 1868. Built in Nova Scotia in 1851 and owned by Robert Robinson of Middlesbrough, she was on passage from Middlesbrough for London, under the command of a Captain Ridley and carrying a cargo of coal and a crew of seven. Her crew took to the boat and were picked up by a Filey fishing-coble, while the *Beale* sank by the stern and became a total loss. The vessel was insured for £1,000 and sailors from

Scarborough and Filey saved most of her sails and rigging. A snow looks very similar to a brig from a distance, but has her spanker/gaff sail set on a small mast, just abaft the main mast.

Wreck-site

The co-authors of the book *Shipwrecks of the Yorkshire Coast*, Arthur Godfrey and Peter Lassey, first discovered the wreck in 1969 and extensively surveyed the area. Among the finds they made was a bronze signal cannon, a mound of cast iron ingots, a battered soup-ladle bearing the insignia of the Volunteer Rifle Brigade, and a worn old ship's bell, believed to have come off the *John Ray*, which was wrecked here in 1912. All the vessels are now totally collapsed and well dispersed beneath the seaweed amongst the rocks and boulders in a depth of 3-5m, being about the lowest astronomical depth. Tidal streams are reasonably moderate and it would be possible to visit the site at most states of the tide. However, on the seaward or outer side of Old Horse Rocks, tidal streams are very strong indeed, with the boulders coated in a fine array of soft corals. Here great care is required and the use of a surface-marker buoy essential. Underwater visibility is usually rather poor most of the year, but greatly improves during the summer months. For those divers with a good eye, small crustaceans can be found in the surrounding reefs and boulders, and there is still the odd chance of finding more of the ship's lost artefacts.

Numerous other vessels have also come to grief in this location over the past century or so, including:

Wilne, a wooden schooner from Brancaster, was wrecked in this area in September 1833, with the loss of all of her crew.

Hambro, a wooden brig from Middlesbrough, met her fate there in September 1851.

On 20 December 1868, the Sunderland-registered 225-ton collier brig *Beale*, built in Nova Scotia in 1851, ended her days on the Old Horse Rocks during thick fog, but without any loss of life.

In a storm during March 1883, the German wooden schooner *Emmanuel* was driven ashore and wrecked, but luckily her crew were able to walk ashore at low water.

The 104-ton paddle-driven steam trawler *Chevy Chase* ran onto the reef on 6 October 1886 to become a total wreck, but her skipper Henry Thompson and the crew of eight were all rescued by a Filey fishing-coble. The *Chevy Chase* was valued at £1,500, which was a lot of money in those days. She was built by J. Eltringham and owned by W. Adey of Sunderland at the time of loss. She measured 29.5m in length, with a 6.5m beam and a 2.7m draught.

Another paddle-driven steam trawler that came to an untimely end on the reefs was the 112-ton *Iron King*. She was built by Eltringham's at South Shields in 1880 and owned by F. Warren, also of South Shields. She measured 30.8m in length, with a beam of 5.5m and a draught of 3.0m.

Thick coastal fog and severe weather conditions were the main reasons why so many vessels ended up on the Old Horse Rocks, which lie in position N54 14 114 W000 18 380.

BALLOGIE, ex ANTWERPEN, ex BULL, ex MITTELWEG
Wreck: ★★★
Depth: 24m
Reference: N54 13 896 W000 14 812
Location: 1.16 miles NE of Filey Brigg

The *Ballogie* was an iron 1,207-ton British steamship registered at the port of Aberdeen. She was 73.15m long with a 10.01m beam and a 4.39m draught. Short Brothers built and launched her as the *Mittelweg* at Sunderland in 1889 for J. H. Lorentzen and Co. of Hamburg Germany, with O. Demsat as captain. Her single iron screw propeller was powered by a 3-cylinder triple expansion steam engine that developed 202hp using two 2SB 6PF boilers and she had cylinder sizes measuring: 50.80cm, 83.82cm and 137.16cm-99.06cm, (20in, 33in and 54-39in). J. Dickinson built her machinery at Sunderland. She had one iron deck, web-frames, six cemented bulkheads, a well deck and a superstructure consisting of a 7.01m poopdeck, 20.42m quarterdeck, 16.46m-bridgedeck and 6.71m forecastle. She was also armed with one stern positioned gun that fired 90mm shells (3.54in). In 1894 she was sold to J. Watson & Co. at Middlesbrough and renamed *Bull*, with C. Bilton the captain and registered at Middlesbrough. A new donkey boiler was fitted in 1904. In 1912 she was sold to Maritime Walford (Soc. Anon.), registered at Antwerp, Belgium and renamed *Antwerpen* with signal letters MBRN, with M. Canfrère the captain. In 1912 she was fitted with electric lights. She became the *Ballogie* in 1915 when J.&D. Davidson Ltd, the owners at the time of loss, bought her and employed G. Cook as the captain.

At 4.10 p.m. on 9 November 1917, the *Ballogie* was on passage from Middlesbrough for Dunkirk when she was torpedoed and sunk by SM UC 47, an Imperial German submarine. The steamer was carrying an unspecified cargo of slag and a crew of nineteen, under the command of Captain G. Cook. The vessel went down almost immediately and the captain and twelve of the crew, including all of the officers, lost their lives either in the huge explosion or when they went into the sea. A patrol boat picked up six men alive, then recovered the bodies of the captain and steward and landed them at Grimsby.

Wreck-site

The wreck of the *Ballogie* was referred to as the 'Two Boiler Wreck' for many years, until two Filey divers, Dave Hunter and Chris Truelove, positively identified her in 1986. She lies on a seabed of sand, gravel and mud, in a general depth of 24m, the lowest astronomical depth. She is now decayed and totally collapsed, with her bows lying over to starboard. Amidships to stern section is flattened and broken up, while her engine is lying on its side. A number of crustaceans have adopted the wreck as a sanctuary, but very few fish have been observed on, or around her. Tidal streams are fairly strong and visibility is usually poor or grim most of the year. Local divers recovered the 90mm stern-gun some time ago and presented it to the local Sea Cadet Corps.

ARDENS, ex UNIVERSAL
Wreck: ★★★
Depth: 28m
Reference: N54 13 679 W000 13 054
Location: 1.93 miles ENE of Filey

The *Ardens* (Official No.68968) was an iron 1,274-ton British steamship registered at the port of London. She was 73.2m long, with a 10.05m beam and a draught of 5.41m. Short Brothers built her as Yard No.85 at Sunderland in 1878 and launched her as the *Universal* for Taylor & Sanderson of Sunderland. On 23 March 1916 she was acquired by the Gas Light & Coke Co. and renamed *Ardens*. She had one deck, a well deck and a superstructure consisting of a 28.65m quarterdeck, 12.80m bridge deck and 8.23m forecastle. Her single iron screw propeller was powered by a 2-cylinder compound steam engine that developed 140hp using one 1SB 4PF boiler. Her cylinders measured 73.66cm and 139.70cm-91.44cm. George Clark built her machinery at Sunderland. She was armed with a stern-mounted howitzer that fired 2.72kg shells (6 pounders). In 1900 the owners became Taylor & Sanderson Steamshipping Co. Ltd, with Taylor & Sanderson as managers.

At 10.30 a.m. on 30 June 1917, twelve miles south of Flamborough Head, while on passage for Beckton with a cargo of coal, the steamship *Ardens* was attacked by a U-boat. The submarine fired two torpedoes at her and luckily for the *Ardens* both the torpedoes missed. The U-boat then surfaced to put an end to the steamship with her deck-gun, but before she could do so, the *Ardens* opened fire first with her own gun. The *Ardens'* captain believed that his crew had sunk the U-boat, because two violent explosions followed the second and third shots and the submarine disappeared beneath the surface. However, the Government's assessment of the action was that this was highly improbable. Even after the war, German records could not show any U-boat to have been lost in that vicinity, but the Imperial German U-boat SM UC 63 did happen to be in the area at the time of the incident. However the captain and DEMS gunners (these were Royal Navy or Royal Artillery gunners carried on merchant ships during both wars) were still duly awarded DSMs. During 1917, collier captains made a whole spate of claims, honestly believing they had sank enemy submarines with gunfire, but very few in fact turned out to be true.

Luck ran out for the *Ardens* at 6.15 p.m. on 18 August 1917, when she was torpedoed and sunk by SM UC 16. The steamer was on passage from Sunderland for London, under the command of Captain J.W. Dinneen and carrying an unspecified cargo of gas-coal and a crew of nineteen. Some of the crew saw the wake of the missile, but there was insufficient time to take avoiding action, before it detonated on the port side. The huge explosion killed the engine room donkey-man, tore out the ship's side and caused the mainmast to crash down on deck. The eighteen survivors, including two injured crewmen, immediately abandoned ship in the boats and rowed towards land. Ten minutes later they watched their vessel roll over to one side and break in two. In a gush of steam and a mass of bubbles, she slipped out of sight. After about five minutes of rowing, the submarine's periscope was sighted as it followed the boats, but when a patrol-boat approached, it disappeared. The self-righting ten-oared lifeboat from Filey, *Hollon the Third*, was launched at 6.15 p.m. She rescued ten of the men from one boat and the rest were picked up by other vessels and landed at Filey. SM UC 16 was presumed mined off Boulogne on 3 March 1917.

Wreck-site

The wreck, known by local fishermen as the 'Reasty', lies north-west to south-east, on a seabed of mud and sand, in a general depth of 28m, being about the lowest astronomical depth, 1.8 miles from the nearest land at Filey. She is broken into two halves, with her bows and stern lying folded together, but leaning outwards and rather collapsed down. Her engine and boiler are visible and soft corals adorn the upper structures. The vessel's gun has been recovered at some time, but live shells can be found close to the stern section. Crustaceans and numerous fish have been observed on and around the wreck, but visibility is poor and tidal streams are very strong. This site should make a good boat-angling venue when weather conditions permit.

MEKONG, HM Yacht, ex MAUND

Wreck: ★
Scenery: ★★★
Depth: 3m
Reference: N54 13 720 W000 18 421
Location: Southern part of Gristhorpe Wyke

The *Mekong* (Official No.119732) was a steel 903-ton luxury steam yacht that was designed by Cox & King of Falmouth and sails supplied by Madder. She measured 60.8m in length, with a 9.22m beam and a 5.41m draught. Ramage & Ferguson built her as the *Maund* at Leith and she was completed in March 1916 for Adam Singer (of sewing machine fame). She was registered at Southampton, but spent most of her time around the French Riviera. Her single screw propeller, possibly bronze was powered by a 3-cylinder triple expansion steam engine that developed 204nhp using one boiler, with a working pressure of 12.41 bar. The upper deck-houses were built of teak and she was fitted with electric lights. The yacht was sold to a member of the French aristocracy, the Duc de Montpensier, then in 1912 was renamed *Mekong*. This was probably influenced by France's connections with Vietnam, as the French controlled the country for many years. On 14 April 1915, the Royal Navy, which was the owner at the time of loss, hired the yacht as an armed auxiliary patrol vessel and equipped her with two deck-guns that fired 7.62cm (3in) shells. Her signal letters were HGBV.

At 4.50 a.m. on 12 March 1916, HM Trawler *Mekong* was on patrol in Humber area No.9, when, during a north-east gale, driving rain, hail and snow, she drove ashore under the cliffs at Gristhorpe Wyke (another report has the wind direction as east-south-east). She was the flagship of the 49th Patrol Unit, made up of six trawlers and the armed yacht. She was carrying a crew of fifty-nine (another report says forty-six), under the command of sixty-five-year-old Admiral Frank Finnis CVO, who volunteered to come out of retirement to join the war effort. When the vessel came ashore one of her guns was fired to attract attention and summon assistance. A crewman, stoker Chapel, attached a line around his waist and tried to swim ashore, but drowned in the attempt; his body was later found on the rocks. Able seaman Piper made a gallant effort, but he too perished. Filey Rocket Brigade had been alerted and was searching for the yacht. Another attempt to swim to shore, this time successful, was made by a greaser, Thorn, who also managed to scale the 30m cliffs to raise the alarm. The brigade soon got rockets aboard and set up a breeches buoy, hauling the rest of the crew up the high cliffs. Unfortunately, one man, Quartermaster Davies, fell to his death from the buoy and immediately disappeared from sight.

Wreck-site

The wreck is now totally collapsed and well dispersed and scattered under the seaweed, amongst the surrounding rocks and boulders of the Wyke. She lay forgotten until around 1958-1960, when it was reported that local diving enthusiasts from York and Scarborough had found large quantities live shells rolling around in the remains of the yacht. The Royal Navy was called in to remove them and they dispersed the *Mekong* with explosives. All that remains of her today are two upturned boilers and some bottom plates. Occasionally brass shells can be found, but very little else now remains of the once proud vessel. However, in 1986 one lucky diver discovered a battered gold Krugerrand in the wreck, so the area is still worth a visit during the summer months. The wreck is reported to be owned by the authors of 'Dive Yorkshire'. The two boilers were reported to break the surface at low water and could be a navigation hazard to small boats when visiting the wreck. Tidal streams are fairly moderate, although visibility is usually rather poor, with the best time to see anything after a spell of dry settled weather and westerly winds.

LAILA, ex H. HEITMANN, ex THOMAS LEIGH

Wreck: ★★★★
Depth: 51m
Reference: N54 13 873 E000 00 409
Location: 9.72 miles E by N of Filey Brigg

The *Laila* was a steel 809-ton Norwegian steamship that was registered at the port of Bergen. She measured 57.91m in length, with a 9.19m beam and a draught of 3.96m. Ritson & Co. built her at Maryport as the *Thomas Leigh* in 1899 for H. Podeus at Wismar in Germany. Her single iron screw propeller was powered by an 87hp 3-cylinder triple expansion steam engine that used one boiler. W.B. McKie & Baxter built her machinery at Glasgow. She had one deck and her cylinders measured 39.37cm, 63.50cm and 104.14cm-68.58cm. In 1909-1910, Dampskipsaksjeselskap H. Heitmann Steamship Co. Ltd of Christiania in Norway purchased her and renamed the vessel *H. Heitmann*, while H. Heitmann & Son also managed her. In 1916-1917, she was sold to A/S D/S Laila of Bergen in Norway and she was renamed *Laila*. The managers became W. Hansen of Bergen.

On 24 October 1916, the *Laila* was on passage from Archangel for Hull when she was torpedoed and sunk by the Imperial German submarine SM U 57. She was under the command of Captain O.O. Apold and carrying a cargo of wood. SM U 57 went on to survive the ravages of the First World War and surrendered to the Allies, to become French reparation and was broken up at Cherbourg in 1921.

Wreck-site

The wreck, possibly that of the steamship *Laila*, lies on a seabed of sand and stone, in a general depth of 51m, the lowest astronomical depth. She is still reasonably substantial, standing upright and intact, but collapsed and broken, with the highest structures of 5m being around amidships to stern. The ship's bell, if recovered, will almost certainly be inscribed with '*Thomas Leigh*' and the date she was built, '1899'. This wreck should make an interesting boat angling venue, but she is quite a long way from shore. A large trawl net is reported as being snagged up near to the stern end, so a lot of care will be required when diving the site. Tidal streams are very strong and underwater visibility is usually rather poor and often grim.

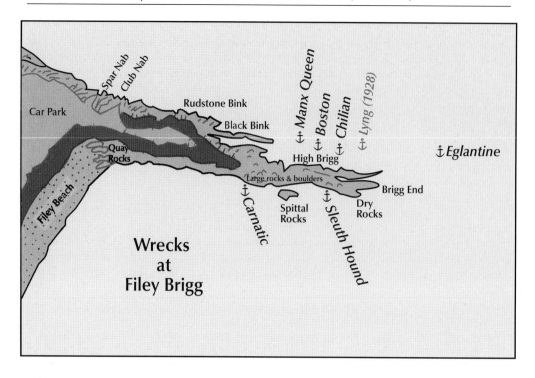

MANX QUEEN, HM Trawler
Wreck: ★
Scenery: ★★★
Depth: 5m
Reference: N54 12 989 W000 15 676 (approx.)
Location: Off High Brigg, north side of Filey Brigg

The *Manx Queen* was a steel 234-ton British steam fishing trawler that was registered at Grimsby as trawler No.GY491. She measured 36.6m in length and had a 6.7m beam. The vessel was built at Selby in 1915 for W.H. Beeley, but requisitioned by the Admiralty to use as an auxiliary patrol vessel and equipped with a deck-gun that fired 2.72kg shells (6 pounders). Her single iron screw propeller was powered by a 3-cylinder triple expansion steam engine that developed 75hp using one boiler, giving her a maximum speed of 10.5 knots.

At 3.30 a.m. on 1 March 1916, the *Manx Queen* was on patrol duties carrying a crew of thirteen when, during dense fog and heavy weather, she drove ashore on the north side of Filey Brigg. Attempts to pull her off were unsuccessful, as her bows were hard aground, but she stayed afloat for quite some time. However, the hull had been damaged and water was flooding in. The ten-oared, self-righting lifeboat from Filey, *Hollon the Third* was launched at 3.50 a.m. She got in close and rescued ten of the men, but the captain and two others remained on the vessel. In the meantime, the Rocket Brigade had managed to fire a rocket over the vessel and rigged up a breeches buoy. When all hope of saving the vessel had gone the three remaining men were brought ashore. The *Manx Queen* eventually settled on the bottom and became a total loss.

Wreck-site
The co-ordinates place the wreck to the left of the High Brigg and two thirds of the way along Filey Brigg, in a general depth of 5m. She is totally collapsed and well dispersed among the rocks and boulders under a carpet of seaweed. She has never been positively identified to my

knowledge, but should make an interesting forage dive where anything could turn up. Many vessels have met their fate along this stretch of coastline over the past few centuries. Tidal streams are reasonable close in to the reef but significantly stronger further away. Visibility is usually very poor but it improves during the summer following a spell of dry settled weather on neap tides.

ISABELLA
Wreck: ★★★
Depth: 26m
Reference: N54 13 013 W000 13 104
Location: 1.5 mile E of Filey Brigg

The *Isabella* was a steel 2,466-ton French steamship registered at the port of Nantes. She was 87.2m long with a 13.1m beam and a 7.0m draught. Atel. & Ch. de la Loire built her at Nantes in 1913 and Compagnie Auxiliaire de Navigation owned her at the time of loss. Her single iron screw propeller was powered by a 3-cylinder triple expansion steam engine that developed 148hp using two boilers. She was armed with two 90mm (3.54-inch) cannon. Her bridge equipment included a brass pedestal-mounted telegraph and pedestal-mounted steering helm. She also had one stern-mounted iron steering helm.

On 9 November 1917, the *Isabella* was in convoy on passage from the Tyne for Rouen when she was torpedoed by SM UC 47. The steamer was carrying 3,700 tons of coal and a crew of thirty-three when the torpedo hit her port side at 8.05 p.m., killing six men. With a huge breach in her side and her engine out of action, the vessel was seriously damaged, but she stayed afloat. The British convoy ship HMS *Swallow* took off the twenty-seven survivors and took her in tow. The two vessels then proceeded towards the shallow water of Filey Bay, but at 1.20 a.m. the following morning and one mile east of Filey Brigg, the *Isabella* heeled over and sank.

Wreck-site
Some years ago, a local fisherman fouled his net on something one mile off the Brigg. When local sport divers went to recover it for him, they discovered the wreck of the *Isabella*. She lies on a seabed of sand, shells and stone, in a general depth of 26m, about the lowest astronomical depth. The wreck was reported to be upright and in one piece, with one of the two 90mm cannon clearly visible. She is now believed to be totally collapsed and broken up, with her boilers and engine exposed and surrounded by masses of twisted broken debris, intermingled with bent and flattened copper pipes. It is doubtful that any interesting equipment is still to be seen, but the wreck is reported to make a nice dive when conditions are right. Visibility is usually rather poor and tidal streams very strong most of the time. Crustaceans and a few fish are sometimes present. The remains should be treated as a grave and given respect by anyone visiting the site.

Chapter 3

Filey To Flamborough Head

Area 3 (N54 13' to N54 06')

CHILIAN
Wreck: ★
Depth: 5-6m
Reference: N54 12 980 W000 15 580 (approx.)
Location: Off High Brigg, north side of Filey Brigg

The *Chilian* was an iron 161-ton British steam fishing trawler registered at Grimsby. She was 32.6m long with a 6.2m beam. She was built at North Shields, probably by Smith's Dock, in 1893 and owned by the Great Grimsby Co-op Box & Fish Carrying Co. Ltd, Grimsby at the time of loss. Her single iron screw propeller was powered by a 3-cylinder triple expansion steam engine that developed 45hp using one boiler, which gave the vessel a maximum speed of 10 knots.

The *Chilian* was returning from the Icelandic fishing grounds in thick fog on 8 April 1894 when she ran aground at Filey Brigg at 3.30 a.m., midway between High Brigg and the Brigg end. Skipper J.K. Little put the vessel hard astern in an attempt to pull her clear, but it was to no avail as the his vessel held fast. She was badly holed and going down, so six of the crew of eleven took to the boat and disappeared into the fog, never to be seen alive again. The tide was at half flood and the *Chilian* settled on a ledge with her rigging standing proud. Skipper Little and the other four crewmembers had no alternative but to climb into it and they hung there until daybreak, when local fishing cobles came to their rescue.

Wreck-site
The wreck, which eventually fell off the ledge into deeper water, is now totally collapsed, well broken up and rather dispersed amongst the rocks in a general depth of around 5-6m being about the lowest astronomical depth. Very little remains now, except a few rusting iron plates and unrecognisable pieces of ironwork, which often shelter little green shore crabs. Small colefish or saithe have been reported swimming in huge shoals around the area during the spring and summer months. Underwater visibility, like with the rest of this part of the coastline, is usually very poor, but significantly improves in the summer to give a few metres.

BOSTON
Wreck: ★
Scenery: ★★★
Depth: 5m
Reference: N54 12 989 W00015 635 (approx.)
Location: Off High Brigg, north side of Filey Brigg

The *Boston* was a steel 1,168-ton Norwegian steamship that was registered at the port of Christiania. She measured 68.58m in length, with a 10.23m beam and a draught of 3.83m. Nylands Vaerksted built her at Christiania in 1905 and her owner at the time of loss was A/S D/S Boston, however, another report says Fred Olsen. Her single bronze screw was powered by a 3-cylinder triple expansion steam engine that developed 119hp using one boiler. Her cylinders measured 40.64cm, 68.58cm and 111.76cm-81.28cm (16in, 27in and 44-32in). Nylands Voerksted at Christiana also built her machinery.

On 22 December 1914, the *Boston* was on passage from Bremen for London when she detonated a German mine just north of Scarborough, leaving her seriously disabled. She was under the command of Captain A.J. Olsen, carrying a cargo of wood pulp, plain and printed paper and a crew of eighteen. (A further report has her master recorded as T.H. Johansen.) Shortly after the explosion, ten of the crew abandoned ship and took to the boats, while the captain and eight others stayed on board the stricken steamship. She carried on drifting south in the strong east-north-easterly wind and eventually ground ashore on Filey Brigg, late that afternoon. The remaining crew lowered the ship's other boat just as the *Boston* began to go down by the head in the heavy seas. The self-righting ten-oared lifeboat from Filey, *Hollon the Third*, was launched at 7.30 a.m. and rescued the nine men on board, while the other boat with ten men in it managed to reach Scarborough safely under their own power. The German Imperial Navy Light Cruiser SMS *Kolberg* laid the mine.

Wreck-site
The wreck, which now lies outside a gully between High Brigg and the foot of Carr Naze, is totally collapsed, broken up and scattered amongst the rocks and reefs in shallow water. The battered single boiler is the highest piece of her and this breaks the surface during spring tides. Very little remains except an iron bollard, an anchor, a few battered steel plates/ribs and unrecognisable pieces of broken machinery. A few crustaceans can be found in the clefts of rock and boulders. Tidal streams are rather strong in this area of shallow water where the currents run around the Brigg and visibility is usually poor. However during the summer months it significantly improves following a spell of westerly wind and settled dry weather.

CARNATIC
Wreck: *
Scenery: **
Depth: 4m
Reference: N54 12 884 W000 15 827 (approx.)
Location: Inside Spittal Rocks, south side of Filey Brigg

The *Carnatic* was a wooden 654-ton British sailing barque that was registered at the port of London. She measured 48.5m in length, with a 10.2m beam and a draught of 5.8m. It was thought that she had been built in London in 1834, but another report suggests she was built in America in 1847. G. Hicks of London owned her at the time of loss and was classed at Lloyd's as A1 for London-Australia.

On 29 January 1859 the *Carnatic* sailed from Malta in ballast under the command of Captain Thomas Price, on passage for Newcastle-upon-Tyne. The journey was uneventful and as she passed Flamborough Head on 25 February at 11 p.m. Captain Price left the mate in charge and went below, leaving instructions for him to steer a course, north-north-west. The weather turned worse, with a hazy fog enveloping the vessel. Another ship was sighted at 12.15 a.m. and the captain was called back on deck. Soon after, a light was seen at three points on the port bow. Captain Price was unaware of the distance they had travelled and thought it was the Scarborough light. The vessel pressed on and within half an hour land was sighted, just two cables (518m) away and directly ahead. Her wheel was put hard to port, her main yards squared and the mizzen sheet loosened, but all to no avail as the majestic vessel ground to a shuddering halt on rocks at the south side of Filey Brigg. The crew made tremendous efforts to refloat her by throwing out the ballast, while local boats assisted in laying out kedge anchors, but she held fast. With seawater pouring through the shattered hull planks, she settled down and soon became a total wreck.

The two Justices of the Peace, Mr John Wharton and Mr S.S. Byron, residing at the Court of Inquiry for the North Riding of Yorkshire, found Captain Price was at fault for neglecting the ship's reckoning after passing Flamborough Head and guilty of not using the lead and line to check for depth. The captain admitted that had he used the lead and line he would have soon realised his ship was heading for a collision course with the Brigg. His Master's certificate was then immediately cancelled and he lost his employment.

The wreck is probably that of the sailing barque *Carnatic*, but she has not been positively identified yet. However, there is the possibility that she could also be one of the following two vessels:

(1) The *Cesare Beccaria* was a 594-ton Italian wooden sailing barque that measured 46.51m in length, with a 9.40m beam and draught of 5.63m. The vessel was in collision with the steamship *Conservator* while at sea on 11 March 1875. She was so badly damaged that her master, Captain Palorino, and his crew took to the boats and landed safely at Filey, leaving the vessel to the elements. She eventually drove ashore on the inside of Filey Brigg, close to where the *Carnatic* had stood twelve years earlier, and soon became a total wreck. The ship's stores were then consequently salvaged and sold for £200.

2) The *Unico* was a 364-ton Italian wooden sailing schooner that measured 37.6m in length, with a 7.87m beam and a draught of 5.30m. On 16 January 1871, she was on passage from North Shields for Genoa with a 600-ton cargo of coal and a crew of fourteen. A Tyne pilot called Corbett had piloted her down the north-east coast, but because of strong southerly winds, the schooner anchored in Filey Bay. However, during the night an increase in the wind to force twelve caught the crew by surprise and in their haste, or panic, attempts were made to steer her out to sea. Being in the Bay, the *Unico* drove directly onto the rocks of Filey Brigg where she was dashed to pieces. Thirteen of the crew died and only one person survived. Rumours abounded locally that the captain and officers were all drunk at the time of the incident and soon after a bell buoy was placed in position to mark the end of the Brigg.

Wreck-site

The wreck, or what remains of it, lies on the inside and south side of Filey Brigg, inside the Spittal Rocks, in a general depth of 4m, being about the lowest astronomical depth. All that is visible are a few sections of wooden planking, held together by some large copper rivets, but who knows what else may turn up in the future. Tidal streams are very moderate, while visibility is usually poor, but significantly improves during the summer months. A bonus at this wreck-site is that the occasional crustacean can be found amongst the rocks and boulders of the Brigg.

EGLANTINE
Wreck: *
Scenery: **
Depth: 8m
Reference: N54 12 915 W000 15 000 (approx.)
Location: Off the south tip of Filey Brigg

The *Eglantine* (Official No.79212) was an iron 1,312-ton British steamship that was registered at North Shields. She measured 76.38m in length, with a 9.70m beam and a draught of 6.41m. Tyne Iron Shipbuilding Co. built her at Newcastle-upon-Tyne and launched her in August

1878 for John Robinson & Co. The ship cost £20,780 and on delivery was insured for £23,000. On 2 September 1895 she was transferred to Stag Line Co. Then in 1898 she was sold to Tyneside Line Ltd who owned her at the time of loss. J. Ridley, Son & Tully managed her. Her single iron screw propeller was powered by a 2-cylinder compound steam engine that developed 130hp using two 2SB 4PF boilers. Her cylinders measured 63.50cm and 137.16cm-83.82cm. North Eastern Marine Engineering built her machinery at Sunderland. She had one deck, four bulkheads and a superstructure consisting of a 5.18m bridge deck.

In the early hours of 16 April 1915 the *Eglantine*, which was on passage from the Tyne for Le Havre with a cargo of coal and a crew of eighteen, struck Filey Brigg. The *Eglantine's* master, Captain T.R. Thompson believed a German submarine had launched a torpedo at his ship, but his evasive action turned his vessel into the treacherous rocks of Filey Brigg. The crew took to the ship's boat and were picked up by the ten-oared self-righting lifeboat from Filey, *Hollon the Third*, which had been launched at 1.45 a.m. The crew were landed safely at Filey, but their vessel was submerged within a few hours of striking the rocks and became a total wreck.

Wreck-site
The wreck, which lies between the bell buoy and the end of the Brigg is totally collapsed, well broken up and rather scattered amongst the many rocks and large boulders, in a general depth of 8m, being about the lowest astronomical depth. The highest pieces of the wreck are her boilers and engine, but the winches, anchors, bollards and lots of broken bottom-plates surround them, making the site quite an interesting place to explore. However, the tidal streams which tear around the Brigg are not for the faint hearted. The underwater visibility is also usually very poor, but improves during the summer months. The best and probably only time to visit the wreck-site is at slack water on a neap tide, after a spell of settled westerly winds and dry weather. A fair number of crustaceans can also be found hiding under and amongst the rocks and boulders.

SLEUTH HOUND
Wreck: *
Scenery: ***
Depth: 3-4m
Reference: N54 12 860 W00015 662 (approx.)
Location: South side of Filey Brigg

The *Sleuth Hound* (Official No.98709) was a steel 153-ton British steam fishing trawler that was registered at Hull. She was 30.8m long and had a 6.25m beam. Cook, Welton & Gemmell built her at Hull as Yard 65 in 1890. She was launched as the *Sleuth Hound* and registered as H114 for Humber Steam Trawling Co. Ltd of Hull on 13 November 1890. Her single iron screw propeller was powered by a 3-cylinder triple expansion steam engine that developed 45hp using one boiler, giving her a maximum speed of 10 knots. Bailey & Leetham of Hull built the machinery.

Early on 27 October 1897, the *Sleuth Hound* was returning from a successful fishing voyage under the command of Captain Charles Neilson with a crew of nine. During a thick fog, she ran aground and stranded at the extreme eastern end of the Spittalls, on Filey Brigg. Attempts were made to reverse her off, but she held fast. A number of distress signals were made but with the dense fog, ebbing tide and the crew having no idea of their location, the skipper decided there was little else they could do until high tide. By lunchtime the fog had cleared, the sea was like a mirror and numerous curious onlookers flocked to see the *Sleuth Hound's* predicament. By this time, her engine room had flooded and things looked bleak so arrangements were made with local boats to ferry her valuable cargo of fish ashore. At high tide a harbour tug from Scarborough, the SS *Cambria*, arrived and tried to tow her off, then the steam paddle trawlers *Dandy*, *Dunrobin* and *Star* tried, but the *Sleuth Hound's* hull had settled on the bottom and was well jammed into the rocks. All attempts to move her failed and she was eventually written off as a total wreck.

Wreck-site

The wreck is now totally collapsed, well broken up and rather dispersed at the seaward end of the Spittall Rocks and a little to the right of the rocks, on the inland side of the reef, where parts of her stern end can still be seen. Her engine, bits of broken machinery and pieces of steel plating can also be found under the seaweed at the other side, in what is known locally as Crab Hole. A few crustaceans can also be observed hiding under the steel debris and surrounding rocks. Tidal streams in this area are very reasonable, but visibility usually poor, except during the summer months when it is possible to see a few metres.

AMSTELDAM

Wreck: ★★★
Depth: 49m
Reference: N54 12 662 W00003 427
Location: 5.55 miles NNE of Flamborough Head

The *Amsteldam* (Official No.132870) was a steel 1,233-ton British steamship that was registered at Cardiff. She measured 69.92m in length, with a beam of 10.46m and a 4.87m draught. The Campbeltown Shipbuilding Co. built her as Yard No.78 at Campbeltown in 1907 for Stoomvaart Maatschappi Amstel of Amsterdam, Holland. Hayman & Schuuman Ltd of Amsterdam managed her. In 1912, she was sold to Pomaron Steamship Co. Ltd and managed by William H. Vernall of London. Later that year, the Guardiana Steamship Co. Ltd became the new owner and she was managed by William H. Vernall, but in Cardiff. In 1913, Fisher, Renwick & Co. of Newcastle purchased her and then South Metropolitan Gas Co., which owned her at the time of loss, acquired her on 4 March 1915. Her single iron screw propeller was powered by a 3-cylinder triple expansion steam engine that developed 130hp using one 1SB 3CF boiler. Her cylinders measured 45.72cm, 68.58cm and 114.30cm-83.82cm. Hutson & Sons Ltd built her machinery at Glasgow. She had one deck, a well deck and a superstructure consisting of a 24.08m quarterdeck, 17.68m bridge deck and 8.53m forecastle. The vessel was also armed with one stern-mounted howitzer gun that fired 2.72kg shells (6 pounders). The South Metropolitan Gas Co.'s first ships, the steamers *Amsteldam* and *Broompark*, were bought in March 1915, followed later that year by the *Glenpark* and the *Togston*.

   At 4.30 p.m. on 18 October 1917, the *Amsteldam* was in convoy steaming south at 8 knots, on passage from South Shields for London, when she was torpedoed and sunk by SM UB 21, an Imperial German submarine that survived the First World War. The U-boat commander, Oblt.z. S. Walter Scheffler, gave no warning and at no time did the steamship's crew sight her. Under the command of Captain Letonge, the *Amsteldam* was carrying a crew of twenty and a 1,900-ton cargo of coal. Some of the crew had seen the unmistakable track of the torpedo before it hit the vessel, but there was insufficient time to take avoiding action. When it detonated in the boiler-room on the port side, four men were killed, some in the engine room and some on deck, while Captain Letonge was blown clear overboard. Within five minutes, the crew had abandoned ship, some in the lifeboat, while others, some including the injured chief officer, took to a life raft. The crew in the ship's boat picked up the captain, who was by then swimming around. A British warship picked up all the survivors and landed them at Grimsby.

Wreck-site

The wreck, possibly that of the steamship *Amsteldam*, lies east-south-east to west-north-west on a seabed of sand, shells and stone in a general depth of 49m, the lowest astronomical depth. She stands some 4.5m at the highest point, is broken into two main sections and covers an area of seabed measuring about 66m by 9m, with a 1m scour surrounding her. Much of the wreck is totally collapsed and well broken up with sand encroaching over the north and south sides. The highest sections are covered in a nice colourful array of soft corals, with swarms of pout whiting swimming around. Tidal streams are very strong and underwater visibility is usually bad, but it vastly improves during the summer months after a spell of dry settled weather. The wreck may also be worth adding to the boat-angling venues, because there should be some large cod under the debris, which is strewn around on both sides of the main wreck. For divers who are prepared to leave the wreck, there is always the chance of picking up a few scallops that can be found in this vicinity. The wreck should be treated as a grave because brave men died on the ship during the conflict.

ALADDIN
Wreck: ★★★
Depth: 43m
Reference: N54 12 8013 W000 08 104 (approx.)
Location: 5.33 miles NNW of Flamborough Head

The *Aladdin* was a steel 753-ton Norwegian steamship that was registered at the port of Stavanger. She measured 59.48m in length, with a 9.16m beam and draught of 3.35m. Stavanger Stoberi & Dok built her at Stavanger in 1902 and D/S A/S Aladdin of Stavanger owned her at the time of loss. Her single iron screw propeller was powered by a 3-cylinder triple expansion steam engine that developed 75hp using one boiler. She had cylinder sizes measuring 35.56cm, 58.42cm and 96.52cm-68.58cm. The vessel also had one deck.

On 8 September 1917, the *Aladdin* was on passage from Newcastle-upon-Tyne for Treport when she was torpedoed and sunk by SM UB 34, an Imperial German submarine that survived the First World War. She was carrying an unspecified cargo of coal under the command of Captain M.H. Westergaard. Available records do not say if anyone was lost when the *Aladdin* went down.

Wreck-site
The wreck of the *Aladdin* lies on a seabed of sand, stone and gravel in a depth of 43m, the lowest astronomical depth. She is reasonably intact, upright and standing some 4m high from just passed amidships to her stern end. She has collapsed and is broken up, but the highest sections are covered in an array of soft corals. Most, if not all of her interesting equipment and the ship's bell should still be there to see, so the wreck will be a good one to explore. The wreck frequently has trawl nets or cod nets draped over her so great care will be required in the gloomy water. This wreck should make an excellent boat-angling venue when conditions are right. Tidal streams are rather strong and the underwater visibility usually very poor to dismal, but it gradually improves during the summer months.

LEERSUM
Wreck: ★★★★
Depth: 46m
Reference: N54 11 548 W000 00 236
Location: 5.25 miles NNE of Flamborough Head

The *Leersum* was a steel 1,455-ton Dutch steamship that was registered at the port of Amsterdam. She measured 73.2m in length, with a beam of 11.3m and draught of 4.75m. She was built in 1898 by Sunderland Shipbuilding Co. Stoomvaart Maatschappij Oostzee owned her at the time of loss and Vinck & Co. managed her. Her single iron screw propeller was powered by a 3-cylinder triple expansion steam engine that used one 2SB 4PF boiler. Her cylinders measured 46.99cm, 76.20cm and 124.46cm-83.82cm. McColl & Pollock built her machinery at Sunderland.

On 16 December 1914, the SS *Leersum* foundered and was lost off Flamborough Head after detonating a German mine. She was on passage from Rotterdam for Newcastle-upon-Tyne carrying a general cargo and a crew of ten, under the command of Captain G. Stekelenburg.

Wreck-site
This wreck could possibly be that of the Dutch steamer, but she has not been positively identified. She lies north-east to south-west on a seabed of mud, sand, gravel and shells, in a general depth of 46m, the lowest astronomical depth. The wreck is quite substantial, is collapsed, upright and intact, standing 5m high amidships to her stern. Plenty of marine life can be found on and around the wreckage and numerous cod have been observed, so this should make a nice boat-angling venue. Tidal streams are very strong and underwater visibility is usually poor to grim, but improves during the summer months after a spell of dry settled weather.

LEDA
Wreck: ★★★★
Depth: 17m
Reference: N54 11 516 W000 13 576
Location: 2.13 miles SSE of Filey Brigg

The *Leda* was a steel 1,140-ton Dutch steamship that was registered at the port of Rotterdam. She measured 69.5m in length, with a 9.7m beam and a 5.5m draught. Rijkee & Co. built her at Rotterdam in 1898 and Koninklijke Nederlandsche Stoomb Maats owned her at the time of loss. Her single iron screw propeller was powered by a 3-cylinder triple expansion steam engine that used one boiler. Her cylinders measured 43.18cm, 71.12cm and 114.30cm.

On 6 December 1917, the *Leda* was torpedoed by SM UC 49, an Imperial German submarine, and sank two miles south, south-east from Filey. She was on passage from Methil for Amsterdam with a cargo of coal and six of her crew died in the explosion. (SM UC 49 was sunk by depth charges and gunfire from Royal Navy ships on 8 August 1918.)

Wreck-site
The wreck of the *Leda* has never been officially located, but there are the remains of an unknown wreck lying 2.13 miles south, south-east from Filey Brigg. The wreck is now totally collapsed, well broken up, partially buried and quite dispersed over the surrounding seabed. Very little remains of the vessel, which appears to have been dispersed at some time or other. She lies on a seabed of sand and shells, in a general depth of 17m, the lowest astronomical depth.

GEMMA, ex KONIGSAU
Wreck: ★★★
Depth: 36m
Reference: N54 10 846 W000 06 831
Location: 3.84 miles NNW of Flamborough Head

The *Gemma* was a steel 1,385-ton British steamship that was registered at the port of London. She measured 78.05m in length, with a 10.89m beam and a 4.62m draught. Flensburger Schiffsb. Ges of Flensburg built her as the *Konigsau* in 1904. In 1914 she was requisitioned by the Admiralty as a collier, but managed by Everett. Her single iron screw propeller was powered by a 3-cylinder triple expansion steam engine that developed 106hp using one boiler. She had one deck and a superstructure consisting of a 4.88m poop deck, 19.81m quarterdeck, 34.14m bridge deck and 9.14m forecastle. The vessel was also armed with one 406kg stern-mounted deck-gun that fired 5.44kg shells (12 pounders).

At 4.30 p.m. on 19 October 1917, the *Gemma* was on passage from Blyth for the Tyne when she was torpedoed by SM UB 21. She was under the command of Captain W.J.W. Sutton, carrying a 2,100-ton cargo of coal and a crew of twenty-one. The explosion tore a gaping hole in her side and killed one gunner, a fireman, the second engineer and the second mate. She went down in five minutes and the rest of the crew went into the sea. A Royal Navy motor-launch rescued twelve men and picked the second mate's body up and landed them at Bridlington. The steamship *Tay & Tyne* picked up the captain and three crewmen and took them to Grimsby while two others, one of whom died later, were rescued by the steamship *General Havelock* and taken to London. Following the armistice SM UB 21 was surrendered to the French. She was sunk somewhere along the English East Coast in 1920, en route to being broken up.

Wreck-site

The wreck lies orientated in a north-west to south-east direction, on a seabed of sand, black shells and stone, in a general depth of 36m, the lowest astronomical depth. The wreck covers a large area of seabed, is very substantial and stands some 5m high, but is collapsed and broken up amidships, where her boiler and engine are exposed. The bow and stern are reported to be reasonably intact and covered in an array of soft corals, mostly on the upper structures. It is not known how much of her interesting bridge equipment is still around, or whether the vessel's bell has been located, but she should make an interesting one to explore. Tidal streams are quite brisk and underwater visibility is usually poor to grim, but can be reasonable during the summer on neap tides and westerly winds. Men died on this ship, so the wreck should be treated with respect.

HANNA, ex AGHIOS IOANNIS, ex TRANSITION

Wreck: ★★★★★
Depth: 46m
Reference: N54 10 647 W000 02 097
Location: 3.91 miles NNE of Flamborough Head

The *Hanna* (Official No.3586) was a steel-hulled 1,598-ton Swedish steamship that was registered at the port of Helsingborg. She measured 83.9m in length, with an 11.0m beam and a 5.5m draught. R. Dixon & Co. built her at Middlesbrough as the *Transition* in 1885 for J.M. Lennard & Sons. Her single screw propeller, possibly bronze, was powered by a 3-cylinder triple expansion steam engine that used two boilers. Blair & Co. at Stockton built her machinery. It is also understood that the vessel was equipped with a brass pedestal-mounted telegraph and brass pedestal-mounted steering helm, plus a stern-positioned iron steering helm.

In 1892 she was sold to C. Nicolaidis, Sons & Co. of Cephalonia in Greece and renamed *Aghios Ioannis*. Later that year she was sold to Vagliano Bros, and registered at Argostoli in Greece who kept her until 1897 and sold her back to C. Nicolaidis, Sons & Co. Rederiaktieb AB Henckel purchased the vessel last, while N.P. Swensen managed her.

The *Hanna* left the Tyne at 12.05, together with the Swedish steamship *August Leffler*. The *Hanna* was on passage for Las Palmas carrying a 1,950-ton cargo of coal and a crew of twenty. They were both being navigated by an English pilot, when an explosion in the bow section at 12.50 a.m. on 13 March 1915 rocked the *Hanna*. They were close to Flamborough Head and whatever it was blew most of the vessel's bow-stem away. The second officer on watch said that he had seen what he believed to be the wake of a torpedo, a white trace at the port side shortly before the explosion, but he was not sure. Six out of the eight men who were asleep in the forecastle were killed outright and the *Hanna* immediately began to sink. The fourteen surviving crewmen took to the boats after abandoning ship and were picked up by steamship *Gylier* and landed at Hull later that day. The *Hanna* was a neutral ship and had her identity plainly painted on the ship's hull in large letters. Although it was probably a mine, to this day, no one seems sure whether she detonated a mine or a torpedo sank her.

Wreck-site

The wreck, possibly that of the Swedish steamship *Hanna*, lies east-south-east to west-north-west on a seabed of coarse sand, mud and shells, in a general depth of 46m, the lowest astronomical depth. The wreck-site is very substantial, partially buried, lying in two main sections, collapsed and broken, with the highest section of 4.7m being around amidships to stern. Her engine and boilers are now exposed and surrounded by mounds of broken debris. The wreck-site covers an area of seabed measuring 90m by 23m and is thought to have seen very few divers, making her an interesting one to explore. Tidal streams are very strong and underwater visibility usually poor. This wreck should also make an excellent boat-angling venue, but she is in the main shipping lanes.

TRONGATE

Wreck: ★★★★
Depth: 31m
Reference: N54 10 600 W000 07 242
Location: 3.78 miles NNW of Flamborough Head

The *Trongate* was a steel 2,553-ton British steamship that was registered at the port of London. She measured 94.48m in length, with a 13.41m beam and a draught of 6.19m. T. Turnbull & Son of Whitby built her in 1897 and the Turnbull, Scott Shipping Co. Ltd owned her at the time of loss. Her single iron screw propeller was powered by a 3-cylinder triple expansion steam engine that developed 235hp using two 2SB 6CF boilers. Her cylinders measured 58.42cm, 93.98cm and 154.94cm-99.06cm. Blair & Co. built her machinery at Stockton-on-Tees. In 1911, the vessel was valued at £13,000. She had one deck and a superstructure consisting of a 9.45m poop deck, an 18.59m bridge deck and a 10.67m forecastle. The vessel was also armed with one 610kg stern-mounted deck-gun that fired 5.44kg shells (12 pounders).

At 3.30 p.m. on 22 September 1917, the SS *Trongate* was on passage from South Shields for Rocheford via Ipswich when she was torpedoed and sunk by SM U 71, an Imperial German submarine. The U-boat was never sighted and remained submerged during the attack on the steamer. *Trongate* was under the command of Captain H.M. Brown and was carrying a 3,800-ton cargo of coal and a crew of twenty-eight. Two of her crew were killed when the torpedo detonated amidships and the rest took to the boat after abandoning ship at 3.35 p.m., the *Trongate* going down soon after. A torpedo boat destroyer picked up the survivors and landed them at Immingham later that evening. SM U 71 surrendered to the Allies at the end of the First World War and became French reparation. She was broken up at Cherbourg in 1921.

Wreck-site

The wreck lies on a seabed of rough sand, stone and black shell, in a general depth of 31m, the lowest astronomical depth. She is still very substantial, covering an area of seabed measuring 95m by 15m, but now collapsed and well broken up, with her boilers and engine exposed amidships. The upper structures are coated in an array of soft corals, being a sure sign of the strong tidal stream that flow over the wreck-site and underwater visibility is usually very poor to grim, but during the summer months it greatly improves. The ship was fitted with a pedestal-mounted telegraph and steering helm, plus a stern-positioned iron steering helm, making her an interesting one to look at and explore. There are also no reports of the ship's bell being recovered and it is uncertain how the wreck was identified. A few large lobsters have been observed sheltering among the steel debris etc., and due to her size, she should also make an interesting boat-angling venue when weather conditions allow.

LIFEGUARD
Wreck: ★★★
Depth: 47m
Reference: N54 10 920 E000 02 261
Location: 5.73 miles NE of Flamborough Head

The *Lifeguard* was an iron brigg-rigged 491-ton British auxiliary steamship that was registered at the port of Newcastle-upon-Tyne. Her dimensions were 50.49m in length, a 7.49m beam and a draught of 4.08m. Laing & Co. built her at Newcastle-upon-Tyne in 1857 and a Newcastle company owned her at the time of loss. An auxiliary 80hp 2-cylinder compound steam engine that used one boiler powered a single iron screw propeller. The vessel had five bulkheads and was classed at Lloyd's as A1.

On 20 December 1862, the SS *Lifeguard* was on passage from Newcastle-upon-Tyne for London when, during the night, she disappeared off Flamborough Head in unknown circumstances. She was under the command of Captain Cracknell, carrying an unspecified general cargo, twenty-two crew and thirty passengers, all of whom were lost. The vessel had left the River Tyne down at the stern and deeply laden, with her gunwales barely 30cm clear of the water. The master of the steamship *Newcastle* later reported that during the night he had seen the lights of two steamers going towards Flamborough. He said the weather was dreadful at the time and that the lights of one of the vessels suddenly disappeared, while the lights of the other one, were seen for some time after. A few days later, the fishing-smack *Idra* picked up a box from the sea, containing Christmas presents, poultry and a letter from London and wreckage also began drifting ashore. The *Scarborough Gazette* reported on New Year's Day 1863 that, 'It is the general opinion of nautical men that she had been pooped by the sea, which put out the fires, leaving her at the mercy of one of the most terrible seas known for some many years past.'

Wreck-site
There is a wreck in the position above, which could possibly be the remains of the steamship *Lifeguard*. The wreck has not been positively identified, but what is left is that of a very old steamship. She is totally collapsed and well broken up, standing about 2m high amidships around a single boiler and engine. If the bell is recovered, it will certainly make good reading in the local press and solve this long-standing mystery as to what happened to the *Lifeguard* on that ill-fated night on 20 December 1862. Tidal streams are very strong in this area and underwater visibility unfortunately, is usually pretty grim most of the year.

SEISTAN, ex HEADLEY
Wreck: ★★★★★
Depth: 26m
Reference: N54 10 408 W000 08 633
Location: 3.95 miles NNW of Flamborough Head

The *Seistan* (Official No.123779) was a steel 4,238-ton British steamship registered at Swansea. Her dimensions measured 110.94m in length, with a 15.24m beam and a draught of 5.41m. William Gray & Co. Ltd built her as Yard No.737 and launched her as the *Headley* in December 1906. In February 1907 she was completed for the Mitre Shipping Co. Ltd of London, with Houlder, Middleton & Co. as the managers. Her single screw, possibly bronze, was powered by a 3-cylinder triple expansion steam engine that developed 408hp using three 3SB 9RF boilers. Her cylinders measured 66.04cm, 109.22cm and 182.88cm-114.30cm. Central Marine Engineering Works Ltd in West Hartlepool built her machinery. Her superstructure consisted of an 8.23m poop deck, a 33.53m bridge deck and a 10.06m forecastle. She was also armed with a 610kg stern-mounted deck-gun that fired 5.44kg shells (12 pounders). She was sold to the Anglo-

Algerian Steamship Co. (1896) Ltd in 1912 who renamed her *Seistan*. On 1 January 1913 the Anglo-Algerian Steamship Co. merged with La Commerciale Steam Navigation Co. Ltd to form the Strick Line Ltd and ownership passed to that company, who owned her at the time of loss.

At 5.30 p.m. on 23 October 1917, the *Seistan* was on passage from the Tyne for Alexandria via Falmouth when she was torpedoed and sunk by the U-boat SM UB 57. The U-boat remained submerged during the attack and no warning was issued. The steamer was under the command of Captain R.R. Forbes, carrying a 5,440-ton cargo of Government-owned coal and a crew of fifty-nine. The torpedo detonated on her starboard side, causing a massive explosion, which practically blew the ship to pieces. The blast was so great that it killed the third engineer and four lascar seamen who were down below, with even her starboard lifeboat being totally wrecked. The crew of fifty-four who survived, including five that were injured, immediately abandoned ship in three boats and got clear. At 4.02 p.m., they watched at a distance as the *Seistan* went down, taking the confidential papers and wartime codebooks with her. Patrol boats picked up the survivors and landed them at Bridlington later that evening. SM UB 57 was presumed mined off Zeebrugge on 14 August 1918.

On 17 February 1958 the second ship to be named *Seistan*, which was built at Redheads, was six months old when fire broke out in her No.5 hold beneath the explosive magazine, while on passage from London for Khorramshahr. Her cargo included 170 tons of explosives, fuses and detonators. The following day she anchored two miles east from South Sitra Beacon, Bahrain. While fire fighting continued, 75 tons of explosives were transferred to a barge. The following day, the fire spread to the magazine, which exploded, destroying the superstructure and after part of the vessel and killing fifty-three members of the crew including the master and four crewmen on a tug. The forepart of the vessel eventually sank, but was raised in 1959 and towed to Italy where it was broken up. A photograph of this vessel is now in the South Tyneside Museum.

Wreck-site
The wreck lies on a seabed of sand, stone and black shells in a general depth of 26m, the lowest astronomical depth. The latest reports (2002) are that she is upright and intact, with her stern section standing 10m proud of the seabed at the highest point and listing to starboard, but amidships is collapsed and well broken up, where the torpedo detonated. The bow section is also reasonably intact and her boilers and engine are exposed through a mass of broken steel plates and framework. Huge bent and often flattened copper pipes with large brass valves and flanges attached to the ends were visible, some poking out from the mound of debris amidships. The wreck should be a nice one to explore; however, it is a matter of 'look but don't touch', because she is owned by Arthur Godfrey, co-author of the book *Shipwrecks of the Yorkshire Coast*. A fair amount of salvage has taken place, so it is unlikely that her bell and other interesting equipment will still be around to see. A number of crustaceans and numerous large cod have been observed, which should also make this an excellent boat-angling venue. The tidal streams are very strong and underwater visibility usually rather grim most of the year, but slightly improve during the summer months. Men went down with this vessel, so her remains should be treated with respect
.

CLAUDIA
Wreck: ★★
Depth: 30m
Reference: N54 10 283 W000 09 400
Location: 4.9 miles NW of Flamborough Head

The *Claudia* (Official No.102967) was a steel 149-ton British steam fishing trawler that was registered at Hull. She measured 31.24m in length and had a 6.25m-beam. Cook, Welton & Gemmell built her as Yard No.127 at Hull and launched her as the *Claudia* for Charles Hellyer of Hull in 1894. The vessel was registered as Hull trawler No.H263 on 18 September 1894.

Her single iron screw propeller was powered by a 3-cylinder triple expansion steam engine that developed 45nhp using one boiler, which gave her a maximum speed of 10 knots. Charles D. Holmes built her machinery at Hull. She had one deck and a small superstructure/wheelhouse. On 5 August 1895, the boat was sold to Hellyer Steam Fishing Co. Ltd at Hull.

On 29 December 1895 the trawler was on a return fishing voyage from Hull when, during thick fog, she was stranded on rocks near Buckton Hall, south of Filey. On 3 January 1896, tugs arrived and towed her off the rocks, but with her hull fractured and letting in water, she soon foundered and was lost in deeper water further offshore.

Wreck-site
The wreck has never been positively identified, but there is a possibility that this may be the wreck of the *Claudia*. She is now totally collapsed, well broken up and rather dispersed, with the highest sections being around the engine and boiler. A small mound of iron debris litters the seabed around the engine. She lies in a general depth of 30m, the lowest astronomical depth. Tidal streams are very strong, while under water visibility is usually very poor and often grim.

LADY JOSYAN
Wreck: ★★★
Depth: 43m & 20m
Reference: N54 10 103 W000 02 890
Location: 3.23 miles NNE of Flamborough Head
Also given: N54 07 013 W000 04 104
Location: 0.25 miles NE of Flamborough Head

The *Lady Josyan* was an iron 1,054-ton British steamship that was registered at the port of London. She measured 68.5m in length, with a 9.58m beam and a draught of 5.84m. Pearce & Co. of Stockton built her in 1872 and R. Gordon of London owned her at the time of loss. Her single iron screw propeller was powered by a 2-cylinder compound steam engine that used one boiler. Her cylinders measured 66.04cm and 132.08cm-91.44cm. Day, Summers & Co. built her machinery at Stockton-on-Tees.

On 26 October 1884, the *Lady Josyan* was on passage from the Tyne for London with an unspecified cargo of coal, one passenger and a crew of sixteen, when she foundered following a collision with Middlesbrough-registered steamship *Hero*, three miles off Flamborough Head.

Wreck-site
Two positions have been suggested for the wreck of the old steamer *Lady Josyan*, and only a few dives on the remains would verify which one is which.

The first co-ordinates have her lying north-east to south-west on a seabed of sand, stone and shells, in a general depth of 43m, the lowest astronomical depth. The wreck is partially buried, upright and intact, standing no more than 2.4m high and covering an area of seabed measuring 65m by 10m. It is very doubtful if the site has seen any divers, so it should be a very interesting one to investigate and explore. She will be totally collapsed and well broken up, probably with her engine and boiler exposed. Tidal streams are very brisk in this vicinity and underwater visibility usually poor to grim, but it vastly improves during the mid summer months. Because of her size, she is not likely to make a very good boat-angling venue.

The second set of co-ordinates places her about a quarter of a mile north-east of Flamborough Head, lying on a hard seabed of sand and stone, in a general depth of 20m, the lowest astronomical depth. All that remains is some scattered wreckage, with little standing more than half a metre proud of the seabed. Tidal streams are extremely strong and underwater visibility is usually very poor to grim most of the year.

H142 *Diamond*. Built 1891 by Mackie & Thompson, Govan. Length: 100ft 5in, Gross Tonnage: 149. Wrecked at Speeton Cliffs, 9 January 1912. *(Courtesy Jonathan Grobler Collection)*

DIAMOND
Wreck: ★
Depth: 1m
Reference: N54 09 503 W000 12 588 (approx.)
Location: 0.5 miles S of King & Queen Rock, near Speeton Village

The *Diamond* (Official No.98739) was an iron 149-ton British trawler that was registered at the port of Hull as trawler No.H142. She measured 30.5m in length and a beam of 20.4m. She was built in 1892 at Govan on the Clyde for the Kingston Steam Trawling Co. of Hull, who was the owner at the time of loss. Her single iron screw propeller was powered by a 2-cylinder compound steam engine that developed 45hp using one boiler.

On 9 January 1912, the *Diamond* was on a return voyage to Hull from the fishing grounds when she drove ashore under Speeton Cliffs in thick fog. With the hull badly damaged and water flooding her engine room, the crew took to the trawler's own boat and were picked up by Flamborough lifeboat. The *Diamond* submerged on the incoming tide and became a total loss.

Wreck-site
The wreck lies at the end of the long stretch of sand where the rocky beach begins, about 750m south of King & Queen Rocks and not far from Speeton village. She dries at low water and is, or was, visible at most states of the tide, but in recent years has broken up somewhat. It is also possible to walk to the wreck at low spring tides and she can be dived at high tide from the seaward side of the wreck. There is now very little of interest to see, but will make an interesting foray for trainee divers or snorkel-swimmers.

HAWKWOOD
Wreck: ★
Scenery: ★★
Depth: 3-4m
Reference: N54 09 598 W000 12 650 (approx.)
Location: Under Speeton Cliffs, Filey Bay

The *Hawkwood* was a steel-hulled 1,155-ton (902 tons under deck) British schooner-rigged steam collier that was registered at the port of London. She measured 71.63m in length, with a beam of 10.08m and a 4.40m draught. J. Blumer & Co. built her in eleven months at Sunderland in 1899 for William France, Fenwick & Co. of London, who also owned her at the time of loss. Her single iron screw propeller was powered by a 3-cylinder triple expansion steam engine that developed 179hp using two single-ended boilers with plain furnace. Her cylinders measured 50.80cm, 82.55cm and 134.62cm-91.44cm. J. Dickinson & Sons Ltd built her machinery at Sunderland. She had a flat keel, four cemented bulkheads, one part iron deck with web frames, a well deck and a superstructure consisting of a 5.18m poop deck, a 21.64m quarterdeck, a 14.63m bridge deck and a 6.71m forecastle. Her water ballast consisted of cellular double bottoms with 19.81m aft, 10.67m under engines and boilers and 21.64m forward, giving 487 tons. She also had an after peak tank of 40 tons. Lloyd's classed her as 100 A1. The registration letters in 1912-1913 were RKGT. The vessel had two captains during her fourteen years: Captain J. Lumsden up to 1903 and Captain R. Harrison from 1903.

On 12 January 1913, the *Hawkwood*, valued at £14,000, was on passage from Granton for London carrying an unspecified cargo of coal and a crew of seventeen when she drove ashore under Speeton Cliffs, in a south-easterly gale. Early that day, the steamer *Newark* off Flamborough Head had seen her. The *Hawkwood* had a heavy list to port and even though her lights were still blazing, there were no other signs of life on board. The *Newark* went in as close as she dared and the crew noticed that some of the vessel's lifeboats were missing and the falls were hanging down by the side of the ship. A big sea was running and there was nothing anyone could do. Eventually she was blown ashore in front of Brecon Hole, a little south of King & Queen Rocks and almost immediately capsized. As she started to break up in the surf, her cargo of coal was washed all over the beach. Like that of the *Marie Celeste* nothing was ever found of her crew, but the ship's empty boats were washed ashore later. The ship was salvaged at a later date.

Wreck-site
After being heavily salvaged, very little remains of her today and what there is left, is hardly worthy of a visit. The reason I have included her in the book is because of the mystery surrounding her, and her crew of seventeen souls, who seemed to have sadly disappeared from the face of the earth.

An interesting theory to the vessel's fate seems to lie in a design fault in the position and size of her bunker-space and donkey boiler. It seems that her sister ship *Glow*, ex *Monkwood*, which sank four miles south-east of Robin Hood's Bay, also had the fault. They had to continuously be trimmed as the fuel was used up, or the vessel took on a serious list, which, if not rectified in heavy weather, could have resulted in the vessel capsizing. Maybe the crew panicked and left in the boats, but why no bodies?

ALFA, ex NORMANDIET, ex ROLLON, ex SICILIAN

Wreck: *
Scenery: ***
Depth: 3-5m
Reference: N54 09 538 W000 11 660 (approx.)
Location: 3 miles SSE of Filey, under Speeton Cliffs

The *Alfa* was an iron-hulled 1,195-ton (1,021-ton under deck) Danish schooner-rigged steamship registered at Copenhagen. Her dimensions were 74.19m in length, with a 9.75m beam and a 5.56m draught. E. Withy & Co. built her in eleven months as the *Sicilian* at Hartlepool in 1877 for Blaik & Co. at Leith. Her single iron screw propeller was powered by a 2-cylinder compound steam engine that developed 149hp using two single-ended boilers, with four plain furnaces having a grate-surface of 149.86cm. Her cylinders measured 66.04cm, 143.18cm-83.82cm. T. Richardson & Sons built her machinery at Hartlepool. She had one deck made up of two tiers of beams, a well deck, four cemented bulkheads and a superstructure consisting of a 25.60m quarterdeck, a 20.12m bridge deck and 9.45m forecastle. She had water ballast in double bottoms, which were 22.25m aft, 26.21m forward and 11.58m under engine and boilers giving 311 tons of ballast. In 1899 she was sold to G. Vallee of Rouen in France and renamed *Rollon*, with her master being Captain Burrolaud and signal letters KTSC. In 1903-1904 Aktieseeskabet Det Dansk-Franske Dampskibs renamed her *Normandiet*, with N.W. Schmidt the manager; she was then registered in Copenhagen. Her master was Captain H. Schmidt. In 1903 A.N. Petersen became the manager, with the same owner, and she was registered at Esbjerg. In 1915-1916 she was renamed *Alfa* when A/S D/S Absalon of Copenhagen bought her and owned her at the time of loss. The vessel was classed as 100 A1 at her last inspection in March 1915 at Helsingør.

On 13 July 1916, in dense fog and a heavy sea, the *Alfa* became stranded under Speeton Cliffs, 2.5 miles south-south-east of Filey. She was on passage from Hudiksvall for London, under the command of Captain S. Clausen, carrying a crew of sixteen and an unspecified cargo of wood. The crew abandoned ship in their boat, but experienced great difficulty in clearing the ship. However, the ten-oared self-righting lifeboat *Hollon the Third* from Filey was launched at 6.50 a.m. and despite the huge seas that pounded the vessel, she got alongside the boat and rescued the sixteen crew. Within minutes of the lifeboat leaving the scene, the steamer broke in two and became a total wreck. Her cargo littered the coastline for many months after and was often collected by local people to keep the home fires burning.

Wreck-site

The wreck is now totally collapsed, broken up and dispersed under the weed, among the rocks, reef and boulders, in a general depth of between 3 and 5m. A propeller, parts of her boilers and the remnants of her engine can still be made out, but very little else is said to remain. Tidal streams are very reasonable close to the shore, but underwater visibility is usually very poor, but significantly improves during the summer months after a spell of dry settled weather and south-westerly winds. The occasional edible crab and even lobsters can sometimes be found sheltering under the surrounding rocks and boulders. The ship's bell if recovered will almost certainly be inscribed 'Sicilian' with the date she was built '1877'.

H285 *Pelican*. Built C.W. & G., Hull, 1895 for St Andrews S.F. Co. (Hull). Yard no.145. Length: 104ft 3in, Gross Tonnage: 156. Wrecked off Bempton Cliffs on passage from Farne Islands to Hull, 30 December 1909. *(Courtesy Jonathan Grobler Collection)*

PELICAN
Wreck: ★
Scenery: ★★★
Depth: 5m
Reference: N54 09 149 W000 10 241
Location: Below Bempton Cliffs, 3.63 miles NW of Flamborough Head

The *Pelican* (Official No.105046) was an iron 156-ton British steam fishing trawler that measured 31.77m in length and had a beam of 6.30m. Cook, Welton & Gemmell built her as Yard No.145 at Hull and launched her on 5 May 1895. The new owners, St Andrews Steam Fishing Co. Ltd, which was also the owner at the time of loss, registered her at Hull as trawler H285 on 25 June 1895. Her single iron screw propeller was powered by a 3-cylinder triple expansion steam engine that developed 50hp using one boiler. Charles D. Holmes built the machinery that gave her a speed of 10 knots.

On 30 December 1909, the *Pelican* was returning to Hull from a fishing voyage off the Farne Islands when she drove onto rocks beneath Bempton Cliffs in thick fog. The boat quickly filled up and sank, but the Flamborough lifeboat *Forester* rescued all her crew of nine who were found, in total darkness, clinging to the rigging of the sunken boat.

Wreck-site
The wreck is now totally collapsed, well broken up and dispersed under the seaweed amongst the rocks and boulders, at the base and offshore from Bempton Cliffs. She lies in a general depth of 5m, the lowest astronomical depth. Just a few remnants of broken machinery, iron ribs and plates are to be seen, but the area makes a nice rummage dive for crustaceans, which can be found amongst the rocks and boulders. Tidal streams are fairly reasonable close inshore, but underwater visibility is usually rather poor most of the year.

WAPPING
Wreck: *
Scenery: ★★★
Depth: 2m
Reference: N54 09 00 W00 10 00 (approx.)
Location: Just N of Scale Nab, near Flamborough Head

The *Wapping* was an iron 688-ton British steamship that was registered at the port of London. She measured 48.76m in length, with a 10.66m beam and draught of 4.41m. William Gray & Co. built her at West Hartlepool in 1886-1887 for F. Green & Co. of London. The *Wapping* was one of three steamships built together for a total of £33,250. The others were the *Stepney* and the slightly larger *Poplar*, and all three were built to ship coal from the Marquis of Londonderry's purpose built harbour at Seaham, to London. The vessels were known as 'up-river colliers', but seamen referred to them as 'flat-irons', because of their very low superstructure and masts that could be lowered to allow them to pass under all of the bridges over the navigable stretches of the River Thames. She was later sold to H.C. Pelly of London who owned her at the time of loss. Her single iron screw propeller was powered by a 2-cylinder compound steam engine that developed 120hp using one boiler. Her cylinders measured 68.58cm, and 127.00cm-83.82cm. Central Marine Engine Works Co. Ltd built her machinery at West Hartlepool. She had one deck, four bulkheads and superstructure consisting of a 5.18m poop deck and 2.13m bridge deck.

On 29 November 1891, the *Wapping* was on passage from West Hartlepool for London with a cargo of coal, under the command of Captain G. Skelton, when she drove ashore near Bempton, in dense fog. The sea was calm at the time, with very little wind, which allowed Captain Skelton and his fourteen-man crew to reach shore safely in their own boat. The coxswain of Flamborough lifeboat was informed of the stranding and set off in a gig to summon tugs to the scene in order to tow her off. Five paddle tugs responded, but on arrival they found the *Wapping* badly holed and full of water and decided it would have been a fruitless exercise. In a few short weeks, the stricken vessel soon became a total wreck and Captain Skelton had his certificate suspended for three months, as a result of his carelessness.

Wreck-site
What remains of the *Wapping* is believed to lie at the northern end of what is known as Old Roll Up, just north of Scale Nab (Staple Nook) and close to the wreck of the *Radium*. Her battered boiler is visible, but most of the rest of the vessel is totally collapsed, well broken up and dispersed under the seaweed, among the rocks and boulders. Although the general depth is very shallow, 2m being about the lowest astronomical depth, the area around the wreckage is reported to make a very interesting dive, with plenty of nice underwater scenery. Crustaceans can be found and Ballan wrasses also frequent the area. Access is only by boat and the best time to visit the site is after a spell of settled dry weather and light westerly winds.

APHELION, ex VOCATES, ex ULLAPOOL
Wreck: ★★★
Depth: 53m
Reference: N54 08 955 E000 25 949
Location: 18.12 miles E from Flamborough Head

The *Aphelion* was steel 197-ton British steam fishing trawler that was registered at Grimsby. She measured 33.65m in length, with a 6.45m beam and a 3.4m draught. Earle's Shipbuilding Co. Ltd at Hull built her as the *Ullapool* in 1899. Her single iron screw propeller was powered by a 55hp 3-cylinder triple expansion steam engine that used one boiler. She had one deck and as superstructure consisting of a 14.02m quarterdeck and a 5.49m forecastle. She was later sold to another company who renamed her *Vocates*. Grimsby & North Sea Trawling Co., which was the owner at the time of loss, then purchased her and renamed the boat *Aphelion*.

On 24 September 1916, the *Aphelion* was on a return fishing voyage from Grimsby, under the command of Captain W. Evans, when she was captured by the Imperial German submarine, SM U 57. Her crew were ordered to abandon ship by the U-boat captain, which they did in their own boat, and the trawler was then sunk by gunfire. SM U 57 went on to survive the ravages of the First World War and surrendered to the Allies, to become French reparation. She was broken up at Cherbourg in 1921.

Wreck-site

The wreck, probably that of the trawler *Aphelion*, lies on a seabed of sand and shells, in a general depth of 53m, the lowest astronomical depth. She is collapsed and well broken up, standing 3m high amidships to stern, with her boiler and engine exposed. The bow section is completely flattened and bridge structure is totally collapsed around the engine. The top and highest parts are covered in a well-established colourful array of soft corals, with a shoal of resident pout whiting swarming over them. If her bell is located, it will almost certainly be inscribed '*Ullapool*' and '1899', the date she was built. Tidal streams are very brisk and underwater visibility is usually very gloomy, dark and eerie.

LINDUM, ex FINSEN, ex SIR GALAHAD

Wreck: ★
Scenery: ★★★
Depth: 1m–2m
Reference: N54 08 980 W000 06 404 (approx.)
Location: 182m off Thornwick Nab, North Cliff Rocks, near Flamborough Head

The *Lindum* was a steel 156-ton steam fishing trawler that was registered at the port of Grimsby. Her dimensions measured 32m in length, with a 6.27m beam and a 3.27m draught. Edwards Brothers of North Shields built her as the *Sir Galahad* in 1899 and R.D. Clarke of Boston owned her at the time of loss. Her single iron screw propeller was powered by a 3-cylinder triple expansion steam engine that developed 45hp using one 1SB 2PF boiler. Her cylinders measured 30.48cm, 45.72cm and 76.20cm. Baird & Barnsley built her aft-positioned machinery at North Shields. She had one deck and a superstructure consisting of a 5.49m-quarterdeck and a 5.79m-forecastle.

On 3 October 1916, the *Lindum* was on a return fishing voyage from Boston, Lincolnshire, with a crew of nine, when she stranded off Thornwick Nab and became a total loss. Her skipper, W. Smith, was fined £20 and had his fishing certificate suspended for six months for his 'un-seamanlike conduct' and carelessness in losing his vessel.

Wreck-site

The wreck is below the massive cliffs and some 182m from shore, lying amongst rocky outcrops and small reefs, in a general depth of 1m–2m, the lowest astronomical depth. She is now totally collapsed, well broken up and dispersed. All that remains of her are some small unrecognisable pieces of broken machinery, mixed up with steel debris lying under the seaweed and surrounding rocks. If her bell is ever recovered it will probably be inscribed '*Sir Galahad*' plus the date she was built, '1899'. Tidal streams are moderate except on spring tides, but it becomes very strong a little further away from the shore. Underwater visibility is usually poor, but significantly improves following a spell of dry, settled weather and westerly winds during the summer months.

JESSIE

Wreck: *
Scenery: ***
Depth: 3-5m & 4m
Reference: N54 08 885 W000 09 597 (approx.)
Location: 2.5 miles NW of Flamborough Head, under Bempton Cliffs
Also given: N54 09 597 W000 12 788 (approx.)
Location: Near Speeton Village

The *Jessie* was a steel 332-ton British steamship that was registered at Grangemouth. She measured 44.72m in length, with a 7.34m beam and a draught of 3.12m. S. MacKnight and Co. Ltd built her at Ayre in 1901 for the Shield Steamship Co. Ltd which was the owner at the time of loss. Walker & Bain of Grangemouth managed her. Her single screw propeller was powered by a 2-cylinder compound steam engine that developed 86hp using one 1SB 2PF boiler. Her cylinders measured 45.72cm and 35.56cm. Ross & Duncan of Glasgow built her aft-positioned machinery. She had one deck, a well deck and a superstructure consisting of a 16.46m quarterdeck, 4.27m bridge deck and an 8.23m forecastle.

On 2 November 1917, the *Jessie* was under the command of Captain J. Gorman and carrying a crew of ten, on passage from Calais for Middlesbrough. She had called at Bridlington and was making about 8 knots at 4 a.m., when suddenly from astern, an unidentified German submarine surfaced and shelled her with its deck-gun. She was hit several times and suffered significant damage, so Captain Gorman turned the bow of the ship towards shore, but then left the bridge and hastened to one of the ship's boats in an attempt to get away, along with the chief engineer and two seamen. However in their haste, they had neglected to stop her engine before abandoning ship. The *Jessie* was still travelling at nearly 8 knots and the boat capsized as it was being lowered into the sea. Unfortunately, the four occupants were then drawn under the ship and drowned. Meanwhile the U-boat kept up its attack and shells continued to rain down, hitting her several more times and causing considerable damage. The rest of the survivors, including the mate, decided then that they had had enough and after the second engineer had stopped her engine, they all abandoned ship in the other boat, reaching Filey safely later that morning. The *Jessie* just drifted with wind and tide, before striking rocks below Bempton Cliffs, where she quickly broke up and became a total loss. After the war ended, the U-boat was identified as SM UB 35, which was sunk by depth charges dropped by HMS *Leven*, just to the north of Calais on 26 January 1917.

Wreck-site

The first co-ordinates are for what is believed to be the position of the wrecked steamer. The report says she is now totally collapsed, well broken up and scattered under the weed, amongst the rocks, reefs and boulders in a general depth of 3-5m. Very little remains of her today, except a few unrecognisable pieces of broken machinery, twisted steel plates and the green hue of broken copper pipes. One report says that a propeller and the remains of her boiler, which has split open and is now mostly flattened, can still be found. Tidal streams are fairly moderate close to the shore, but access is from the sea only. The underwater visibility is usually on the poor side but improves considerably during the summer months after a spell of dry settled weather and south-westerly winds.

The second position offered suggests the wreck lies below the cliffs near Speeton, in a general depth of 4m, the lowest astronomical depth. Very little is known about her, but being so close inshore, the wreck will now be totally collapsed, well broken up and fairly dispersed among the rocks and boulders. Tidal streams are reasonably moderate, but will significantly increase further to seaward. Access to this site is only by sea.

HARBOURNE
Wreck: ★★
Depth: 42m
Reference: N54 08 823 W000 02 273
Location: 2.32 miles NE of Flamborough Head

The *Harbourne* was a steel 1,158-ton British steamship that measured 74.4m in length, with a beam of 10.3m and draught of 5.2m. S.P. Austin & Son built her at Sunderland in 1883 and J. & C. Harrison owned her at the time of loss. Her single iron screw propeller was powered by a 3-cylinder triple expansion steam engine that used one 1SB boiler. Her cylinders measured 45.72cm, 76.20cm and 124.46cm.

On 29 March 1894, the *Harbourne* was on passage from Blyth for London with a cargo of coal when she foundered off Flamborough Head, following a collision with the steamship *Eppleton*.

Wreck-site
The wreck has never been located, but the author suggests that there is a possibility that this wreck could be the remains of the *Harbourne*. The position given has the wreck lying on a seabed of mud, stone and shingle in a general depth of 42m, the lowest astronomical depth. The remains are now totally collapsed, partially buried, well decomposed and rather scattered, with the highest section standing no more than 3m. Little else is known about the site, but it should be well worth investigating. Tidal streams are pretty ferocious and underwater visibility usually very poor to dismal, but improves slightly during the summer months. Very little marine life has been observed around the debris and she is hardly worth a visit for either diving or boat angling.

GRELTORIA
Wreck: ★★★★
Depth: 24m
Reference: N54 08 825 W000 06 365
Location: 1.93 miles NNW of Flamborough Head

The *Greltoria* was a steel 5,143-ton British steamship that was registered at the port of Cardiff. She measured 114.3m in length, with a 15.54m beam and a 9.75m draught. Northumberland Shipbuilding Co. Ltd at Newcastle-upon-Tyne built her in 1917 and Griffiths Lewis S.N. Co. Ltd in Cardiff owned her at the time of loss. Her single iron screw propeller was powered by a 3-cylinder triple expansion steam engine that used three 3SB 9CF boilers. Her cylinders measured 63.50cm, 104.14cm and 175.26cm-121.92cm. North Eastern Marine Engineering Co. Ltd built her engine at Sunderland and she was classed as a 'Lewis' scheme ship. The vessel was also armed with one CP Mk 1 anti-submarine stern-mounted gun that fired 10.16cm shells (4in).

At 3 p.m. on 27 September 1917, the *Greltoria* was in convoy, just north of Flamborough Head when she was torpedoed and sunk by the U-boat SM UB 34. The U-boat remained submerged and unseen during the attack and no warning was issued. She was on passage from the Tyne for Naples, carrying a 6,624-ton cargo of coal and a crew of thirty-eight, when the missile detonated on her port side. The captain turned his ship towards land in an attempt to beach her in shallow water, but she was going down too fast and he ordered the crew to abandon ship. They took to the boats at 3.20 p.m. and watched their vessel sink within five minutes of leaving.

SM UB 34 surrendered to the Allies at the end of the First World War and became British war reparation. She was scrapped at Canning Town in 1922.

Wreck-site

The wreck of the steamship *Greltoria* is owned by Bridlington Diving Services for the purpose of salvaging her. In 1960 the wreck stood some 6m proud of the seabed with a derrick visible above the surface and she was buoyed; however, the buoy was later removed or lost. In 1978, she was reported as being silted over nearly to the top of her boilers. She lies on the seabed next to the edge of some outcropping bedrock and orientated in a north–north-east to south–south-west direction, in a general depth of 24m, the lowest astronomical depth. The wreck, which covers an area of seabed measuring 117m by 28m, is now totally collapsed and well broken up, with very bad damage amidships. The highest section, being around her boilers, stands no more than 3.3m high. It is also unlikely that there will be any of the vessel's interesting navigation equipment still to be seen. Tidal streams are fairly brisk and underwater visibility usually very poor most of the year, except in midsummer when it greatly improves. There have been no reports of any marine life about, but it would be surprising if there were not a few crustaceans under the debris, especially during the summer months.

At the end of summer 1982, members of Hull British Sub Aqua Club (BSAC) Branch No.14 located the wreck. The following season they identified her as the *Greltoria* and found her deck-gun still intact. Then a team of the club's divers, including Mike Petherbridge and Tom Hewson and about twenty other divers, set about raising the gun with the intention of offering it to Hull City Council as a display in the city's marina. Whether the gun is on display today is not known.

ROYALLIEU
Wreck: *
Scenery: ***
Depth: 1m
Reference: N54 08 778 W000 09 473 (approx.)
Location: 0.25 miles S of Staple Nook, under Bempton Cliffs, Flamborough Head

The *Royallieu* (Official No.113197) was an iron 203-ton British steam fishing trawler that measured 34.42m in length, with a beam of 6.52m and a draught of 3.25m. Cook, Welton & Gemmel built her at Hull as Yard No.269 and launched her on 11 July 1900 for William Grant of Grimsby. On 15 August 1900 the owner registered her as Grimsby trawler GY1191. Her single iron screw propeller was powered by a 3-cylinder triple expansion steam engine that developed 60hp using one boiler, which gave her a maximum speed of 10.5 knots. Charles D. Holmes built her machinery at Hull. On 16 May 1905, she was sold to the Pelham Steam Fishing Co. Ltd in Grimsby.

On 6 May 1906, the *Royallieu* was in ballast on a fishing voyage from her home port of Grimsby, when she became stranded on rocks near Wandale Nab, under Bempton cliffs, during a light southerly wind and dense fog. She was under the command of Captain N. Cook and carrying a crew of nine. The crew managed to reach shore safely, but the vessel, which was holed, soon began to break up and became a total loss.

Wreck-site

The wreck is now totally collapsed, broken up and well dispersed under the seaweed, amongst the rocks and boulders, in a general depth of 1-2m, the lowest astronomical depth. Sections of her ribs and part of the boiler and engine are reported to be still visible, but there is not much else of interest, although the surrounding reefs and boulders are a favourite hiding place for crustaceans, which can be an added bonus for anyone visiting the site. The wreck was positively identified when a Filey sport diver recovered the builder's plate with the yard number engraved on it. Tidal streams are reasonable close to shore, but get considerably stronger after a few metres further out. Underwater visibility is usually poor to grim, but improves during the summer months after a spell of settled westerly winds and dry weather.

ARTIC
Wreck: ★★★
Depth: 49m
Reference: N54 07 730 E000 07 065
Location: 7.02 miles E of Flamborough Head

The *Artic* was an iron 154-ton British steam fishing trawler that was registered at the port of Grimsby. She measured 30.65m in length and 6.1m by beam with a draught of 3.45m. Earle's Ship Building & Engine Co. built her at Hull in 1888 and the Grimsby Steam Fishing Co. owned her at the time of loss. Her single iron screw propeller was powered by a 3-cylinder triple expansion steam engine that developed 45hp using one-single ended 155LB boiler. Her cylinders measured 26.04cm, 45.72cm and 76.20cm-45.72cm.

On 19 January 1909, the *Artic* was on a return voyage from the Icelandic fishing grounds with a crew of thirteen, when she was in collision with the Grimsby steamship *Haverstoe*, six miles east by south from Flamborough Head. The weather and visibility were good at the time, and there must have been some considerable negligence on behalf of the lookouts on both of the vessels involved. They passed so close together that the propeller on the *Haverstoe* ripped through the hull plates of the 154-ton steam trawler. She was sent down to the bottom in less than four minutes, taking two of the crew down with her.

Wreck-site
The wreck, believed to be that of the small trawler, lies more or less east to west on a seabed of mud, small broken black shells, gravel and coarse sand, in a general depth of 49m, the lowest astronomical depth. She has totally collapsed, and is partially buried and well broken up, standing no more than 1.5m high amidships, where her single boiler and engine are exposed. She is surrounded by a mound of broken and concreting iron debris. Soft corals encrust the highest section of the wreck and a number of crustaceans have been observed, but very few fish. Tidal streams are exceptionally strong, but underwater visibility is reported to be surprisingly good during the summer months. A good lookout is also required at all times, because the site is well into the main shipping channels.

FRITHJOF EIDE, ex TROJA, ex ÖSTERGÖTLAND
Wreck: ★★★★
Depth: 42m
Reference: N54 08 037 W00 00 127
Location: 3 miles ENE of Flamborough Head

The *Frithjof Eide* was a 1,207-ton steel Norwegian steamship that measured 69.03m in length, with a 10.51m beam and a draught of 4.72m. Howaldtswerke built her at Kiel as Yard No.401 in 1904 and launched her as the *Östergötland* for A/B Östergötland of Norrköping. Her single iron screw propeller was powered by a 3-cylinder triple expansion steam engine that used one boiler. Howaldtswerke also built the machinery. In December 1915, A/S Troja (Johs. Lindvig) of Kragerø, Norway, bought the vessel and renamed her *Troja*. She was sold to A/S D/S Fridtjof Eide (Birger Pedersen & Son), of Hauesund, Norway in May 1916, who was the owner at the time of loss and renamed *Frithjof Eide*. (Note the different spelling of the ship and the company.)

On 9 November 1917, the *Frithjof Eide* was on passage from Skien for London with a cargo of saltpetre when she was torpedoed and sunk by SM UB 75, an Imperial German submarine. The U-boat was lost one month later in extensive British minefields off Flamborough Head, on 13 December 1917.

Wreck-site

The wreck believed to be the *Frithjof Eide* lies on a seabed of gravel, stone and sand in a general depth of 42m, being about the lowest astronomical depth. She is quite substantial, with her stern and bows reasonably intact and standing some 4m high amidships, where she has collapsed, exposing her boiler and engine. The amidships to bows section is a mound of broken, decaying steel debris, with lengths of bent, flattened copper piping protruding from it; however, she is still an interesting wreck to explore, with plenty of marine life about, both swimming and crawling. The vessel's bell and navigation equipment should still be around so she will be interesting to look at. Her bell will probably be inscribed 'Östergötland' and '1904', the date she was built. Tidal streams are very strong and visibility is usually poor to rather grim, with most of the wreck covered in a layer of sediment. The wreck is in the main shipping channels, so a good lookout will also be required by anyone either angling or diving on the remains. It is believed that her crew was lost when the vessel sank, so her remains should be treated with the utmost respect.

RUBY SCHULTZ, ex FINCHALE

Wreck: ★
Scenery: ★★★
Depth: 3-5m
Reference: N54 08 249 W000 07 695 (approx.)
Location: 1.25 miles NW of Flamborough Head, under Bempton Cliffs

The *Ruby Schultz* (Official No.62526) was an iron 729-ton (654-ton under deck) Belgian schooner-rigged steamship that was registered at the port of Antwerp, with signal letters JDSW. She measured 59.97m in length, with an 8.84m beam and a 5.06m draught. J. Laing & Co. built her as the *Finchale* in 1869 for Lambton Collieries with T. Nicholson as manager. Her single iron screw propeller was powered by a 4-cylinder compound steam engine that developed 90rhp using one boiler and a new boiler was fitted in 1974. Her cylinders measured 48.26cm and 96.52cm-71.12cm. She had one deck, four cemented bulkheads and a super-structure consisting of a 6.71m quarterdeck and North East Marine Engineering Co. Ltd at Sunderland built her machinery. Schultz Steamship Co. Ltd of Antwerp, who owned her at the time of loss, purchased her in 1899 and renamed the vessel *Ruby Schultz*, with Captain C. Mellentin serving as her master from 1884 to at least 1899.

On 12 February 1904, the *Ruby Schultz* was on passage from Leith for Cullera and Valencia with a general cargo of nitrate of soda and sulphates, when she stranded and was lost under Bempton Cliffs during thick fog. She was under the command of Captain J.E. Muyllaert and carrying a crew of fourteen. Her £10,000 cargo of chemicals was lost with the vessel, but the crew was rescued by local fishing cobles.

Wreck-site

The wreck is totally collapsed, broken up and dispersed under the seaweed, amongst the rocks and small reefs, in a general depth of between 3m and 6m, some 100m out from the cliffs. Very little remains now, except her iron propeller, small pieces of battered iron plates and the occasional glint of flattened copper pipes under the kelp strands. There is also the possibility that her bell is still buried somewhere in the surrounding debris and if it is recovered, it should be inscribed 'Finchale' and the date she was built, '1869'. Crustaceans can sometimes be found among the rocks, but visibility is usually very poor. Tidal streams are reasonable, but become very strong a little further out from shore.

KEPIER

Wreck: ★
Scenery: ★★★
Depth: 5-7m
Reference: N54 08 149 W000 06 975 (approx.)
Location: 0.5 miles NW from North Landing, Flamborough
Head

The *Kepier* was an iron 703-ton British schooner-rigged steamship that was registered at the port of Sunderland. She measured 57.5m in length, with a 9.10m beam and a 4.1m draught. J. Laing built her at Sunderland in 1869 and Langton & Co. of Sunderland owned her at the time of loss. Her single iron screw propeller was powered by a 2-cylinder compound steam engine that used one boiler. Her cylinders measured 63.50cm and 109.22cm-91.44cm. T. Richardson built her machinery at Hartlepool.

Early in the morning of 12 February 1886, the *Kepier* was on passage from Sunderland for London with a cargo of coal when she drove ashore and stranded, half a mile north of the North Landing, during thick fog and heavy seas. Later that day at high tide, she had settled on the bottom, with the whole of her forepart submerged and the bows pointing upwards. With huge seas running, by the following morning, 13 February, she had began to break up and a section of the vessel's hull and two of the crew's sea chests were washed onto the shore. It is not known if any of her crew survived the disaster.

Wreck-site

The wreck is totally collapsed, well broken up and dispersed under the kelp, amongst the rocks and reefs, in a general depth of between 5m and 7m. Very little remains of the wreck, which is now lying mixed up with the remnants of the steamship *Crosby*, except an iron propeller, part of a collapsed boiler and remnants of their shattered hull plates. An added bonus to any divers visiting this site is that they stand a chance of catching one of the nice crustaceans to be found around this area. Also, with a little bit of time and patience, a trawl reasonably close inshore with a magnetometer should find of a few of the many other shipwrecks that litter the seabed off this part of the Yorkshire coast. Tidal streams are fairly brisk away from the shoreline and underwater visibility is usually very poor, but improves slightly during the summer months.

CROSBY, ex LEUTWEIN, ex SCHALDIS

Wreck: ★
Scenery: ★★★
Depth: 5m
Reference: N54 08 149 W000 06 975 (approx.)
Location: 0.5 miles NW of North Landing, Flamborough Head

The *Crosby* was a steel-hulled 324-ton (242-ton under deck) British three-masted schooner-rigged steamship that was registered at the port of London. She measured 42.74m in length, with a 6.75m beam and a draught of 3.14m. J.T. Eltringham & Co. built her at South Shields as the *Schaldis* in 1891 for De Clerc & Van Hemelrijck of Antwerp in Belgium, who renamed her *Leutwein*. Shipping Investments Ltd, which purchased her and owned her at the time of loss, renamed the boat *Crosby*, while Messrs C.H. Pyle of London managed her. Messrs Hutchinson of Hull chartered the boat from the owner. The single iron screw propeller was powered by a 3-cylinder triple expansion steam engine that developed 35hp using one single-ended boiler, with two plain furnaces, a grate surface of 53.34cm and a donkey boiler of 36.29kg. Her cylinders measured 27.31cm, 43.18cm and 71.12cm-53.34cm. North East Marine Co. Ltd built her machinery at Sunderland. She had a 17.78cm bar keel, one iron deck, three cemented bulkheads and a superstructure consisting of a 14.02m quarterdeck, 2.13m bridge deck and 4.88m forecastle. She also had water ballast in a fore peak tank of 45 tons and four part tanks of 6 tons. The vessel was also classed at Lloyd's as 100 A1.

At 6 a.m. on 9 January 1903, the *Crosby* was on passage from Middlesbrough for Ramsgate when, two hours before daylight, she drove ashore in dense fog and heavy weather, half a mile north of the North Landing, near Flamborough Head. She had left Middlesbrough on the evening of 8 January, under the command of Captain J.M. Henderson, carrying a crew of ten and a cargo of cast-iron water pipes. The vessel struck the rocks with a shuddering halt, about 550m offshore, but minutes later she heeled over to starboard. The crew immediately scrambled to launch the starboard boat, but then suddenly the ship lurched over to port, swamping the men in the process and washing the boat away. Captain Henderson dived into the sea, swam to the boat and sculled it back to the stranded ship. The mate and two other crewmen climbed into the boat, but just as they did so, a large wave picked it up and smashed it against the side of the steamer, cracking the boat's hull in the process. However with water flooding in, they still managed to row north, landing at a place known as White Rocks, where they were faced with a three mile hike back to civilization to get help. With snow falling heavily and in chest deep icy water, the rest of the men desperately clung onto ropes, hanging from the wrecked steamer, until eventually a local fishing-coble, the *Etna*, came alongside, rescued them and landed them safely at Flamborough. Unfortunately, Thomas Campbell, the second engineer succumbed to the freezing conditions and died before help could arrive. By noon of that same day, the steamer had disappeared from sight. Captain Henderson said later, he believed that the twenty-four cast-iron pipes she was carrying on deck might have affected the ship's compass, which took her off course and onto the rocks.

Wreck-site

The wreck is now totally collapsed, broken up and well dispersed under the weed-covered rocks in a general depth of about 5m, the lowest astronomical depth. Her remains lie mixed up with the few battered steel plates from the 703-ton schooner-rigged steamship *Kepier*, which came to grief in that position on 12 February 1886. Except for one propeller, the remnants of a boiler and a few pieces of rusting steel plate and debris, almost nothing remains of the two vessels today, however the surrounding reefs and rocks offer a bonus in the form of some nice crustaceans during the summer months. Tidal streams are fairly brisk and underwater visibility generally rather poor at most times of the year, but improve after a spell of dry settled weather between July and August.

ROBERT DICKINSON
Wreck: *
Scenery: ***
Depth: 3m
Reference: N54 08 085 W000 06 885 (approx.)
Location: Sanwick Nook, Flamborough Head

The *Robert Dickinson* was an iron 1,706-ton British steamship that was registered at the port of London. She measured 79.55m in length, with a 10.36m beam and a draught of 6.7m. A. Leslie & Co. built and completed her at Newcastle-upon-Tyne for J. Bell & Symonds of Newcastle in 1879. Her single iron screw propeller was powered by a 3-cylinder triple expansion steam engine that developed 200hp using two boilers. J. Dickinson & Co. Ltd built her machinery at Sunderland. She had one deck, five bulkheads and a superstructure consisting of a 24.99m bridge deck and a 9.75m forecastle.

Having successfully completed her sea trials on 24 April 1879, the *Robert Dickinson* left South Shields on her maiden voyage three days later, on passage for Naples. Insured for a value of

The SS *Caenwood* aground at North Landing in November 1905. *(Author's Collection)*

£25,000, she was under the command of Captain R. Fuller, carrying an unspecified cargo of bricks and a crew of twenty-two. At 4 a.m. on 27 April, she encountered dense fog with force four north-easterly winds off the Yorkshire coast. Having been employed at sea for just twelve hours, she drove ashore at Sanwick Nook, the third little bay from Thornwick Bay. A kedge anchor was laid, but all efforts to refloat her were in vain, despite a steam tug being employed and divers being sent down from the Tyne to repair the damaged hull plates. The following week, gales developed and the vessel broke her back, then broke in two and became a total loss, after heavy seas battered the coastline for many days.

Wreck-site
The wreck is said to lie in a general depth of 3m, the lowest astronomical depth about 50m offshore in Sanwick Nook. She is now totally collapsed, well broken up and dispersed over an area of 100m, with most of the remains concreting into the rocky seabed. Part of a broken boiler and an iron propeller are the largest pieces visible, but the surrounding area makes an interesting dive after a spell of dry settled weather. Tidal streams are fairly reasonable, but get much stronger a little further seaward.

CAENWOOD
Wreck: ★
Scenery: ★★
Depth: 6m
Reference: N54 08 082 W000 06 200 (approx.)
Location: Off North Landing, Flamborough Head

The *Caenwood* was a steel 1,191-ton British steamship that was registered at the port of London. She measured 68.58m in length, by an 11.15m beam with a draught of 4.06m. S.P. Austin & Son built her at Sunderland in 1902 for William Cory & Son, who owned her at the time of loss, and G. Alder of London managed her. Her single iron screw propeller was powered by a 3-cylinder triple expansion steam engine that developed 170hp using one 1SB 4PF boiler. Her cylinders measured 50.80cm, 83.82cm and 137.16cm-83.82cm. George Clark & Co. Ltd built her machinery at Sunderland. She had one deck, a well deck, four bulkheads and a super-structure consisting of a 6.10m poop deck, 20.73m quarterdeck, 5.49m bridge deck and 8.53m forecastle.

On 21 November 1905, the *Caenwood* ran ashore near North Landing at Flamborough Head, during dense fog, a light westerly wind and flat calm sea. She was under the command of Captain W.J. Baxter, on passage from Tyne Dock for Devonport with an unspecified cargo of coal and a crew of seventeen. The impact of striking the jagged rocks tore a huge hole forward and she filled up at once and settled on the bottom. Local fishing cobles rescued the crew, but within one week, the *Caenwood* broke up and became a total wreck. Just two days later, Tommy Round, a local salvage man, purchased the wreck for £100 and work on dismantling her started almost at once.

Wreck-site
The wreck lies just off the north-west corner of North Landing, in a general depth of 6m, the lowest astronomical depth. What remains of the wreck is now totally collapsed, well broken up and dispersed amongst the rocks and boulders with little of interest to see. However, reports say that this area makes a nice rummage dive, because over the years a number of other vessels have also been lost in this vicinity and you can never tell what may turn up. Tidal streams are fairly strong, but significantly more so a little further seaward. Shoals of small saithe are also common-place around the site during the summer months.

PRINCESS
Wreck: *
Scenery: **
Depth: 2m
Reference: N54 08 016 W000 06 350 (approx.)
Location: Between North Landing and Thornwick Bay, Flamborough Head

The *Princess* was an iron 2,094-ton British steamship that was registered at Sunderland. She measured 87.17m in length by 11.73m beam with a draught of 6.24m. Short Brothers built her at Sunderland in 1883 and Taylor & Sanderson of Sunderland owned her at the time of loss. Her single iron screw propeller was powered by a 2-cylinder compound steam engine that developed 180hp using two boilers. Carr & Co. of Sunderland built her machinery. She had one deck and four bulkheads and was classed at Lloyd's as A1.

At around 1 a.m. on 19 November 1893, the *Princess* was on passage from Bilbao for Sunderland when she ran into a raging north-easterly storm as she rounded Flamborough Head. The steamer was under the command of Captain C. McCormick, carrying a cargo of iron ore and a crew of nineteen. Eye witnesses reported that to the north of the Head there were walls of foaming white water as far as the eye could see, and the wind had whipped up waves so huge that they were crashing over the coastguard station, more than 30m above sea level. She turned head to the wind, but gradually the power of storm and mountainous waves drove the vessel back towards rocks below the towering cliffs. When her crew realised the inevitable was about to happen, they took to the rigging, some lashing themselves on. Coastguard observers on the cliff tops had been watching the situation and attempted to fire rocket lines over her, but it was useless as the force of the wind just blew them all back. At around 2 a.m., she smashed onto the treacherously jagged shoreline and went to pieces within minutes. None of her crew survived and it took days for most of the bodies to be recovered.

Wreck-site

What remains of the wreck lies between North Landing and Thornwick Bay, in a general depth of 2m, the lowest astronomical depth. She is totally collapsed, well broken up and fairly dispersed under the seaweed, amongst the surrounding rocks and not far from the scattered remains of the *Caenwood*. For many years her two boilers were visible at low water, but eventually the elements took their toll and now all that remains are some unrecognisable pieces of broken machinery, a few bits of iron plating and ribs. Tidal streams can be rather strong at times, especially on high spring tides and visibility is usually poor, but improves during the summer months.

BLONDE

Wreck: *
Scenery: ***
Depth: 2-3m
Reference: N54 07 945 W000 06 200 (approx.)
Location: East Scar Rock, North Landing at Flamborough
Head

The *Blonde* (signal letters HFQK), was an iron 613-ton British schooner-rigged steamship that was registered at the port of London. She measured: 53.34m in length, with a beam of 8.71m and a draught of 4.67m. C. Lungley of London built her in 1863 for Theodor Rodenacker, who owned her until 1904. Her single screw, possibly bronze, was powered by a 4-cylinder quadruple compound steam engine that developed 112hp using one single-ended boiler. Her cylinders measured 40.64cm and 91.44cm-68.58cm. She had one deck and aft-positioned machinery built by C. Lungley. The vessel was sold to the German company of Danziger Rhederei AG in 1904 and that company owned her from 1904 until 1914, when she was interned. The Royal Navy, which was the owner at the time of loss, requisitioned her as fleet collier CT 22 for the East Coast run.

On 28 December 1916, the old steamship was on passage from North Shields for London when she ran aground at low water during dense fog at East Scar Rock, North Landing, at Flamborough Head. She was under the command of Captain A.B. Milne (although another report says Alex J. Ervine), carrying an unspecified cargo of coal and a crew of seventeen. The *Blonde* was badly holed and with water rapidly pouring in, local fishermen, led by the Flamborough lifeboat coxswain, Richard Chadwick, took off her captain and crew. At high tide she was completely submerged except for her smokestack and masts, and within a few days these had broken off and disappeared. The vessel gradually broke up over a few weeks, but her cargo of coal was being washed ashore for many months afterwards.

At the Court of Inquiry, the master attributed the stranding and loss of his vessel to the 'abnormal eastward set of the current'; however he was still censured.

Wreck-site

The remains of the *Blonde* lie close to East Scar Rock, in a general depth of 2-3m, being about the lowest astronomical depth. She is now totally collapsed, well broken up and dispersed over a wide area. Except for an anchor, a short length of chain and a few pieces of iron debris, very little remains. However, the surrounding rocks make an interesting forage dive, where a few crustaceans can still be found. Tidal streams are very strong away from the rocks and shore, while underwater visibility is usually poor, but improves during the summer months after a spell of dry settled weather.

DUNDEE
Wreck: *
Depth: 2m
Reference: N54 07 900 W000 05 882 (approx.)
Location: Between East Scar & Newcombe Hope, Flamborough Head

The *Dundee* was a steel 839-ton British steamship that was registered at the port of Glasgow. She measured 68.3m in length by 8.8m beam with a draught of 4.2m. John Key & Sons built her in 1890 for J. Rankine & Son of Grangemouth, as that company's first passenger steamer at Kinghorn, Kirkcaldy. Later she was sold to T. MacGill of Glasgow, who was the owner at the time of loss. Her single screw propeller was powered by a 3-cylinder triple expansion steam engine that used one 2SB 4RF boiler. Her cylinders measured 48.26cm, 81.28cm and 132.08cm. J. Scott & Co. built her machinery at Kirkcaldy.

In the early hours of 26 January 1896, the *Dundee* was on passage from Grangemouth for Rotterdam when she ran aground just north of Flamborough Head, during a dense fog and force two easterly wind. She was under the command of Captain J. Gentle and carrying an unspecified general cargo and a crew of twenty. Captain Gentle sent the whole crew ashore in their own boat, but remained on board with the other officers; however, he requested that the lifeboat stand by until he had communicated with Lloyd's agent. The vessel's hull was badly holed in the stranding and gradually she settled on the bottom. By the time coastguard officers arrived on the scene, much of the *Dundee* was under water and waves were sweeping her decks. The men soon realised that the vessel was beyond hope and it was decided to abandon ship. By daylight, some of her general cargo, including large bales of cloth, was being washed ashore. Not surprisingly, news of the stranding had by this time spread far and wide, attracting not only the revenue men, but also vast crowds of people. They carried away the cloth in big bundles by wrapping it around their bodies beneath very baggy skirts. Within days, the *Dundee* had begun to break up and soon became a total wreck.

Wreck-site
The remains of the wreck, which was well salvaged, lie between East Scar and Newcombe Hope, a few hundred metres south of North Landing. She is now totally collapsed and well dispersed over a wide area, lying in a general depth of 2m, the lowest astronomical depth. Nothing of any significance remains, but the few battered steel plates and ribs often shelter a few nice juicy crustaceans. Tidal streams can by fairly strong and get significantly more so, further seaward.

BIRTLEY
Wreck: *
Scenery: **
Depth: 2-4m
Reference: N54 07 582 W000 05 115 (approx.)
Location: 1 mile N from Flamborough Head

The *Birtley* was a steel 1,029-ton British steamship that was registered at Newcastle-upon-Tyne. She measured 67.05m in length, with a 10.1m beam and a draught of 4.34m. Wood, Skinner & Co. Ltd built her at Newcastle in 1900 for the Burnett Steamship Co. Ltd who owned her at the time of loss. Her single iron screw propeller was powered by a 3-cylinder triple expansion steam engine that developed 133hp using one 1SB 4PF boiler. Her cylinders measured 43.18cm, 71.12cm and 116.84cm-83.82cm. North Eastern Marine Engineering Co. Ltd built her machinery at Newcastle-upon-Tyne. She had one deck, four bulkheads, a well deck and a superstructure consisting of a 33.53m quarterdeck, a 3.05m bridge deck and a 7.62m forecastle.

On 10 November 1905, the *Birtley* was on passage from South Shields for London when she ran aground and stranded, just north of Cradle Head and 1 mile north of Flamborough Head. She was under the command of Captain John Haddon Taylor, carrying an unspecified cargo of coal and a crew of sixteen, all of who got safely ashore. It was believed that the vessel would be refloated later, but a north-easterly gale developed. The huge waves, which built up battered the stricken ship, taking away her smokestack and wheelhouse, then she broke in two and became a total wreck. The local salvage company of Tommy Round bought the wreck on the 30 November and work dismantling her commenced almost at once. For their carelessness, Captain Taylor and the first mate had their certificates suspended for three months.

Wreck-site
The wreck lies just north-west of Cradle Head and very close to the remains of the steamship *Wandle*, in a general depth of 2-4m, the lowest astronomical depth. She is now totally collapsed, well broken up and dispersed under a covering of seaweed among rocks and boulders. Very little is recognisable of the wreck these days and it is difficult to distinguish which is the wreck of the *Birtley*, because iron and steel debris is so scattered. There is also not a lot to see between the wrecks, although large shoals of saithe visit the area during the summer months, so it maybe worth taking a look at as a boat-angling venue.

WANDLE
Wreck: *
Scenery: **
Depth: 2-4m
Reference: N54 07 553 W000 05 464 (approx.)
Location: 1 mile N of Flamborough Head

The *Wandle* was a steel 889-ton British steamship that was registered at the port of London. She measured 62.53m in length, with a beam of 9.77m and a draught of 4.36m. W. Dobson & Co. of Newcastle-upon-Tyne built her in 1909 and Wandsworth, Wimbledon & Epsom Gas Co. owned her at the time of loss. This vessel may have been originally built for Wandsworth Gas Light & Coke Co. in London. Her single iron screw propeller was powered by a 3-cylinder triple expansion steam engine that developed 178hp using one boiler. P. Rennoldson & Sons built her aft-positioned machinery at South Shields. She had one deck, four bulkheads and a superstructure consisting of a 4.57m poop deck, a 5.18m bridge deck and a 7.01m forecastle.

On 29 April 1916 the *Wandle* was on passage for the Thames when she sighted a German submarine on the surface, rigged up with a sail as a deception. The *Wandle* steamed straight at the U-boat in an attempt to ram her, however the submarine, realizing the steamer's intention, fired at her with shells from its deck-gun before diving for cover. The *Wandle* came so close to the U-boat the crew thought they had struck her a fatal blow as she went down. This caused great excitement on board, and a great fuss was made when they arrived in the Thames. However, at the end of the First World War, records showed that in fact the submarine, which turned out to be the Imperial German U-boat SM UB 27 was not even damaged in the incident and had actually dived only because other British ships were approaching the scene. SM UB 27 was later rammed, depth charged and sunk on 19 July 1917.

The *Wandle*'s luck ran out on her 500th voyage the following year when, in dense fog on 12 December 1917, she ran aground between Breil Head and Cradle Head. She was under the command of Captain G.R.A. Mastin, on passage from the Tyne for Wandsworth carrying a crew of nineteen and an unspecified cargo of coal. The crew took to the boats and landed safely, but the vessel soon broke up after being holed and became a total wreck. She was later sold to the local salvage man, Tommy Round, as were the majority of wrecks in this vicinity.

Wreck-site

The wreck is now totally collapsed and well dispersed under the seaweed amongst the rocks. Very little is left to distinguish her from the nearby wreck of the *Birtley*. Just a few sections of broken steel hull plates, ribs and unrecognisable lumps of machinery lie concreting into the surrounding rocks. As a wreck-site she is not worth visiting, but who knows what could turn up after a winter storm? A few crustaceans can sometimes be found and shoals of saithe visit the area during the summer months. Tidal streams are fairly strong at high tide and increase significantly during springs.

APOLLONIA, ex GALATA, ex PAROS, ex BELLAGIO, ex VENETIA II
Wreck: ★★★
Depth: 21m
Reference: N54 07 443 W000 03 931
Location: 0.65 mile ENE of Flamborough Head

The *Apollonia* was a steel 2,891-ton Italian steamship measuring 97.54m in length, with a beam of 12.19m and a draught of 8.23m. Reihersteig Schiffswerke built her as the *Venetia II* at Hamburg in 1891. She was a passenger liner built for the Hamburg to New York run. Her single iron screw propeller was powered by a 3-cylinder triple expansion steam engine that developed 350hp using three boilers, which gave the vessel a maximum speed of 10 knots. Reihersteig Schiffswereke built her machinery, with cylinders measuring 64.11cm, 104.14cm and 163.17cm. She had two decks and a superstructure consisting of a 15.24m forecastle and a 57.91m bridge and poop deck. Robert Sloman of Hamburg bought her in 1897 and renamed her *Bellagio*, then sold her to the Italian company Deutsche Levant in 1900, which renamed the vessel *Paros*. In 1906, they changed her name again to *Galata*, but in 1913 she was sold to Società di Navigazione Sicilia of Palermo, which was the owner at the time of loss, and became the *Apollonia*.

On 1 March 1917, the *Apollonia* was carrying munitions when she foundered and was lost, following a large explosion caused by a German laid mine off Flamborough Head. Flamborough lifeboat was launched and saved seven of the steamship's crew. SM UC 32 laid the mine in Barrier 51. UC 32 was lost off the River Wear at Sunderland, on 23 February 1917, when one of her mines detonated prematurely.

Wreck-site

The wreck of the *Apollonia* lies south-east to north-west on a hard rocky shelf, in a general depth of 21m, the lowest astronomical depth. She covers a huge area of seabed, measuring some 100m by 60m, is totally collapsed, well broken up and scattered, with the highest point around the centre, which stands 6.3m high. If her bell is recovered, it will almost certainly be inscribed 'Venetia II 1891'. Quite a few brass shell cases, both live and empty, have been found around the site in recent years and she still makes a nice forage dive. Fair numbers of crustaceans have been reported amongst the debris, but tidal streams are very strong and underwater visibility is usually pretty grim.

DUNSTAFFNAGE
Wreck: ★★★
Depth :16m
Reference: N54 07 197 W000 04 285
Location: 0.29 miles ENE of Flamborough Head cliffs

The *Dunstaffnage* was a steel 1,395-ton British steamship that was registered at Glasgow. She measured 72.23m in length, with a beam of 10.38m and a draught of 5.18m. Mackie &

Thomson built her at Glasgow in 1894 and the Scottish Navigation Co. owned her at the time of loss. Her single iron screw propeller was powered by a 3-cylinder triple expansion steam engine that used two 2SB 4PF boilers. Her cylinders measured 43.18cm, 68.58cm and 114.30cm-91.44cm. Muir & Houston of Glasgow built her machinery.

During dense fog and a light northerly wind on 1 October 1908, the *Dunstaffnage* drove ashore on the rocks and stranded, immediately in front of the old Coastguard lookout station at Dyke End, near Speeton. She was on passage from Sunderland for Oporto with a 2,000-ton cargo of coal and carrying a crew of eighteen. Shortly after the stranding, a Scottish fishing vessel amazingly passed between her and the cliffs, without even touching bottom. About two weeks later, salvage crews patched her up and managed to refloat her. However, the damage to her hull had been too great and she foundered soon after leaving the rocks, with the crew managing to leave the ship before she went down.

Wreck-site
A Bridlington diver, Mike Radley, who discovered her engine-maker's plate, has just recently identified the wreck as that of *Dunstaffnage*, which, for reasons unknown, has always been referred to as the 'Hospital Ship'. She lies north to south on a hard seabed of sand and stones, in a general depth of 16m, the lowest astronomical depth. The wreck is totally collapsed, well broken up and scattered. Her two boilers are the highest parts, with little else standing proud of the seabed. The site is very popular with local divers, but tidal streams can be extremely strong, in fact so powerful that one unlucky group of visiting divers had their rigid-hulled inflatable boat pulled under the surface after the anchor became fastened on the flood spring tide. Visibility is usually very poor to grim most of the year, but improves during the summer months.

The wreck was thought to lie close inshore at Dyke End, having gone down immediately after being refloated, but then her top structures would have been visible on the surface at the time and there were no reports of this. Records do not say how far the *Dunstaffnage* was able to travel before she finally went down to the bottom, so the author thought that the unknown wreck lying in position: N54 09 498 W000 09 251 could have possibly been her remains. It is some 1.5 miles east of Speeton Village, lying in a general depth of 19m, the lowest astronomical depth. She is now totally collapsed and well broken up and surrounded by a mound of broken plates and machinery, but the report doesn't say how many boilers there are on this wreck. The remains, although now known not to be the aforementioned vessel, may still be worth investigating. Tidal streams are quite strong and visibility usually very poor to grim, but the visibility improves significantly during the summer months.

GRAAFJELD, ex ALFRED DUMOIS
Wreck: ★★★★
Depth: 43m
Reference: N54 07 094 E000 00 875
Location: 3.4 miles E of Flamborough Head

The *Graafjeld* was a steel 728-ton Norwegian steamship and measured 53.41m in length, with a beam of 8.5m and a 3.6m draught. Blackwood & Gordon built her as Yard No.217 and launched her as the *Alfred Dumois* at Port Glasgow in 1890 for Jacob Christensen of Bergen. Her single iron screw propeller was powered by a 3-cylinder triple expansion steam engine that used one boiler. The vessel was not classed at Lloyd's. In 1898 she was sold to Carl Traae of Bergen. In 1916 A/S Sjofart (Skogland & Rasmussen) of Haugesund purchased her and she was renamed *Graafjeld*.

On 15 January 1917, the SS *Graafjeld* was on passage from Aalesund for Hull with a cargo of herring and salt, when she detonated a mine laid by the Imperial German submarine SM UC 43. Eight of her crew of thirteen were killed, including the captain, and the five survivors, all Norwegian seamen, were brought ashore in an exhausted condition at Bridlington. The men had been in the freezing water for an hour before being picked up. UC 43 was later torpedoed by British submarine off Muckle Flugga, Shetland on 10 March 1917.

Wreck-site

The wreck, believed to be that of the *Graafjeld*, lies east to west on a hard, flat seabed of coarse sand and gravel, in a general depth of 43m, the lowest astronomical depth. She is reported as intact, upright, standing 6m high from amidships to stern, with her boiler visible, but her super-structure and forepart now collapsed almost to the seabed. It is possible that the vessel's bell and interesting navigation equipment are still there somewhere, so she should be a nice wreck to explore. The bell, if located, will almost certainly be inscribed '*Alfred Dumois* 1890'. Tidal streams are very strong and underwater visibility is usually extremely poor to grim most of the year. No fish have been reported around the site, but she will certainly be worth investigating as a boat-angling venue. However, a good lookout will be required, because she lies in the main shipping lanes. The wreck should also be treated with the utmost respect because she is the grave of eight of her crew who died on the vessel.

MAZEPPA

Wreck: ★★
Scenery: ★★★
Depth: 5m
Reference: N54 07 069 W000 04 560 (approx.)
Location: South corner of Selwick's Bay at Flamborough Head

The *Mazeppa* was an iron 1,164-ton British three-masted, schooner-rigged steamship that was registered at Newcastle-upon-Tyne. She measured 78.3m in length, a beam of 9.1m and a draught of 5.2m. Palmers built her at Jarrow-on-Tyne in 1872 and Renwick Wilton & Co. of Newcastle-upon-Tyne owned her at the time of loss. Her single screw, possibly bronze, was powered by a 2-cylinder compound steam engine that developed 134hp using one 1SB 4PF boiler. Her cylinders measured 76.20cm and 139.70cm-83.82cm. Palmers also built her machinery at Jarrow-on-Tyne. A new double boiler was installed in the vessel in 1888.

On 24 June 1908, the *Mazeppa* was on passage from the Tyne for Dartmouth carrying a cargo of coal when she encountered dense fog off Flamborough Head and drove ashore at the corner of Selwick's Bay. It is understood that the crew got safely ashore in their own boats, but the vessel settled on the bottom in about 5m and soon became a total loss. Since then her remains have been well salvaged by the local firm of Tommy Round.

Wreck-site

The wreck is now totally collapsed, well broken up and dispersed over an area of about 100m of seabed, just off the south corner of Selwick's Bay, (locally referred to as 'Silex-Bay'). Two iron bollards, pieces of her rib frames, battered hull plates and broken unrecognisable lumps of machinery stand no more than about 2.5m high among the rocks and boulders. A few crus-taceans can often be found around the wreck-site, albeit usually rather small, while during the summer months, large shoals of saithe and individual ballan-wrasse can sometimes be observed. She lies in a general depth of 5m, about the lowest astronomical depth. Tidal streams are fairly moderate, but increase dramatically as you move seaward and underwater visibility is usually poor to grim but significantly improves during the summer months.

Chapter 4

Flamborough Head to Withernsea

Area 4 (N54 06′ to N53 43′)

NITEDAL, ex HERO
Wreck: ★★★★
Depth: 41m
Reference: N54 05 741 E000 01 667
Location: 3.98 miles ESE of Flamborough Head

The *Nitedal* was a steel-hulled 1,714-ton Norwegian steamship that was registered at the port of Christiania. She measured 81.73m in length, with an 11.78m beam and a draught of 5.25m. Laxevaags Maskin & Jernskibs of Bergen, Norway, built her as the *Hero* in 1903 for Kjaer & Isdahl of Bergen, who owned her until 1916. Dpsk. Akties. Ostlandet Christiania purchased her in 1916, renamed her *Nitedal* and owned the vessel at the time of loss. T. Sagen of Christiania managed her. The single iron screw propeller was powered by a 3-cylinder triple expansion steam engine that developed 149hp using two boilers. Her cylinders measured 48.26cm, 78.74cm and 129.54cm-83.82cm. She had one deck and Laxevaags Maskin & Jernskibs, the builders, built her machinery.

On 20 October 1917, the SS *Nitedal* was torpedoed and sunk by the Imperial German submarine SM UB 57, some four miles east-south-east of Flamborough Head. The steamship was under the command of Captain T. Evenson, carrying a 2,500-ton cargo of coal, on passage from the River Tyne for Rouen. The vessel is reported to have gone down in less than three minutes following the explosion. SM UB 57 was the first submarine to be lost to a ground magnetic mine, when she disappeared off Zeebrugge on 14 August 1918.

Wreck-site
The wreck of the *Nitedal* has never positively identified. The officially recognised location for the wreck was given as: N54 01 12 W000 02 08 and four miles east-south-east of Flamborough Head. However those co-ordinates would place her about six miles south of Flamborough Head, lying in a general depth of 16m, the lowest astronomical depth, but the only wreck in that vicinity is the *Tredegar Hall*. The author believes the wreck most likely to be the *Nitedal* is the one in the position given above. She lies on a seabed of coarse sand, gravel, pebbles, small broken black shells and mud, in a general depth of 41m, the lowest astronomical tide. The wreck is very substantial, standing around 6m high, but the upper superstructure is collapsed. Tidal streams are extremely strong and underwater visibility is usually poor to grim, but improves significantly during the summer months. Lion's mane jellyfish will be rather a hazard while decompressing during the months of July and August. The wreck attracts large numbers of fish, so she will make an excellent boat-angling venue when conditions permit.

MARY

Wreck: ★
Scenery: ★★
Depth: 3m
Reference: N54 06 338 W000 05 497
Location: 0.7 miles SW of Flamborough Head

The *Mary* was an iron 1,124-ton schooner-rigged Russian steamship that was registered at the port of Riga. She measured 71.01m in length by 9.52m beam with a draught of 4.74m. Helsingørs Jrnsk. Bygeri built her at Helsingør in 1897 and Helmsing & Grimm of Riga (now in Latvia) owned her at the time of loss. Her single iron screw propeller was powered by a 2-cylinder compound steam engine that developed 125hp using one boiler. Her cylinders measured 66.04cm and 129.54cm-83.82cm. Helsingørs Jrnsk. Bygeri also built her machinery. She had one deck and a superstructure consisting of a 21.03m quarterdeck and an 8.23m forecastle.

The SS *Mary* had sealed orders when she left North Shields for an unknown destination. She was under the command of Captain J. Jankowsky, carrying a crew of nineteen and an unspecified cargo of coal. The SS *Mary* steamed south until she rounded Flamborough Head during the early hours of 2 March 1916 then, for reasons unknown (possibly fog) she ran aground on rocks between the Head and South Landing. The vessel was left badly damaged, with a gaping hole torn through the hull plates, but when the lifeboat *Matthew Middlewood* arrived on the scene, the crew stubbornly refused to abandon her. However, as water poured in through the damaged plates, leaving nearly 4m of water in the aft part of the ship, the wind picked up and developed into a north-westerly gale. When all hope of saving her seemed lost and she began to break up, the lifeboat took off her crew and left the vessel to the elements.

Wreck-site

It is understood that the vessel was heavily salvaged soon after she was wrecked. She lies in a general depth of 3m, the lowest astronomical depth, and what remains of her is now well broken up and dispersed. Just a few rusting iron plates and small pieces of unrecognisable broken machinery can be seen concreting into the surrounding rocks and sand. Small green shore crabs are commonplace around the site, but there is very little else of interest for the diver; it is also possible to snorkel-dive the area with a little care. Tidal streams are reasonable close to the shore, but underwater visibility is usually poor most of the year.

OSCAR

Wreck: ★★
Depth: 31m & 17m
Reference: N54 06 596 W000 01 991
Location: 1.60 miles ESE of Flamborough Head
Also given: N54 08 166 W000 05 083
Location: 0.75 miles NNW of Flamborough Head

The *Oscar* was a very old iron 330-ton British steamship that was registered at the port of Grangemouth. She measured 47.5m in length, with a 7m beam and a 3.9m draught. William Denny built her in 1856 (other sources say 1850) at Dumbarton for R. Henderson of Belfast. In 1858, the vessel was sold to W. Sloan & Co. Then in 1870 she was sold to the Dingwall & Skye Railway Co. who bought her to use in their ferry service. However, on 9 November that year, she ran aground at Applecross and was abandoned to the Underwriters. They had her repaired and refloated, then the *Oscar* was sold on to G.G. MacKay of Grangemouth, who was the owner at the time of loss. Her single iron screw propeller was originally powered by a 2-

cylinder compound steam engine that developed 75hp using one boiler. However, after a number of years, the vessel was lengthened to 48.7m and her machinery changed to a smaller 50hp 2-cylinder compound steam engine, making her more efficient.

On 15 July 1881, the SS *Oscar* was on passage from London for Middlesbrough when she foundered and was lost following a collision with the West Hartlepool steamer *Breeze* off Flamborough Head. The SS *Oscar* was in ballast, under the command of Captain P. Keir and carrying a crew of thirteen. The wind at the time was a light south-south-easterly force two, but the visibility was poor due to a coastal fog.

Wreck-site

The wreck of the SS *Oscar* has not been found to date, but I suggest the two sets of co-ordinates above, because they are the positions of two very old wrecks and may prove worthwhile.

The first co-ordinates are for a wreck positioned 1.6 miles east-south-east of Flamborough Head. She lies on a seabed of sand and pebbles, in a general depth of 31m, the lowest astronomical depth. The wreck is totally collapsed and well broken up, with the highest section standing no more than 2m around a single boiler and engine. Lots of broken iron plates and bits of machinery are strewn around, with much of it now beginning to concrete into the stony seabed. Tidal streams are exceptionally strong, but the wreckage will be worth looking for.

The second co-ordinates are for a wreck lying on a seabed of sand, rock and stone, in a general depth of 17m, the lowest astronomical depth. The wreck is totally collapsed, well broken up and scattered, with the highest section of 2.5m being around her boiler and the scattered remnants of her engine, which is now concreting into the seabed. There are no reports of marine life around the site. Tidal streams are very strong and underwater visibility is usually poor to grim, however it improves during the summer months following a spell of dry settled weather and on neap tides.

MANCHESTER ENGINEER II

Wreck: ★★★★★
Depth: 41m
Reference: N54 05 378 E000 01 776
Location: 4.12 miles ESE of Flamborough Head

The *Manchester Engineer II* (Official No.121260) was a steel hulled 4,465-ton British schooner-rigged steamship registered at Manchester. She was 115.23m long with a 15.26m beam, a 5.49m draught and a 6.73m moulded depth. D.&W. Henderson & Co. at Glasgow built her in five months, completing her in September 1905 as the *Craigvar* for the West of Scotland Steamship Co. Briggart, Fulton & Grier of Glasgow managed her. Her single, possibly bronze, screw was powered by a 3-cylinder triple expansion steam engine that developed 379hp using three single-ended 3SB 9CF boilers, giving a 13.03-bar (189lb) pressure. There were nine corrugated furnaces and grate surface of 52.73m. Her cylinders sizes measured: 63.50cm, 104.14cm and 170.18cm with a 121.92cm stroke, (25in, 41in and 67in with a 48in stroke). D.&W. Henderson manufactured the machinery giving her a speed of 10.5 knots. She had a flat keel, four-bulkheads to spar-deck, and two bulkheads to main deck cemented, one steel deck and a superstructure consisting of a 9.49m-poopdeck, 29.87m bridgedeck and a 12.19m forecastle. She had water ballast, with 36.88m cellular double bottom aft, 11.28m under engine and boilers and forward 50.29m giving 1,011 tons of ballast, aft peak tank 122 tons. She was equipped with one-stern mounted 11.94cm (4.7in) deck gun.

In 1910 she was sold to W. Thaner & Co. of Liverpool and renamed *Nation*, signal letters HDMB. Treasury Steamship Co. Ltd purchased her in 1911, with the managers as W. Thomas & Sons, Liverpool. In 1917, Manchester Liners Ltd, who was the owner at the time of loss, purchased the ship and renamed her *Manchester Engineer II* and R.B. Stoker became the managers. Captain H. Jones was the master from 1913 until 1917 and she was captained by Captain

Owens when Manchester Liners Ltd took over the ownership. She was the second vessel of that name, belonging to the company, the other, *Manchester Engineer I*, was torpedoed by SM U 44 off the Irish coast near Waterford on 27 March 1916.

At 6.05 p.m. on 16 August 1917 the SS *Manchester Engineer II* was on passage from Archangel via South Shields for St Nazaire when SM UC 16, a Kaiserliche Deutsche Marine U-boat, torpedoed her off Flamborough Head. The U-boat remained submerged during the attack and gave no warning of the impending attack. The steamship was under the command of Captain Owens, carrying a cargo of coal, the pilot and a crew of forty-two. She was steaming at full speed along the war-channel, an area cleared of mines, when the pilot observed a periscope about 150m off the port beam. The ship was still turning, after her helm had been put hard-to-port, when a torpedo detonated on the aft port side, leaving a gaping hole in the area of the bulkhead level with No.4 hold. The vessel took on a heavy list and settled by the stern, as walls of water flooded in, while the crew took to the boats, abandoning ship at 6.15 p.m. Two minutes later, the big steamer heaved up out of the water in a mass of gushing steam and bubbles and disappeared beneath the surface, taking the confidential papers and Wartime Codebooks with her. All of the crew, including the pilot, were picked up by motor launches and landed at Bridlington later that day. In Artic waters two months earlier, the *Manchester Engineer II* had a lucky escape when chased by a U-boat.

Under the command of Oblt.z.S. Georg Reichmarus and carrying a crew of twenty-seven, SM UC 16 left her base at Zeebrugge on October 1917, but was never seen, or heard of again. On 26 October 1917 a crewman's body from the U-boat was washed ashore at Noordwijk in Holland.

Wreck-site

The wreck lies north-north-west to south-south-east on a seabed of sand, gravel and fine black shells, in a general depth of 41m, the lowest astronomical depth. She is very substantial, standing some 7m high amidships, with the upper structures collapsed and broken, but covered in a colourful array of soft corals. Lots of marine life has been reported all around the wreck, but she has numerous nets snagged on the jagged steel structures. Tidal streams are very strong and underwater visibility is usually pretty grim, but significantly improves during the summer months. This wreck should make an excellent and exciting boat-angling venue when conditions permit. She is also a first-class dive site because the ship was equipped with two pedestal-mounted telegraphs and steering helms, one of which was situated at the stern of the vessel. She will be a nice one to visit although the wreck-site is very dark and gloomy. The wreck of the SS *Manchester Engineer* is owned by three divers from Manchester. They also own the SS *Keynes*, SS *Grangemouth* and the SS *Catford* and operate an ex-Naval fleet tender, *Sultan Adventurer*, the ex MS *Meavy*, which is based at Grimsby.

SM UB 75

Wreck: ★★★★
Depth: 47m
Reference: N54 04 714 E000 05 54
Also: N54 04 724 E000 05 564
Location: 6.42 miles ESE of Flamborough Head

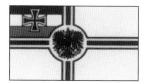

SM UB 75 was a UB III-class attack submarine of the SM UB75-UB79 type, built by Blohm & Voss at Hamburg for the Imperial German Navy. She was launched on 5 May 1917, commissioned on 11 September 1917 and was a double-hulled boat capable of being used in the Atlantic Ocean. She measured 55.3m in length, with a 5.78m beam and a draught of 3.65m. Two 550hp diesel/oil engines powered her two bronze screw propellers, giving her a maximum speed of 13.6 knots. Rows of lead-acid batteries powered her two 394hp electric motors for running submerged, giving her a maximum speed of 7.8 knots. The boat had an endurance distance of around 8,000 miles and carried 34 tons of fuel oil. SM UB 75's armament consisted of one stern and four bow torpedo tubes, one 88mm deck-gun and ten torpedoes. Her normal complement was three officers and thirty-one crewmen.

Under the command of Oberleutnant zur See F. Walther and carrying a crew of thirty-four, SM UB75 left Borkum on 29 September 1917 for a war patrol off the Yorkshire coast. In early December, she arrived off Whitby and created mayhem amongst the Allied ships in the first few days, by sinking the 1,780-ton steamship *Highgate* on 7 December, the 2,220-ton SS *Lampada* on the 9th and then the following day the 3,596-ton SS *Venetia*. The U-boat seemed to be having a good time, but from then on nothing was seen or heard from her again. She failed to answer all signals and on 13 December 1917, when she was due back at her base, she was presumed lost in the area off Flamborough Head, which had extensive British minefields.

Wreck-site
The wreck is not yet identified but is believed to be that of the U-boat. She lies south-south-east to north-north-west in a general depth of 47m, the lowest astronomical depth. She is upright but broken in two, with the highest section standing some 4.3m high. The wreck is on a flat seabed of sand, smooth gravel, broken black shells and mud covering an area 57m by 9.5m. It is doubtful if there will be very much marine life around the wreck, which is swept by very strong tidal streams and where underwater visibility is usually very poor for the majority of the year. Visibility improves significantly during the summer months after a spell of dry settled weather and on neap tides. This wreck will make an interesting club project, especially if it is the U-boat in question.

BORDEAUX
Wreck: ★
Depth: 7m
Reference: N54 04 619 W000 05 89
Location: 2.38 miles SSW of Flamborough Head near South Smithic Sandbank

The *Bordeaux* was an iron 320-ton British steamship that was registered at the port of Glasgow. She measured 43.4m in length, by 6.7m beam with a 3.35m draught. A.F. Blackwater of Glasgow owned her at the time of loss. Her single iron screw propeller was powered by a 2-cylinder compound steam engine that used one boiler.

On 29 November 1897, the SS *Bordeaux* was in ballast and carrying a crew of twelve, on passage from London for Methil. She was under the command of her master, Captain J. Phillips, as she steamed north from London. However, a force nine north-north-westerly storm developed and the SS *Bordeaux* attempted to seek shelter in Bridlington Bay, but she got into serious difficulties while approaching Flamborough. Watchers on the cliff tops reported that she was 'pitching fearfully' in massive rolling waves and mountainous walls of foaming water. Soon afterwards she was driven ashore and stranded on the Stack Rocks near Flamborough Head. She no sooner struck the rocks than, badly holed, she was driven back off in a sinking position. Distress signals were sent up and Flamborough lifeboat was launched, but she was unable to get through the huge seas. The Bridlington lifeboat was also alerted to the situation, but the secretary decided that it would be suicidal to attempt a rescue in the prevailing conditions. The SS *Bordeaux* sank in the early hours, with the loss of all her crew of twelve. By daybreak, her two masts were all that could be seen from the shore.

The disaster caused great concern amongst local folk, but when they discovered that the lifeboat secretary had made the decision not to launch the lifeboat, young men around the district burnt effigies of him in the streets and blamed him for the loss of the SS *Bordeaux*'s crew. However, the subsequent inquiry vindicated the Bridlington secretary, calling it a 'brave decision', but because the vessel was reported to be in danger close to the cliffs earlier on, the Flamborough lifeboat was censured for failing to launch at that time, even though the lifeboat crew and launchers had at least tried to get her out to sea.

Wreck-site
The wreck believed to be the remains of the SS *Bordeaux* lies close to the sandbank known as South Smithic, just off Bridlington. She lies north to south on a shifting seabed of soft sand, in a general depth of around 7m. The wreck, which covers an area of approximately 20m by 7m, is totally collapsed, well broken up and usually mostly covered in sand, with just a few plates, ribs and girders showing above it. Spring tides and storms often move vast masses of the sandbank, sometimes revealing up to half of the wreck at different times of the year. Tidal streams are quite severe most of the time and underwater visibility usually poor to grim, but visibility improves slightly during the summer months. The majority of this area is also fairly shallow with lots of confused currents.

POTOMAC
Wreck: *
Depth: 5m
Reference: N54 03 182 W000 10 575
Location: 1.07 miles off South Beach, Bridlington Bay

The *Potomac* was an iron 1,832-ton British brig-rigged steamship registered at the port of London. She was 80.06m long with a 10.08m beam with a 7.46m draught. London & Glasgow Engineering Co. built her at Glasgow in 1872 for the Merchantile Steamship Co. Ltd of London which was the owner at the time of loss. Her single iron screw propeller was powered by a 2-cylinder compound steam engine that developed 150hp using two boilers and her cylinders measured 78.74cm and 137.16cm-83.82cm. She had two decks and five bulkheads.

On 21 November 1893, the old brig-rigged steamer was off Bridlington, on passage from Odessa for Aberdeen, when she was found to have a serious leak. She was under the command of Captain H.C. Barcham, carrying a cargo of wheat and a crew of twenty. Tugs towed her into shallower water, but with a force six east-north-easterly, she could not be saved and sank when about seven cables south-south-east of Bridlington pier light. Local boatmen salvaged some of her cargo of wheat, but the majority of it was lost to the sea. The *Potomac* became a total wreck and gradually collapsed.

Wreck-site
The wreck remained a navigational hazard until 1971, when the salvage company Risdon & Beazley salvaged and dispersed her remains. They employed their *Topmast 18* vessel and left what there is of the wreck almost buried, in a depth of 5m, although it is still described as a 'foul area' today. She is now totally collapsed, well broken up, dispersed and mostly buried, but storms often expose her remains at different times of the year, leaving large bottom sections visible on a seabed of sand in a general depth of 5m. This whole area is sandy and very shallow and of very little interest to divers, but various flatfish can be caught around the bay during the summer months.

BRABANT
Wreck: **
Depth: 6m
Reference: N54 03 529 W000 05 813
Location: 3.45 miles ESE of Bridlington Quay Light

The *Brabant* was a steel 1,492-ton Norwegian steamship that was registered at the port of Christiania. She measured 73.58m in length, with a beam of 10.69m and a draught of 6.22m. Fredriksstad Mek. Vaeks built her at Fredriksstad in 1907 and A/S Granger Rolf owned her at the time of loss. Her single iron screw propeller was powered by a 3-cylinder triple expansion steam engine that developed 150hp using two boilers and her cylinders measured 45.72cm, 73.66cm and 127.00cm. Fredriksstad Mek. Vaeks also built her machinery and she had one deck.

On 15 January 1917, the SS *Brabant* was on passage from Christiania for London when she foundered and was lost east of South Smithic Sands, after detonating a mine laid by SM UC 43, an Imperial German submarine. The steamer was under the command of Captain P. Michaelsen and carrying a 696-ton cargo of wood pulp. It is understood that her crew took to the boats, but the vessel settled on the bottom in shallow water, with her two masts, smoke stack and upper structures showing and awash above the surface. UC 43 was sunk off Muckle Flagga, Shetland Islands when a British submarine torpedoed her on 10 March 1917.

Wreck-site
The wreck is now lying in a 2m scour, totally collapsed, well broken up and partially buried. She is on a seabed of soft sand, in a general depth of 6m, the lowest astronomical depth. The wreck is now very silted, with usually little more than 1m of her showing above the shifting sand. There is very little to interest the serious diver on this wreck, but she makes a reasonable second dive. Tidal streams are very strong and can be quite dangerous, with various currents criss-crossing each other, especially during spring tides. Vast shoals of mackerel visit the shallow area around Bridlington Bay during the summer months, which can make a nice boat-angling venue, however the deep-water wrecks off Flamborough Head, are a much more interesting place for the serious angler.

FELTRE, ex RHENANIA
Wreck: ★★★★
Depth: 36m
Reference: N54 02 399 E000 01 749
Location: 5.93 miles SSE of Flamborough Head

The *Feltre* was a steel 6,455-ton Italian passenger steamship that measured 124.76m in length by 16.5m beam with a draught of 8.53m. She was built for the German-Africa Line as a passenger liner called *Rhenania* by Bremer Vulkan of Vegesack in Germany in 1904 and was designed to carry 260 passengers. However at the outbreak of the First World War, she was laid up in Naples, where the Italian Government requisitioned her and renamed the vessel *Feltre*. She was then turned over to the Italian State Railways, which owned her at the time of loss. Her single bronze screw was powered by a 4-cylinder quadruple expansion steam engine that developed 387hp. She had two decks and a superstructure that consisted of a 77.72m poop deck and 14.02m forecastle.

On 26 August 1917, the SS *Feltre* was on passage from Villaricos for the Tees, carrying a cargo of iron ore, when she was torpedoed and sunk off Flamborough head by the Imperial German submarine SM UB 32. The U-boat was later bombed by a flying-boat in the English Channel on 22 September 1917.

Wreck-site
Local fishermen refer to this wreck as 'Catmerole' or 'Cattle Mere Hole' from marks on the cliffs. She lies north-north-east to south-south-west on a flat seabed of sand and small pebbles, in a general depth of 36m, the lowest astronomical depth. She is intact, leaning on her starboard side in a half metre scour and standing some 6m high amidships. Not very long ago, she stood almost 15m high but now most of the wreck has collapsed in a jumbled heap, with part of her cargo and fishing equipment scattered all around. She is said to be an excellent dive when visibility is good, which is not very often, but in bad visibility, she can be a 'heart stopper'. Lots of marine life has been reported on and around the wreck-site, so she will make an excellent

boat-angling venue when weather conditions permit. Her bell, bearing the inscription 'Rhenania 1904', was recovered in recent times. The vessel was equipped with at least two brass pedestal-mounted telegraphs and two pedestal-mounted steering helms, one of which was situated at the stern end. There are no reports that these have ever been removed, so they will be very interesting to see. The best time to visit the wreck for diving is 1.5-2 hours after slack water at Bridlington, preferably on a low neap tide. Tidal streams are quite strong and under-water visibility usually poor, but it vastly improves during the summer months after a spell of dry settled weather and westerly winds.

BREMA, ex MECKLENBURG
Wreck: ★★★★
Depth: 33m
Reference: N54 59 036 E000 07 184
Location: 10.45 miles SSE of Flamborough Head

The *Brema* was a steel 1,537-ton British steamship and measured 79.6m in length, with an 11.6m beam and a draught of 5.2m. AG Neptun built her as the *Mecklenburg* at Rostock, Germany, in 1904 for H. Podeus of Wismar, Germany. Her single iron screw propeller was powered by a 3-cylinder triple expansion steam engine that developed 162hp using two boilers and her cylinders measured 50.80cm, 81.28cm and 132.08cm-91.44cm. The vessel was later sold for 465,000 marks to the famous German company, Argo Reederei of Bremen, and placed on the Italian route, together with another vessel the company had bought, the steamship *Lestris*. She was purchased from a shipping company in Cork in Ireland and renamed *Condor*. The *Mecklenburg* was the last vessel to sail on the Italian line when it finished in 1908. On 19 December 1908, she transported 3,693 sacks of phosphate from Italy to Bremen. From then on she was put into the tramp business, together with six other ships. In 1914, Argo Reederei had a total of thirty vessels (44,504 tons in total) in the Linienfakt (a steady route to a country or certain harbour). Until then, eleven of the ships went to England and twelve went to Russia. In August 1914, the *Mecklenburg* docked at Swansea just as war broke out and she was taken as a prize of war. The Admiralty then requisitioned her to use as a fleet collier and renamed her *Brema*.

At 3 p.m. on 19 August 1917, the SS *Brema* was steaming at 8 knots along the cleared war channel when SM UC 17 torpedoed her. The U-boat, which survived the First World War, was unseen and gave no warning of the impending attack. The steamship was on passage from Sunderland for London, carrying an unspecified cargo of coal and a crew of twenty-one. The torpedo detonated on the port side close to the No.2 hatch, causing a massive explosion which tore a large hole in the hull and smashed the port lifeboat to pieces. The vessel immediately began to settle by the stern. The crew lowered the starboard boat and all but the captain and two others managed to scramble in and quickly cleared the ship. The three men left on board had to jump into the sea and were very soon picked up by the boat. The bow of the SS *Brema* lifted up slightly and she slipped below the surface at 3.03 p.m., just three minutes after the explosion. The crew saw the submarine's periscope about 275m away and it was believed at the time she was manoeuvring to attack another vessel, but no more were recorded as lost in that vicinity. The survivors were picked up by the Port of London Authority's hopper-barge No.21 and landed at Grimsby.

Wreck-site
The wreck of the *Brema* is something of a mystery, because the position of sinking has been given as the same as that of the *Tredegar Hall*. The author has suggested that there is a possibility that this wreck may be hers. She lies on a seabed of sand, gravel and shells, in a general depth of 33m, the lowest astronomical depth. The wreck is upright and basically intact, but collapsed and broken up, with the largest part standing about 4m high around amidships with a trawl-net entangled close

to the engine area. If her bell is located, it will probably be inscribed '*Mecklenburg* 1904'. Tidal streams are quite brisk and underwater visibility is usually poor to dismal, but the visibility improves significantly during the summer months. The wreck is fairly large, so she will almost certainly attract large numbers of various kinds of fish, making the site a good boat-angling venue.

VILLE DE VALENCIENNES
Wreck: ★★★★
Scenery: ★
Depth: 35m
Reference: N54 01 785 E000 02 984
Location: 6.78 miles SE of Flamborough Head

The *Ville de Valenciennes* was a steel 1,734-ton French steamship that was registered at Dunkirk. She measured 83.51m in length, by a 10.69 beam and a draught of 4.9m. J. Redhead & Sons built her at South Shields in 1897 and Cie. des Bateaux à Vapeur du Nord owned her at the time of loss. Her single iron screw propeller was powered by a 3-cylinder triple expansion steam engine that developed 234hp using two boilers and her cylinders measured 58.42cm, 93.96cm and 154.94cm-99.06cm. She had one deck and a superstructure consisting of a 13.41m bridge deck and a 5.18m forecastle.

On 22 September 1917, the French collier was torpedoed and sunk off Flamborough Head by SM UC 64, an Imperial German U-boat. The steamer was under the command of a Captain Boulogne and carrying an unspecified cargo of coal from the Tyne for Bordeaux. SM UC 64 was depth-charged and sunk between Folkestone and the Varne on 20 June 1917.

Wreck-site
The wreck has been known locally as 'Ted's wreck' for many years and it has always been thought to be that of the steamship *Brema*. Recently the bell from the SS *Ville de Valenciennes* was recovered from the wreck-site, confirming her position. she lies north-west to south-east on a seabed of sand, gravel, pebbles and small black shells, in a general depth of 35m, the lowest astronomical depth. She is reported as being in a small scour, intact and standing about 5m high amidships, but collapsed and broken. Tidal streams are very strong and underwater visibility usually grim to poor, significantly improving during the summer months, especially during neap tides and following a spell of dry settled weather. The wreck should also make an interesting boat-angling venue when conditions allow due to a number of large cod and decent sized pollack among and above the steel debris. Various crustaceans have also been observed sheltering in pipes and overhangs.

IDA
Wreck: ★★★★
Depth: 45m
Reference: N54 02 043 E000 07 849
Location: 8.88 miles SE of Flamborough Head

The *Ida* was an iron 1,172-ton Norwegian steamship that was registered at the port of Langesund, Norway. She measured 73.07m in length, with a 10.36m beam and a draught of 4.9m. A. Hall & Co. of Aberdeen built her in 1882 and H. Skougaard owned her at the time of loss. Her single iron screw propeller was powered by a 143hp 2-cylinder compound steam engine that used two boilers. Blair & Co. Ltd built her machinery at Stockton-on-Tees. She had one deck, a 28.04m quarterdeck, a 15.85m bridge deck and a 9.75m forecastle.

On 8 February 1917, the *Ida* was in ballast on passage from Leith for London when the Imperial German submarine UC 39 stopped her. Captain C. Nilsson and his crew were forced to abandon ship in the boats, while the Germans placed explosive scuttling charges in their vessel and she sank soon after. Earlier that day, the U-boat sank the British-registered 1,311-ton steamship *Hanna Larsen* by gunfire and explosive scuttling charges. UC 39 was sunk by the destroyer HMS *Thrasher* using gunfire and depth charges later that day. The destroyer sighted her when she was in the process of sinking the steam collier *Hornsey*.

Wreck-site
The wreck, probably that of this Norwegian steamship, lies north-north-west to south-south-east on a seabed of sand, gravel, black shells, small pebbles and mud, in a general depth of 45m, the lowest astronomical depth. She is still fairly substantial, standing upright and reasonably intact, but with the bridge structures totally collapsed. The highest 5m section is amidships, where two trawl nets lie snagged in the tangle of debris. Lots of fish have been reported over and around the wreck, so she will make an interesting boat-angling venue. Soft corals are well established on the upper most exposed areas and numerous crustaceans have been sighted. Tidal streams are very strong, while underwater visibility is usually poor most of the year.

KNUTHENBORG
Wreck: ★★★★
Depth: 36m
Reference: N54 01 413 E000 03 725
Location: 7.35 miles SE of Flamborough Head

The *Knuthenborg* was an iron 517-ton Danish steamship that was registered at the port of Odense. She measured 54.91m in length, by 8.02m beam with a 4.03m draught. Kockums Mek. Verk built her at Malmö in 1880 and Det Forenede Dampskibs Selskab owned her at the time of loss. Her single iron screw propeller was powered by a 2-cylinder compound steam engine that developed 105hp using one boiler. The vessel had one deck.

On 27 June 1916, the SS *Knuthenborg* was in ballast when she foundered and was lost following a collision with the Danish-registered steamship *Rhône*. The *Knuthenborg* was on passage from Grimsby for Newcastle-upon-Tyne and under the command of Captain O. Holm.

Wreck-site
The wreck lies on a seabed of sand, gravel, pebbles and small broken black shells, in a general depth of 36m, the lowest astronomical depth. The wreck is now partially buried, totally collapsed and well broken up, with her boiler and engine exposed. She makes a nice rummage dive, where practically anything may turn up, however the remains have been well dived. Most of the vessel's interesting navigational equipment will probably have been destroyed when the wreck collapsed down, but she is said to be still worth a visit. A number of large crustaceans and cod have been observed around the wreck-site, so weather conditions permitting, she may be worth adding to the list of boat-angling venues. Tidal streams are very strong and under-water visibility is usually poor, but improves during the summer months.

CYNTHIA
Wreck: ★
Depth: 43m
Reference: N54 00 946 E000 33 398
Location: 23.29 miles E by S of Flamborough Head

The *Cynthia* was an iron 133-ton British steam fishing trawler that was registered at Grimsby. She measured 29.38m in length, with a 7.08m beam and a 3.22m draught. Raylton Dixon & Co.

built her at Middlesbrough in 1891 and the Allen Steam Fishing Co. Ltd owned her at the time of loss. Her single iron screw propeller was powered by a 40hp 3-cylinder triple expansion steam engine that used one boiler. Westgarth, English & Co. built her machinery at Middlesbrough. She had one deck and a superstructure consisting of a 6.10m quarterdeck and a 5.79m forecastle.

On 25 September 1916, the trawler was on a return fishing voyage from Grimsby, under the command of Captain D. Appleyard, when she was sunk by gunfire from the Imperial German submarine U 57. The crew left safely in their own boat after being ordered to abandon ship by the U-boat captain. SM U 57 went on to survive the ravages of the First World War and surrendered to the Allies, to become French reparation and was broken up at Cherbourg in 1921.

Wreck-site
The wreck lies on a seabed of fine sand and small black shells, in a general depth of 43m, the lowest astronomical depth. She is totally collapsed, well broken up and partially buried, with the highest section amidships, where her engine/boiler are located, protruding some 1m above the seabed. A few bits of broken debris surround the wreck-site, but there is little else to see and not much marine life. Tidal streams are very brisk and underwater visibility is usually rather poor most of the year.

TREDEGAR HALL
Wreck: ★★★
Depth: 21m
Reference: N54 00 815 W000 00 388
Location: 6.46 miles ESE of Flamborough Head

The *Tredegar Hall* was a steel 3,764-ton British steamship that was registered at the port of London. She measured 104.26m in length by 14.17m beam with a draught of 7.51m. William Doxford & Sons Ltd built her at Sunderland in 1906 for E. Nicholl of Cardiff, but the Tredegar Hall Steamship Co. Ltd owned her at the time of loss. Her single iron screw propeller was powered by a 3-cylinder triple expansion steam engine that developed 300hp using two boilers. Her cylinders measured 66.04cm, 116.84cm and 172.72cm-106.68cm (26in, 46in and 68in-42in). She had one deck and a superstructure that consisted of a 6.40m poop deck and a 10.67m forecastle. She was also equipped with one 11.94cm quick-firing stern-mounted gun.

On 23 October 1917, the SS *Tredegar Hall* was on passage from Melilla for Middlesbrough, when SM UB 57 torpedoed her. The steamship was under the command of Captain A.O. Welch, carrying a crew of thirty-three and a cargo of iron ore. The torpedo detonated in the port side of the engine room at 6.40 a.m., killing the second engineer and an Arab coal-trimmer, while a third man, a donkey-man, drowned later after having to jump overboard. The ship's port boats were destroyed in the explosion, but the chief officer and twenty-four other crewmembers managed to launch the starboard boat and safely clear the ship. The captain and other survivors, were in the process of lowering the ship's dinghy when she sank, forcing them to jump into the sea. The ship's lifeboat picked up those in the water some forty minutes later, and a minesweeper took the crew and boat on board and the men were landed at Grimsby. The confidential papers and wartime codebook went down with the ship. SM UB 57 was the first submarine to be lost to magnetic mines on 18 August 1918, when she disappeared off Zeebrugge.

Wreck-site
The wreck, known locally as the 'Ore-ship', for obvious reasons, lies east to west on a seabed of sand, gravel and black shells, in a general depth of 21m, the lowest astronomical depth. She is now partially buried, totally collapsed and well broken up, with her bows lying across the tidal run and pointing to the west. Around amidships, a pile of steel debris and broken machinery surrounds her engine and two upended, exposed boilers. Her 4.57m iron screw

propeller is visible at the stern, and between it and her engine and boilers lies a huge mound of the cargo of iron ore, where various species of marine life can be found. Large cod are in evidence all around the wreck-site, so she will make a nice boat-angling venue when the weather permits. Tidal streams are fairly strong and often confused, while the underwater visibility is usually poor, but significantly improves during the summer months, following a spell of dry settled weather and westerly winds. The best time to visit the site for diving is one hour after low water at Bridlington, on a neap tide.

LEKA, ex ZOE
Wreck: ★★★★★
Depth: 37m
Reference: N54 00 721 E000 07 932
Location: 9.64 miles SE of Flamborough Head

The *Leka* was an iron 1,845-ton Norwegian steamship that was registered at the port of Christiania. She measured 82.39m in length, with an 11.13m beam and a 5.02m draught. Richardson Duck & Co. built her at Stockton-on-Tees as the *Zoe* in 1892 for C.T. Gogstad. Dmpsk. Akties of Laly in Norway, which owned her at the time of loss, purchased her and renamed her *Leka*. A 3-cylinder triple expansion stream engine that developed 193hp using one 1DB 4CF boiler powered her single iron screw propeller. Her cylinders measured 53.34cm, 88.90cm and 144.78cm-91.44cm. Blair & Co. of Stockton-on-Tees built her machinery.

On 24 September 1917, the *Leka* was torpedoed and sunk by the mine-laying German submarine SM UC 71, commanded by Steindorff. The steamer was under the command of Captain S. Schettelvig and carrying a cargo of iron ore on passage from Santander for Sunderland. SM UC 71 survived the First World War.

Wreck-site
The wreck, probably that of the steamship *Leka*, lies almost south-east to north-west on a seabed of sand, broken black shells, gravel and small pebbles, in a general depth of 38m, the lowest astronomical tide. She is very substantial, upright, partially buried, with her top structures now very collapsed and the wreck broken in two at the forward hold. Lots of marine life has been observed on and around this wreck, so she will make an excellent boat-angling venue when conditions permit. If the ship's bell is located, it should be inscribed 'Zoe 1892'. Slack water occurs around two hours after it does at Bridlington, which is the best time to visit the site. Tidal streams are very strong and underwater visibility is usually poor to grim, but significantly improves following a spell of dry settled weather, during neap tides, in the summer months. Lion's mane jellyfish can also be a nuisance when decompressing during the months of July and August.

SM UC 47
Wreck: ★★★★
Depth: 50m & 52m
Reference: N54 00 437 E000 23 582 (possibly)
Also given: N54 01 248 E000 20 577 (probably)
Location: 15.19 miles ESE of Flamborough Head

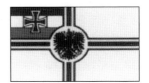

SM UC 47 was a class UC11 mine-laying boat of the SM UC46-UC48 type, built by A.G. Weser at Bremen for the Imperial German Navy. This was a double-hulled offshore boat, capable of being used in Atlantic waters. Her keel was laid on 1 February 1916 and she was launched on 30 August 1916 and commissioned for service on 13 October 1916. She had a surface displacement of 420 tons, 502 tons submerged, and measured 51.85m in length by 5.22m beam with a draught of 3.6m. Two 300hp diesel oil engines powered her two bronze screw propellers, giving her a maximum speed of 11.7 knots. Rows of lead-acid batteries powered her two 230hp electric motors for running submerged, giving her a speed under water of 6.9 knots. The UC 47 had an endurance range of some 7,280 sea miles at a steady 7 knots, using 47-64 tons of fuel. Submerged, she was capable of covering a distance of some fifty-four sea miles at a steady 4 knots using her battery power. Maximum diving depth was 50m and it took her just thirty-three seconds to dive. The boat had an armament consisting of one stern and two bow torpedo tubes, one 88mm deck-gun, six vertically inclined mine tubes, eighteen UC200 mines for laying and seven torpedoes. The boat's normal complement was three officers and twenty-three crewmen.

SM UC 47 left her base at Zeebrugge for a war patrol on 17 November 1917, under the command of Oberleutnant zur See von Wigankow and carrying a crew of twenty-eight. Wigankow's instructions were to attack and sink Allied ships between the Humber and Flamborough Head. On his first mission to the Yorkshire coast in October that year, SM UC 47, under the command of Wigankow, torpedoed and sank two British steamships on the 18th, the 1,075-ton SS *Togston* with five crew lost and the 1,879-ton SS *Cadmus*. Then on his second mission to that area, Wigankow sent the French 2,466-ton steamship *Isabelle* to the bottom on 9 November, along with the 1,207-ton British steamer SS *Ballogie* when five crewmen were lost. Two days later, on 11 November, he torpedoed the 1,620-ton Swedish SS *Dana* and sent her to a watery grave.

SM UC 47 had made her way safely across the North Sea and through the minefields that littered British coastal waters, arriving at a position east-south-east of Flamborough Head. It was still dark just before dawn on 18 November and for reasons which have only now become a bit clearer SM UC 47 was travelling on the surface. The British patrol-boat, HMS *P57*, command by H.C. Birnie, had just challenged an Allied steamship by scanning it in her search-lights, but moved on after realising the vessel was friendly. No sooner had the searchlight been turned out at 6.23 a.m., than one of the crew of HMS *P57* shouted that there was a large buoy on the port bow. Realising there should be no buoys in that particular area, Birnie closed in to further investigate the low-lying object. The officer of the watch, Lt Isdale, and Commander Birnie almost instantly realised that what they were looking at just 200m away was the conning tower of a U-boat. The patrol boat was then immediately swung hard-to-port towards the submarine and her engines put at full speed. It only took about fifteen seconds before the bows of HMS *P57* had ripped into the submarine, just before the conning tower and almost at a right angle. The force of the impact pushed SM UC 47 forward and down, but with the submarine still travelling, she began to pass astern of the patrol-boat. Quickly a depth charge was released, then HMS *P57* turned and came racing back to drop another one over the submarine. Commander Birnie turned once again and dropped a marker-buoy where oil and bubbles soon rose to the surface, then, another depth charge was dropped in the middle of the oily-slick, along with a second buoy. All day and the following night, HMS *P57* patrolled around the area, but none of the U-boat's twenty-eight crew came to the surface. Later that day, a minesweeper arrived on the scene, hooked the wreck with an explosive chain-sweep and detonated it. Royal Navy divers in hard-hat gear then went down to the wreck later that day and entered the submarine. They recovered publications and papers, which identified her as SM UC 47, but even more important, valuable charts, listing all of the minefields she had laid on her previous missions, were also recovered. For his quick action in sinking the U-boat, Commander Birnie was awarded the DSO and the crew of HMS *P57* took an equal share of the £1,000 offered by the Admiralty. A £1,000 reward was given to the crew of any vessel, including merchant ships, for destroying an enemy submarine.

Oberleutnant zur See von Wigankow was a very experienced U-boat commander, having previously been in command of two attack boats, SM UB 12 and SM UB 17, so, until recently, it has always been a bit of a mystery why he got caught on the surface by a British patrol boat.

The headquarters of SM UC 47, being part of the Flanders Flotilla, was at Bruges, and when the boats were operating in the North Sea, communication between them and headquarters was always difficult. The wireless/radio mast situated on the low hull of a U-boat only had a range of some thirty miles and without the use of a telescopic extension, the captain would have had to rely on passing messages via other boats closer to home. The telescope for the mast could be fully extended by the use of small electric motors inside the boat, which increased her wireless range up to about 100 miles. Local divers from Bridlington have reported finding the fully extended mast on the wreck, so it is almost certain now that Wigankow was using it to pass a message on, when HMS *P57* caught him on the surface – hence the mystery is finally solved.

HMS *P57* was one of sixty such vessels, purposely built, capable of a maximum speed of 20 knots and with bows of hardened steel, designed for ramming U-boats. They were also fairly well equipped, having one gun that fired 10.2cm shells, pom-pom guns and two special depth-charge throwers.

Wreck-site

The wreck of SM UC 47 has only recently been located and reports about the expeditions to the site appeared in the monthly *Diver* magazine in summer 2001. However, the position for the wreck offered by the visiting divers was rather vague. They mentioned in the article that it is difficult to find amongst the sand peaks. The position given was N54 01 00 E00 20 00 and the closest positive wreck to those co-ordinates, is at N54 01 248 E000 20 577. She lies south-south-east to north-north-west direction, on an undulating seabed of sand peaks and dunes, consisting of fine sand, broken black shells and small pebbles, in a general depth of 52m, the lowest astronomical depth. The wreck is intact and has the same proportions as a First World War U-boat, being 50m in length by 5m beam, but she is also partially buried, with just 1.7m of her showing in a sand wave.

The divers report her as lying with her bows buried so deep in the sand that only her conning tower, the 88mm deck-gun and a telescopic wireless mast are visible above it. Her stern-end stands 6m clear and the twin three-bladed bronze propellers are still both attached to the shafts. The stern torpedo tube, which is empty, lies on the sand and completely clear of the wreck on her starboard side. (It is believed that this was blown clean out of the submarine by the depth charge that followed her down from HMS *P57*.) Near to the stern on the port side, there is a large hole in the hull, also probably caused by one of the depth charges. The aft hatch near to the engine room is still closed and a little way forward there is extensive damage to the outer casing, which runs all the way to the bow. The conning tower and control room periscopes are lying on the seabed, pointing aft on the starboard side. The conning tower hatch is open, probably where the Royal Navy divers entered the boat to retrieve the valuable documents. Her 88mm gun is still attached to the wreck, with live and spent shell-cases lie scattered around. The hatch covers on the six mine chutes are close to but clear of the sand, while between the fourth and fifth chutes, her extended telescopic wireless mast towers 7m above the hull casing. The outer hull casing and twin torpedo tubes at the bow are all torn off the wreck, but her pressure casing inside is still intact. There is the probability that the U-boat's seven unexploded torpedoes also remain inside the boat, because her torpedo tube doors are closed tight shut. Her starboard side air ballast tank has a large hole in it. The wreck is very badly silted up, with sand coming to within 1.5m of her hatch cover, so there is no way anyone could now attempt to enter the submarine, which is officially classified as a war grave.

DRYADE
Wreck: ★★★★
Depth: 31m
Reference: N53 59 335 E000 04 439
Location: 9.27 miles SE of Flamborough Head

The *Dryade* was a steel 1,833-ton British steamship that was registered at the port of London. She measured 76.68m in length by 11.32m beam with a draught of 4.49m. A.G. Neptun built her at Rostock in 1906 for a German company, but she was seized as a prize of war and requisitioned by the Admiralty to use as a collier, under the management of Everitt & Newbiggin. She had one deck and her single iron screw propeller was powered by a 3-cylinder triple expansion steam engine that developed 133hp using one boiler. Her cylinders measured 43.18cm, 76.20cm and 121.92cm-83.82cm. J. Dickinson of Sunderland built her machinery. The vessel was equipped with one stern-mounted Hotchkiss gun that fired 1.36kg shells.

On 7 June 1917, a torpedo fired by U-boat SM UB 21 hit the *Sir Francis*. The ship was two miles north-east of Scarborough and the submarine remained submerged during the attack and was never observed by the steamer's crew. The torpedo detonated under the No.3 hold and the vessel immediately began to settle by the stern, so the twenty-two crewmen began to lower the ship's boats, in order to abandon ship. However, Captain C. Jeffers of the SS *Dryade*, also happened to be close to the scene, but he actually saw the submarine. He also saw UB 21 fire a second torpedo, but this time he knew it was aimed at his own vessel. Whether it was by his evasive actions, or by a stroke of luck on his behalf, the torpedo whirred past the *Dryade* by a few metres, but detonated under the bridge of the SS *Sir Francis*. Ten of her crew were killed or drowned, including the captain and the ship then sank almost at once. Other ships, including the SS *Dryade*, picked up twelve survivors, and landed them at South Shields. (Following the armistice, UB 21 was surrendered to the French and was sunk somewhere along the English East Coast in 1920, en route to being broken up.)

On 8 December 1917, Captain C. Jeffers and the *Dryade* weren't so lucky when the ship foundered off Flamborough Head, following a collision with the London-registered steamship *Upminster*. She was on passage from the Tyne for London, carrying an unspecified cargo of coal and a crew of twenty-three. It is understood that there was no loss of life and that her crew were all taken on board the SS *Upminster*.

Wreck-site
This wreck has recently been positively identified as that of the *Dryade* by the cylinder sizes and her German-built machinery, according to local diver Mike Bradley of Bridlington. She lies in a slight scour almost east to west on a seabed of sand, gravel, pebbles and small black broken shells, in a general depth of 31m, the lowest astronomical depth. The wreck is partially buried, very substantial, standing upright across the tide and broken amidships, but still around 5m high. The vessel was known to have been equipped with a brass pedestal-mounted steering helm and telegraph and had a stern-mounted steering helm, so she will be interesting to explore. The depth is also in a reasonable range for most club and sport divers. Lots of marine life has been reported, including some large cod and pollack, so the wreck should make an excellent boat-angling venue when the weather permits. Tidal streams are fairly strong and underwater visibility is usually poor to grim, however the visibility improves significantly during the summer months on neap tides and following a spell of dry settled weather. Large stinging jellyfish, probably Lion's mane, can be a nuisance during the months of July and August. Slack water occurs two hours after it does at Bridlington and local divers say there is more slack water on high tides, than low.

FOREST QUEEN
Wreck: ★★★
Depth: 32m
Reference: N53 59 812 E000 07 348
Location: 9.98 miles SE of Flamborough Head

The *Forest Queen* was an iron 446-ton British steamship that was registered at Hull. She measured 52.22m in length, by 7.49m beam with a draught of 4.01m. Henderson & Colborn & Co. built her at Renfrew in 1863 and W. Rawson & J. Robinson of Hull owned her at the time of loss. Her single iron screw propeller was powered by a 2-cylinder compound steam engine that developed 90hp using one boiler. Gilbert & Cooper at Hull built her machinery. She had one deck, four bulkheads and a superstructure consisting of a 9.7m poop deck.

On 24 February 1892, the SS *Forest Queen* was on passage from Hull for Stockton-on-Tees when she foundered following a collision with the 733-ton steamship *Loughbrow*, ten miles south-east of Flamborough Head. The SS *Loughbrow* picked up her master, but all twelve crewmen and the two passengers were drowned. The *Forest Queen* was under the command of Captain R. Lawson and carrying a cargo of railway rails and iron ore.

Wreck-site
The wreck lies on a seabed of sand, fine black-shells, pebbles and gravel, in a general depth of 32m, the lowest astronomical depth. She was positively identified recently when the ship's bell was recovered. she is now totally collapsed, well broken up and partially buried, with the highest structure standing about 1.5m. The exposed boiler stands to the port side of the wreck and furnace bricks are scattered around the site. She is a dark dive, with fairly strong tidal streams and visibility is usually very gloomy. Little marine life has been reported, but it would be expected that a few cod would be sheltering amongst the debris. For boat-angling the much larger wrecks that can be found not too far away are much better venues. The best time to visit the wreck for diving will be on a neap low tide and about 1.5-2 hours after low tide at Bridlington.

This wreck should be treated with respect, in honour of the fourteen people who died on her.

FALMOUTH, HMS
Wreck: ★★★
Depth: 16m
Reference: N53 59 295 W000 04 400
Location: 4.51 miles E of Skipsea and 7.53 miles S off
Flamborough Head

The *Falmouth* was a steel 5,250-ton British Weymouth-class cruiser that measured 131.06m in length, by 14.75m beam with a draught of 5.3m. W. Beardmore & Co. built her in 1910 and the Royal Navy owned her at the time of loss. Her twin bronze screw propellers were powered by steam turbines that developed 22,000hp using twelve Yarrow boilers. Parsons built her machinery that gave the vessel a maximum speed of 27 knots. She had an armament of eight 15.24cm guns, four that fired 1.36kg shells (3 pounders), two torpedo tubes and one 7.62cm anti-aircraft gun.

On 19 August 1916 HMS *Falmouth*, part of the 3rd Light Cruiser Squadron, was under the command of Captain J.D. Edwards RN and with 433 (other sources quote 376) crew. The warship was part of a cruiser screen protecting the North Sea Battle Fleet; however, two German Zeppelin airships were shadowing the fleet of British warships so HMS *Falmouth* left the fleet and engaged the enemy, but without success. Having lost the Zeppelins, the cruiser turned back at 4.45 p.m., to close with her consorts again. She steamed into a trap when she ran across the line of fire of SM U 66, commanded by Oberleutnant Von Bothner. The U-boat disappeared off the Dogger Bank in the North Sea during September 1917. SM U 66 fired two

HMS *Falmouth*, lost in Bridlington Bay in August 1916. *(Author's Collection)*

torpedoes at less than 1,000 yards range, both of which struck HMS *Falmouth*. They detonated on her starboard side, one at the bow and the other at the stern. The cruiser was badly damaged, but the use of a six destroyer screen protected her from any more attacks by SM U 66 and SM U 49. The destroyers used a pattern of depth charges to prevent the submarines from finishing off HMS *Falmouth* and after two hours the submarines backed off. She was then able to proceed under her own steam at 6 knots throughout the following night. Early the next morning, two tugs from Immingham took her in tow and headed for the relative safety of the Humber. However, unknown to the British Admiralty, the Germans had established a line of U-boats, running out from Flamborough Head, to intercept any shipping approaching or leaving the River Humber. Despite the screen of six destroyers, the unsuspecting HMS *Falmouth* then became an easy target for Otto Schultz in SM U 63. The U-boat was part of the line of submarines off the Humber, and she let loose two torpedoes at the cruiser. Both struck the ship and detonated, but still she refused to sink. After having been torpedoed four times without loss of life, she remained afloat for a further eight hours, until eventually sinking just over 7.5 miles south of Flamborough Head. The escorting destroyers took off all the crew, although one man, a stoker, died later from the injuries he had received in the second attack. SM U 63 survived until the end of the First World War and surrendered to the Allies..

Wreck-site
The wreck of HMS *Falmouth* was dispersed by four tons of gelignite soon after the war ended and the remains were laid low to the seabed, because she was a navigational hazard. She was fairly well salvaged and her large bronze propellers recovered. The wreck now lies almost north to south on a seabed of coarse sand, gravel and small pebbles, in a general depth of 16m, the lowest astronomical depth. She has 1m scour on the west and landward side, is totally collapsed, well broken up and barely recognisable as a ship. The steel wreckage and debris cover an extensive area of approximately 200m, with the highest parts about 3m, but is said to be a fascinating dive-site where all kinds of artefacts turn up from time to time. Explosives were reported as being used on the wreck on 19 July 1985 and in 1986 a steel plate bearing the ship's name in brass letters was discovered, but souvenir hunters damaged this. Tidal streams are reasonably strong and underwater visibility is usually very poor most of the year, but improves during the summer.

Note
The telegraph was recovered from the wreck and now has pride of place in Bridlington Harbour Museum.

MARKERSDAL, ex ELLEN JENSEN, ex HAAKON

Wreck: ★★★★
Depth: 31m
Reference: N53 57 116 E000 08 863
Location: 12.53 miles SSE of Flamborough Head

The *Markersdal* was a 1,640-ton Danish steamship that was registered at the port of Copenhagen. She had dimensions of 82.16m in length, with an 11.93m beam and a draught of 5.48m. Akties Burmeistr & Wain built her as the *Haakon* at Copenhagen in 1907 for Dampsk. Acties St Olaf, in Arendal, Norway. Her single iron screw propeller was powered by a 144hp 3-cylinder triple expansion steam engine that used two boilers. Burmeister & Wain of Copenhagen built her machinery. Her cylinders measured 45.72cm, 73.66cm and 127cm-83.82cm. Chr. Th. Boe & Son managed her until 1915.

Acties Dampsk. Selsk. of Aegir purchased the vessel in 1915, renamed her *Ellen Jensen*, with H. Jensen the manager until 1916. Akties Dampsks. Rodbyhavn at the Danish port, Rodbyhavn, took the ownership over in 1917, changed her name to *Markersdal* and A. Andersen became the new manager.

On 30 June 1917, the *Markersdal* was torpedoed and sunk off Hornsea by a U-boat, SM UC 63. The steamship was under the control of Captain N.P. Danholt and carrying a 2,500-ton cargo of coal on passage from Dunston-on-Tyne for Rouen.

The British submarine HMS E52 attacked and sank SM UC 63, on 1 November 1917.

Wreck-site

The wreck lies north-west to south-east on a seabed of sand, gravel, small black shells and mud, in a general depth of 31m, the lowest astronomical depth. She is broken into two sections, with a deep scour of almost 2m around them. The wreck sections are now rather collapsed, but the highest part, which is nearly 6m high, lies to the north. A few portholes and the majority of her most interesting equipment have been recovered from the site in recent years. If her bell has been recovered it will almost certainly have been inscribed 'Haakon 1907'. The wreck still makes an enjoyable dive and is worth adding to the boat-angling venues, because quite a few fair-sized cod have been observed, along with some juicy crustaceans. Tidal streams are very strong and underwater visibility is usually poor to grim, but improves during neap tides and the summer months following a spell of dry settled weather.

ACKLAMD

Wreck: ★★★
Depth: 48m
Reference: N53 56 632 E000 25 576
Location: 18.88 miles NE of Withernsea

The *Acklamd* was an iron 508-ton British steamship that was registered at Middlesbrough. She measured 50.49m in length, with a 7.49m beam and a draught of 4.08m. Dixon & Co. Ltd built her at Middlesbrough in 1876 and W. Rayner & Murray of Middlesbrough owned her at the time of loss. Her 68hp 2-cylinder compound steam engine that used one boiler powered a single iron screw propeller. Blair & Co. Ltd built her machinery at Stockton-on-Tees. The vessel was classed at Lloyd's as A1 and had one deck, four bulkheads, an 11.58m reinforced quarterdeck and a 6.10m forecastle.

On 6 September 1878, the SS *Acklamd* foundered and was lost with two of her crew, following a collision with the Dundee-registered steamer *Emerald*. The *Acklamd* was on passage from Drompheim for Lowestoft with a cargo of sulphur, under the command of Captain J. Hancy, carrying one passenger and a crew of fourteen.

Wreck-site

This wreck could possibly be that of the old steamer. She lies north-west to south-east, with her bows to the south, on a hard seabed of fine sand, black shells and gravel, in a general depth of 48m, the lowest astronomical depth. The wreck is collapsed and broken, but stands some 5m high amidships around her boiler and engine, which are all exposed. A large mound of iron plates, broken machinery and lengths of bent and twisted copper piping surround the engine. This is a very dark and eerie dive, where tidal streams are quite brisk and underwater visibility is usually poor, but it significantly improves during the summer months. The wreck should also make an interesting boat-angling venue when weather conditions permit, because there are sure to be some big fish on and around the site.

DANA, ex CLIVEDEN

Wreck: ★★★★
Depth: 46m
Reference: N53 56 163 E000 14 814
Location: 15.75 miles SE of Flamborough Head

The *Dana* (Official No.5240) was an iron 1,620-ton (1,127 tons net) Swedish steamship registered at the port of Norrköping. She was 78.64m long with a 10.97m beam and a draught of 4.88m. J. Blumer & Co. Ltd built her at Sunderland as the *Cliveden* in 1883 for Rederi AB Motala Ström of Sweden. A 2-cylinder compound steam engine that developed 178nhp using two 2SB 6PF boilers powered her single iron screw propeller. Her cylinders measured 81.28cm and 152.40cm-99.06cm. North Eastern Marine Engineering Co. Ltd built her machinery at Sunderland. R. Gohle, who owned her at the time of loss, purchased her and renamed her *Dana*.

On 11 November 1917, the *Dana* was on passage from Gothenburg for Hull via Kirkwall when she foundered and was lost with eight of her crew following a torpedo attack by the SM UC 47. The steamship left Gothenburg on Friday 2 November with a 688-ton cargo of iron and paper pulp and a deck-cargo of 563 standards of (sawn) timber. She was under the command of Captain A. Rasmusson and carrying a crew of twenty.

The journey across the North Sea to Kirkwall and south as far as the Tyne was undertaken in a convoy without any problems. From the Tyne, at around 11.30 a.m. on Sunday 11 November, the convoy split up. *Dana* then headed south, hugging the coastline, together with other vessels, but without an escort. It was a dark evening when they passed Flamborough Head sometime before 8 p.m., with a light fog, calm water and just little ripples and a weak wind blowing from the land. She sailed with both navigational lights and an anchor-light showing when, just a few minutes before eight, there was an almighty explosion on her port side. The ship was blown to pieces amidships as soon as the torpedo struck her. Captain Rasmusson and the first mate, Erik Johansson, were both on the bridg together with the helmsman, S. Pettersson. The three men immediately rushed down from the bridge, the captain to get the ship's papers and the first mate to watch over the lowering of the boats

The port-side boat and the jolly boat were destroyed in the explosion. Both boats were on the after deck and were buried under her deck cargo of wood, which had shifted and collapsed under the explosion. Only the starboard boat could be used, so the first mate ordered the crew to man this boat. Stoker Alex Lundvall, who at the time of the explosion was on watch in the stoke hold, must have been killed instantly. The second engineer, A. Walden, who was reading at the time of the explosion, rushed up on deck and met the first engineer and donkey-man Mr Nordqvist on the way up. Engineer Walden ran straight to the starboard boat, where Simonsson the cook, Stoker Andersson and Wenngren, the cabin boy, together with Seaman Blomgren had already taken their places. Mr Johansson and sailor Linden were standing on the deck next to Albin Jonsson, the second mate, who was lowering the front ropes, when the steamship suddenly broke in two. The bow and aft sections then both lifted high into the sky, after which the steamer slipped down in the wink of an eye. The boat, which had not been properly set loose from the ship, filled with water halfway above the waterline, but stayed in an upright position. However everyone on board was thrown into the sea. Able Seaman Blomgren was sucked down by the vortex and was never seen again, while the others clung desperately onto the half sunken boat. The mate must have died when the *Dana* broke up, after which he would have been buried under the deck cargo of wood. Linden, one of the crew who was on the bridge deck at the time of the explosion, had rushed to the main deck in an attempt to reach the boat on starboard side. The ship broke in two and sank before he could reach it and he was pulled down by the suction, but resurfaced soon after and managed to reach a piece of floating wood from the deck cargo. Henricksson, the boatswain, was also on the bridge deck near Linden and he reached the main deck, but when the ship broke up he was forced to jump into the sea. Like Linden, he was sucked under and resurfaced and reached the same piece of wood as his crew-mate. Both men paddled over to one of the life rafts and floated about for forty-nine hours before an English trawler rescued them and put them ashore at Grimsby. The explosion blew both helmsman Pettersson and the lookout-seaman Bystedt up in the air, but neither was injured. After collecting their senses, they rushed towards the front deck to board the starboard boat. Seaman Bystedt met the captain on deck who was proceeding to amidships carrying the confidential papers under his arm and he instructed Bystedt to get into the boat. It was at that moment that the steamer broke in two, so Bystedt and Pettersson, together with four other crewmen: Johansson the stoker, Lampman, Lyche and Svensson and a young cabin-boy called Sjoberg, all ran to the front-deck, where they clung to a liferaft. The raft was set loose and stayed afloat when the ship sank. Captain Rasmusson, 1st Engineer Jansson, Nordqvist the donkeyman and Larsson the steward, who were all amidships, were sucked down deep and drowned.

At 6 a.m. an English torpedo boat picked up the crew who had clung to the half sunken starboard boat; while Engineer Walden, who managed to cling to a plank of wood from the deck-cargo, was rescued by a trawler, the same one which had previously picked up the other six men. Pieces of wreckage and deck cargo were found on the beach at Bridlington the day after the incident and the body of a Swedish seaman, who was later identified as the donkeyman Erik Nordqvist, was buried at Bridlington. The convoy had carried on oblivious to the situation, because none of the other vessels had heard the explosion. The eight casualties were:

Anders Rasmussen (Captain, born 1 October 1882, a married man from Malmö)
Erik August Nathanael Johansson (First Mate, born 10 January 1891, from Karlskrona)
Albin Jonsson (Second Mate, born 15 January 1892, single, from Mjallby, Blekinge)
Efraim Jansson (Chief Engineer, born 17 September 1867, married, from Gothenburg)
Anders Olsson-Blomgren (Able Seaman, born 7 May 1865, single, from Nattraby)
Axel Viktor Lundvall (Stoker, born 1 January 1899, single, from Gothenburg)
Erik Valfrid Olsson-Nordqvist (Donkeyman, born 11 April 1884, from Solvesborg)
Karl Alfred Larsson (Steward, born 17 September 1878, from Solvesborg)
SM UC 47 was rammed, depth-charged and snk by the British patrol-boat HMS *P57*, exactly one week later, on 18 November 1917.

Wreck-site
The wreck, although not positively identified, could possibly be that of the steamer *Dana*. She lies north to south on a seabed of sand, black shells and gravel, in a general depth of 46m, the lowest astronomical depth. The wreck is quite substantial, standing 6m high amidships, where her boilers and engine are exposed. She is fairly intact, but collapsed at each side of where her superstructure once stood. Masses of non-ferrous metal can be seen amongst the collapsed iron. If her bell is recovered, it will probably be inscribed 'Cliveden 1883'. Soft corals and anemones are well established on the upper and most exposed sections and lots of fish have been observed. This wreck will make an interesting one to explore and to visit as a boat-angling venue. Tidal streams are quite strong and visibility is usually very dark and gloomy.

SM UC 39
Wreck: ★★★
Depth: 24m
Reference: N53 55 523 E000 04 562
Location: 8.43 miles E from Hornsea

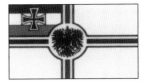

SM UC 39 was a UC11-class mine-laying submarine of the SM UC34-UC39 type, built by Blohm & Voss at Hamburg for the Imperial German Navy. She was launched on 25 June 1916 and commissioned for service on 29 October 1916 and was one of the double-hulled offshore boats, capable of being used in Atlantic waters. She had a surface displacement of 427 tons (509 tons submerged) and measured 50.35m in length. Two 300hp diesel engines powered her two bronze screw propellers, giving her a surface speed of 11.9 knots. Rows of lead-acid batteries powered her two 230hp electric motors for running submerged, which gave her a maximum speed of 6.8 knots. UC 39 had an armament consisting of one 8.8mm deck-gun, one stern and two bow torpedo tubes and six mine chutes. She also carried seven torpedoes and eighteen UC200 mines. Her normal complement was three officers and twenty-three crewmen.

Kapitänleutnant Otto Tornow was the boat's first commanding officer, followed by Oberleutnant zur See Otto Ehrentraut, who assumed command on 1 February 1917 and took the boat from Kiel to Flanders that same day, being the boat's first patrol.

On her second patrol, Otto Ehrentraut took UC 39 out into the North Sea and off the English East Coast where he sank three ships. However, on 8 February 1917, the destroyer HMS *Thrasher* sighted UC 39 while she lay stopped on the surface in the process of sinking the British steam collier *Hornsey* with gunfire (another report says *Ida*). *Thrasher* fired a volley of shells at the U-boat from some distance away, which took Ehrentraut by surprise. With shells exploding all around him and seeing the British warship thundering towards him at full speed, Ehrentraut made an emergency dive, but the U-boat left a large swirl on the surface. The destroyer ran over the position where the boat had submerged and dropped a single depth charge in an estimated position, just ahead of the swirl. The explosion badly damaged the boat and caused volumes of seawater to pour into the control room. She was then forced to surface, whence *Thrasher* immediately commenced a heavy volley of gunfire. The aim was so accurate that the first of the submarine's crew who clambered onto the casing, including Oberleutnant zur See Ehrentraut, were killed in the barrage. The destroyer's gun-crew finally ceased firing when Captain J. Souter, master of the Swedish steamship *Larsen*, appeared, bravely waving a white flag. He had been taken prisoner earlier that day after the U-boat sank his ship and emerged from the hatch on the U-boat's conning tower, in an attempt to prevent any more bloodshed. Seven of the U-boat's crew were killed, but HMS *Thrasher* rescued two British prisoners of war and seventeen of the boat's crew. Another destroyer, HMS *Itchen* was called in and took UC 39 in tow, but she sank soon afterwards. In May the same year another destroyer located the U-boat's wreck. Her divers were sent down to inspect it and found the wreck already covered in barnacles after just four months.

Wreck-site
The wreck of the U-boat lies east to west on a seabed of sand, gravel, pebbles and small broken black shells, in a general depth of 22m, the lowest astronomical depth. Graham Garner, a Leeds diver, reported that early in 2001 the wreck was sitting upright and as you swam along the casing, you could look down inside where the mines came out (probably the mine-chutes). He said he never saw the conning tower, but her forward hatch was open and shells visible inside, although everything was covered in silt. One of the hatches was lying on the seabed on the port side and the brass mechanism was missing. Brass taps, wheels and various pieces of the submarine's machinery were also lying on the seabed. Inside the boat was what appeared to be one of her telegraphs, but after further inspection it turned out to be part of the brass mechanism that operated the hydroplanes and was well bolted to the hull. Another report says

she was recently blown apart using explosives and is partially buried and difficult to find. Most of the interesting artefacts have been removed, although in 2000 divers removed a number of small copper boxes, the contents of which are not known. Her two bronze propellers have also been recovered and one of them is on display in Bridlington Harbour Museum, along with a large brass shell casing. Underwater visibility is usually poor to dismal, but improves significantly during the summer months, but tidal streams are fairly brisk. There is very little marine life on or around the wreck, but the occasional crustacean can be found. The best time to visit the wreck-site is at low water on a neap tide following a spell of dry settled weather and light westerly winds.

SNA-III, ex CLINCHFIELD, ex INTERNATIONAL

Wreck: ★★★★
Depth: 27m
Reference: N53 54 907 E000 07 568
Location: 10.20 miles E of Hornsea

The *SNA-III* was a steel 1,709-ton French steamship that was registered at the port of Le Havre. She measured 78.03m in length, with a 13.11m beam and a draught of 5.18m. The Great Lakes Engineering Works built her as the *International* in Michigan, USA, in 1915 for the River Lawrence & Coasting Services to the West Indies. Her single screw propeller, reported as bronze, was powered by an aft-positioned 3-cylinder triple expansion steam engine that used two 2SB 4CF boilers. The ship's builders built her machinery and her cylinders measured 40.64cm, 66.04cm and 114.30-43.18cm. Her name was changed to *Clinchfield* when Clinchfield Navigation Co. purchased her and Moore & McCormack Co. Inc. managed her. Later, Société Nationale d'Affrements of France, who was the owner at the time of loss, purchased the vessel and renamed her *Sna-III*.

On 26 September 1917, the *Sna III* was carrying a cargo of coal, on passage from the Tyne for Rouen when the Imperial German submarine SM UB 30 torpedoed and sank her, ten miles east of Hornsea. SM UB 30 was depth charged and sunk by Royal Navy trawlers off Whitby on 13 August 1918.

Wreck-site

The wreck lies in a north-east to south-west direction, on a seabed of sand, gravel, small pebbles and broken black shells, in a general depth of 27m, the lowest astronomical depth. She is collapsed and well broken up, with the highest section standing just over 4m high. Her propeller, said to be bronze, was reported as still being attached to the stern, but all or most of the interesting artefacts have now been removed. There are no reports of her bell being recovered to date, but if it is, it will probably be inscribed '*International* 1915'. She makes an interesting dive, with a fair amount of marine life to be seen. Large cod up to about 5 kilos have been observed, so she may well be worth considering as a boat-angling venue. Visibility is usually very poor, but significantly improves during the summers. Tidal streams are quite strong and the best time to visit the site is on a low neap tide after a spell of dry settled weather with light westerly winds.

CELTIC
Wreck: ★★
Depth: 28m
Reference: N53 54 486 E000 07 801
Location: 10.27 miles E by S of Hornsea

The *Celtic* was an iron 170-ton British steam fishing trawler registered at the port of Grimsby. She measured 32.31m in length, with a beam of 6.10m and a 3.35m draught. She was built by Earles at Hull in 1889 and owned at the time of loss by the Grimsby Steam Fishing Co. Ltd. A 3-cylinder triple expansion steam engine that used one 1SB 2CF boiler powered her single iron screw propeller. Her cylinders measured 25.40cm, 50.80cm and 81.28cm-55.88cm. (*Shipwreck Index* claims she had a 2-cylinder compound steam engine.) S. Amos at Hull built her machinery.

On 1 December 1906, the trawler was in ballast, on a return fishing voyage from Grimsby, when she sank, fifteen miles north of Spurn Point, following a collision with the Danish-registered steamship *Jagersborg*. One crewman was lost, but thirteen were rescued. Wind conditions at the time were force nine northerly.

Wreck-site
Local diver Peter Fergus positively identified the wreck when he saw the unusual steel telegraph which read 'Slow Ahead'. She is now totally collapsed, well broken up and almost level with the seabed, with very little of interest to be seen. The wreck lies on a seabed of coarse sand, small pebbles, mud and broken black shells in a general depth of 28m, the lowest astronomical tide. Very little marine life can be found on or around the wreck-site, but in early spring, the occasional lobster can be observed sheltering under the iron debris. Tidal streams are quite brisk and underwater visibility is usually very poor, but improves during the summer months.

BRITON
Wreck ★★
Depth 46m
Reference: N53 54 210 E000 21 855
Location: 15.56 miles NE from Withernsea

The *Briton* was an iron 134-ton British steam fishing trawler that was registered at Grimsby. She measured 29.33m in length, with a 6.17m beam and a draught of 3.22m. R. Dixon & Co. Ltd built her at Middlesbrough in 1891 and Mrs J. Green of Grimsby owned her as GY374 at the time of loss. A 40hp 3-cylinder triple expansion steam engine that used one boiler powered her single iron screw propeller. Westgarth, English & Co. built her machinery at Middlesbrough. She had one deck, a 6.10m quarterdeck and a 5.79m forecastle.

On 24 September 1916, the *Briton* was on a return fishing voyage from Grimsby, when she was sunk by gunfire fired from the Imperial German submarine SM U 57.

SM U 57 went on to survive the ravages of the First World War and surrendered to the Allies, to become French-reparation and was broken up at Cherbourg in 1921.

Wreck-site
The wreck, almost certainly that of the *Briton*, lies on a seabed of shingle, gravel and fine sand, in a general depth of 46m, the lowest astronomical depth. She is collapsed, partially buried, well broken up and almost level with the surrounding seabed. The highest section is her boiler and machinery, which is surrounded by a scattered mound of iron debris, intermingled with pieces of non-ferrous metal. There appears to be very little of interest to see and the marine life is conspicuous by its absence. Tidal streams are very strong and the wreck-site is very gloomy.

TOGSTON
Wreck ★★★★
Depth 29m
Reference: N53 53 999 E000 12 014
Location: 11.74 miles NE from Withernsea

The *Togston* was a steel 1,057-ton British steamship that was registered at the port of London. She measured 64.13m in length, with a 10.1m beam and a draught of 4.11m. Osbourne, Graham & Co. built her at Sunderland in 1909 and the South Metropolitan Gas Co. owned her at the time of loss. A 3-cylinder triple expansion steam engine that developed 106hp using one boiler powered her single iron screw propeller. Her cylinders measured 40.64cm, 68.58cm and 111.76cm-76.20cm, (16in, 27in and 44in-30in). Richardsons, Westgarth & Co. Ltd built her machinery at Sunderland. She had one deck, a well deck, and a superstructure consisting of a 32.92m quarterdeck, a 3.05m bridgedeck and a 6.10m forecastle. The vessel was also armed with one stern-mounted Howitzer gun that fired 1.36 kilo shells (3-pounders).

On 6 June 1915, the SS *Togston* was in a collision with the wooden 501-ton Norwegian barque *Cito*, while 12.5 miles north-east from Dimlington High Land, near Spurn Head. The *Cito* foundered and was lost, but it is understood that all of her crew were taken on board the *Togston*. However on 18 October 1917, at 7.15 p.m., the *Togston* was on passage from the Tyne for London with a 1,400-ton cargo of coal, when the Imperial German submarine UC 47 torpedoed her. The *Togston* was under the command of Captain A. Harvey and carrying a crew of eighteen. The vessel was making 8.5 knots when the torpedo detonated on the port side near to the engine room, killing five of the steamships' crew. She immediately began to sink, forcing the survivors to abandon ship by jumping into the sea, where one of the men drowned. Some of them managed to cling to an upturned lifeboat and were amazed when the U-boat surfaced close-by and asked for details of their ship. The steamer *Cadmus* was within sight of the men in the water and they watched as the submarine made off in her direction and sent a torpedo into her soon after. Survivors from the *Togston* were later picked up by the SS *Johan Siem* and landed at Middlesbrough. On 11 November UC 47 was rammed, depth-charged and sunk by the British patrol-boat HMS P57.

Wreck-site
The wreck lies orientated in a north-west to south-east direction on a seabed of fine sand, mud, gravel, small pebbles and black shells, in a general depth of 29m, the lowest astronomical depth. She is fairly substantial, but collapsed and broken up in a 1m scour, with the highest section of about 4m amidships around her boiler and engine. The wreck is still a nice dive, but most of the interesting artefacts have been removed in recent years. Tidal streams are very strong, while underwater visibility is usually poor to grim, but improves significantly during the summer months. The wreck may be worth visiting as a boat-angling venue too, because some decent-sized cod have been reported on and around her.

GAINSBOROUGH
Wreck ★★★
Depth 26.5m
Reference: N53 53 546 E000 07 540
Location: 15.7 miles SSE from Flamborough Head

The *Gainsborough* was an iron 1,081-ton three-masted British passenger steamship that was registered at Grimsby. She measured 70.45m in length, with a 9.21m beam and a draught of 5.06m. Earle's Shipbuilding Co. built her at Hull and launched her on 20 December 1880. The Manchester, Sheffield & Lincolnshire Railway Co., who ordered her in June 1880, also owned her at the time of loss. The vessel cost just £21,000 when she was built and could accommodate forty First Class passengers in the saloon and stateroom and had enough accommodation for a large number of emigrants. She was also fitted with cattle pens on deck and under deck, amidships. Her 900ihp compound inverted steam engines that used one double-ended boiler, with a working-pressure of 4.83 bar (70lb per square inch), powered a single (probably bronze) screw propeller. Her maximum speed was 12 knots. She was also equipped with a brass pedestal-mounted telegraph and one brass pedestal-mounted steering helm, plus one stern-positioned iron steering helm.

On 27 December 1883 the SS *Gainsborough* was on her regular run, on passage for Grimsby from Hamburg, when she foundered after being run down by the Sunderland-bound steamship *Wear*. The *Gainsborough* was under the command of Captain A.C. Hawkins, carrying an unspecified general cargo, seven passengers and a crew of twenty-three, all whom were picked up by the *Wear*.

Wreck-site
Although the wreck has not yet been positively identified, it is very likely that of the 120-year-old steamship *Gainsborough*. She is orientated in a north, north-west to south, south-east direction, with her bows to the south, south-east. The wreck lies on a seabed of sand, shells and gravel, in a general depth of 26.5m, the lowest astronomical depth. She is totally collapsed, well broken up and standing some 3m amidships, where her boiler and engine are now exposed. For such an old wreck, she is still fairly substantial and lots of copper and brass is visible amongst the pile of broken debris. A number of decent-sized lobsters were observed near the boiler and a large shoal of small saithe swarmed around the engine area, but nothing of a decent size.

Tidal streams area very strong and underwater visibility is usually poor most of the year.

ROCHESTER
Wreck ★★
Depth 39m
Reference: N53 53 270 E000 42 235
Location: 25.52 miles ENE from Withernsea

The *Rochester* was a steel 165-ton British steam fishing trawler that was registered at Lowestoft. She measured 31.75m in length, with a 6.4m beam and a 3.22m draught. Mackie & Thomson built her at Govan in 1898 and the Consolidated Fisheries Co. of Grimsby, who owned her at the time of loss, kept her Lowestoft registration No.LT 153. A 45hp 3-cylinder triple expansion steam engine that used one boiler powered her single iron screw propeller.

On 27 February 1944 the trawler was returning to Hull from a fishing voyage with twenty kits of fish when she detonated a German-laid mine. She foundered and was lost with one of her crew of twelve, while the survivors took to the boat.

Wreck-site
This small wreck lies on a seabed of sand, gravel and black shells, in a general depth of 39m, the lowest astronomical depth. She is now partially buried, totally collapsed, well broken up and standing 1.5m high around her boiler and engine, surrounded by battered iron and steel debris. There is very little of interest and marine life is quite conspicuous by its absence. This is rather a dark wreck-site and tidal streams are very strong, however visibility can be excellent during the summer months.

LONGBENTON
Wreck **
Depth 11m
Reference: N53 53 124 W000 00 420
Location: 5.67 miles ESE from Horsea and 13.98 miles S by E from Flamborough Head

The *Longbenton* was a steel 924-ton British steamship that was registered at Newcastle-upon-Tyne. She measured 64.21m in length, with a 9.14m beam and a draught of 4.16m. Blyth Shipbuilding Co. Ltd built her at Blyth in 1898 and Harris Brothers & Co. of Swansea owned her at the time of loss. Her single iron screw propeller was powered by a 99hp 3-cylinder triple expansion steam engine that used one 1SB 3PF boiler. Her cylinders measured 43.18cm, 71.12cm and 116.84-76.20cm, (17in, 28in and 46-30in). North East Marine Engineering Co. Ltd built her machinery at Newcastle-upon-Tyne. She had one deck, a well deck, and a super-structure consisting of a 31.39m quarterdeck, a 2.74m bridgedeck and a 6.71m forecastle.

On 27 June 1917 the *Longbenton* was making 7.5 knots on passage from Newcastle-upon-Tyne for Devonport when she was torpedoed and sunk by SM UC 63, an Imperial German submarine. Captain J. Kinley was in command of the steamer, which was carrying a 1,200-ton cargo of coal and a crew of fourteen. The track of the missile was observed moments before it detonated level with the No.2 hold at 8 p.m., but there was insufficient time for anyone to do anything about it. The entire crew managed to abandon ship safely and got away in the boats, being picked up by the Aberdeen-registered steamship *Hogarth*. The SS *Longbenton* went down by the head, just two minutes after the explosion. The British submarine HMS E52 attacked and sunk UC 63 on 1 November 1917.

The crew of the 1,231-ton steamship *Hogarth*, built by Hall, Russell & Co. in 1883 for the Aberdeen Steam Navigation Co. Ltd, were not so lucky as those of the *Longbenton*. On 7 June 1918, she was on passage from London for Aberdeen with a general cargo, when she was torpedoed and sunk by the Imperial German submarine UB 107, ten miles south of the Farne Islands. Captain D. Stephen and twenty-six crewmen were lost. Just the senior gunner managed to survive. Fortunately he happened to be in his cabin when the torpedo detonated. All he could remember was a flash and almighty explosion and he found himself clinging to some wreckage in the sea. Then he watched his ship disappear rapidly in just a few minutes. Two days later at 8.30 p.m. the exhausted, but extremely lucky, man was found by a patrol-vessel, picked up and landed at Newcastle-upon-Tyne.

Wreck-site
The wreck thought to be that of the SS *Longbenton*, is orientated in a north, north-east to south, south-west direction. She lies on a seabed of coarse sand, small pebbles and broken black shells, in a general depth of 10m, the lowest astronomical depth. The wreck is totally collapsed, well broken up and fairly dispersed, with her boiler and engine all exposed. There is a scour to the east side (seaward) and the highest part is around the boiler/engine area. Much of the wreckage is partially buried, but steel debris is strewn around. The wreck has been well dived over a number of years and very little in the way of artefacts can be found on her. She is, or was, owned by a local diver called Peter Fergus, who operates the dive-boat *Storm Drift*. Tidal streams are reasonable and it is possible to visit the site at most times, but underwater visibility is usually poor to grim, except during the summer months following a spell of dry settled weather and light westerly winds.

ELLINGTON
Wreck ★★★
Depth 27m
Reference: N53 51 632 E000 10 313
Location: 9.19 miles NE from Withersea

The *Ellington* was an iron 703-ton British steamship registered at Aberdeen. She measured 56.21m in length, with a 9.24m beam and a draught of 3.96m. D. Baxter & Co. Ltd built her at Sunderland in 1882 and J.A. Davidson Ltd owned her at the time of loss. A 2-cylinder compound stream engine that developed 95hp using one 1SB 3PF boiler powered her single iron screw propeller. Baird & Barnsley of North Shields built her machinery and her cylinders measured 60.96cm, 121.92cm-83.82cm, (24in, 48in-33in). She had one deck, four-bulkheads and a superstructure consisting of a 28.96m quarterdeck, a 5.49m bridgedeck and a 6.71m fore-castle. The vessel was armed with one stern-mounted deck-gun that fired 11.94cm (4.7in) shells.

On 16 November 1917, the *Ellington* was on passage from Leith for St Malo with a cargo of pitch when she foundered following a collision with the French steamship *Cabourg*. The *Ellington* was under the command of Captain J. Stephen and carrying a crew of sixteen, all of whom were rescued.

Wreck-site
The wreck lies orientated in a north, north-west to south, south-east direction, on a seabed of fine sand, black shells and stone, in a general depth of 27m, the lowest astronomical depth. She is now totally collapsed, well broken up and standing no more than about 2m high, with her engine and boiler exposed. Much of the wreck is level to the seabed and almost, if not all of her portholes and interesting steering and navigational equipment has been recovered. The wreck, which has been fairly well dived, was positively identified in the 1980s by divers from Humberside. Tidal streams are fairly strong and like most of this coastline the underwater visibility is often non-existent, but improves a little during the summer months.

RAGNHILD, ex CARBONIA, ex FINLAND
Wreck ★★★★
Depth 21m
Reference: N53 51 502 E000 07 008
Location: 8.29 miles NNE from Withernsea

The *Ragnhild* was a steel 1,495-ton British steamship that was registered at the port of Copenhagen. She measured 73.05m in length, with a 10.43m beam and a draught of 6.32m. Flensburger Schifbau Gesellschaft built her as the *Finland* in 1895 for Dampskibsseelskabet 'Nordsoen' and A. Christensen in Denmark managed her. Her single iron screw propeller was powered by a 3-cylinder triple expansion steam engine that developed 106hp using two boilers. Her cylinders measured 40.64cm, 66.04cm and 109.22cm-83.82cm, (16in, 26in and 43-33in). The vessel was armed for defence with a stern-mounted deck-gun that fired 6.80 kilo shells (15-pounders). In 1906 she was taken over by Dampskibssclskabcd 'Inga', managed by P.L. Fisker in Denmark and renamed *Carbonia* until 1910. Dampskibs Selsk 'Torm' purchased the vessel in 1911 and C. Kraemer of Copenhagen managed her. However, on 22 May 1917, she was taken as a prize of war by the British and renamed *Ragnhild*. Pelton Steamship Co. Ltd became the new owner and was the owner at the time of loss.

On 3 September 1917, the *Ragnhild* was on passage from Jarrow-on-Tyne for Rouen when SM UB 30 torpedoed her at 7.45 a.m. The steamship was carrying a cargo of coal and a crew of nineteen, under the command of Captain A. Schultz. An able seaman who was helmsman and on watch when she was hit and survived the sinking, said later that the captain had ordered him to put the helm hard over to starboard, because he had seen the track of the torpedo heading towards them. The chief engineer was in his bunk when the detonation took place and said later, 'seawater poured rapidly into the ship and she looked in danger of going down quickly. All the crew then rushed to the starboard lifeboat, clambered in and lowered it down, the port one having been totally smashed in the explosion'. He said, 'unfortunately the boat then capsized, drowning Captain Schulz and fourteen of the men, but him and three other survivors clung on to the upturned lifeboat. The ship, although half full of water, was still afloat, so one of the men courageously swam back to her, managed to launch the jollyboat and rescued the others'. Two hours later, at 10.15 a.m., a torpedo boat destroyer arrived at the scene and picked up the men. They took the *Ragnhild* in tow, but had no sooner got under way when the steamer sank. The four crewmen were landed at Grimsby, later that day. SM UB 30 was lost with her crew of twenty-six off Whitby on 13 August 1918, when RN trawlers depth charged and shelled her.

Wreck-site

The wreck most likely to be the *Ragnhild* is orientated in a north, north-west to south, south-east direction, with her bow to the south, south-east. She lies on a seabed of sand, black shells, gravel and mud, in a general depth of 21m, the lowest astronomical depth. She is largely intact, upright, but with her superstructures collapsed and broken and standing some 6m high from amidships to stern. The top structures are ablaze with soft corals and colourful anemones and lots of fish have been reported around the wreck-site. It would be very surprising if her bell has not been recovered, which will probably be inscribed '*Finland*' and '1895', the year she was built. This should make an excellent boat-angling venue when weather conditions permit. The vessel was equipped with a pedestal-mounted telegraph and steering helm, plus a stern-mounted steering helm and will be an interesting wreck to explore. Tidal streams are very strong and underwater visibility is usually rather poor to grim, but significantly improves during the summer months.

CADMUS

Wreck ★★★★
Scenery ★
Depth 25m
Reference: N53 50 950 E000 12 344
Location: 18.97 miles SSE from Flamborough Head and 9.32 miles NE from Withernsea

The *Cadmus* was a steel 1,879-ton British steamship that was registered at Leith. She measured 85.04m in length, with a beam of 12.21m and a draught of 5.61m. Irvines Ship Building & Dry Dock Co. Ltd built her at West Hartlepool in 1911 for J. Gaff & Co. In 1915 Christian Salvesen & Co., who owned her at the time of loss, purchased her for £44,505. Her single iron screw propeller was powered by a 3-cylinder triple expansion steam engine that developed 175hp using two boilers. Richardson Westgarth & Co. built her machinery.

At 8.40 p.m. on 18 October 1917, the *Cadmus* was torpedoed and sunk by the Imperial German U-boat SM UC 47. Under the command of Captain M. Morilla, the SS *Cadmus* was on passage from Dunkirk for Blyth after picking up a valuable 900-ton cargo of empty brass shell cases for recycling from the Western Front. Before firing the torpedo, the U-boat had shadowed the steamer for some time and on a parallel course without navigation lights. Some of the crew actually saw the wake of the approaching missile. However, there was insufficient time to take evasive action before it detonated in the No.2 hold. The explosion caused such a massive hole below the waterline that the steamship immediately settled to port and started to sink. Her crew of twenty-two at once abandoned ship in the two boats and sat watching their vessel go down in just ten minutes following the explosion. The enemy-raider surfaced and stayed in the vicinity for a further twenty-five minutes, but made no further effort to bother the survivors. Luckily weather conditions were reasonable and the crew in the master's boat were picked up off Spurn and landed at Immingham. The other boat carrying the mate was picked up by a patrol-boat and landed at Grimsby.

The SS *Cadmus* was insured under the Government's war risk scheme and Christian Salvesen received £93,000 for her, making a profit of £48,495 from her loss. SM UC 47 was later rammed and sunk off Flamborough Head on 18 November 1917.

Footnote

Christian Salvesen & Co. was quite a large company that also indulged in whaling, to a large extent, even until fairly recent times. They regularly rejuvenated their mercantile fleet by buying many more vessels, before and during the Great War of 1914–1918, because high profits were possible. During the First World War twenty-one vessels were purchased, and by January 1918 the average age of the fleet had been reduced to eight years. With many of their ships falling victim to the German U-boat scourge, there was a need to replace many of them. One of the first vessels to go down as a result of the U-boats was the SS *Glitra*. Salvesen's next loss was the SS *Ailsa*, sunk by a U-boat off Bell Rock in June 1915. Then, on 12 March 1917, the SS *Marna* was torpedoed and sunk, without loss of life, while on passage from Leith for Norway. A German surface-raider shelled and sunk Salvesen's steamship *Katherine*, just outside the River Plate Estuary, in February 1917, but her crew were all captured and taken back to Germany for internment. It was that year that the Germans intensified their U-boat campaign, which resulted in the loss of the SS *Coronda*. She was torpedoed some 300 miles west of Ireland, while bound for South Georgia with a cargo of general goods and barrels. Unfortunately the barrels may have been indirectly responsible for the lives of five of her crew when many of the barrels were washed clear off the SS *Coronda'* decks. The U-boat commander thought there was something suspicious about the objects floating around close to the men in the water, so he immediately dived and left the men to fend for themselves, hence five of them were lost, although twenty survivors were picked up and landed at Halifax in Nova Scotia. In May 1917 the SS *Fernley*, purchased by Salversen in 1915 and requisitioned by The Shipping Controller, was torpedoed off Ireland, but was successfully towed into Queenstown without any casualties. The SS *Cadmus*, purchased in 1915, was the next to go on 18 October 1917. Two more of the company's requisitioned ships were sunk in 1918. The first of them was the SS *Ardandearg*, which was torpedoed and lost in the Mediterranean sometime in March. The captain of the SS *Ardandearg* had taken the lead-weighted covers off the secret Codebooks to make them lighter for removal and had forgotten about them when the torpedo detonated against his ship, causing it to lurch from side to side. Believing she was going to go down, he rushed to abandon ship, but then remembered about the wartime codebooks and went back to collect them. Unfortunately, without warning, the steamship suddenly reared up and plunged headlong into the depths, taking the master with her.

In August 1917 and just some six months before the SS *Ardandearg* sank, her captain then was John Begg. The time was 1.16 p.m. when the crew sighted the periscope of a German submarine about 1,000 yards (914.4m) on the starboard beam. Expecting the worst, the helm was immediately put hard to port and a torpedo that had been fired just missed the vessel by a few yards. The submarine then dived and came up 2,000 yards (1,828.80m) astern of the steamer. Both vessels then opened fire with their deck-guns, with the submarine firing one round and the steamship seven. After the third shot from the steamer, smoke boxes were put over. The sixth round from the SS *Ardandearg* was a direct hit, detonating on the U-boat's conning tower, whereupon the submarine dived and was never seen again. For his part in this gallant action, Captain Begg was awarded the D.S.C. and the gun layer, Leading Seaman W. Jennings, received the DSM.

Captain Begg also received Lloyd's Silver Medal for Meritorious Services, the V.C. of the Merchant Navy, and he was commended in the London Gazette for his actions on 1 May 1918. On that occasion he was master of the SS *Ravenstone*, a requisitioned vessel taken over by The Shipping Controller in 1915, which had been fitted out as a 'Q' ship with a Royal Navy crew on board, as a vessel used as a decoy for U-boats. She was also under the management of Christian Salvesen & Co. with Captain Begg in command. At a later date she went back into commerce. Begg and his crew caught a U-boat by surprise and the SS *Ravenstone'* armaments so heavily damaged the submarine's hull that it made off as quickly as it could go, much to the joy of the steamer's crew.

Most of the ships that were lost were insured under the Government's war-risk scheme, but Salvesen's were not happy about the compensation paid, which was based upon the estimated future earnings, at requisitioned rates. However, Christian Salvesen & Co. appears to have made a fortune out of the loss and even sale of vessels during the First World War. As an example: the SS *Ardandearg* was purchased for £61,500 and £77,500 was paid out when she was lost. SS *Katherine* was bought for £33,000 and they received £80,000, SS *Cadmus* cost £44,505 and the company was paid £93,000. As the war went on and more ships were lost, inflation increased with supply and demand and Christian Salvesen & Co. took advantage of the situation by disposing of some of their old vessels. The SS *Giralda*, which was purchased in 1893 for £9,180 was sold for the grand sum of £33,000 in 1917. The SS *Alharna* was bought for £37,375 on 25 January 1915 and sold to another company eight days later, after never entering service, for an extra £5,125. The SS *Fernley* cost £40,000 in April 1915 and Salvesen & Co. sold her in June 1918 for £83,500.

Finally, many of the Salvesen family served in the armed forces during the Great War and Thomas Salvesen, one of the partners of the company, lost two of his sons. His oldest son Christian, named after his grandfather, was killed in a train crash at Gretna in Scotland while on his way to Gallipoli and his second son Eric was killed in France in April 1917. To honour his sons, Thomas gave £1,000 towards the erection of two homes for Scottish war veterans. The family also gave Christian's house in Trinity to the Royal Navy Benevolent Fund as a home for orphans, but during the war it was used as a convalescent hospital for wounded troops.

Wreck-site

The wreck lies orientated in a north-east to south-west direction, on a seabed of fine sand, small black shells and stones, in a general depth of 25m, the lowest astronomical depth. She has been commercially salvaged in recent times, but much of her cargo, which includes boxes of live shells and empty 8.16 kilos (18lb) shells are still scattered around. Locally she is now referred to as 'the shell-case-supermarket', but local divers ration themselves to two shells per person. There is so much of the cargo left, that at one time, the authorities considered declaring her a prohibited site to sport-divers. Large amounts of the wreck are now partially buried and the upper structures are collapsed and broken. She is lying in two halves near the boiler and engines, and large loose coils of steel wire, empty shell cases and other debris lie between the two major sections. A spare propeller lies aft of the boiler. The hold still contains many complete boxes of shell cases in good condition and only recently the ship's compass was recovered among the shell cases. Fair numbers of cod have been observed and it is not unusual to encounter 3 kilo lobsters amongst the steel debris. Tidal streams are very strong and underwater visibility poor to grim on average, but improve during the summer months, especially on neap tides after a spell of dry settled weather.

MEMBLAND
Wreck ★★★★
Depth 37m
Reference: N53 50 926 E000 29 211
Location: 17.50 miles NE by E from Withernsea

The *Membland* was a 3,027-ton British steamship that was registered at West Hartlepool. Her dimensions measured: 100.68m in length, with a 14.35m beam and a draught of 6.8m.

William Gray & Co. Ltd built her at West Hartlepool in 1900 and Macbeth & Co. (Pyman Steamship Co. Ltd) owned her at the time of loss. Her single iron screw propeller was powered by a 3-cylinder triple expansion steam engine that developed 262hp using two boilers, which gave a maximum speed of 10 knots. Central Marine Engineering Works Ltd at West Hartlepool built the machinery. She had one deck, five bulkheads and a superstructure consisting of an 8.23m poop deck, a 25.60m bridgedeck and a 9.75m forecastle.

The SS *Membland* left Hull at 8 a.m. on 15 February 1915, in ballast and on passage for the Tyne, but when she disappeared between Spurn Head and Flamborough Head, it was presumed she had been mined. She was under the command of Captain Brochie and carrying a crew of twenty, all of who were lost.

On the night of 25/26 August 1914, in the area limited by N53 50 to N53 40 and E00 33 to E00 38, SMS *Nautilus*, an Imperial German Navy minelayer, laid a minefield and it is most probable that the *Membland* detonated one of those.

Wreck-site
There is a large 'unknown' wreck lying 17.50 miles north by north-east from Spurn Point, which could possibly be this large steamship that has never been located, to date. The wreck lies on a seabed of fine sand, black broken shells, coarse sand, pebbles and gravel, in a general depth of 37m, the lowest astronomical depth. She is very substantial, standing 6m high from amidships to stern, but with the upper structure collapsed and broken. A colourful array of anemones and soft corals adorn the most exposed parts and a large shoal of pout whiting swarm over the top of the wreck. This site should make an excellent boat-angling venue, although she is a long way from shore. A point to remember is that twenty crewmen were lost with this ship, so her remains should be treated with the utmost respect. Tidal streams are very strong, but the underwater visibility is reasonably good during the summer months.

EARL OF BEACONSFIELD, ex CUBA
Wreck ★★
Depth 2m
Reference: N53 49 107 W000 03 768
Location: Near Aldbrough, 400m offshore

The *Earl of Beaconsfield* was an iron 2,488-ton four-masted sailing barque that measured 103.02m in length, with a 12.80m beam and a draught of 8.23m. Todd & McGregor built her as an auxiliary steam-powered sailing barque and launched her as the *Cuba* at Glasgow in 1864 for the Cunard Line. Her single iron screw propeller was powered by an auxiliary 2-cylinder compound steam engine. However, D. Brown of London purchased the vessel in 1882 and had the propeller and part of her steam engine removed, but kept the donkey-engine/boiler to operate lifting/lowering equipment. The Earl of Beaconsfield Shipping Co. of London, who owned her at the time of loss, renamed her *Earl of Beaconsfield*.

On 6 November 1887, the four-masted, squared-rigged vessel was on passage from Hull for Calcutta with a cargo of grain when, in dense fog, she ran aground a quarter-mile offshore near Aldbrough and six miles north of Withernsea. A passing fishing-smack sighted the distressed vessel and sent its small boat ashore to alert the authorities to the problem and the company's agent in Hull was then sent a telegram. Several small boats immediately put out to the stranded vessel, but on arrival they found the ship's master in the process of dumping her cargo over the side, using the lifting gear operated by the donkey engine. By the fourth day, three tugs had arrived and efforts were made to pull her clear of the sand, but the wind had increased to a strong easterly. The large sailing barque was going nowhere, except further inshore, driven by the elements. The master finally fired his rockets and local pulling/rowing lifeboats took off her crew of twenty-seven and the vessel was then abandoned. The hull soon flooded and she broke up and became a total wreck.

Wreck-site

It is said that it would be possible to dive this wreck from the shore, but access to this part of the beach via the cliffs is an almost impossible task, especially humping heavy diving equipment. The wreck is, as would be expected, totally collapsed, well broken up and rather dispersed, about 400m offshore, although parts of her are still dry on a low spring tide. A few portholes have been recovered in recent years, but there are no reports of her bell ever having been recovered, which will probably be inscribed '*Cuba*' and '1864', the date she was built. There is not really a lot left of her to see, but she makes a nice novice dive when weather conditions permit. Tidal streams are reasonable, but underwater visibility is usually rather poor to non-existent most of the year. However, visibility improves significantly during the summer months on neap tides, following a spell of dry settled weather and light westerly winds.

C29, HM Submarine
Wreck ★★★★
Depth 36m
Reference: N53 48 790 E01 06 030
Also given: N53 58 750 E001 23 786 (Hydrographic position)
Location: 37 miles ENE from Spurn Head

HM Submarine C29 was a Type 'C' Class British coastal submarine of the Group-2 design. She measured 43.59m in length, with a 4.11m beam and a 3.51m draught. Vickers built her at Barrow-in-Furness in 1909 for the Royal Navy, who owned her at the time of loss. She had a surface displacement of 290 tons and 321 tons submerged. A 600hp 16-cylinder Vickers petrol engine powered her single bronze screw on the surface, which gave a maximum speed of 12 knots. Rows of lead/acid batteries powered her 200hp electric motor for running submerged and gave her a maximum speed of 6.5 knots. She carried 15 ½ tons of fuel/petrol, giving her a range of 740 nautical miles at 12 knots on the surface, or a range of 1,000 nautical miles at 8.7 knots and an endurance of ten days. Her armament consisted of two 45.72cm (18in) torpedo tubes. She had a normal complement of two officers and fourteen ratings. The 'C' Class submarine represented the final development of the original Holland class of boat. The 'C' Class was the last to be equipped with petrol engines, while the Group-Two of the class were also the first British submarines, twenty in all, to be designed with forward hydroplanes. Group-Two boats were built at two yards: Vickers at Barrow-in-Furness between 1908 and 1910 and HM Naval Dockyard at Chatham between 1908 and 1909. The boats operated extensively throughout the First World War from East Coast ports or from Dover. Out of the total of thirty-eight 'C' Class boats built, thirteen were lost.

HM Submarines in port at Dundee Naval Base, 1912. *(Courtesy Richard Driuer Collection, USA)*

British Submarines C28 and C29 at Dundee Naval Base 1912.

HM Submarine C29 was part of the 8th Flotilla, based at Harwich. She was part of a trawler-submarine team set up to trick U-boats into thinking the trawler was by herself and an easy target, a kind of Q-ship duet. The submarine was trimmed down so that her deck casing was awash, while being towed by a disguised trawler. Then when an enemy vessel was sighted, the tow was slipped and the submarine would go in for the kill, catching the German U-boat, or any other enemy vessel by surprise.

On 29 August 1915, the disguised trawler *Ariadine* was towing HMS C29 when she inadvertently strayed into a minefield. Unfortunately the submarine, which was in telephone contact with the trawler at the time, detonated one of the mines. She blew up and was lost in seconds with her crew of sixteen, including her commander, Lt W.R. Schofield RN. This system of trawler-submarine ploy was discontinued soon after this accident.

Wreck-site

The wreck lies on a seabed of sand, gravel and small pebbles, in a general depth of 36m. She is largely intact, but the casing is beginning to corrode allowing the engine-cylinders to be observed through holes which have appeared in it. Her bronze propeller is still in place and the rear fins are reported to be like a 1950s Dan Dare Rocket. The conning tower, which has been pulled off to starboard, probably by a trawler, makes the hull look like a rocket. The bow section brings home the reality of what happened on that fateful day, when she detonated a mine which blew her to bits. The fore end on the upper side, just behind the hydroplanes, is blown open. The hydroplanes are missing but some of the gearing is present, situated on the upper side of the hull, (all heavy bronze shafts and gears.) What these gears were, and their position on the upper side of the vessel, confused the diving party until they looked at a sectional line drawing of this class of boat. The gearing and the position they observed was as shown on the drawing in the upper structure above the main pressure hull and served the front hydroplanes. All gears were stamped with the broad arrow. The forward torpedoes were exposed and directly under them when looking at the hydroplane gearing. Two torpedo tubes still contain corroded weapons, making this not a very safe place to be in. You can look inside the hull, but it would be a very tight squeeze. However this is a classified war grave and should be treated with the utmost respect. Tidal streams are very strong and confused, but underwater visibility can be a staggering 25m at times.

PARACIERS, Ex TIDJITT, ex SYRA, ex HALIFAX CITY, ex SYRACUSA, ex JOHN COCKERILL
Wreck ★★★★
Depth 18m
Reference: N53 45 377 E000 12 591
Location: 6.35 miles ENE from Withernsea

The *Paraciers* was a steel 2,634-ton French steamship that was registered at Boulogne. She measured 97.84m in length, with a 12.25m beam and a draught of 7.22m. Soc. Anon. John Cockerill, Hoboken, Antwerp built her as the *John Cockerill* in 1895 at the Seraing Plant. Her single iron screw propeller was powered by an 825nhp 3-cylinder triple expansion steam engine that used two boilers. Her cylinders measured 68.58cm, 111.76cm and 177.80cm-111.76cm, (27in, 44in and 70in-44in). In 1900-1901, she was sold to Robert M. Sloman & Co. of Hamburg who renamed her *Syracusa* until 1903 when Damfschiffs-Rhederei 'Union', Hamburg, took over. She was later sold to Grofbritannien and renamed *Halifax City* in 1906 and *Syra* in 1911. She was sold to France-Mostagnemoise d'Armement and registered as the *Tijditt* at Mostaganem in France in 1915-1916. Soc. Anon. des Acieries de Paris & d'Outreau in France, who owned her at the time of loss, later bought her and renamed her *Paraciers*.

On 17 September 1917, this French steamship was on passage from Newcastle-upon-Tyne for Boulogne with an unspecified cargo of coal when she was torpedoed and sunk by SM UC 64, a submarine of the Kaiserliche Deutschen Marine.

On 20 June 1918, UC 64 was lost when she was depth-charged by Royal Navy vessels, after she had detonated a mine in the Straight of Dover.

Wreck-site
The wreck is orientated in a north-west to south-east direction, lying on a seabed of sand, black shells, pebbles and short weed. She is on her side with the bows facing north, in a general depth of 18m, the lowest astronomical depth. The wreck is now totally collapsed and well broken up, with the highest section standing no more than some 3m at the stern. A few bent and flattened copper pipes are visible, but most of the interesting artefacts will probably have long since gone. Steel plating and broken machinery litter the site, but it is still an interesting dive, where anything could turn up. There are no reports of the ship's bell being recovered and it will probably be inscribed '*John Cockerill*' and '1895', the date she was built. However, it is possible that the bell was changed at some time or other, with the vessel having so many names! Fair numbers of crustaceans can be found hiding amongst the debris, particularly during the early months of spring. Visibility is usually very poor to grim, but vastly improves during the summer months, while tidal streams are mostly very strong and she is best dived at low slack water.

LISMORE
Wreck ★★★
Depth 30m
Reference: N53 45 312 E000 32 216
Location: 18.76 miles NE by E from Spurn Point

The *Lismore* was a ketch-rigged iron 198-ton (178 under-deck tons) British steam fishing trawler that was registered at the port of Grimsby. She measured 34.29m in length, with a 6.40m beam and a draught of 3.48m. In 1900 Cochrane & Cooper built her in seven months at Selby for Lindsey Steam Fishing Co. Ltd of Grimsby, who owned her at the time of loss, and E. Bacon managed the boat. Her single iron screw propeller was powered by a 3-cylinder triple expansion steam engine that developed 55rhp using one single-ended boiler. There were two corrugated furnaces, a grate surface of 73.66cm (29in) and a heating surface of 23.37m (920in). Her cylinders measured 30.48cm, 50.17cm and 81.28cm-58.42cm, (12in, 19.75in and 32in-23in). Charles D. Holmes & Co. built her machinery at Hull. She had one deck, four bulkheads cemented, a 14.63m quarterdeck, a 6.71m forecastle, a bar-keel of 19.05cm (7.5in) and a moulded depth of 3.73m (12.25ft). A special survey was carried out at Grimsby as a steam trawler in December 1903.

On 11 May 1907, the *Lismore* was in ballast on a return fishing voyage from Grimsby when she foundered and was lost following a collision with the Norwegian steamer *Eva*. She was carrying a crew of nine who, it is understood, were picked up by the steamship. Wind conditions at the time were south, south-east force one, with a dense fog enveloping the coast.

Wreck-site

The wreck thought to be that of the trawler, lies on a seabed of pebbles, small black shells, sand and gravel, in a general depth of 30m, the lowest astronomical depth. She is totally collapsed, well broken up and standing 2.5m high amidships, around her boiler and engine. A partially buried mound of iron debris, broken machinery and bits of non-ferrous piping, surrounds these. The whole outline of the wreck can be made out, but there appears to be little of interest, except for one or two crustaceans. Tidal streams are very strong, but underwater visibility is usually rather good, especially during neap tides during the summer months, when visibility can reach as much as 15-20m at times.

MODIVA

Wreck ★★★
Depth 19m
Reference: N53 45 182 E000 17 833
Location: 9.37 miles E from Withernsea

The *Modiva* was a steel 1,276-ton Norwegian steamship that was registered at Christiania, which is now Oslo. She measured 69.85m in length, with a 10.79m beam and a draught of 4.47m. Antwerp Engineering Co. Ltd of Hoboken built her in 1911 and A/S Modiva owned her at the time of loss. Her single iron screw propeller was powered by a 3-cylinder triple expansion steam engine that developed 142hp using one 1SB 3CF boiler. Her cylinders measured 43.18cm, 71.12cm 116.84cm-58.42cm, (17in, 28in, 46in-23in).

On 31 January 1917, the SS *Modiva* foundered east from Withernsea after detonating a mine placed by the Imperial German submarine SM UC 47. The steamer was under the command of Captain F. Arentz, carrying an unspecified cargo of coal, on passage from Hartlepool for Rouen. SM UC 47 was later rammed and sunk by HMS P57 on 18 November 1917.

Wreck-site

Local divers positively identified the wreck during the summer of 1986. She lies in a north-west to south-east direction, on a seabed of coarse sand, broken black shells and small pebbles, in a general depth of 19m, the lowest astronomical depth. The wreck is totally collapsed, well broken up and partially buried, with her boiler, engine and donkey boiler exposed and surrounded by a mass of broken debris. A spare propeller lies just aft of the engine and two stockless anchors are (or were) reported visible at the bow section. The propeller shaft is prominent and leads right up to the stern, with steel plating, ribs and girders strewn all around. Very few artefacts can be seen, but a number of crustaceans can be found early in the summer months. The wreck still makes an interesting dive-site, in a depth suited to most sport-divers. However tidal streams are fairly strong and underwater visibility is usually very poor to grim, though the visibility improves during the middle of the summer months. Apart from the occasional small codling that has been observed, the wreck has not much scope as a boat-angling venue.

EMPRESS, ex CADIZ, ex EMPRESS
Wreck ★★★
Depth 16m
Reference: N53 45 157 E000 09 242
Location: 4.42 miles ESE from Withernsea

The *Empress* was a 2,914-ton steel British steamship that was registered at Cardiff. She measured 95.7m in length, with a 12.31m beam and a draught of 6.5m. Furness, Withy & Co. Ltd of West Hartlepool built her as the *Empress* in 1893 for the Imperial Steamship Co. Ltd in West Hartlepool and Sivewright, Bacon & Co., also of West Hartlepool, managed her. A 3-cylinder triple expansion steam engine that developed 249hp using two 2SB 6CF boilers powered her single iron screw propeller, which gave her a maximum speed of 9 knots. Her cylinders measured 53.34cm, 96.52cm and 157.48cm-106.68cm, (21in, 38in and 62-42in). T. Richardson built her machinery at Hartlepool. The vessel was armed with one stern-mounted deck-gun that fired 5.90 kilo shells (13 pounders). She had one deck, six bulkheads and a super-structure consisting of a 39.93m quarterdeck. In 1900, the vessel was sold to another company and she was renamed *Cadiz*. Between 1906 and 1911, the ship was owned by the Ogmore Steamship (1899) Co. Ltd and G. Chitham of Cardiff managed her. Amaryllis Shipping Co. Ltd of Newcastle-upon-Tyne, who was the owner at the time of loss, purchased her in 1912 and changed her name back to *Empress*.

At 5 a.m. on 31 July 1917, the *Empress* was on passage from the Tyne for Southend-on-Sea when she detonated a mine laid by the Imperial German submarine SM UC 63. The steamship was on Italian government service, carrying a 3,760-ton cargo of coal and a crew of twenty-six, under the command of Captain A. Armstrong. Being in imminent danger of going down, the mixed cosmopolitan crew abandoned ship in the boats, but one boat was smashed while being lowered and another capsized, drowning five of its occupants. The rest of the crew, which consisted of two Swedish men, one Russian, three Norwegians, one Portugese, one Spaniard, one Dane, one Dutchman, fourteen British citizens and two Argentinians were picked up by a patrol vessel and landed at Grimsby. The *Empress* went down at 5.30 a.m., taking most of the confidential papers with her, however Captain Armstrong, who was among the survivors, managed to save the ship's secret sailing orders. Although she was an Italian vessel, the British government was responsible to the ship's owners for war-risk insurance, which was duly paid out. A British submarine near the Goodwin Sands sank SM UC 63 on 1 November, later that year.

Wreck-site
When the ship went down, she stood for quite a time with both of her two masts showing above the surface. However, the wreck is now totally collapsed, partially buried, well broken up and rather dispersed, with the highest parts being no more than about 2.5m. She lies on an undulating seabed of coarse sand, small black shells and pebbles, in a general depth of 16m, the lowest astronomical tide. Very few of the vessel's interesting equipment still remain to be found, but early in the summer months the debris of the wreck-site attracts a number of decent crus-taceans. If her bell were to be recovered, it will be inscribed '*Empress*' and '1893', the date she was built. Visibility is usually very poor; however, during neap tides and following a spell of light westerly winds, this significantly improves. Tidal streams are quite brisk.

GEORGIOS ANTIPPA, ex ELPINIKI, ex PRINS WILLEM III
Wreck ★★★
Scenery ★
Depth 17m
Reference: N53 44 933 E000 12 412
Location: 6.20 miles E from Withernsea

The *Georgios Antippa* was a steel 1,951-ton Greek steamship that measured 80.89m in length, with a 10.85m beam and a draught of 6.37m. Nederlandssche Stoomboot Maatschappij in Rotterdam built her as the *Prins Willem III* in 1890 for the Dutch company N.V. Koninklijke West-Indische Maildienst, which was put under direction of the Dutch K.N.S.M. in 1912, (a lot of the ships were called after Dutch Royalty). A 3-cylinder triple expansion steam engine that used two boilers powered her single iron screw, which gave her a maximum speed of 10 knots. In 1909 she was fitted with a new double boiler and her cylinders sizes measured 55.88cm, 86.36cm and 142.24cm-101.60cm, (22in, 34in and 56-40in). The machinery was built by 242 NPK and she carried forty-two passengers. Calling signal was PQRT and, for protection, she was armed with a large machine-gun amidships and one 90mm (3.54in) breech-loading cannon forward. She was sold in 1913 to Achaia Steamship Co. in Piraeus, Greece, and renamed *Elpiniki*. In 1916 the vessel was purchased by S.G. Antippa in Argostoli, Greece, and renamed *Georgios Antippa*. However, in March 1917 she was confiscated by the British and put under management of the British company Cairns Noble & Co. of Newcastle-upon-Tyne.

There was some confusion over the details of this vessel and after much research, it turns out that there were two vessels of that name built around the same time! The other boat was Georgios Antippa, *a 3,188-ton Greek steamship that was registered at the port of Piraeus and measured 103.63m in length, with a 13.84m beam and a draught of 7.13m. William Doxford & Sons Ltd built her as the* Progressist *at Sunderland in 1894 for the Angier Line (1887) Ltd, London. J. Holman & Sons in London purchased her in 1898 and renamed her* Beltor. *In 1900 she was sold to Manar Steamship Co. Ltd and was managed by Moody & Lyngaas, Newcastle. Resold to R.H. Holman in 1912, Antippa Freres (Bros) of Piraeus, Greece, purchased her in 1913 and changed the vessel's name to* Georgios Antippa. *She was sold again in 1916 to A.B. Aaby in Norway and renamed* Drammenseren. *In 1917, she was taken over by the British government and managed by the Shipping Controller, then placed under the management of Yeoward Brothers. She returned to E.B. Aaby in 1918. In 1923 she was sold to Schroder, Holken & Fischer in Germany and renamed* Jacob Schroder.*

She had a 300hp 3-cylinder triple expansion steam engine that used three boilers, had two decks, three masts and an unusual turret deck. This ship was also armed with one stern-mounted deck-gun that fired 8.16 kilo (18lb) shells). The vessel was broken up in 1925.

On 28 November 1917, the *Georgios Antippa* most probably detonated a possible British-laid mine and sank, while on passage from Sunderland for Rouen. Most references to the ship say an Imperial German submarine torpedoed her, but U-boat records don't show her as being torpedoed! The steamship was carrying an unspecified cargo of coal and a crew of twenty-seven, under the command of Captain N.T. Phocas. At 1.50 p.m. a violent explosion occurred between the fore-rigging and the boiler-room, causing the vessel to list and settle almost immediately. All of the crew, except the captain, managed to abandon ship in the boats. The captain, being the last to leave, had to leap into the sea as his ship went down, just seven minutes after the explosion. One of the ship's boats picked up the captain, while the Spanish-registered steamship *Astondo Mendi* rescued the rest of the crew and landed them at Grimsby later that day. The Wartime Codebooks and confidential papers were lost with the ship, which was operating under the British flag when she was sunk.

Wreck-site

The wreck, believed to be that of the steamship *Georgios Antippa,* is orientated in a north, north-west to south, south-east direction, with her bows to the north, north-west. She lies in a small scour, on a seabed of coarse sand, broken black shells and small pebbles, in a general depth of 17m, at the lowest astronomical tide. The wreck is reported to be just over 6m high, but broken in two halves, with her boilers and engine exposed and surrounded by mounds of broken steel debris. She is still quite substantial but most, if not all, of the interesting navigation and steering equipment has been removed in recent years. It is likely that if her bell is recovered, the inscription will be: '*Prins Willem III.* 1890', the date she was built. Underwater visibility on the wreck-site is usually very poor to grim, but it significantly improves during the summer months. She can be dived at most states of the tide, but the best time is on a low neap tide, after a spell of dry settled weather and westerly winds. Tidal streams are very brisk during spring tides.

LYRA
Wreck ★★
Depth 13m
Reference: N53 44 913 E000 07 321
Location: 3.20 miles ESE from Withersea

The *Lyra* was a steel 1,141-ton Norwegian steamship that measured 72.42m in length, with an 11.06m beam and a 5.06m draught. Afties Moss Voerft built her in 1917 and C.T. Gogstad & Co. owned her at the time of loss. Her single iron screw propeller was powered by a 3-cylinder triple expansion steam engine that developed 97nhp using one boiler. Her cylinders measured 40.64cm, 63.50cm and 106.68cm-76.20cm, (16in, 25in and 42-30in).

On 4 November 1917 the SS *Lyra* foundered and was lost with her crew after she detonated a mine, laid by the Imperial German submarine SM UC 63. The steamship was on passage from Skien for Rouen with an unspecified cargo of nitrate of soda and aluminium ingots.

SM UC 63 had already met her end three days earlier, when a British submarine torpedoed and sank her on 1 November 1917.

Wreck-site

The wreck, which was positively identified by a local diver, is now totally collapsed, well broken up and rather dispersed. She lies on a seabed of coarse sand and small pebbles, in a general depth of 13m, the lowest astronomical depth. Much of the wreck is partially buried and about all that remains of her is the boiler and engine, with a few bits of scattered debris. Evidence of her cargo of aluminium ingots, some of which have turned into a mushy white and black substance, can be seen scattered over the seabed. Tidal streams are moderate, but visibility is usually poor, improving during the summer months, following a spell of dry settled weather and on neap tides. Very little marine life can be seen around the wreck-site, except for a few small resident saithe (a member of the cod family).

CORINTH
Wreck ★★★★★
Depth 20m
Reference: N53 44 794 E000 15 940
Location: 8.18 miles E from Withernsea

The *Corinth* was a steel 3,669-ton British steamship that was registered at Liverpool. She measured 105.58m in length, with a 15.44m beam and draught of 7.01m. J.L. Thompson & Sons Ltd built her at Sunderland in 1904 and the Corinthian Shipping Co. Ltd of Liverpool owned her at the time of loss. A 3-cylinder triple expansion steam engine that developed 307hp using two 2SB 8PF boilers powered her single iron screw propeller. Her cylinders measured 60.96cm, 101.60cm and 167.64cm, (24in, 40in and 66in). This vessel was equipped with a stern-positioned iron steering helm, plus a brass pedestal-mounted steering helm and brass pedestal-mounted telegraph in the wheelhouse.

On 12 November 1916 the *Corinth* was on passage from Blyth for Rochfort with a 5,500-ton cargo of coal when the Imperial German submarine SM UB 39 surfaced close alongside her. The *Corinth* was under the command of Captain J. Reed and carrying a crew of twenty-six. The U-boat fired a single shot at the steamer from her deck-gun. Captain Reed altered course for the shore and sounded his ship's siren with three long blasts, however the submarine fired a second direct shot and hit the steamer. When more shells were fired at her and one hit the foremast, Captain Reed stopped his engines and ordered the ship's boats lowered. However, while they were abandoning ship, more shells rained down on her, with one causing a direct hit on the bridge derrick. The crew got safely away and watched the U-boat's crew use one of their ship's boats to board the steamer. They then pillaged the vessel of food, clocks, clothing, brass and copper, lamps, boots and even the knives and forks, before hanging explosive charges over the ship's side, causing her to sink. The U-boat crew had just re-boarded their boat when a Royal Navy destroyer appeared on the scene, forcing the U-boat to make a hasty retreat. The destroyer picked up the survivors and landed them at Grimsby.

SM UB 39 disappeared in the English Channel on 14-15 May 1917. It was believed that she had detonated a mine and was lost with her crew of twenty-four.

Wreck-site

The wreck that is thought to be that of the *Corinth* is orientated in a north-east to south-west direction (045/225 degrees). She lies on a seabed of coarse sand, black shells, small pebbles and gravel, in a general depth of 20m, the lowest astronomical depth. The wreck is very substantial and covers an area of some 200m. She lies in a half metre scour, is broken into three main sections, with the highest part, 5.7m, being around amidships where one of her boilers is exposed. There are fair amounts of copper piping with brass flanges attached and brass junction-valves to be seen in amongst the mound of debris towards the stern half. Quite a few large fish have also been observed around the wreck, so she should make a decent boat-angling venue when conditions permit. Tidal streams are quite strong and underwater visibility usually rather poor, but improve during the summer months.

MODIG
Wreck ★★★
Depth 20m
Reference: N53 44 498 E000 16 607
Location: 8.60 miles E from Withernsea

The *Modig* was a steel 1,704-ton Norwegian steamship that was registered at the port of Christiania. She measured 80.69m in length, with a 12.24m beam and a draught of 5.63m. Nylands Vaerksted built her at Christiania in 1913 and I.An. Christensen of Rederi owned her at the time of loss. Her single iron screw propeller was powered by a 152hp 3-cylinder triple expansion steam engine that used two boilers. Nylands Verksted of Xania built her machinery. Her cylinders measured 48.26cm, 78.74cm and 129.54cm-83.82cm, (19in, 31in and 51in-33in). She had one deck and a superstructure consisting of a 14.94m poop deck, an 18.59m bridgedeck and an 8.84m forecastle.

On 21 December 1916, the *Modig* was on passage from the Tyne for Rouen when she foundered and was lost after detonating a mine laid by the Kaiserliche Deutschen Marine U-boat SM UC 46. The *Modig* was under the command of Captain O.J. Vaarli and carrying a

2,400-ton cargo of coal. She had previously been captured and taken to Swinemunde, before being released back into Norwegian service again.

SM UC 46 sank with the loss of all twenty-three hands on 8 February 1917 when the British destroyer HMS *Liberty* rammed her south-east of the Goodwin Sands, in position N51 07 E01 39.

Wreck-site

The wreck lies in a north to south direction, with her bows to the south. She lies on a seabed of coarse sand, black shells and small pebbles, in a general depth of 20m, the lowest astronomical depth. When she sank around Christmas 1916, her two masts were visible above the surface, but she was dispersed using explosives in 1917. Now, the remains of the *Modig* are partially buried, totally collapsed and well broken up with her engine and boilers exposed and one of the boilers half buried in the seabed. Much of the non-ferrous metal has been picked clean, along with the most interesting wheelhouse/bridge equipment. Originally the vessel was equipped with a pedestal-mounted steering helm and pedestal-mounted telegraph. Tidal streams are very strong and underwater visibility usually poor. There are also no reports of any fish around the wreck.

PORTIA
Wreck ★★★
Depth 19m
Reference: N53 44 694 E000 16 914
Location: 8.81 miles E from Withernsea

The *Portia* was a steel 1,127-ton Norwegian steamship that measured 68.9 8m in length, with an 11.13m beam and a draught of 4.79m. Trondhjems Mek. Verksted built her at Trondhjems, Norway, in 1914 and J. Lund & Co. owned her at the time of loss. A 3-cylinder triple expansion steam engine that developed 116nhp using one boiler powered her single iron screw propeller. Her cylinders sizes measured 43.18cm, 68.58cm and 116.84cm-76.20cm, (17in, 27in and 46in-30in). The vessel had one deck and a centrally-positioned bridge structure.

On 1 February 1917 the SS *Portia* was lost off Withernsea after she detonated a mine laid by SM UC 47, an Imperial German U-boat. The mine detonated on the starboard side near the forward mast and she sunk in seven minutes, however her crew were rescued by a British vessel. She was on passage from Sunderland for Bilbao with a 1,600-ton cargo of coal.

(The U-boat was rammed and depth-charged by the British patrol-boat HMS P57 off Flamborough Head and sunk on 18 November 1917.)

Wreck-site

The wreck sits in a half-metre scour, is orientated in a north to south direction, with her bows to the south. She lies on a seabed of coarse sand, black shells and small pebbles in a general depth of 19m, the lowest astronomical depth. The wreck is now totally collapsed and well broken up, with the highest part, of just over 2m amidships, around her broken machinery. Lots of steel debris, battered plates, ribs, iron bollards, anchor chain, anchors and bits of machinery, etc., surround these. Except for a few small crabs, very little marine life has been reported on or around the wreck-site. Tidal streams are fairly strong and underwater visibility is usually very poor most of the year.

DERWENT
Wreck ★★★
Depth 16m
Reference: N53 44 075 E000 12 536
Location: 6.18 miles E from Withernsea

The *Derwent* was a steel 417-ton British steamship that was registered at Scarborough. She measured 43.9m in length, with a 6.7m beam and a 3.5m draught. W. Gray & Co. built her at Hartlepool in 1884 at a cost of £8,100 for the Scarborough Steamshipping Co., the owner at the time of loss. Her single iron screw propeller was powered by a 2-cylinder compound steam engine that developed 70nhp using one boiler. T. Richardson & Co. built her machinery. The vessel was delivered to her new owner in October 1884 and made fifty-one voyages between the North East and London until she was lost. In 1881 the Scarborough Steamship Co. was formed to carry passengers and cargo between the North-east and London, their first vessel being the steamship *Balaclava*.

On 23 October 1885 the *Derwent* left West Hartlepool on passage for Chatham with a cargo of coal and a crew of twelve, under the command of Captain Henry Price. She encountered a storm force ten en-route and disappeared with her crew, never being seen, or heard of, again. However, a lifebelt bearing her name was washed up on the Lincolnshire coast and a bucket also bearing her name was washed up near Spurn Point. The Board of Inquiry revealed later that she left West Hartlepool with just 0.48m (19in) of freeboard, although this was considered adequate at the time.

Wreck-site
The wreck was discovered by a group of sport-divers from Hartlepool and Withernsea and was positively identified through the ship's bell on 6 October 1986. She lies on a seabed of coarse sand, shells and gravel, in a general depth of 16m, the lowest astronomical depth. The wreck is now totally collapsed and well broken up, with the highest section around her engine and boiler. Local divers report that she is still quite an interesting dive and worthy of a visit, being in a depth that is suitable for most sport-divers. Tidal streams are reasonably strong and the best time to visit the site is at low slack water, on a neap tide, following a spell of light westerly winds during the summer months. Visibility is usually on the poor side.

ARNSTRV (Unknown)
Wreck ★★★
Depth 25m
Reference: N53 43 455 E000 24 077
Location: 12.90 miles E from Withernsea

This is an unknown steamship on which a ship's bell bearing the inscription '*Arnstrv*' was found. The vessel had a length of about 45-46m, with a single iron screw propeller that was driven by a compound steam engine using one boiler.

Wreck-site
The wreck is orientated in a north-east to south-west direction, lying on a seabed of sand, shells and gravel, in a general depth of 25m, the lowest astronomical depth. She is reported as lying on her side, standing 4.2m high around the boiler/engine, with the rest of the vessel totally collapsed and well broken up. Tidal streams are fairly brisk and underwater visibility is usually very poor most of the year. There have been no reports of marine life on or around the wreck-site.

CRUX
Wreck ★
Depth 3m
Reference: N53 43 212 E000 03 862
Location: 1.15 miles SE from Withernsea

The *Crux* was a steel 132-ton British steam fishing trawler registered at Grimsby. She was 30.25m long, with a 6.12m beam and a draught of 3.14m. She was built at Govan in 1896 and owned at the time of loss by the Grimsby & North Sea Steam Trawling Co. A 3-cylinder triple expansion steam engine that developed 45hp using one boiler powered her single iron screw propeller.

On 10 January 1912 the *Crux* was on a fishing voyage from Grimsby when she ran ashore at Out Newton. The local lifeboat, which launched through heavy surf, made a desperate attempt to reach the stricken trawler but had to turn back due to the adverse seas. Meanwhile, the Rocket Brigade arrived at the scene and succeeded in getting a line over the wreck. Captain Warner and nine crew were winched to safety, although one man was swept off and drowned.

Wreck-site
The wreck lies in a small scour, is orientated in an east to west direction, and lies in a general depth of 3m, this being about the lowest astronomical depth. As would be expected, she is now totally collapsed and well broken up, with the highest part being the remains of her battered boiler and engine. All there is to be seen of the rest of her are some bottom plates, ribs and the propeller shaft. On a calm day it is possible to visit the site at any state of the tide, but visibility is usually rather poor, although this clears up significantly during the summer months.

Chapter 5

Withernsea to The Humber

Area-5 (N53 43′ to N53 37′)

REVIGO
Wreck ★★★
Depth 26m
Reference: N53 42 948 E100 00 708
Location: 33.19 miles ENE from Spurn Point

The *Revigo* (Official No.125068) was a steel 230-ton British steam fishing trawler registered at Grimsby. She was 35.66m long with a 6.7m beam and a draught of 3.53m. Cook, Welton & Gemmell built her at Beverley as Yard No.145 and launched her on 15 April 1907 for George F. Sleight of Grimsby. On 10 August 1907, she was registered as Grimsby trawler No.GY296. A 3-cylinder triple expansion steam engine that developed 63nhp using one boiler powered her single iron screw propeller and gave her a maximum speed of 10.5 knots. Charles D. Holms & Co. Ltd built her machinery at Hull. She was classed at Lloyd's as 100 A1 and had one deck, four bulkheads and a superstructure consisting of a 17.98m quarterdeck and a 5.49m forecastle.

On 7 September 1914, the *Revigo* detonated a German-laid mine thirty-three miles east-north-east from Spurn Point. She was on a return fishing voyage from Grimsby under the command of Skipper W. Lewis. It is believed that her crew abandoned ship in the lifeboats.

Wreck-site
This wreck, possibly that of the *Revigo*, lies on a seabed of muddy sand, broken black shells, gravel and small pebbles, in a general depth of 26m, the lowest astronomical depth. She is upright, intact but collapsed and broken, with the highest sections of 3.5m being at her bows and amidships to stern, where her engine and boiler are exposed. Everything is covered in a colourful array of soft corals and huge plumose anemones, a sure sign of the strong confused tidal streams that sweep around the wreck. Visibility is usually very good to excellent during the summer months, but the site is best avoided following a spell of heavy stormy weather.

JERSEY
Wreck ★★
Depth 26m
Reference: N53 42 907 E000 37 199
Location: 20.08 miles NE by E from Spurn Head

The *Jersey* was a steel 161-ton British steam fishing trawler that was registered at Grimsby. She measured 31.75m in length, with a 6.22m beam and a draught of 3.22m. Mackie & Thomson built her at Glasgow in 1896 for Hagerup, Doughty & Co. of Jersey. A 3-cylinder triple expansion steam engine that developed 45hp using one boiler powered her single iron screw propeller. Muir & Houston Ltd built her machinery at Glasgow. She had one deck, four bulkheads and a superstructure consisting of a 5.18m quarterdeck and a 5.79m forecastle. She was purchased by the Consolidated Steam Fishing & Ice Co., who owned her at the time of loss.

On 4 October 1916 the *Jersey* on a return fishing voyage from Grimsby under the command of Skipper S. Rye when SM UB 19 stopped her, came up alongside, and ordered the crew to abandon ship. The vessel was then sunk when explosive scuttling-charges were placed below her deck and detonated. SM UB 19 was lost with eight of her crew on 30 November 1916 when she was sunk by gunfire from the Q-ship *Penshurst* in the English Channel.

Wreck-site

The wreck is orientated in an east to west direction, lying on a seabed of fine mud and sand, black shells and small pebbles, in a general depth of 26m, the lowest astronomical depth. She is now partially buried, well collapsed and broken up and standing 2.5m high at the stern half, around her boiler and engine. The upper structures are well coated in a colourful array of soft corals and shoals of small fish swarm over and around the wreck. Being such a small vessel and being half buried, there is very little else of interest to be seen. Tidal streams are quite strong and underwater visibility is often excellent during the summer months.

RADO

Wreck ★★★
Depth 25m
Reference: N53 42 711 E000 36 760
Location: 19.80 miles NE by E from Spurn Head

The *Rado* (Official No.118769) was an iron 182-ton British steam fishing trawler that was regis-tered at Grimsby. She measured 32m in length, with a 6.4m beam and a draught of 3.35m. Cook, Welton & Gemmell built her as Yard No.352 at Hull and launched her as the *Rado* on 27 August 1903 for George Frederick Sleight of Grimsby. The new owner registered her as Grimsby trawler No.GY1272 on 27 July 1903. Her single iron screw propeller was powered by a 3-cylinder triple expansion steam engine that developed 55hp using one boiler, which gave her a maximum speed of 9.5 knots. Charles D. Holmes built her machinery at Hull. She had one deck, four-bulkheads, a 14.02m quarterdeck and a 5.49m forecastle.

On 4 October 1916 the *Rado* was on a return fishing voyage from Grimsby, under the command of Skipper G.W. Thomas, when the Imperial German submarine UB 19 stopped her. The crew were then ordered to abandon ship in the boats and the vessel was sunk when explosive scuttling-charges were detonated below her deck. Two months later, on 30 November 1916, the U-boat was lost in the English Channel with eight of her crew when gunfire from the decoy-vessel *Penshurst* sank her.

Wreck-site

The wreck, believed to be that of the trawler *Rado*, lies on a seabed of muddy sand, small pebbles and black shells, in a general depth of 25m, the lowest astronomical depth. She is partially buried, upright and fairly intact, but with her structures collapsed. The highest 4m sections are at the stern half and her bow, which are coated in soft corals and plumose anemones. Quite a few fish have been reported around the wreck, which could make an interesting boat-angling venue, although they are supposedly rather on the small side. Tidal streams are quite strong and rather confused, but underwater visibility is excellent during the summer months.

HOMER

Wreck ★★★★
Depth 26m
Reference: N53 42 101 E000 32 396
Location: 17.20 miles ENE from Spurn Head

The *Homer* was an iron 1,308-ton British steamship that was registered at the port of London. She measured 76.2m in length, with a 10.41m beam and a draught of 5.28m. J. Redhead & Co. Ltd built her at Newcastle-upon-Tyne in 1881 and the Elliott Steam Tug Co. Ltd owned her at the time of loss, Dick & Page managed her. Her single iron screw propeller was powered by a 2-cylinder compound steam engine that developed 151hp using two boilers. Her cylinders measured 76.20cm and 144.78cm-96.52cm, (30in and 57in-36in). She had one deck, a well deck, four bulkheads and a superstructure consisting of a 28.96m quarterdeck, a 15.24m bridgedeck and a 7.62m forecastle.

On 15 February 1901 SS *Homer* was on passage from London for the Tyne when she foundered and was lost following a collision with the Russian barque *Hoppet*. Wind conditions were strong westerly force six and it was dark. As the two vessels collided, an English able seaman, who was the only survivor from the steamship, leapt from the bow of the *Homer* onto the barque, a decision that saved his life. At that same instant, the Russian captain leapt the other way onto the *Homer*, and he went down with the steamer. The SS *Homer* was in ballast, under the command of Captain R.J. Gant and carrying a crew of seventeen. The barque, which was in ballast and on passage to the USA, made a search for survivors, but none were found.

Wreck-site

The wreck is orientated in a north, north-east to south, south-west direction, with her bows to the south-west. She lies on a seabed of mud, sand, broken shells and small pebbles, in a general depth of 26m, the lowest astronomical depth. The wreck is collapsed and covers an area of seabed measuring 81.4m by 21.6m. She is upright, but lying slightly to one side and standing some 4.03m high amidships around her exposed engine and boilers. A mound of collapsed superstructure and broken debris surrounds these. Soft corals and hard, white marine worm casings cover the wreckage, which is swept by strong tidal streams. Underwater visibility is usually rather poor and often dismal at times.

BERNADOTTE

Wreck ★★★
Depth 24m
Reference: N53 41 922 E000 54 917
Location: 29.69 miles ENE from Spurn Head

The *Bernadotte* (Signal letters JWPK) was an iron 413-ton Norwegian steamship registered at the port of Stavanger. She measured 44.04m in length, with a 7.39m beam and a draught of 3.58m. Bergens Mek Verk built and completed her at Bergen in 1889 and A/S Bernadotte was the owner at the time of loss, while Sigval Beresen of Stavanger managed her. Her single iron screw propeller was powered by a 3-cylinder triple expansion steam engine that used one boiler.

On 29 December 1909 the steamer was in ballast on passage from Hull for Stromstad when she struck a submerged wreck, foundered and was lost. It is believed that her crew safely abandoned ship in the vessel's own boat.

Wreck-site

The wreck thought to be that of the small steamer *Bernadotte*, lies on a seabed of gravel, coarse sand and small black shells, in a general depth of 24m, the lowest astronomical depth. She is partially buried, totally collapsed, well broken up and standing some 3m at the highest point amidships. A mound of iron debris surrounds her boiler and engine, which are now exposed. An anchor and chain, her propeller and a pair of iron bollards are all visible, but most of the wreck is broken debris. Tidal streams are quite strong and underwater visibility is usually rather poor, but this improves significantly during the summer months and can often reach 15m. Very little marine life was observed, but the wreck has a coating of soft corals.

EARL HOWARD
Wreck ★★★
Depth 23.5m
Reference: N53 41 457 E000 26 124
Location: 13.62 miles NE from Spurn Point

The *Earl Howard* (Official No.137009) was a steel 226-ton British steam fishing trawler that was registered at Grimsby and measured 35.66m in length with a 6.71m beam. Cook, Welton & Gemmell built her as Yard No.304 at Beverley and launched her on 27 July 1914 for the Earl Steam Fishing Co. Ltd of Grimsby. She was then registered as Grimsby trawler No.GY332 on 22 October 1914. Her single iron screw propeller was powered by a 75nhp 3-cylinder triple expansion steam engine that used one boiler, which gave her a maximum speed of 10 knots. Charles D. Holmes built her machinery at Hull.

On 11 December 1914, just seven weeks after being registered, the *Earl Howard* was posted missing with all hands, presumed mined, north-east from Spurn Head. On the night of 25-26 August 1914, in the area limited by N53 50' to N53 40' and E00 33' to E00 38', the Imperial German Navy minelayer SMS *Nautilus* laid a minefield and it is most probable that the *Earl Howard* detonated one of those.

Wreck-site
This wreck has not been positively identified to date, but there is the possibility that this may be the final resting place of the steam trawler *Earl Howard* and her crew. She lies on a seabed of sand, gravel and small pebbles in a general depth of 23.5m, the lowest astronomical depth. The wreck is totally collapsed, well broken up, with the highest 2m section being around her exposed boiler and engine towards the stern. A small mound of steel debris and broken machinery litters the site around the boiler and small donkey-boiler.

Tidal streams are very strong and underwater visibility is usually rather dark, with lots of suspended sediment spoiling the visibility, although this improves during the summer months.

REBONO
Wreck ★★★
Depth 24m
Reference: N53 41 294 E000 49 606
Location: 26.40 miles ENE from Spurn Point

The *Rebono* (Official No.134739) was a steel 176-ton British steam fishing trawler that was registered at Grimsby. She measured 32m in length, with a beam of 6.4m and a draught of 3.27m. Cook, Welton & Gemmell built her as Yard No.247 at Beverley and launched her as the *Rebono* on 18 July 1912 for George F. Sleight of Grimsby. She was registered as Grimsby trawler No.GY731 on 23 August 1912. Her single iron screw propeller was powered by a 3-cylinder triple expansion steam engine that developed 60nhp using one boiler, giving her a maximum speed of 10 knots. Charles D. Holmes & Co. built her machinery at Hull. She was classed at Lloyd's as 100 A1 and had one deck, four bulkheads and a 17.37m quarterdeck.

On 23 September 1914, the *Rebono* was on a return fishing voyage from Grimsby, under the command of Skipper G. Burgess, when she detonated a German-laid mine, foundered and was lost with one of her crew.

SMS *Nautilus*, a Kaiserliche Deutsche Marine minelayer, laid a minefield on the night of 25–26 August 1914 in the area limited by N53 50' to N53 40' and E00 33' to E00 38'. It is most likely that the *Rebono* detonated one of those mines. On the same night as *Nautilus* laid her mines, the Imperial minelayer SMS *Albatros* also laid mines during the same operation, but in the area N54 55' to N55 08' and W01 09' to W01 17' off the Tyne.

Wreck-site
The wreck, probably that of the Grimsby trawler, lies on a seabed of black shells, coarse sand and gravel, in a general depth of 24m, the lowest astronomical depth. The bow section seems reasonably intact, but the majority of her is collapsed and well broken up. The highest structures of 3m are around her boiler and engine, which are now exposed. Soft corals are well established on the debris and everything is coated with hard, white marine worm casings. Tidal streams are very strong, but underwater visibility is usually quite good during the summer months after a spell of calm settled weather.

LINDSELL, HM Drifter
Wreck *
Depth 24m
Reference: N53 41 139 E000 59 199
Location: 200m NE from HMS *Speedy* and 31.98 miles ENE from Spurn Point

The *Lindsell* (Port No.322) was a steel 88-ton steam fishing drifter hired by the Admiralty as an armed patrol/minesweeper and commissioned in September 1914. Her single iron screw propeller was powered by a 3-cylinder triple expansion steam engine that used one boiler.

On 3 September 1914, HM Drifter *Lindsell* detonated a mine and sank with the loss of four of her crew, those being:

E. Bailet (deckhand) RNR No.901.D.A.
A. Baker (deckhand) RNR No.905.D.A.
A. Sharman (2nd-hand) RNR No.253.S.A.
B.W. Sharman (engineman) RNR No.477.E.S.
Six crewmen survived.

See the full story of her sinking under **HMS SPEEDY**

Wreck-site
She lies on a fairly hard seabed of coarse sand, black shells and gravel, in a general depth of 24m, the lowest astronomical depth. All that remains of this small boat is her boiler and a few bits of iron debris scattered around. Visibility can be excellent during the summer months, but Lion's mane jellyfish can be a bit of a nuisance. Tidal streams are very strong and the wreck-site is a long way from land.

SPEEDY, HMS
Wreck ****
Depth 24m
Reference: N53 41 101 E000 59 027
Location: 31.97 miles ENE from Spurn Point

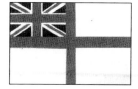

Torpedo boat destroyer HMS *Speedy*. *(Author's Collection)*

The *Speedy* was an 810-ton steel 'Alarm' Class British torpedo boat destroyer that measured 8.23m in length, with an 8.22m beam and a 3.66m draught. J.I. Thornycroft & Co. Ltd built her at Chiswick for the Royal Navy. She was launched on 18 May 1893 and completed on 20 February 1894. Her two bronze screw propellers and two shafts were powered by two triple expansion reciprocating steam engines that developed 3,150ihp, using four Thornycroft coal-fired boilers. She was capable of 18.7 knots maximum speed and had forced draught ventilation. Her armament consisted of three 45.72cm (18in) torpedo tubes – (one bow-mounted and one amidships, port and starboard), four single 1.36 kilo QF guns (3-pounders) and one Gardner machine-gun. Her main armament was either two single 11.94cm (4.7in) QF guns or 11.94cm (4.7in) BL guns, however under the circumstances, they were probably QF guns.

A QF gun fired rounds, which had the cordite in a brass case with the shell attached. This enabled the round to be loaded and fired very quickly, hence the abbreviation QF – quick-firing. A BL gun, on the other hand, had a separate shell and cordite charge loaded, shell first, into the breech, hence the term BL – breech-loading. This ammunition was also very unsafe as in action these cordite charges would be exposed in the ready-use lockers and would readily ignite if the gun mounting were hit by enemy fire or shrapnel.

This type of vessel was designed and built to counter attacks by torpedo boats but they were not a success in this role due to their unreliability and their failure to maintain their designed speed. The vessel's maximum speed was far less than that of contemporary torpedo boats, which meant that they were unable to match the speed of their intended targets, let alone stand a chance of catching them. It was not, at that time, generally appreciated that torpedo boats would not be able to attain high speeds in heavy seas. HMS *Speedy* was the most successful of her class, principally due to the reliability of her boilers, which were much more dependable than the locomotive type fitted to her sister ships. She was also the only one to have three funnels.

Her service history, post-1900:

She commissioned for service with the Mediterranean Fleet at Chatham on 16 January 1900 and was refitted at Chatham for services with the Fishery Protection Squadron at Harwich, being completed on 6 June 1905. During this refit, her torpedo tubes were removed. She was damaged in collision with a merchant ship in June 1906. After service with the Home Fleet between 1907-1909, the boat was re-converted into a Minesweeper. In the August 1914 Navy List, she is listed as being under the orders of the Admiral Commanding Coastguard and Reserves, North Sea Fisheries, having re-commissioned at Sheerness on 4 March 1914.

On the night of 25-26 August 1914, the Imperial German Navy Minelayer SMS *Nautilus* laid a minefield off the Humber in the area limited by N53 50 to N53 40 and E00 33 to E00 38. When this became known, SNO North Sea Fisheries, Lowestoft, on 31 August, they dispatched HMS *Speedy* to find and clear this field, under the command of Lieutenant-Commander E.M.C. Rutherford RN with ten hired drifters. On 2 September, HM Drifter *Eyrie* (Adm. No.214) struck a mine, which exploded aft, blowing off her stern and sinking her almost immediately. Six of her crew, including Skipper T. Scarll RNR, were lost, but four survivors were picked up.

The next day, HMS *Speedy*, in company with HM Drifters *Lindsell* (Adm. No.224), *Wishful* (Adm. No.218) and *Achievable* (Adm. No.212) continued the work until about 1100 hours when *Lindsell* struck a mine aft, which exploded and sank her with the loss of four of her crew. *Speedy* launched her boats to recover the survivors from *Lindsell* when she too detonated a mine aft, shortly afterwards. The resulting explosion blew off most of her stern and keel aft and she sank rapidly. Officer Steward 2nd-Class E.A. Claxton was lost with the ship and several of the crew were injured – Gunner A.C. Bright RN severely so. Boats from other vessels rescued the survivors and HMS *Spanker*, another former Torpedo-gunboat that had been converted to a Minesweeper, took the injured from both ships to Grimsby. It is also believed that another crewmember of *Speedy* subsequently succumbed to his injuries.

Many trawlers and drifters were lost after mines struck the vessels aft. This was because the draught aft was some 1.83m to 2.13m (6-7ft) more than the draught forward.

Wreck-site

The wreck, which may be classed as a war grave, is orientated in a north, north-east to south, south-west direction (030/210 degrees). She lies on a fairly hard seabed of coarse sand, black shells and gravel, in a general depth of 24m, the lowest astronomical depth. It is collapsed, standing 2.3m high amidships to the bows, but the stern end is well broken up. All her guns are visible forward, amidships and aft and her three magazines are all full. She is said to be a very interesting dive. There are no reports of the ship's bell having been recovered, but both of her bronze propellers have been removed. Large sections of her wooden hull are in place, but most of the boat is collapsed down on herself. Visibility can be excellent during the summer months, but Lion's mane jellyfish can be a bit of a nuisance. Tidal streams are very strong and the wreck-site is a long way from land.

GIUSEPPE

Wreck ★★
Depth17m
Reference: N53 40 596 E000 18 347
Location: 9.37 miles NE from Spurn Point

The *Giuseppe* was an old iron steamship approximately 64m in length and a 10m beam. Her single iron screw propeller was powered by a 2-cylinder compound steam engine.

She was discovered on 27 February 1978 and the ship's bell was located on 6 November 1978, however the vessel still remains a mystery. Even after extensive research nothing has come up to say where she came from, who built her or anything else.

Wreck-site

The wreck is orientated in a south, south-east to north, north-west direction. She lies on a seabed of sand, shells and gravel, in a general depth of 17m, the lowest astronomical depth. The wreck is totally collapsed, well broken up and dispersed. Her boiler and engine are the highest parts at 2m and stand amidst a mound of broken debris. The iron propeller and shaft also remain, but most of the wreck is iron plates and broken ribs. Tidal streams are fairly strong and underwater visibility is usually poor.

EDWIN

Wreck ★★★★
Depth 24m
Reference: N53 40 333 E000 51 884
Location: 27.57 miles ENE from Spurn Point

The *Edwin* was a 1,860-ton iron British steamship registered at North Shields. She was 86.91m long with a 10.54m beam and a 7.36m draught. A. Leslie & Co. of Newcastle built her in 1878 and H.E.P. Adamson of Newcastle owned her at the time of loss. A 2-cylinder compound steam engine that developed 201hp using one boiler, powered her single iron screw propeller. R. & W. Hawthorn built her machinery at Newcastle. She had two decks, a 12.19m poop deck and a 12.19m forecastle. She was fitted with a stern-positioned second iron steering helm.

On 3 August 1899, the SS *Edwin* was on passage from Bona for Leith when she foundered and was lost following a collision with the Newcastle-registered steamship *Chipchase*. The *Edwin* had a crew of twenty-five under the command of Captain T. Matthews and a cargo of Phosphate and Esparto grass. The crew safely abandoned ship and were picked up by the *Chipchase*.

Wreck-site

The wreck is orientated in a north-west to south-east direction, with her bow to the north-west. She lies in a 1m scour, on a seabed of gravel, coarse sand, black shells and small pebbles, in a general depth of 22m, the lowest astronomical depth. The wreck is partially buried, upright, still reasonably intact, but collapsed and broken and standing around 3.5m high amidships, where her boiler/engine are located and exposed. A large iron anchor and some bollards are visible at the bows, which are collapsed and lots of heavy rusting chain is spread out on the seabed. Lengths of copper piping are intermingled with lots of iron debris from amidships to stern. Tidal streams are very strong and underwater visibility is usually quite reasonable during the summer months.

MERCHISTON

Wreck ★★★
Depth 19m
Reference: N53 39 601 E000 31 427
Location: 15.68 miles ENE from Spurn Head

The *Merchiston* was a steel 1,840-ton British steamship that was registered at West Hartlepool. She measured 85.34m in length, with a 12.24m beam and a draught of 5.56m. W. Gray & Co. Ltd built her at West Hartlepool in 1901 and the Merchiston Steamship Co. Ltd owned her at the time of loss. Her single iron screw propeller was powered by a 165hp 3-cylinder triple expansion steam engine that used two boilers. Central Marine Engineering Works Ltd built her machinery at West Hartlepool. She had one deck, four bulkheads and a superstructure consisting of a 22.56m bridgedeck and an 8.23m forecastle. The vessel had a stern-mounted iron steering helm as well as her bridge/wheelhouse equipment.

During wind conditions north-east force four on 31 March 1906, the SS *Merchiston* was on passage from Bilbao for Middlesbrough when she foundered and was lost following a collision with the London-registered steamship *Eda*. The *Merchiston* was under the command of Captain F.W. Weeks, with a crew of twenty and a cargo of iron ore. Her crew were taken on the *Eda*.

Wreck-site

The wreck is orientated in a south-east to north-west direction, with her bows to the north-west. She lies on a seabed of coarse sand shells and stone, in a general depth of 19m, the lowest astronomical depth. She is totally collapsed and well broken up, with the highest 3.6m section amidships, where her boiler and engine are located, being partially intact. A mound of broken steel debris surrounds the engine and boilers with twisted copper pipes protruding out of it. The vessel was equipped with a brass pedestal-mounted steering helm, but this is unlikely to still be around. Little else of interest remains to be seen except for the occasional juicy crustacean hiding beneath the debris. Not many fish have been reported. Tidal streams are quite strong and underwater visibility usually poor, but this improves significantly during the summer months.

MARSHALL

Wreck **
Depth 15m
Reference: N53 39 534 E000 16 929
Location: 8.5 miles NE from Spurn Head

The *Marshall*, (also called *Marchell* in the Admiralty register of 1853) was an early iron 307-ton German steamship registered at the port of Hamburg. She was 39.62m long with a 7.4m beam. She was built at South Shields in 1846 for the Elbe & Hambro Steam Navigation Co. Her single iron screw propeller was powered by an 80rhp 2-cylinder compound steam engine that used one boiler and gave her a maximum speed of 9 knots. She was classed at Lloyd's as A1-Hull-Hambro.

The *Marshall* left Hamburg on 26 November 1853, on passage for Hull, with an unspecified cargo, forty-two passengers and a crew of eighteen, under the command of Captain J. Rohrs. On 28 November, while approaching the mouth of the Humber at night in thick fog, the *Marshall* ran into the wooden barque *Woodhouse*. The barque, under the command of Captain Catgens on passage from Stockholm for Hull, was struck heavily on her starboard bow. Catgens hailed the steamship her to reverse her engines. There was no reply and the *Marshall* swung around and struck the *Woodhouse* another heavy blow on the stern. This was all that was ever seen of the *Marshall* and it was presumed she sank. The two vessels collided off Kinsea, five miles from the Newsand Float, near the mouth of the River Humber. The *Woodhouse* lost her fore-top gallant mast and her jib boom and one young apprentice was drowned when he fell overboard. Later that day, some North Sea fishermen reported that they had seen the tops of her masts off Kilnsea at low water and a fishing-smack found one of her boats. Sixty-one people were lost: the eighteen crew and forty-two passengers on the *Marshall* and the young lad from the barque.

Wreck-site

The wreck, probably that of the *Marshall*, lies in a small scour, on a seabed of shells and sand, in a general depth of 15m, the lowest astronomical depth. She is totally collapsed and well broken up, with the highest point being about 2.4m around her upright boiler and engine. Battered iron plates, ribs and pieces of broken machinery etc., surround these. The site could well be worth investigating, because one never knows what interesting artefacts may turn up. Very little marine life has been observed on and around the wreck. Tidal streams are fairly strong and underwater visibility usually very poor most times of the year.

HANNA LARSEN, Ex ROBERT KOPPEN, ex FRIDERUN, ex MULHEIM, ex HEDWIG MENZELL

Wreck ★★★
Depth 24m
Reference: N53 38 205 E000 39 477
Location: 19.95 miles ENE from Spurn Head

The *Hanna Larsen* was a steel 1,311-ton British steamship registered at the port of London. She was 74.86m long, with a 10.82m beam and a draught of 4.63m. Flensburger Schiffbau Ges built her as the 1,547-ton *Hedwig Menzell* at Flensburg in 1903. Chinesische Kustenfaht Ges. (Menzell & Co.) at Hamburg owned her until 1908-1909, when the Hamburg-Afrika Line AG purchased her and renamed the vessel *Friderun*. In 1912, she was renamed *Mulheim* when Midgard Deutsche Seeverkehr Akties Ges. of Bremen bought her. In 1912 she was renamed *Robert Koppen* when Robert Koppen purchased her. In 1913-1914 she was sold to F.W. Fisher and renamed *Hanna Larsen*. The Admiralty requisitioned the vessel and placed her under the management of Everett & Newbigin of London. A 3-cylinder triple expansion steam engine that developed 120hp using one boiler, powered the single iron screw propeller. Her cylinders measured 38.10cm, 64.14cm and 115.09cm-87.63cm, (15in, 25.25in and 45.31in-34.5-in). Flensburger Schiffbau Ges also built her machinery. Sometime during her ownership she was lightened by 236 tons.

At 11.20 p.m. on 7 February 1917, the *Hanna Larsen* was in ballast on passage from London for the Tyne to load up with coal when UC 39 fired four shells at her. Captain J. Souter, in command of the steamship, stopped her engines. Fifteen minutes later he restarted the engines and ordered full-steam ahead in an attempt to get clear of the submarine but, when another shell was fired, the engines were stopped again. This time he ordered the men to abandon ship, but while they were doing so more shells rained down, injuring four of them and leaving one man so badly injured that he later died. Just before midnight the U-boat drew alongside the lifeboats and took the master and chief engineer prisoner. The German crew plundered the vessel before attempting to sink her with bombs and explosive scuttling charges. The submarine stood off for a while, but when the bombs failed to sink her they returned to finish the looting and place explosives on board. The *Hanna Larsen* blew up and sank early in the morning of 8 February. Later that day the British destroyer HMS *Thrasher* caught UC 39 on the surface. The submarine was shelled and depth charged and her captain, Oberleutnant zur See Ehrentraut, and six men were killed while clambering onto the casing. The gunfire ceased when the two English prisoners taken earlier from the *Hanna Larsen* appeared on the conning tower, waving white rags and the U-boat was captured. She sank while being towed back to port by the destroyer HMS *Itchen*.

Wreck-site

The wreck lies on a seabed of shells, gravel, mud and sand, in a general depth of 24m, the lowest astronomical depth. She is upright, but now totally collapsed and well broken up, standing 2m high amidships, with her boiler and engine exposed. She was equipped with a brass pedestal-mounted telegraph and steering helm so she could still be quite interesting to explore. Her bell, if discovered, will probably be inscribed '*Hedwig Menzell* 1903', the date she was built. The wreck-site covers an area of 75m by 18m, with lots of visible broken debris. Visibility can be excellent during the summer months, often reaching 20m, but tidal streams are very strong. Lion's mane jellyfish can be quite a nuisance during the July to September.

HVITVEIS
Wreck ★
Depth 13m
Reference: N53 37 967 W000 09 303
Location: River Humber, opposite Immingham Oil
Terminal, 10.2 miles WNW from Spurn Point

The *Hvitveis* was a 650-ton steel Norwegian schooner registered at the port of Bergen. She was 55.06m long with a 9.16m beam. Porsgrund Mek Vaerk built her at Porsgrund in 1915 for A/S Hvitveis, who was the owner at the time of loss. She was a fully equipped sailing schooner fitted with an aft-positioned oil/diesel-powered auxiliary engine built by Germaniawerft at Kiel. She had one deck and a superstructure consisting of a 15.24m poop deck and a 7.32m forecastle.

On 27 November 1915, *Hvitveis* was on passage from Hull for Rouen when she collided with Danish-registered steamship *Ulla* near the No.7 Holme Ridge buoy on the Humber and sank.

Wreck-site
The wreck is now totally collapsed, partially buried and well broken up, standing no more than 2m high from the riverbed, in a general depth of 13m at the lowest tide. The full shape of the vessel can be seen, but there is little of interest for the diver. Anyone thinking of visiting the wreck, which lies in the fairway, would be wise to seek permission from the River Authority.

HAWK
Wreck ★★★
Depth 27m
Reference: N53 37 551 E000 20 762
Location: 9.05 miles ENE from Spurn Point

The *Hawk* was an iron 181-ton British steam fishing trawler that was registered at Hull. She measured 33.52m in length, with a 6.4m beam and a draught of 3.42m. Cook, Welton & Gemmell built her as Yard No.200 at Hull and launched her on 27 January 1898 for St Andrews Steam Fishing Co. Ltd at Hull. She was registered as Hull trawler No.H389 on 25 March 1898. Her single iron screw propeller was powered by a 3 cylinder triple expansion steam engine that developed 58nhp using one boiler. Charles D. Holmes & Co. Ltd built her machinery at Hull. She was classed at Lloyd's as 100 A1 and had one deck, three-bulkheads and a 6.10m quarterdeck.

On 19 April 1916, the *Hawk* was on a return fishing voyage from Hull for Iceland when, following a collision off the Humber with the Brazilian-registered steamship *Corovado*, she foundered and was lost with four of her crew. The trawler was under the command of Skipper T.W. Firber and carrying a crew of ten.

Wreck-site
The wreck, most probably that of the *Hawk*, lies in a deep 2m scour, on the western side and edge of the long trench known as the New Sand Hole, situated some seven to eight miles east, north-east from the Spurn Head. She is broken into three sections, with the bows complete and lying some 13.72m away from the main part of the wreck, on the starboard side. The highest section is around her engine, boiler and the bow section, which stands about 4m. Two large winches and some broken derricks can be seen towards the bows. Quite a lot of marine life has been observed, including some large crustaceans, which were seen hiding in amongst the wreckage. Tidal streams are very strong and confused, with fairly powerful downward pushing currents in places. Visibility is usually poor, but this improves significantly during the summer months, following a spell of dry weather. This site is very close to the main shipping lanes, so a good lookout is required by anyone thinking of visiting her.

SS Dido. (Courtesy Arthur Credland, Hull Maritime Museum)

DIDO
Wreck ★★★
Depth 13m
Reference: N53 37 298 E000 15 144
Location: 5.93 miles NNE from Spurn Lightvessel

The *Dido* was a steel 4,769-ton British steamship that was registered at Hull. She measured 122.09m in length, with a 14.63m beam and a draught of 8.73m. Earle's Ship Building Co. Ltd built her at Hull in 1896 for Thomas Wilson Sons & Co. Ltd of Hull. A 3-cylinder triple expansion steam engine that developed 339hp using three boilers powered her single iron screw propeller. Her cylinders measured 63.50cm, 101.60cm and 177.80cm-121.92cm, (25in, 40in and 70in-48in). Earle's Ship Building Co. Ltd also built her machinery at Hull. She had two decks and a superstructure consisting of a 13.41m poop deck, 32.31m bridgedeck and an 11.89m forecastle. The vessel was also said to have been equipped with a brass pedestal-mounted steering helm and pedestal-mounted telegraph, plus a stern-positioned iron steering helm.

At 6.15 a.m. on 26 February 1916, while lying at anchor during a raging gale and heavy snow showers, just north of the Humber, a violent explosion rocked the *Dido* on her port-side up forward, She was carrying one passenger, who also happened to be a stowaway, a crew of thirty and an unspecified general cargo, while on passage from Middlesbrough for Bombay. Captain Taylor instructed the chief officer to lower a boat and have the damaged area examined. The chief and two crewmen climbed in, but as the boat reached the water, the battering from choppy waves broke it adrift. The men tried desperately to row back to the steamship, but in the thick squally snow, they lost sight of the ship and were soon driven away by a strong tide and the wind. The Belgian steamship *Martha* actually found the three men and headed over to the *Dido* to see what assistance could be rendered. The *Dido* was gradually sinking and some of the men had gone into the sea by the time the *Martha* reached the vessel. Attempts were made to rescue the men by throwing ropes, but the icy water had left them too weak and exhausted to grab hold of the ropes. A lifeboat was then lowered from the Belgian steamer, but the freezing conditions were also affecting the rescuers and the squally, lumpy sea made rescue almost impossible. At 7.20 a.m., with the *Martha* standing by, the *Dido* heaved up and went down to the bottom, taking the confidential papers down with her. In total, twenty-seven people were lost; the stowaway and twenty-six crewmen. The *Martha* then proceeded on her voyage to Hull, where she landed the three survivors. Later, it was discovered that the vessel had detonated a mine placed by SM UC 7.

Four months later, on 6 July 1916, the submarine was also lost with her crew of eighteen, when it is believed she detonated a newly laid British mine, between Thornton Bank and

Zeebrugge in the English Channel, although she may have been lost by accident, resulting from mechanical or drill failure. SM UC 7 was under the command of Oberleutnant zur See G. Haag, who was also lost with the boat.

Wreck-site

The wreck is orientated in an east to west direction, lying on a seabed of muddy sand and short weed, in a general depth of 13m, the lowest astronomical depth. She is now totally collapsed, well broken up and thoroughly dispersed, with the highest piece standing no more than 2m. The whole wreck is just a large mound of broken steel debris and bits of machinery, covering an area of some 200m by 25m or so. One larger piece lies some 50m over to the west of the main part of the wreckage. It would be possible to visit the site at most states of the tide, although springs should be avoided. Underwater visibility is usually rather poor and often grim, but improves during the summer months.

Chapter 6

The Humber Estuary to Skegness

Area-6 (N53 37 to N53 10)

COURTIER, HM Trawler
Wreck ★★★
Depth 12m
Reference: N53 36 665 E000 15 830
Location: 6.01 miles ENE from Spurn Point

The *Courtier* was a steel 181-ton British steam fishing trawler that measured 33.35m in length and had a 6.40m beam. Cook, Welton & Gemmell built her as Yard No.203 at Beverley and launched her on 25 June 1910 for the Queen Steam Fishing Co. Ltd of Grimsby. The owners then registered her as Grimsby trawler No.GY564 on 8 August 1910. Her single iron screw propeller was powered by a 3-cylinder triple expansion steam engine that developed 55nhp using one boiler, which gave her a maximum speed of 10 knots. Charles D. Holmes & Co. built her machinery at Hull. In January 1915, the Admiralty requisitioned the boat and converted her as minesweeper No.FY 449.

On 6 January 1916, HM Trawler *Courtier* was on minesweeping duties off Kilnsea when she foundered and was lost after detonating a German-laid mine. The mine has never been credited to any U-boat or surface warship, so it is presumed that she detonated either a British mine, or one that was actually drifting.

Wreck-site
The wreck, probably that of HMT *Courtier*, lies on a seabed of sand, shells and gravel, in a general depth of 12m, the lowest astronomical depth. She is totally collapsed, well broken up and rather dispersed with the highest section of 2m being around the boiler and engine. These are surrounded by lots of battered steel plates, ribs and broken machinery. The wreck was dispersed by explosives and is generally a mound of debris, but her outline can still be made out. Tidal streams are fairly strong, while underwater visibility is usually murky and grim most of the year, but clears a little during the summer months.

FERMO
Wreck ★★★
Depth 13m
Reference: N53 35 732 E000 15 844
Location: 5.72 miles ENE from Spurn Point

The *Fermo* was an iron 175-ton British steam fishing trawler that was registered at Grimsby. She measured 30.53m in length, with a 6.4m beam and a 3.5m draught. Cochrane & Cooper Ltd built her at Selby in 1898 and Ocean Steam Fishing Co. Ltd at Grimsby owned her at the time of loss. A 3-cylinder triple expansion steam engine that developed 45hp using one boiler

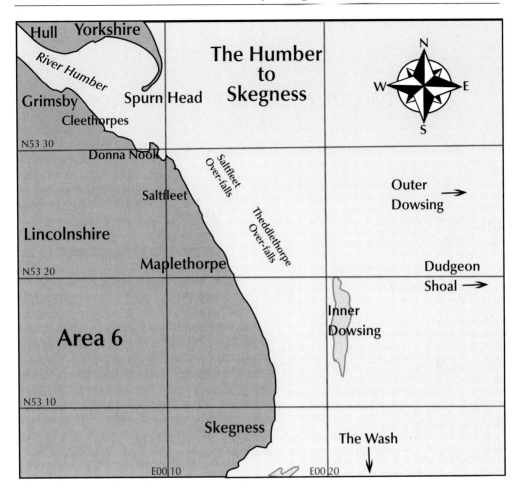

powered her single iron screw propeller. Amos & Smith Co. built her machinery at Hull. She had one deck, three bulkheads, a 13.72m quarterdeck and a 5.49m forecastle.

On 10 November 1917 the *Fermo* was on a return fishing voyage from Grimsby when she foundered and was lost following a collision with the Norwegian-registered steamship *Breidablik*. The trawler was under the command of Skipper F. Jacobson and carrying a crew of ten. It is understood that the Norwegian vessel took the crew on board and landed them at Grimsby.

Wreck-site
Steve Cooper, a local diver, is reported to have identified the wreck in 1986 by her name on the bows. She lies on a hard, flat seabed of sand and gravel, in a general depth of 13m, the lowest astronomical depth. The wreck is collapsed and well broken up, with the highest 3m section being around the boiler and engine. This is a small wreck and, being a trawler, the most interesting part to look at is the stern section, although there is very little to see. Most of the site is just a mass of broken battered iron debris. The tidal streams are fairly brisk and underwater visibility is usually very poor.

RICHARD, ex GWENLLIAN THOMAS
Wreck *
Depth 19m
Reference: N53 32 968 E000 10 480
Location: In the Humber Estuary, 2.74 miles SE from Spurn Point

The *Richard* (signal letters: MCPN) was an iron 1,082-ton Norwegian steamship that measured 68.70m in length, with a 9.53m beam and a 5.18m draught. Palmers completed building her as the *Gwenllian Thomas* at Newcastle-upon-Tyne in 1882 and she was owned at the time of loss by A/S D/S Richerd. Albr. W. Selmer of Trondhjem was her manager. A 2-cylinder compound steam engine that developed 118nhp using one boiler, also built by Palmers, powered her single iron screw propeller. She had one deck and a superstructure consisting of a 34.44m quarterdeck, a 13.41m bridgedeck and an 8.53m forecastle.

On 20 January 1911, the *Richard* was in ballast on passage from Antwerp for Grimsby when she foundered and was lost following a collision with the steamship *Aaro*. The *Aaro* saved all of her crew.

Wreck-site
The wreck, which is possibly that of the *Richard*, lies in a small scour, in a general depth of 19m, the lowest astronomical depth. The remains are totally collapsed, well broken up and dispersed, standing no more than 1-2m, with just a few sections of iron plate, ribs and broken unrecognisable bits of machinery left of her. If the ship's bell is still around, it will probably be inscribed 'Gwenllian Thomas' and '1882', the date she was built. Tidal streams are fairly strong and underwater visibility is usually very poor most of the year.

VALPA, HM Trawler
Wreck *
Depth 10m
Reference: N53 33 848 E000 12 477
Location: 3.59 miles E by S from Spurn Point

The *Valpa* was a steel 230-ton British steam fishing trawler that measured 37.66m in length, with a 6.73m beam and a draught of 3.55m. J. Duthie, Torry Shipbuilding Co., built her at Aberdeen. The vessel originally belonged to Clifton Steam Trawlers Ltd of Fleetwood but The Admiralty, who was the owner at the time of loss, hired her as an auxiliary patrol vessel in 1915. Her single iron screw propeller was powered by a 75hp 3-cylinder triple expansion steam engine that used one boiler. Lidgerwood Ltd built her machinery at Glasgow. She had one deck, three bulkheads and a superstructure consisting of a 23.47m quarterdeck, a 4.88m forecastle and was classed at Lloyd's as 100 A1.

The trawler was on patrol duties off the Humber Estuary when she detonated a German-laid mine on 19 March 1916, foundered and was lost.

Wreck-site
The wreck lies on a seabed of sand and shell, in a general depth of 10m, the lowest astronomical depth. She is totally collapsed, broken up and well dispersed, with very little remaining except some bits of steel plates and unrecognisable pieces of broken machinery. The site is now marked down on the charts as being a 'foul' ground, meaning nothing remains over 2m high. Tidal streams are quite strong and underwater visibility is usually very poor to grim most of the year. The wreck-site is also in the main shipping channel, so anyone contemplating a dive should keep a good lookout.

H75 *Foxhound*. Built by C.W. & G., Hull, 1889, for Humber Steam Trawling Co. (Hull). Yard no.39. Length: 100ft 7in, Gross Tonnage: 140. Sunk in collision with GY62 *Olympia* off Spurn Head, 27 January 1909. *(Courtesy Jonathan Grobler Collection)*

FOXHOUND
Wreck ★★
Depth 15m
Reference: N53 33 801 E000 08 696
Location: 1.40 miles SE from Spurn Point

The *Foxhound* (Official No.95803) was an iron 140-ton British steam fishing trawler that was registered at Hull. She measured 30.69m in length with a 6.37m beam. Cook, Welton & Gemmell built her as Yard No.39 at Hull and launched her as the *Foxhound* on 26 August 1889. The new owner, Humber Steam Trawling Co. Ltd at Hull, who was the owner at the time of loss, registered her as Hull trawler No.H75 on 10 September 1889. A 3-cylinder triple expansion steam engine that developed 45nhp using one boiler powered her single iron screw propeller, which gave her a maximum speed of 10 knots. Bailey & Leetham built her machinery at Hull.

On 27 January 1909, the *Foxhound* was on a return fishing voyage from Hull when she foundered and was lost off Spurn Head, following a collision with the 221-ton Grimsby-registered trawler *Olympia* (No.GY62). The *Olympia* was also badly damaged, but was able to reach Grimsby under her own steam. However seven years later, on 3 August 1916, she was on a return fishing voyage from Grimsby when an Imperial German submarine captured her 3.5 miles east from Coquet Island. Captain A. Smith and his crew were ordered to abandon ship and the trawler was sunk by gunfire.

Wreck-site
The wreck, possibly that of the *Foxhound*, lies on a seabed of sand, gravel and stone, in a general depth of 15m, the lowest astronomical depth. She is orientated in a north to south direction, lying in a 2m scour. The wreck is totally collapsed, well broken up and standing no more than 4m high around the engine and boiler, which are surrounded by a mound of collapsed broken

iron debris. Tidal streams are quite fierce and underwater visibility is usually very poor. The wreck is situated right in the main fairway, so it would be wise to seek advice before diving.

LAXTON, ex LILLEBONNE
Wreck ★
Depth 10m
Reference: N53 33 731 E000 05 304
Location: 0.94 miles SW from Spurn Point, near Bull Lightvessel

The *Laxton* was a steel 1,017-ton British steamship that was registered at Goole. She measured 67.05m in length, with a 10.38m beam and a draught of 3.98m. Dublin Dockyard Co. built her as the *Lillebonne* at Dublin in 1905. Wetherall Steamship Co. Ltd, who was the owner at the time of loss, purchased her and renamed the vessel *Laxton*. An aft-positioned 127hp 3-cylinder triple expansion steam engine that used one boiler powered her single iron screw propeller. Ross & Duncan built her machinery at Glasgow. She had one deck, four bulkheads, a well deck and a superstructure consisting of a 32.61m quarterdeck, a 4.27m bridgedeck and an 8.23m forecastle.

On 28 December 1916, the SS *Laxton* was on passage from Goole for Treport when she foundered and was lost in the River Humber, possibly following a collision. She was under the command of Captain C.S. Hill and carrying an unspecified cargo of coal and a crew of sixteen, all of whom were saved.

Wreck-site
The wreck is now partially buried, totally collapsed, well broken up and rather dispersed, with the highest parts of her being no more than 1.5m high. The basic structure of the hull can be made out, which is lying in a scour, on a seabed of sand and shells, in a general depth of 10m, the lowest astronomical depth. If her bell is ever recovered, it will be inscribed '*Lillebonne*' and '1905', the date she was built. Anyone contemplating diving the wreck would be advised to seek permission first, because she is in the fairway. Visibility is usually poor to non-existent and tidal streams are fairly brisk, with lots of fresh water mixed with the salt of the sea.

DAYRIAN, ex ANACAONO
Wreck ★★★
Depth 15m
Reference: N53 33 568 E000 07 647
Location: 1.05 miles SE from Spurn Point

The *Dayrian* was a steel 234-ton British steam fishing trawler that was registered at Grimsby. She had dimensions of 39.62m in length, with a 6.73m beam and draught of 3.4m. Goole Ship Builders & Repairing Co. Ltd built her as the *Anacaono* at Goole in 1906 for J. & G. Alward Ltd., who owned her until 1912. (Her tail-shaft was inspected in November 1911.) Great Central Co-operative Engine & Ship Repairing Co. Ltd of Grimsby purchased the boat in 1912 and owned her at the time of loss. The company also owned the following steam trawlers: the 221-ton *Arian*, built in 1910, the 216-ton *Carian*, built in 1911, and the 214-ton *Alysian*, built in 1912. A 3 cylinder triple expansion steam engine that developed 75hp using one boiler powered her single iron screw propeller. Her cylinders measured 31.12cm, 55.88cm and 88.90cm-60.96cm, (12.25in 22in and 35in-24in).

On 29 November 1913, the trawler was on a return fishing trip from Grimsby when, following a collision with the Swansea-registered steam trawler *Xerxes* in heavy fog, she foundered and was lost.

Wreck-site

The wreck is orientated in a north to south direction, lying in a 3m scour, on a lumpy seabed of sand and shells, in a general depth of 15m, the lowest astronomical depth. She covers an area of about 40m by 14m and is totally collapsed and broken up, with the highest section at amidships to stern. Being classed as a navigational hazard, she has been wire swept, so don't expect too much in the way of interest. She is right in the fairway, so anyone thinking of diving the wreck should approach the Humber Dock's Authority & Conservancy Board for permission. Tidal streams are very strong and underwater visibility is at the mercy of the River Humber.

ROSSINI

Wreck ★★★
Depth 24m
Reference: N53 33 323 E000 40 067
Location: 20 miles E from Spurn Head

The *Rossini* was an iron 1,321-ton British steamship registered at the port of London. She was 74.8m long with a 10.23m beam and a 5.48m draught. Bartram, Haswell & Co. built her at Sunderland and the Gordon Steamshipping Co. of London owned her at the time of loss. Her single iron screw propeller was powered by a 3-cylinder triple expansion steam engine that developed 155hp using one boiler. East Coast Engine Co. Ltd built her machinery at South Shields. She had one deck, four bulkheads and a superstructure consisting of a 27.43m quarterdeck, a 15.54m bridgedeck and a 7.92m forecastle.

On 13 July 1904, the *Rossini* was on passage from South Shields for London when, in wind conditions force four south-east, she foundered and was lost. The vessel was under the command of Captain J. West, carrying an unspecified cargo of coal and a crew of seventeen. The reason she foundered or whether any of her crew were lost is not known.

Wreck-site

The wreck, probably that of the old steamship *Rossini*, lies on a seabed of sand, gravel and small pebbles, in a general depth of 24m, the lowest astronomical depth. She is totally collapsed, well broken up and standing 2.5m high amidships, where her boiler and engine are now exposed. Most of the wreck is a mound of debris, with a number of bent and flattened copper pipes protruding from it all. Very little marine life was observed but an iron propeller and a large anchor can still be seen. Tidal streams are quite strong and underwater visibility is usually very poor.

DUNSANY

Wreck ★★
Depth 15m
Reference: N53 33 135 E000 12 479
Location: 3.76 miles ESE from Spurn Point

The *Dunsany* (Official No.70250) was an iron 832-ton (525 net tons) British schooner-rigged steamship registered at Newcastle-upon-Tyne. She measured 64.64m in length, with an 8.58m beam and a draught of 5.28m. She was specially built in 1876 for the coal trade and fitted with Price's patent self-trimming hatches at Newcastle-upon-Tyne in the Low Walker Yard of C. Mitchell & Co. Joseph Reay & Robert Bloomfield and Fenwick of Newcastle jointly owned her at the time of loss. Her single iron screw propeller was powered by a 2 cylinder compound steam engine that developed 98hp using two boilers and she was classed at Lloyd's as A1.

On 14 April 1876 SS *Dunsany* was on passage from Newcastle-upon-Tyne for London when she foundered and was lost.

She had arrived in Tyne Dock on 12 April 1876, her water ballast was pumped out and she was reloaded with 1,070 tons of gas-coal, besides thirty-nine tons of bunker-fuel. At the time, nobody suggested that she was overloaded. The vessel drew 4.88m (16ft) aft and 4.57m (15ft) forward. She sailed on 13 April, under the command of Captain William Ferguson Adams, with a crew of seventeen. The vessel left Tyne Dock on passage for London with a slight list to port. (At the hearing later, witnesses described this as 'nothing to speak of'.) When she sailed down the Tyne, the wind was blowing strong from the east, north-east and soon after crossing the bar, the foretopsail was set and she proceeded on her voyage. The wind continued blowing a strong gale, with very heavy seas and at 10 p.m. the topsail was reefed and subsequently furled. At midnight the ship was hove-to on the port-tack and the sea continued to increase, which caused the vessel to labour and the sea to breach heavily over her. From the constant lurching to one side only, the list considerably increased, and by 4 a.m. on the 14th the weather conditions were so severe that Captain Ferguson Adams decided that, in the interest of the safety of all concerned, they should make full-speed for the shelter of the River Humber. Soon after that, by the evidence available, the ship took four heavy lurches to the starboard and the list greatly increased. Up to that time no water was found inside the ship, but the sea washed up on the lee-side of the deck and covered the bunker hatch and carried away the tarpaulin and the hatch. Efforts to replace it were in vain and water was by this time seen running down the hatch. Very soon after, water flooded into the engine room, causing her list to further increase. The fires gradually went down and couldn't be kept going, then she lost all of her steam. Distress signals were made at 10 a.m. and were quickly answered by guns from the Newsome Lightship, but passing vessels appeared to take no notice of the distressed steamship. After rounding the Spurn Lightvessel, the steam-tug *Monarch of Grimsby* came to their assistance and took them in tow. The *Dunsany* proceeded in tow, but was in imminent danger of sinking and at 1 p.m., with her decks awash, she began to go down. The towrope was quickly cut, in case she dragged the *Monarch of Grimsby* to the bottom with her. With waves lashing the two ships, the stricken steamer went down stern foremost, with her masts careering into the water. Her port lifeboat and a dinghy had been previously got ready and the latter floated off the deck with four men in it. Then the lifeboat, with the captain and other crewmen in, went into the water. However, the suction from the sinking ship caused the boat to capsize and it went down with the men in it. A boat containing just the mate was sighted shortly after, but he was dead, having been crushed by the violence of the sea on the thwarts of the vessel. Finally, the captain and others, except for the second engineer and two others who were missing, were rescued and taken on board the tug.

The Court of Inquiry, held later, decided that it was not prepared to suggest that Price's self-trimming hatches may have attributed to the serious shifting of the cargo and subsequent loss of the vessel, but it would venture to suggest that where these self-trimming hatches were used, as in this case, a strong set of shifting-boards ought also to be fitted. The Court also decided that the ship had been lost by a combination of circumstances over which Captain William Ferguson Adams had no control. He was therefore exonerated from all blame and his certificate of competency returned.

Wreck-site

The wreck is orientated in an east to west direction, with her bows to the west. She lies on the eastern edge of a deep-sloping trench, in a general depth of 15m, the lowest astronomical depth, with a half to one metre scour on the northern side. The wreck is intact, but was dispersed almost to seabed level in May 1970, leaving the largest pieces of her about 1m high. However, a good rummage dive could turn up some long lost artefacts. The surrounding seabed is very undulating and strong tidal streams sweep down the channels. Underwater visibility is usually at the mercy of the River Humber, which means it is nearly always bad. Anyone contemplating diving the site should first seek advice from the Humber Conservancy Board & Humber Docks Authority, because very large ships pass close by. There are no reports of marine life near or around the wreck-site.

CELERITY
Wreck *
Depth 14m
Reference: N53 33 053 E000 07 143
Location: 1.38 miles S from Spurn Point
Also given: N53 32 826 E000 03 402
Location: 1.07 miles NE from Haile Sand Fort
Depth 7m

The *Celerity* was an iron 193-ton British steamship that measured 39.44m in length, with a 6.4m beam and a 3.17m draught. She was registered at Great Yarmouth and built by R.&W. Hawthorn Ltd at Newcastle-upon-Tyne, who also built her machinery in 1878. A. Beckett & Co. owned her at the time of loss. Her single iron screw propeller was powered by a 2 cylinder compound steam engine that developed 50hp using one boiler.

On 24 November 1901, the *Celerity* was on passage from Hull for Plymouth when, in fine weather, she foundered and was lost following a collision in the Humber Estuary. She was under the command of Captain W. Mobbs and carrying a crew of eight and a cargo of iron bars, sheet, rods and tubes.

Wreck-site
The wreck of the *Celerity* is probably in one of the two positions offered above. The first co-ordinates are for a wreck lying in a general depth of 14m, the lowest astronomical depth. The wreck is totally collapsed and well dispersed, with very little standing more than half a metre high. Just a few iron plates, bits of broken machinery and iron ribs protrude from the sand and gravel seabed. The site is situated in the main shipping lane, so permission to dive the site will probably be required by anyone contemplating doing so.

The second position offered is for a wreck lying in a general depth of 7m, being about the lowest astronomical depth and 1.07 miles north-east from Haile Sand Fort. She is no more than 1.5m high, totally collapsed and well dispersed. Underwater visibility at both these wreck-sites is usually very poor to dismal most of the time and tidal streams are quite strong.

ALBERTA, HM Trawler
Wreck *
Depth 9.5m
Reference: N53 32 178 E000 16 448
Location: 6.3 miles ESE from Spurn Point

The *Alberta* was a steel 209-ton British steam fishing trawler that measured 35.2m in length, with a 6.55m beam and a draught of 3.4m. Smith's Dock Co. Ltd built her at North Shields in 1907 for the Dominion Steam Fishing Co. Ltd. Her single iron screw propeller was powered by a 65hp 3-cylinder triple expansion steam engine that used one boiler. Shields Engineering Co. Ltd at North Shields built her machinery. She had one deck, a 19.51m quarterdeck and a 5.79m forecastle. The Royal Navy, who was the owner at the time of loss, hired the trawler in 1914 and converted her into a minesweeper.

On 14 April 1916, under the command of Captain H.W. Perry, the trawler/minesweeper detonated a German-laid contact mine, foundered and was lost off the River Humber. HMT *Orcades* also detonated a mine and was lost in the immediate vicinity.

Wreck-site
The wreck believed to be that of *Alberta*, lies on a seabed of gravel, small pebbles, sand and shells, in a general depth of 9.5m, the lowest astronomical depth. She is now totally collapsed,

broken up and well dispersed, with the highest portion standing no more than 1.5m high. The site is now just marked down on the admiralty chart as 'foul' ground. Scattered bits of steel plates, an anchor, iron propeller and broken machinery litter the area. There is very little of interest and tidal streams are quite strong. Underwater visibility is also usually poor to rather grim most of the year.

ORCADES, HM Trawler
Wreck *
Depth 9m
Reference: N53 32 129 E000 16 284
Location: 6.31 miles ESE from Spurn Point

The *Orcades* was a steel 270-ton British steam fishing trawler that measured 39.09m in length, with a 6.7m beam and a draught of 3.78m. Cochrane & Sons built her at Selby in 1911 for the Artic Steam Fishing Co. Ltd at Grimsby. A 71hp 3-cylinder triple expansion steam engine that used one boiler powered her single iron screw propeller. Amos & Smith Ltd built her machinery at Hull. She had one deck and a 21.03m quarterdeck. The Admiralty, who was the owner at the time of loss, hired the boat in 1914.

On 14 April 1916, HMT *Orcades* foundered and was lost off the Humber after detonating a German-laid contact-mine. She was under the command of Captain A. Intress on Royal Navy service at the time. HMT *Alberta* also detonated a mine and was lost in the immediate vicinity.

Wreck-site
The wreck, believed to be that of the trawler, lies on a seabed of gravel, small pebbles, sand and shells, in a general depth of 9m, the lowest astronomical depth. She is now totally collapsed, broken up and well dispersed, with the highest portion standing no more than 1m high. The site is now just marked down on the admiralty chart as 'foul' ground. Scattered bits of steel plates, ribs and broken machinery litter the area. There is very little of interest and tidal streams are quite strong. Underwater visibility is also usually poor to rather grim most of the year.

EASTERN COUNTIES, ex TRIAL, ex STRAIT FISHER
Wreck **
Depth 19m
Reference: N53 32 351 E000 08 180
Location: 2.26 mile S from Spurn Point

The *Eastern Counties* was an iron British steamship that was registered at Great Yarmouth. She measured 53.19m in length, with a 7.96m beam and a draught of 3.78m. M'ilwaine & McColl built her as the *Strait Fisher* at Belfast in 1890 for Fisher & Sons at Barrow. A 98hp 3-cylinder triple expansion steam engine that used one boiler powered her single iron screw propeller. Her cylinders measured 43.18cm, 68.58cm and 111.76cm-76.20cm, (17in 27in and 44in-30in). Vessel's builders also built her machinery. W.A. Grainger of Belfast purchased the vessel in 1900 and renamed her *Trial*. H. Newhouse & Co. Ltd of Yarmouth, who was the owner at the time of loss, purchased her in 1910 and renamed her *Eastern Counties*.

On 12 October 1911, the steamship *Eastern Counties* was on passage from Great Yarmouth for Hull when she foundered and was lost after capsizing during heavy weather in the Humber Estuary. She was carrying a general cargo, which included mostly fish/Herring.

Wreck-site

This wreck is probably that of the steamer *Eastern Counties*. She lies on a seabed of sand and gravel, in a general depth of 19m, the lowest astronomical depth. She sits in a 2-3m scour, is partially buried, totally collapsed and well broken up and standing some 3m high. The whole area is a mound of iron plates and broken machinery scattered about the seabed, with the remains of a boiler and engine amidst it. If this is the wreck of the *Eastern Counties*, it is most likely that her bell, if recovered, would be inscribed 'Strait Fisher' and the year she was built '1890'. Tidal streams are very strong and it would be wise to seek permission before conducting a dive, because she is in the fairway. Underwater visibility is usually very poor to grim and the best time to dive on the wreck would be after a long spell of dry settled weather.

TRIGNAC

Wreck ★★★★
Depth 19m
Reference: N53 31 925 E000 47 767
Location: 24.68 miles E by S from Spurn Point

The *Trignac* was a steel 2,375-ton French steamship that was registered at the port of Nantes. She measured 86.14m in length, with a 12.37m beam and a draught of 5.97m. Chantiers Nantais de Constructions Maritimes at Nantes built her in 1903 and Soc. Anon des Chargeurs de L'Ouest owned her at the time of loss. Her single iron screw propeller was powered by a 3-cylinder triple expansion steam engine that developed 228hp using two boilers. Schneider & Co. built her machinery at Creusot. She had one deck, a 5.79m poop deck, a 26.82m quarterdeck and an 8.84m forecastle. This vessel was fitted with a stern-positioned iron steering helm, as well as her normal steering.

On 25 February 1916, the SS *Trignac* foundered and was lost when she detonated a mine laid by the Imperial German submarine SM UC 6. The steamship was in ballast, under the command of Captain H. Cauda, while on passage from Nantes for Newcastle-upon-Tyne. It is understood that her crew took to the boats and possibly landed at Grimsby.

SM UC 6 was presumed lost on 27 September 1917 with her crew of sixteen, when she ran into mine nets and detonated about eight mines off the North Foreland in position N51 30 E00 34. This type of small U-boat was not equipped with torpedoes.

Wreck-site

The wreck believed to be that of the French steamer is orientated in a north-west to south-east direction, with her bow to the north-west. She lies on a seabed of muddy sand, black shells and gravel, in a general depth of 19m, the lowest astronomical depth. The wreck sits in a scour, is collapsed, well broken up and standing about 3m high amidships where her boilers and engine are exposed. A large area of debris surrounds the wreck and strong tidal streams sweep over her. Underwater visibility is usually on the poor side, but during the summer months you could expect in excess of 10m.

KILMARNOCK
Wreck ★★
Depth 19m
Reference: N53 31 025 E000 58 324
Location: 30.97 miles ESE from Spurn Point

The *Kilmarnock* was a steel 165-ton British steam fishing trawler that was registered at Grimsby and measured 31.75m in length, with a 6.4m beam and a 3.22m draught. Mackie & Thomson built her at Glasgow and the Consolidated Steam Fishing & Ice Co. owned her at the time of loss. Her single iron screw propeller was powered by a 45hp 3-cylinder triple expansion steam engine that used one boiler. Muir & Houston Ltd built her machinery at Glasgow. She had one deck, four bulkheads and a superstructure consisting of a 5.18m quarterdeck, a 5.49m forecastle and was classed at Lloyd's as 100 A1.

On 22 September 1914, the boat was on a return voyage from Grimsby for the fishing grounds when she detonated a German-laid mine, foundered and was lost. She was under the command of Skipper W.J. Ash and carrying a crew of six, all of who were lost with the boat.

Wreck-site
This wreck could possibly be that of the steam trawler *Kilmarnock* and the grave of the men who died on her. She lies on a hard seabed of silty sand, gravel and small pebbles, in a general depth of 19m, the lowest astronomical depth. She is totally collapsed, well broken up and dispersed, with the two main sections lying about 200m apart. The largest part is 3m high in the position given above, while the other smaller section to the east stands 1.3m high. Iron and steel debris is spread out over a fair part of the seabed, but there is little of interest to see.

Tidal streams are very strong, but underwater visibility can be excellent during the summer months, especially after a spell of calm weather and light westerly winds.

THESSALY
Wreck ★★
Depth 12m
Reference: N53 31 009 E000 23 091
Location: 8.64 miles ESE from Donna Nook

The *Thessaly* was an iron 1,925-ton British steamship that was registered at Liverpool. She measured 88.69m in length, with a 10.36m beam and a draught of 7.62m. Laird Brothers built her in 1877 and the Birkenhead Shipping Co. Ltd of Liverpool owned her at the time of loss. Her single iron screw propeller was powered by a 2-cylinder compound steam engine that developed 220hp using one boiler.

On 28 December 1890 the SS *Thessaly* was on passage from New Orleans for Hamburg when she caught fire off Borkum in the Friesian Islands. She was under the command of Captain J.B. Gordon, carrying a cargo of raw cotton and oil-seed cake, one passenger and a crew of twenty-nine. The crew abandoned ship in the boats, but the passenger, a fisherman who had been picked up en-route, was lost. The burning vessel then drifted right across the North Sea, in wind conditions north-east by east, force four, before sinking off the Humber Estuary.

The wreck was identified in 1988 when divers recovered the ship's bell. She sits in a small scour on a seabed of pebbles, gravel and sand, in a general depth of 12m, the lowest astronomical depth. The wreck is totally collapsed and well broken up, with the highest sections standing up to 2m high surrounded by a mound of broken iron debris. Tidal streams are fairly brisk, but visibility is usually very poor, depending on how much sediment comes from the Humber.

RIEVAULX ABBEY
Wreck ★
Depth 8m
Reference: N53 30 682 E000 17 889
Location: 7.72 miles SE from Spurn Point, and 0.77 miles ENE from Rosse Spit Buoy

The *Rievaulx Abbey* was a steel 1,166-ton British steamship that was registered at Hull. She measured 77.8m in length, with a beam of 10.23m and a draught of 4.67m. Earle's & Co. Ltd built her at Hull in 1908 and J.H.N. Ringrose of the Hull & Netherlands Steamship Co. Ltd at Hull was the owner at the time of loss. A 3-cylinder triple expansion steam engine that developed 499hp using three boilers powered her single iron screw propeller. She had one deck, a well deck, and a superstructure consisting of a 9.14m poop deck, a 12.19m quarterdeck, 27.43m bridgedeck and a 10.16m forecastle. The vessel was fitted with a stern-positioned iron steering helm, as well as her normal steering equipment.

On 3 September 1916, the SS *Rievaulx Abbey* was on passage from Rotterdam for Hull when she foundered and was lost after detonating a mine. The Imperial German submarine UC 10 had laid the mine. The steamer was under the command of Captain H.W. Pearse and carrying an unspecified general cargo. Two of her crew were lost with the ship.

UC 10 had already been lost two weeks earlier, when the British submarine HMS E54 torpedoed her off the Schouwen-Bank in the Dover Strait on 21 August 1916.

Wreck-site
The wreck is orientated in a north-west to south-east direction, with her bows to the north-west. She lies on a seabed of gravel, small pebbles, sand and shells, in a general depth of 8m, being about the lowest astronomical depth. The wreck is now partially buried, totally collapsed, well broken up and rather dispersed, with the highest section of 0.75m being amidships, where the remains of her engine and boiler can be found. Most of the wreck is now flat and level with the surrounding seabed. Tidal streams are rather strong, but it would be possible to visit the site at any state of the tide. However, underwater visibility is usually very poor, with little marine life to be found.

FITTONIA
Wreck ★★★
Depth 19m
Reference: N53 29 494 E000 52 708
Location: 27.95 miles E by S from Spurn Point

The *Fittonia* was an iron 146-ton British steam fishing trawler that was registered at Grimsby as trawler No.GY390. She measured 29.61m in length, with a 6.24m beam and a draught of 3.35m. Cochrane, Cooper & Schofield built her at Beverley in 1891 and North Eastern Steam Fishing Co. Ltd owned her at the time of loss. Her single iron screw propeller was powered by a 3-cylinder triple expansion steam engine that developed 45hp using one boiler, giving her a maximum speed of 10 knots. Charles D. Holmes & Co. built her machinery at Hull. She had one deck, a 5.18m quarterdeck and a 5.18m forecastle.

On 2 September 1914 the *Fittonia* was on a return fishing voyage from Grimsby when she detonated a German-laid mine, foundered and was lost. The mine, which may have been one that had broken loose, was one of the mines laid by the Kaiserliche Deutsche Marine minelayer SMS *Nautilus* on the night of 25-26 August 1914 in the area limited by N53 50' to N53 40' and E00 33' to E00 38'. On the same night, the Imperial minelayer SMS *Albatros* laid mines in the same operation in the area N54 55' to N55 8' and W01 09' to W01 17'.

Wreck-site

The wreck, which is possibly that of the trawler *Fittonia*, is orientated in a north to south direction. She lies on a seabed of loose sandy sediment and gravel, in a general depth of 19m, the lowest astronomical depth. The wreck is partially buried, totally collapsed and well broken up, with the highest section of 1.02m being around the boiler/engine area. Tidal streams are very strong and underwater visibility is rather poor, but can be excellent during the summer months.

KHARTOUM, ex BELTOR

Wreck ★★★★
Depth 16.5m
Reference: N53 28 816 E000 43 991
Location: 22.53 miles ESE from Spurn Point

The *Khartoum* was a steel 3,020-ton British steamship registered at the port of London. She was 96.01m long, with a 12.31m beam and a draught of 6.14m. Ropner & Son built her as the *Beltor* at Stockton-on-Tees in 1893 for J. Holman & Sons of London. Gordon Steamshipping Co. Ltd of London purchased the vessel in 1913-1914 and renamed her *Khartoum*. In 1914, she passed into the ownership of the Anglo-Bretagne Shipping Co. Ltd at Cardiff. Her single iron screw propeller was powered by a 3-cylinder triple expansion steam engine that developed 246hp using two boilers. Blair & Co. Ltd built her machinery at Stockton-on-Tees. She had one deck, five bulkheads and a superstructure that consisted of an 8.84m poop deck and a 28.65m bridgedeck.

At 11.40 a.m. on 26 November 1914, the steamship *Khartoum* was on passage from the Tyne for Oran when she detonated a German-laid mine. She was under the command of Captain C.A. Wilson, carrying a crew of twenty-three and a 4,050-ton cargo of coal. Captain Wilson ordered his crew to abandon ship in the boats when she appeared to be in the process of going down. The captain, being the last man to leave, got into one of the boats at 12.25 p.m. and they stood off. The steamer foundered by the head, exactly twenty minutes later, taking the ship's confidential papers with her. The steam trawler *Onward* picked up the survivors at 2.45 p.m. and landed them at Grimsby later that day.

Wreck-site

The wreck, possibly that of the large steamship, is orientated in a south-east to north-west direction. She lies on a seabed of small pebbles, gravel and sand, in a general depth of 16.5m, the lowest astronomical depth. She is upright, very substantial, standing some 5.5m high amidships, but with her superstructures and hull rather collapsed down. Lots of fish can be found over the wreck, so she will make an excellent boat-angling venue. If this is the wreck of the *Khartoum*, her bell if, or when, recovered will almost certainly be inscribed '*Beltor*' and the date she was built, '1893'. This steamship was equipped with two pedestal-mounted steering helms, one in the wheelhouse and the other on deck at the stern. She also had a brass pedestal-mounted telegraph, so she will be an interesting wreck to explore. Tidal streams are quite strong, but underwater visibility can be excellent during the summer months.

FAUNUS

Wreck ★
Depth 5m
Reference: N53 28 193 E000 17 244
Location: 4.71 miles E by S from Donna Nook

The *Faunus* (Registration No.6) was a steel 806-ton Swedish steamship that measured 60.3m in length, with a beam of 9.2m. She was built in 1891 at the Southampton Naval Works,

Southampton, for Rederi Aktieb Concordia of Gothenburg, who was also the owner at the time of loss. J.A. Waller of Gothenborg was the manager. Her single iron screw propeller was powered by a 3-cylinder triple expansion steam engine that developed 375hp using one boiler. The ship's builders built the machinery. A 2-cylinder compound engine that used one boiler and developed 70nhp was later fitted. This machinery was built by Akt. Lodose Varf at Lodose. (This was also a very strange thing to do, exchanging a more modern 3-cylinder tripe expansion engine for a 2-cylinder compound one.)

The SS *Faunus* left Domsjo on 12 November 1916 on passage for London with a crew of fifteen and a general cargo consisting of 327 pieces of plane wood, of which forty pieces were stowed on her deck. During the voyage across the North Sea, the vessel had to endure some very heavy weather and reached Flamborough Head at 4 p.m. on Monday 21 November. She passed the Head about five miles offshore and from that position Captain T.R. Berntsen altered course to Z-0 Magnetic. The wind moderated to south, westerly and the sea became calm, although visibility was somewhat hazy. It was dark at 6.15 p.m. and the Second Mate was on watch duty. Suddenly, a massive explosion that occurred aft rocked the ship. The *Faunus* had detonated a mine, which completely shattered the vessel's stern end. It was later learnt that the Imperial German submarine SM UC 17 had laid the mine. All of the crew who were on watch at the time, but were resting in a rear compartment/cabin, were killed instantly, while the explosion sent the deck-cargo of wood hurtling 6.10m (20ft) into the air. The engine room and rear cargo-hold immediately filled up with water and caused the steamer to take on a list of 25 degrees. The order was then given to abandon ship and launch the boats. The crew hurriedly scrambled to the boats and rowed a few yards where they stood by, but there was no trace of any of the men on watch. All of the men's personal possessions and ship's confidential papers were left on the vessel, which was underwater but still floating, probably due to her cargo of wood. The Swedish captain was reluctant to leave his ship while she was still afloat. A number of other ships were sighted on the horizon and signals were sent out, but none were answered. Finally, at 9.a.m. the following morning, the Danish-registered steamer *N.A.Christensen* from Copenhagen, spotted their plight and steered a course to where the stricken steamer was protruding from the water. The men were taken on board and the Danish steamer attempted to tow the *Faunus* to Spurn. The list became worse by the moment and was so bad at one particular time that her masts hit the water. Then the tow cable broke at 6 p.m. and she was abandoned. Just at that moment, the *Faunus* capsized, leaving her keel-up in the air before making her final plunge to the bottom. At 10 a.m. that morning of 23 November 1916, the survivors were put on board the British steamship *Glocliffe*, which landed them at Hull at 1.15 p.m.

SM UC 17 went on to survive until the end of the First World War and surrendered post-war. She became British war-reparation and was broken up at Preston in 1919-1920.

Those who died on the *Faunus* were:

Ragnar Leonard Petterson, a married able seaman who was born on 23 July 1888 and lived in Hindas (Alvsborg).
Gustav Herbert Andersson, an unmarried able seaman who was born on 12 June 1892 and lived in Valdemarsvik.
Axel Eggert Orbom, an unmarried able seaman who was born on 2 April 1897 and lived in Vasta, Frolunda (near Goteborg).
Ernst Albin Kohlstrom, an unmarried young cabin boy who lived at Vasteras.
Erik Julius Persson, an unmarried stoker who was born on 18 May 1892 and lived at Fagre (near Skaraborg).
Finally, Herbert Gustav Sjoberg, an unmarried stoker who was born on 7 November 1897 and resided in Stockholm.

Wreck-site

The wreck is now totally collapsed, well broken up and dispersed around the seabed. She lies in a general depth of 5m, the lowest astronomical depth, on a seabed of sand, gravel, small pebbles, shells and weed. There is very little left of the vessel, which is partially buried and dispersed. A few sections of her steel hull plating, bits of broken machinery and parts of her boiler are all that remain. Very little marine life has been reported on the site. Tidal streams are very strong and underwater visibility is usually rather grim, but improves a little during the summer months.

ELBA

Wreck ★★★★
Depth 17m
Reference: N53 28 186 E000 53 008
Location: 28.36 miles E from Spurn Point

The *Elba* was a steel 2,293-ton British steamship registered at London. She was 89.96m long with an 11.63m beam and a draught of 6.14m. R. Dixon & Co. built her at Middlesbrough in 1889 and Bucknall & Nephews owned her at the time of loss. A 300hp 3-cylinder triple expansion steam engine that used one boiler powered her single iron screw propeller. T. Richardson & Sons built her machinery at Hartlepool. She had one deck, a well deck and a superstructure consisting of a 35.36m quarterdeck, a 37.19m bridgedeck and a 9.14m fore-castle.

On 4 July 1893, the SS *Elba* was on passage from Bombay for Hull when she foundered and was lost following a collision in thick fog with the North Shields-registered steamship *William Balls*. The *Elba* was under the command of Captain Warrick and carrying a cargo of wheat. It is understood that the crew abandoned ship safely and took to the boats. The *William Balls* was so badly damaged that she also sank close by, but no one was lost.

Wreck-site

This is possibly the wreck of the large steamer *Elba*. She is orientated in a south, south-east to north, north-west direction and lies on a seabed of loose, sandy silt, gravel and shells, in a general depth of 17m, the lowest astronomical depth. She is upright, but partially buried, collapsed and broken up, with the tallest parts standing some 4.7m high. Iron debris, including an old anchor and parts of a winch can be seen, along with a large mound of broken iron debris. The ship was equipped with two pedestal-mounted steering helms, one in the wheel-house and one on deck at the stern end, so she will be a nice wreck to explore. Soft corals cover much of the highest structures and lots of fish have been observed. Tidal streams are extremely strong and confused with over-falls present on spring tides, but underwater visibility can be tremendous during the summer months, often reaching 25m.

WILLIAM BALLS

Wreck ★★★
Depth 16m
Reference: N53 27 753 E000 51 975
Location: 27.84 miles E from Spurn Point

The *William Balls* was an iron 1,612-ton British steamship that was registered at North Shields. She measured 78.94m in length, with an 11.27m beam and a draught of 5.38m. J. Redhead & Co. built her at South Shields in 1883 and William D.C. Balls & Co. of South Shields owned her at the time of loss. Her single iron screw propeller was powered by a 2-cylinder compound steam engine that developed 150hp using two boilers. Her cylinders measured 76.20cm and 147.32cm-91.44cm, (30in and 58in-36in). She was classed at Lloyd's as 100 A1 and had one deck, a well deck, a 30.18m quarterdeck, a 19.51m bridgedeck and an 8.84m forecastle.

On 4 July 1893, the SS *William Balls* was on passage from South Shields for Smyrna when she sank in thick fog following a collision with the London-registered steamer *Elba*. She was under the command of Captain W.H. Welch and carrying an unspecified cargo of coal. The steamer *Elba* also foundered close by, but both crews abandoned ship safely and took to the boats.

Wreck-site

The wreck, which is possibly that of the steamship *William Balls*, is orientated in a north-east to south-west direction, with her bows to the south-west. She sits in a small scour, on a seabed of loose, sandy silt, gravel and shells, in a general depth of 16m, the lowest astronomical depth. The wreck is collapsed and broken up, but stands some 5.2m high amidships and covers an area of 84m by 24m. Lots of iron debris and broken machinery are strewn around, with soft corals and beautiful plume anemones adorning the pieces of debris. A couple of sets of bollards, a large anchor, chain and one massive iron propeller have all been observed amongst the wreckage. The wreck will make an excellent one to explore, even if she is not the *William Balls*. Tidal streams are exceptionally strong and currents are confused with over-falls present in the immediate vicinity. Underwater visibility compensates for the tides, because it is excellent during the summer months.

HEATHPOOL

Wreck ★★★
Depth 13m
Reference: N53 27 538 E001 05 169
Location: Outer Dowsing Shoal

The *Heathpool* was a steel 3,828-ton British steamship that was registered at Newcastle-upon-Tyne. She measured 103.63m in length, with a 14.36m beam and a draught of 8.35m. Furness, Withy & Co. Ltd of West Hartlepool built her in 1906 and Peareth Steamship Co. Ltd (Beckingham & Co.) at Newcastle-upon-Tyne owned her at the time of loss. A 317nhp 3-cylinder triple expansion steam engine that used two boilers powered her single iron screw propeller. She was equipped with two pedestal-mounted steering helms, one of which was positioned on deck aft, plus at least one brass pedestal-mounted telegraph.

On 9/10 December 1906, the SS *Heathpool* was on passage from Hull for the River Plate, Buenos Aires, when she struck the Outer Dowsing Shoal in squally weather and poor visibility. The vessel stranded, but then slipped back into deeper water and sank, with the loss of her crew of twenty-four. She was under the command of Captain J. Grieves and carrying an unspecified cargo of coal.

Wreck-site

The wreck sits in a scour, is now totally collapsed, well broken up and partially buried. She lies on a seabed of gravel and sand, in a general depth of 13m, the lowest astronomical depth. The wreck stands about 3m high around amidships, where her boilers and engine are exposed and surrounded by lots of broken machinery. Tidal streams are quite notorious, but underwater visibility can be tremendous during the summer months. The wreck will make an interesting forage dive, but should be treated with respect, because it is the grave of a lot of people.

COBRA, HMS
Wreck ★★★★
Depth 38m

Reference: N53 25 900 E001 04 549 (bow section, possibly)
Reference: N53 25 970 E001 02 433 (possibly the other half,
but could be *W.F. Vint*)
Location: 35.53 miles SE from Spurn Point and the west side of the Outer Dowsing Shoal

HMS *Cobra* was one of only two specially designed, new turbine-powered torpedo boat destroyers, built by Messrs Armstrong, Whitworth & Co. at the Elswick Works, Newcastle-upon-Tyne, and launched as a 'stock ship' in June 1899. (Stock ships were vessels laid down as speculations and, when completed, they were offered for sale to the Royal Navy or similar customers.) She was 354 tons and measured 64m in length, with a 6.4m beam and a 2.13m draught. The vessel had four funnels, quadruple shafts, each carrying three (another report says two) bronze screw propellers, powered by 10,000ihp steam turbine engines built by Messrs C.A. Parsons Turbine Co., that made her capable of a maximum speed of 36 knots. This unusual and short-lived arrangement with the propellers was an attempt to reduce the cavitations effect produced by a single screw when the shaft was rotating at the high revs-per-minute, produced by the two new powerful turbine engines. She had an armament consisting of one gun that fired 5.44 kilo (12lb) shells, five guns that fired 2.72 kilo (6lb) shells and two torpedo tubes. She had her first sea trial on 15 July 1899 and twelve sea trials altogether. The twelfth trial was the one carried out by the Admiralty and she reached a speed of 34.8 knots, as the mean average of six runs. *Cobra*, or No.674 as she was then, was damaged in a collision soon after completion and it was not until she had been repaired that the vessel was put up for offers. On 12 December 1899, the Admiralty was informed that two destroyers, No.673 and No.674, were available for purchase. The Admiralty inspected No.674 and found her structurally weak, however after some strengthening work had been carried out they purchased her for £63,500. The Admiralty's main interest in the ship was her new turbine engines, as she was to be used as a second test bed for the turbine, the first being the *Viper*. These two destroyers were not the modern type as we know them, they were more torpedo boat destroyers, light, fast and designed for that particular purpose. Unfortunately, at 5.25 p.m. on 3 August 1901, *Viper*, under the command of Lt Speke, struck the Reconquet Reef in the Channel Islands and ripped her bottom out. On that afternoon, she had been dispatched from Portsmouth to take part in the 1901 manoeuvres, her job being to search for 'enemy' torpedo boats off the Channel Islands. When the weather took a turn for the worse, her speed was reduced from 22 to 16 knots. A dense fog caused more problems, but *Viper* had sighted one of the 'enemy' boats, namely torpedo boat No.81, and increased her speed back up to 22 knots to avoid the other boat. It was then that she went aground, followed by torpedo boat No.81 and both vessels were a total loss. There had been no loss of life, but Lt Speke was reprimanded. The two wrecks were later sold for scrap after they broke up on the Reconquet Reef, part of the Casquets (rocks) at Alderney, soon after.

Cobra was ready for trial by June 1901 and turned in a mean speed of 34.7 knots with a maximum of 35.6 knots. However, her boilers had an insatiable appetite for coal and they needed an enormous increase in engine room staff to keep them supplied. Despite this type of vessel's phenomenal speed, the First Sea Lord was disgruntled at the prospect of having a whole fleet composed of similar vessels, mainly because of the increase in the number of stokers required. It would have meant that she would have had to have as many as eighty crew on board, just to keep her fires burning.

Having been fitted out at the shipyard in Elswick, Newcastle, and following acceptance into naval service by the Admiralty, Lt Bosworth Smith RN was chosen to command her. He left for Newcastle-upon-Tyne to commission the ship, accompanied by a Portsmouth crew of fifty-three. An early start had been planned for 16 September 1901, but this was not possible because all of the navigational equipment had not arrived in time and her compasses had not been swung. Lt Smith's orders were to steam her down to Portsmouth, passing no closer than five miles off Flamborough Head, then to pass between the Outer Dowsing and Dudgeon Shoals, but outside the Gabbard and Galloper Shoals. Lt Smith was also instructed to sail at dawn and anchor for the night, either off Harwich or Great Yarmouth. *Cobra* cleared the mouth of the Tyne at 11 a.m. on 17 October, with fifty-four officers and men and twenty-five contractors from the Parsons Turbine Co., who were under Mr R. Bernard, the works manager. However she spent a considerable time manoeuvring off the Tyne adjusting the compasses and then steamed on south with a heavy sea on her starboard quarter. Later it was found that great difficulty was experienced in manning the stokeholds as she rolled heavily. Due to terrible conditions Lt Smith was forced to reduce her speed from 17 knots to 10 knots, but the vessel was still thrown about violently as she steamed on through the night. Around dawn the weather improved, allowing her speed to be increased again. It was at 7 a.m. on 17 September that, without any real warning, *Cobra* was enveloped in steam, then just buckled up and broke in two, within sight of the Outer Dowsing Lightship.

Samuel Hambling, the mate in charge of the Outer Dowsing Lightship, said later that the destroyer's approach was reported to him at 7 a.m. on 18 September and he saw the *Cobra* going 'north', but noticed how she was 'plunging heavily'. (Mr Hambling said the vessel was going north, but by all accounts she must have been going south.) Fifteen minutes later he saw steam blowing off from her third funnel and immediately after that she was enveloped in a mass of gushing steam issuing from all parts. Mr Hambling said that the destroyer's bearing was at this time west by south from the lightship and at a distance of about two miles. The weather was cloudy, with the wind blowing from the north, north-west. At 7.20 a.m., he saw her settle down amidships, as if she had 'burst' herself and then watched her stern end sink, with about 30ft (9.14m) of stem/bow out of the water, which then drifted south. Hambling said there was nothing he could do to render assistance, so he hoisted distress signals (flags) and compass bearings, then fired four guns to a steamer passing westward, but it took no notice and sailed on. The flags were kept flying, but at 8 a.m., at a distance of three to four miles and bearing south by west, *Cobra* became stationary. Hambling said that, 'She was a danger to other vessels in that position and at 5 p.m. I saw a steamer go to the wreck, which was by that time six miles distant.' When Mr Hambling first saw the warship, he said she was some six miles distant and in the proper track for vessels passing up and down the coast, but when the steam was seen issuing from her, she altered course. At this point, the wind was blowing north, north-west force six, with the flooding tide running south, south-east.

At 6.45 p.m., a steam trawler passed to the westward and the lightship crew hoisted the signal, but she did not respond. Hambling said, 'when the accident happened, HMS *Cobra* was about four to five miles from the lightvessel. Just then, the vessel ported her helm, which brought her round to south-east. When she settled down amidships both ends rose up, as if attached to a hinge, and they both collapsed immediately. The stern-end began to sink and as that part went down, the fore section gradually rose up. After the stern had gone down, the fore part slipped under, but with about 30ft (9.14m) of the bows out of the water. Two of the funnels, No.2 and No.3 approached each other until they almost touched and it was at that point that the two parts of the vessel collapsed. The two funnels crunched together as the bow and stern halves both came together.'

In a report made by the *Cobra's* chief engineer later, he said, 'I remembered feeling a sharp impact, followed by the complete fracture of the hull, only two or three minutes later.' In actual fact, her back had broken across between the two after boilers and her stern section sank almost immediately. The destroyer carried a 4.27m (14ft) dinghy, a naval-whaler (a type of boat) and three collapsible Berthon boats. However, too many men clambered over the gunwale of the whaler and it capsized. Unfortunately, no one could assemble the Berthon collapsible boats and only the rowing-dinghy managed to get clear, with eight men onboard. They were able to haul four more men out of the sea, over the stern of the boat, but conditions were so cramped it made it impossible to row. The little boat, full of men and up to the gunwales in freezing water, floated around in the very rough sea for eleven hours, before the steamship *Harlington* rescued them. Around the wreck there were piteous cries for help when the already fully laden dinghy drew away from the scene. Bodies of the dead and dying floated everywhere and the lifebelts they wore were useless in the gale-force wind, heavy sea and freezing conditions.

Nothing had been heard from the *Cobra* after she left the Tyne until the disaster struck and a brief message was received at Elswick to the effect that the P&O steamer *Harlington* had picked up twelve of the crew in a dinghy and taken them to Middlesbrough. Then a further message was received about noon, informing them that one of Mr Eustace Smith's trawlers had recovered six of the bodies and taken them to Grimsby. The first news received by Portsmouth was a telegram sent at 9.40 a.m. by Mr Percey, chief engineer of the ship, to the offices of the Commander-in-Chief, Admiral Superintendent and others, connected to the warship. Officers at Portsmouth, acquainted with the North Sea, speculated on whether the *Cobra* had struck a rock or was lifted by the heavy seas onto a sandbank, but either way the result would have been the same and that she would have been a total wreck within minutes. On hearing the news, the Admiralty immediately dispatched the cruiser *St George* and torpedo boat destroyers *Jaseur*, *Angler* and *Mallard* to the scene. HMS *Angler* and *Mallard* left Sheerness at 2 p.m. on Thursday and arrived at the scene of the disaster that evening, having made rapid passage from the Medway. However, *St George*, *Angler* and *Mallard* returned to Sheerness and *Jaseur* to Portsmouth on the Saturday, having been unsuccessful in finding any of the missing men.

King Edward sent a telegram to the Admiralty, acknowledging receipt of the terribly sad news at the loss of the *Cobra* and directing that his Majesty's deepest and most heartfelt sympathy be expressed to the relatives of those lost.

Survivor's reports:

A survivor, who was brought ashore at Middlesbrough from the *Harlington* stated:

> *We struck at half-past seven on Wednesday morning. The sea was high and there was a nasty cross-sea. The* Cobra *began to roll very heavily in the middle watch about four o'clock. It was about sunrise. I went up on deck to see what was the matter. The vessel continued to roll and then suddenly struck the shoal and the waves in a moment broke over her. Alarmed by the force of the shock, every man came on deck. Some of the men were in their berths at the time and had no time to dress themselves. The seas began to roll over the forecastle and a few moments later the* Cobra *broke in two, fore and aft. Someone gave the order to clear the boats away, I do not know whom, but I had already commenced to do this. There was a whaler and a dinghy on board and three collapsible boats. Some difficulty was experienced with the latter and I do not know if they were got out or not. The whaler and the dinghy were got out, but I think the latter was swamped. She did not take the water right. I myself cut the dinghy free and as the after part of the vessel was rising, I could see there was no hope of remaining on her and launched the dinghy. Directly she was in the water, several men boarded her from the ship. Most of the remainder of the crew jumped into the sea from fear of being taken down in the vortex, as no one knew the depth of water around. Besides, every moment an explosion from the boilers was feared. Several fortunate fellows, however, stayed on board till the end. Everything seemed to happen so quickly that I cannot tell how it was before we got clear of the ship and wreckage, but I think it would be about five minutes. As we moved away from the* Cobra *we picked up a number of men who were in the water until we had nine on board. Chief Engineer Percey was the last of the nine. Three other men hung onto the side of the dinghy for three hours before we dare bring them in, owing to the rough sea and the danger of swamping the boat, which was built to hold eight. I had, however, thrown all the tackle overboard that was not absolutely necessary and we had remaining two sculls and two oars. As we rowed away from the vessel we kept passing the bodies of drowned men and I feared that all of the crew and contractor's men, except those in the dinghy, perished. Lifebelts were no use. We rowed on all day, but we were unable to make much headway for fear of being swamped. We endeavoured to get in the track of steamers and I tried to attract*

attention by waving a stoker's towel at the end of a boat hook. Several steamers passed by without even noticing us. At length, after a weary and trying ten hours in an open boat, we were rescued by the P&O steamer Harlington.

Crewman stoker John Collins, O.N. 285171, stated:

I was on duty in the stokehold when the vessel struck. The water began to pour in almost immediately and, coming into contact with the boilers, caused clouds of steam to rise. Rushing up on deck in my trousers and singlet, accompanied by other men who were below, a thrilling spectacle met my gaze. Waves were breaking over the doomed ship, and men with cries and shouts were making in a body for the ship's whaler. Hastily snatching a lifebelt, I went in the same direction and found a place in the boat. Others tumbled in one on the other without regard to the appealing cries of those already in the boat warning them that the boat would be overturned. I estimated that forty to fifty men had rushed into the boat, with the result that it overturned and we were thrown into the raging sea. I found that my leg had been injured in the overturning, but I struck out for the dinghy and clung to the stern with two others. The occupants dared not take me on board until calmer water had been reached and it was fully an hour afterwards that I was dragged in, thoroughly exhausted and unable to hold on any longer. I was the last man to be taken into the dinghy. Meanwhile the unfortunate men who had been thrown into the sea from the whaler struggled hard for dear life, but with many of them the struggle was in vain. Numbers of them were already floating on the water, dead, not withstanding the lifebelts they wore, for those waves rendered the lifebelts useless. One man who belonged to Messrs Parson's Works, was heard to cry out just as the waves closed over him, 'Oh my God, my wife and children.' Other of the whaler's victims were sucked in under the vessel and speedily drowned.

Fishing boats were recovering bodies of the dead for weeks after the accident. On one occasion, on 15 October, the body of a sailor wearing a singlet but with no number attached, was sighted about ten miles from the Hasborough Lightship by the captain of the Sunderland-registered steamer *Eider*, which was bound for Ramsgate with a cargo of coal. Members of the crew put off in the ship's boat and found the body, which was in a very decomposed condition. The body, which was undoubtedly one of the crew of HMS *Cobra*, was committed to the sea again. (This was a course of action that would not be allowed to happen today.)

The sunken bow section of the ill-fated destroyer was eventually located by the Neptune Salvage Co.'s vessel *Herakles*, and a Swedish diver working from her made a number of dives on the bow/fore part and examined it. He reported that 'she lay in 15 fathoms (27.43m), with her bottom up and none of her hull-plates stove-in. She was broke in half close to one of the boilers with jagged ends of metal, however the stern section was not found within 60ft of the wreck.' However, he did find an indentation in the keel-plate of about an inch (2.54cm) deep and extending for about a foot (30.48cm) in the immediate neighbourhood of the jagged rent, which divided the halves. The stern has never been found to date, either.

The merchant steamship *Oakwell* later reported that she had steamed over some floating timbers about six miles north-east from the Dudgeon Lightvessel and said it could have possibly been from a wreck. Striking a submerged wreck or a shoal were other reasons which could have caused the warship to sink, according to some official people at the time.

Out of all those men on board, just twelve survived and, having sent many of their best skilled men on the trip, it was a crippling blow to Parsons Turbine Co. There was a public outcry on Tyneside following the loss, which forced a Court of Inquiry. Tests made by Wolf also concluded that the vessel was structurally unsound when she put to sea. Although Parsons' turbine engines were in no way to blame, it was ironic that two similar vessels driven by the new-fangled turbine engines were lost within a few weeks of each other.

A List of Royal Navy Officers & Men on board HMS *Cobra*

Smith, A.W.B.	Lieutenant RN
Wood, Thomas J.	Boatswain
Cole, F.	Boatswain
Percey, J.G.O.	Chief Engineer (saved)
Adams, Richard,	Stoker O.N. 287773
Ashbey, Chas	Stoker O.N. 290564 (saved)
Auld, Thomas Morrow	Stoker O.N. 288307
Barnes, Francis K.	P.O. 1st Class O.N. 128025 (saved)
Barrett, Edward Ludlow	Stoker O.N. 276860
Borrett, Ed.	Stoker O.N. 286217
Bridge, Henry J.	Stoker O.N. 295??5
Burnett, John	Stoker O.N. 288179
Cannon, Michael	Stoker O.N. 287712
Chivers, F.A.	Domestic 2nd Class O.N. 359141 (saved)
Coates, Charles E.	Stoker O.N. 287706
Collins, John	Stoker O.N. 285171 (saved)
Comley, Isaac Allen	Stoker O.N. 294995
Currie, Alex	Stoker O.N. 267867
Davidson, Alexander	Stoker O.N. 286517
Edwards, George J.	Ship's Steward O.N. 158889
Edwards, Henry	Domestic 3rd Class O.N. 100286
Farmer, Walter Edmund	Stoker O.N. 294997
Ford, William O.	Stoker O.N. 287648
Gates, Frederick W.	Stoker O.N. 167194
Griffiths, William	Domestic 1st Class O.N. 123839
Hardy, Charles	Leading stoker 3rd Class O.N. 142959
Redfern, William	Stoker O.N. 281854
Harfield, Joseph	Stoker O.N. 286016
Hayter, William A.	Stoker O.N. 285465
Head, John	Leading stoker 2nd Class O.N. 164211
Hoare, Edwin J.	Leading Signalman O.N. 120667
Hughes Thomas J.	Stoker O.N. 282976
Hutchinson, Henry L.	A.B. O. N. 131554 (saved)
Johnson, Alexander	Leading Signalman
Keirnan, Thomas	Stoker O.N. 278800
Kendall, William T.	Stoker O.N. 294998
King, Charles	Stoker O.N. 115412
Lavender, Ernest	Stoker O.N. 356123
McGinn, Janes	Stoker O.N. 164077
Montague, Fredk P.	A.B. O.N. 163360
Norton, Frederick	Stoker 1st Class O.N. 132576
Osgood, Henry J.	Ship's Cook O.N. 136510 (saved)
Privett, Ernest	Carpenter's Mate O.N. 151469 (saved)
Rose, William Edward	Sick-berth Steward O.N. 138783
Sellings, Henry C.	A.B. O.N. 187890
Seymour, John	Stoker O.N. 288498
Shayler, Benjamin	A.B. O.N. 168397 (saved)
Tuffrey, Leonard	A.B. O.N. 172594
Turvey, Walter	A.B. O.N.177308
Waldron, George	A.B. O.N. 140654
Warrener, F.H.	PO 1st Class O.N. 119950 (saved)

Wassel, Thomas	Stoker O.N. 295002
Webb, Walter John	Chief Engine Room Artificer 2nd Class O.N. 128927
Woolford, George	Leading Stoker 1st class O.N. 142477

Messrs Parsons Turbine Co. staff

Mr Robert Bernard	(Work's Manager) 10 Stanwick St, Tynemouth.
Edward Lee	(Foreman-fitter) 21 Morley St, Heaton, Newcastle.
Ralph Richardson	(Foreman-fitter) 40 Brighton Rd., Gateshead.
John Abel	(Fitter) 44 Denmark St, Heaton, Newcastle.
J.W. Webb	(Fitter) 9 Fifth Avenue, Heaton.
T. Boyd	4 Blindburn St, Heaton.
Walter Bates	(Fitter) 20 Alice St, South Shields (saved).
J. Blacklock	(Fitter) 20 Second St, Bensham, Gateshead (saved).
W.T. Orton	(Fitter) Newcastle.
J. Hamilton	22 Napier St, Jarrow-on-Tyne.
T. Bailbey	56 Woodbine Avenue, Wallsend-on-Tyne.
Robert Mackenzio	(Seaman) 56 Westminster St, Gateshead.
J. Puncheon	(Apprentice-fitter) 32 Catherine St, Jarrow-on-Tyne
George Spillett	(Fireman) 100 Laurel St, Wallsend-on-Tyne.
W. Ewert	6 Artisan Terrace, Wallsend.
Mr Dinning	An engineer from South Shields who went with the vessel for the run.
G. MacGreger	(Apprentice-fitter) 69 Molynoux St, Heaton.
B. Patterson	(Fitter) 13 School St, Bensham.
Mr Crichton	(Fitter) address unknown.
J. Patrick	(Attendant with the electrical dynamos) Richmond St, Gateshead.
Tom Wilcox	(Attendant with the electrical dynamos) Armstrong St, Bensham.
Fred Keeping	South Shields, sailed with *Cobra* on the Tuesday trials.

Some of the latter men were involved with Messrs Higginbottom & Co. of Newcastle who were the caterers for the voyage.

By 15 November 1901, £4,992 16s 4d had been raised for the *Cobra* Disaster Tyneside Fund and this was before the receipts from the concert on 20 November. There was also a collection at the football match between Middlesbrough and Newcastle United on 23 October that raised £79 3s 6d, as well as a variety of collections and events across Tyneside

The court martial of Lt Bosworth Smith RN (deceased) was held on board the *Victory* at Portsmouth, under the presidency of Rear Admiral Pelham Aldrich in mid-October 1901. The court found that *Cobra* did not touch ground or meet with any obstruction and that her loss was not due to any error of navigation, thus vindicating Lt Smith, who went down with the ship. The court sent a message to his relatives and friends conveying 'the highest consolation that it is in human power to give.' The court also found that the loss of the *Cobra* was due to structural weaknesses and that she was weaker than other destroyers. No blame was attached to the chief engineer, Mr Percey, or to any of the other survivors.

Three experts who were called to give evidence at the hearing included a government servant, an independent person from a private company and a designer and builder of ships. They were in fact the helmsman, the diver and Mr P. Watts, Esq. The designer, Mr Watts, stated that 'the vessel did not collapse from wave motion alone, that she was relatively stronger at the section where she parted than at a similar section nearer the middle point of the ship. Also that the section of the plating was weaker, or had less expansive strength on each side of the fracture at the frames than at the actual section of the parted hull, showing that neither hogging nor sagging could account for the disaster.' Secondly, the evidence of the helmsman at the time shows that he received orders 'to put the helm hard-a-starboard, after which he was steering east with the wind north-west,' or thereabouts in nautical terms, 'on the quarter'. He then received orders 'to again put helm hard-a-starboard' with both engines going ahead at what was considered a very high rate of knots. The result of this would be to bring the full force of the wind on the beam or broadside, and ultimately on the bow, but the vessel only came up north-east. Consequently the wind was on the beam in full force with rough seas.' He then received orders to 'stop port engine and go ahead starboard,' but still the vessel refused to come round and fell back to east. Both engines were then ordered 'slow speed ahead,' and soon afterwards the *Cobra* seemed to be on a pivot. It was then that the captain ordered the boats out. Mr Watts stated that, 'now if we consider what the effect of such an evolution would have on this lightly built ship of great length, relative to her amidships section, we may be able to draw a reasonable inference as to the excessive and abnormal strains brought upon this lightly built structure at a very crucial moment of the disaster.' He went on to say that, 'to put a helm hard over under favourable circumstances when a vessel is at a moderate speed, brings considerable strain on the ship at both ends and, in this case, the ship was heading east, with strong wind north-west, with heavy seas running. An attempt was made to alter course suddenly, so by putting the helm hard starboard, the effect of which was to bring the wind full on the beam and, consequently, with the rough sea, it offered an almost rigid obstacle. These actions resulted in excessive and abnormal stresses on the structure in the lateral direction.' After all these years, the circumstances of her loss are still debated today.

In a reassessment of the loss of HMS *Cobra* in 1985, the transactions of Royal Institution of Naval Architects showed that the most likely cause was structural weakness of the deck under compression (in other words buckling), leading to break-up in waves. Authors in the report included world experts in ship structures Prof. D. Faulkner and (the late) Dr C.S. Smith.

Footnote
It may be helpful to take notes from this information for anyone wishing to search for the stern section, or even the bows, which are not guaranteed to be where they are said to be.

The Outer Dowsing Lightvessel at the time was moored at co-ordinates N53 27 00 E01 05' 06' and it was 1 ½ hours before high water, when the depth of water would have been about 24.38m (80ft). Now there is no Outer Dowsing Lightvessel but the head of the shoal, some six to seven miles to the north, is marked by the north Outer Dowsing light buoy and approach to the channel by the Dowsing Lightvessel is on the west side of the channel, not the east side.

The Swedish diver examined the bow/fore section of the wreck in 1901 and reported that it was in 15 fathoms (27-28m). The wreck suggested for the bows lies in a depth of 38m, a considerable difference in depths! Samuel Hambling, mate from the lightship, said that the *Cobra* was about two miles west by south from the lightship when he saw steam coming from her. Then the bow/fore section drifted for three to four miles and even six miles distance when he saw a steamer going to it. There was a north, north-west force six wind blowing and the tide was flooding, running south, south-east, so the wreck would have been blown and drifted, more or less in the same direction at quite a speed, before coming to rest. Another important point to remember is that the vessel was 64m in length and broken in two halves about amidships between No.2 and No.3 funnels, so both halves would have been about the same size, 32m each. Until someone has dived on the two wrecks, we shall probably be all just presuming that this is the *Cobra*.

Wreck-site
The wreck of the bow section, or what is possibly the *Cobra* bow section, is orientated in a south-east to north-west direction. She lies on a seabed of loose sandy sediment, in a general depth of 38m, the lowest astronomical depth. The wreck was reported as being upside down, (or bottoms-up) and broken off in a clean break near the boilers. She is 50m in length, 25m wide and standing some 3.3m high, with little access to the top structures, which are now

partially buried and rather flattened. Tidal streams are very strong and confused, while under-water visibility is quite good to excellent during the summer months, especially on neap tides after a spell of light westerly winds.

The second co-ordinates offered are believed to be those for the small British ferry *W.E. Vint*, however the wreck has similar stern proportions to that of the *Cobra*. The *W.E. Vint* was lost on 12 August 1957 while she was being towed by the steam-tug *George V* from Sunderland to Southend-on-Sea. The vessel, which was approximately 16-18m in length and sank in position N53 26' 00 E01 02' 00, was still above water at the bows. She lies on a seabed of loose, sandy sediment, in a general depth of 15m, the lowest astronomical depth. She is fairly collapsed, standing 2.5m high and covers an area of some 39m by 14m. This wreck will be well worth investigating, being not far from where the *Cobra* went down, because there are no more known wrecks in this vicinity. Tidal streams are very strong but, with a moderate depth, it should be possible to make a good search of the remains.

WENTWORTH
Wreck ★★★
Depth 64m
Reference: N53 25 014 E000 38 626
Location: 21.29 miles SE from Spurn Point and the southern end of the Silver Pit

The *Wentworth* was an iron 411-ton British coastal steamer that was registered at Newcastle-upon-Tyne. She measured 50.9m in length, with a 7.49m beam and a draught of 4.01m. She was built at North Shields in 1866 and was owned at the time of loss by T. & W. Smith of Newcastle-upon-Tyne. Records show her single iron screw propeller was powered by a 50hp 3-cylinder triple expansion steam engine that used one boiler, however this was very early for an engine of this type and it may have been a 2-cylinder compound steam engine. She had one deck, four bulkheads and was classed at Lloyd's as A1 for Newcastle-upon-Tyne-coasting.

On 18 May 1873 the SS *Wentworth* was on passage from Shields for London, carrying a crew of fourteen and a 500-ton cargo of coal, when she foundered and was lost with six of her crew. She was under the command of Captain A. Arkley, who, at the Board of Trade court of inquiry later, was found guilty of gross carelessness and his Master's certificate was suspended for nine months. The vessel encountered heavy cross-seas during her voyage and because her ports had not been properly secured before she sailed, large amounts of water poured into the bilges and engine room. The captain and his crew took no measures to prevent this, nor did they even attempt to find a reason for it. Eventually the *Wentworth* just filled up and sank, causing six men to lose their lives.

Wreck-site
The wreck, probably that of the steamer, is at the bottom and southern-end of the long, deep trench known as the Silver Pit. She lies on a seabed of mud, sand and shells, in a general depth of 64m, the lowest astronomical depth. The wreck is partially buried, collapsed and well broken up, standing up to 2m high amidships, where her boiler and engine are all exposed. Tidal streams are very strong, but the force of the downward and upward pushing currents can be very unnerving. This is a deep and dark wreck-site, which should only be attempted by divers with the proper technology and expertise. The wreck will also be classed as a grave site!

SCHIELAND
Wreck ★★★★
Depth 13m
Reference: N53 24 399 E000 48 316
Location: 26.79 miles ESE from Spurn Lightvessel

The *Schieland* was a steel 1,106-ton Dutch steamship that was registered at the port of Rotterdam. She measured 67.43m in length, with a 10.21m beam and a 3.88m draught. Werf voorheen Rijkee & Co. built her at Rotterdam in 1909 and Scheepvaat en Steenkolen Maats NV owned her at the time of loss. Her single iron screw propeller was powered by a 3-cylinder triple expansion steam engine that developed 150hp using two boilers. Maats de Schelde built her machinery at Flushing. She had one deck, four bulkheads and a superstructure consisting of a 24.08m quarterdeck, a 17.98m bridgedeck and a 7.62m forecastle.

On 1 April 1915 the steamer was on passage from Goole for Rotterdam when she detonated a German-laid mine and foundered. She was under the command of Captain P. Sperling and carrying an unspecified general cargo. It is believed that all of her crew were lost with the vessel.

On 20 June 1941, German aircraft near the Outer Dowsing Lightvessel bombed the company's second vessel named *Schieland*, which was built in 1916. She sank two miles southeast from the East Dudgeon buoy, with the loss of fifteen of her crew. The first mate, being one of the nine survivors landed, died in hospital.

Wreck-site
The wreck, possibly that of the steamer *Schieland*, lies on a seabed of sand, gravel and pebbles, in a general depth of 13m, the lowest astronomical depth. She is totally collapsed, well broken up, standing 3.5m high amidships, where her engine and boilers are exposed. Fair numbers of crustaceans can be found all around the wreck-site, which is covered in soft corals. Tidal streams are very brisk, but underwater visibility is usually quite good during the summer months. The wreck is still fairly substantial and may be worth looking at as a boat-angling venue.

PEEBLES
Wreck ★★★
Depth 14m
Reference: N53 24 194 E000 36 060
Location: 12.54 miles ENE from Mablethorpe and 20.32 miles SE from Spurn Point

The *Peebles* was a steel 4,284-ton British steamship that was registered at Newcastle-upon-Tyne. She measured 115.82m in length, with a 14.93m beam and an 8.1m draught. Northumberland Ship Building Co. Ltd built her at Newcastle-upon-Tyne in 1911 and the Sutherland Steamship Co. Ltd owned her at the time of loss. Her single iron screw propeller was powered by a 3-cylinder triple expansion steam engine that developed 372hp using three boilers. Richardson's, Westgarth & Co. Ltd at Sunderland built her machinery. She had one deck and a superstructure consisting of a 9.45m poop deck, a 28.65m bridgedeck and a 10.06m forecastle. The vessel was armed with one stern-mounted 7.62cm (3in) howitzer.

On 13 October 1917 the SS *Peebles* was on passage from South Shields for Genoa with an unspecified cargo of coal when she was torpedoed by the Imperial German submarine SM UB 18. The explosion took place on the port-quarter at 5.40 p.m., blowing her rudder and propeller to pieces and leaving the ship drifting helplessly. At about 8 p.m., Captain W.E. Carr, master of the *Peebles*, sent out a wartime distress signal, which was answered by the Greek steamship *Dafni*. Fifty-seven of the crew were taken on board the *Dafni*, but Captain Carr and an apprentice remained on the *Peebles* until 8.30 p.m. However a fire, which had broken out in the aft section, got out of control and fifteen minutes later the two men were forced to abandon ship. The *Dafni* took all the men and landed them at Bridlington. Meanwhile the *Peebles*, which was not seen to sink, drifted away in the tide. The following day a minesweeper picked up the men and took them to Grimsby, but on her way the vessel struck an obstacle on the seabed with its sweeper wires. This was believed to be the wreck of the *Peebles*.

SM UB 18 was lost with all hands when the RN trawler HMT *Ben Lawer* rammed her aft of the conning tower on 9 December 1917.

Wreck-site

If this is the wreck of the *Peebles*, which I have been informed it is, the location is very misleading in comparison to the position where she was attacked by the U-boat, many miles further north. She lies on a seabed of small pebbles, gravel, shells and sand, in a general depth of 14m, the lowest astronomical depth. The wreck is collapsed and broken up, standing no more than 3m high and surrounded by a mound of broken steel debris. Tidal streams are very strong, while the underwater visibility is usually poor and often grim, but this clears significantly during the summer months.

ONESTA, ex MANTINEA

Wreck ★★★★
Depth 21m
Reference: N53 23 562 E000 44 404
Location: 19.57 miles E by S from Saltfleet

The *Onesta* was a steel 2,674-ton Italian steamship registered at Genoa. She was 94.18m long, with a 12.95m beam and a 4.9m draught. Russell & Co. built her at Port Glasgow as the *Mantinea* in 1896 for the Mantinea Steamship Co. of Liverpool. W. Thomson of Liverpool managed her. In 1906-1907 William Thomson & Co. and St John N.B. became the registered managers. The vessel was sold to Beraldo & Devoto of Genoa who renamed her *Onesta* in 1910. In 1913 ownership passed to Fratelli Beraldo of Genoa, who was the owner at the time of loss. A 232nhp 3-cylinder triple expansion steam engine that used two boilers powered her single iron screw propeller. Her cylinders measured 57.66cm, 93.98cm and 154.94cm-106.68cm, (22.7in 37in and 61in-42in). J.G. Kincaid & Co. built her machinery at Greenock. She had one deck, a spar deck, and a superstructure consisting of a 17.68m bridgedeck and a 9.75m forecastle.

On 7 August 1917, the SS *Onesta* was off Norfolk on passage from the Tyne for *Genoa* when the Imperial German submarine SM UC 63 torpedoed her. The steamship made an attempt to reach the safety of the River Humber, but sank before she was able to do so. She was under the command of Captain P. Costa and carrying an unspecified cargo of coal.

The British submarine HMS E52 attacked and sunk SM UC 63 near Goodwin Sands, in the English Channel on 1 November 1917.

Wreck-site

The wreck believed to be that of the Italian steamship lies on a seabed of mud and loose sandy silt, in a general depth of 21m, the lowest astronomical depth. The official position of sinking reads N53 24 30 E00 36 30, but the nearest wreck to that position is the SS *Peebles*. It is orientated in a north-west to south-east direction, with her bows to the north-west. She is collapsed and broken up, but still fairly substantial, standing some 4m high around amidships where her boilers are exposed. The vessel was equipped with two pedestal-mounted steering helms, one at the stern end, plus at least one brass pedestal-mounted telegraph, so she will be an interesting wreck to explore. Tidal streams are extremely strong and underwater visibility is usually very poor.

HERO
Wreck ★★
Depth 11.5m
Reference: N53 22 307 E000 49 784
Location: 20.15 miles E by S from Mablethorpe

The *Hero* was an iron 596-ton British steamship that was registered at Middlesbrough. She measured 56.69m in length, with a 7.51m beam and a draught of 4.39m. Schlesinger, Davis & Co. built her at Newcastle-upon-Tyne in 1866 and E. Harris & Co. of Middlesbrough owned her at the time of loss. She had one deck, three masts and a 2-cylinder compound steam engine that developed 70hp powered her single iron screw, using one boiler. Black Hawthorn & Co. of Gateshead-on-Tyne built her machinery.

On 26 August 1894 the SS *Hero* was on passage from Middlesbrough for Terneuzen when she sprang a leak, foundered and was lost. She was under the command of Captain E.W. Jibber, carrying a cargo of cast iron ingots/pigs, two passengers and a crew of eleven. The crew and passengers abandoned ship and took to the boats.

Wreck-site
The remains of *Hero* are probably those that are lying scattered around in this position. The wreck is now classed as just 'foul' ground, standing no more than about 1-2m high, Bits of iron plates, broken unrecognisable machinery and lots of debris cover an area of around 55m by 20m. She lies on a seabed of sand and gravel in a general depth of 11.5m, the lowest astronomical depth. There is little of interest, but it may be worthwhile searching for her bell, which has never been recovered. Tidal streams are very strong and underwater visibility rather poor, but this significantly improves during the summer months.

TORQUAY, ex ATLAND, ex MARQUIS SCICLUNA
Wreck ★★
Depth 19m
Reference: N53 21 363 E000 59 624
Also given: N53 21 749 E000 58 856
Location: 25.85 miles E from Mablethorpe

The *Torquay* was an iron 1,530-ton Norwegian steamship that was registered at the port of Christiania. She measured 79.25m in length, with an 11.03m beam and a draught of 5.67m. Sunderland Ship Building Co. Ltd built her at Sunderland as the *Marquis Scicluna* in 1883. Her single iron screw propeller was powered by an 187hp 2-cylinder compound steam engine that used two boilers. R. & W. Hawthorn built her machinery at Newcastle-upon-Tyne. Her cylinders measured 81.28cm and 157.48cm-101.60cm, (32in and 62in-40in). She had one deck, five bulkheads, a well deck and she was fitted with electric lights. Lloyd's classified the vessel for carrying petroleum in bulk, the first survey taking place in 1886. C. Tully owned her until 1885 when G.W. Allen took over the ownership. During 1886-1887, the owners became Mutual Shipping & Trading Co. Ltd (G.W. Allen & Co.). Lloyd's registered her as owned by G.W. Allen & Co. until 1895 when Angf. Aktieb Tirfing of Gothenburg purchased the vessel and renamed her *Atland*. A. Brostrom & Son then became the managers. Dampskbs. Torquay (C. Christensen) of Christiania, who was the owner at the time of loss, bought her and renamed the ship *Torquay* in 1910.

On 18 March 1914, the *Torquay* foundered and was lost following a collision with the Boston-registered steam trawler *Carrington*. The *Torquay* was under the command of Captain Christophersen, carrying a crew of eighteen and an unspecified cargo of coal on passage from South Shields for Bordeaux.

Wreck-site

The wreck, probably that of the old steamer, lies on a seabed of loose sandy silt, mud and gravel, in a general depth of 19m, the lowest astronomical depth. She is totally collapsed, well broken up and generally dispersed, with the highest pieces of wreck standing no more than 2m. A set of iron bollards and one large iron propeller can be found amongst bits of broken machinery and iron plates, which are scattered around. There is the possibility that the ship's bell may still be lying around and, if it is, it will probably be inscribed '*Marquis Scicluna*' and '1883', the date she was built. Tidal streams are really horrendous and very confusing, while underwater visibility is usually fairly good, especially during the summer months after a spell of settled weather.

VERNON

Wreck ★★
Depth 17.5m
Reference: N53 20 878 E000 36 348
Location: 11.97 miles E from Mablethorpe

The *Vernon* was an iron 982-ton British steamship that was registered at Newcastle-upon-Tyne. She measured 67.18m in length, with a 9.44m beam and a draught of 5m.

J. Blumer & Co. built her at Sunderland in 1878 and Cory Colliers Ltd owned her at the time of loss. Her single iron screw propeller was powered by a 128hp 2-cylinder compound steam engine that used one boiler. T. Clark & Co. built her machinery at Newcastle-upon-Tyne. She had one deck, a 5.18m poop deck and a 7.32m forecastle.

On 31 August 1917, the *Vernon* was on passage from Seaham for London with an unspecified cargo of coal when SM UB 30 torpedoed and sank her. Captain W.J. Newton was killed in the explosion, but the rest of her crew abandoned ship in the boats. UB 30 was lost with her crew of twenty-six off Whitby on 13 August 1918, when RN trawlers depth charged and shelled her.

Wreck-site

The wreck is orientated in a north-west to south-east direction, with her bows to the south-east. She lies on a seabed of pebbles, mud, gravel and shells, in a general depth of 17.5m, the lowest astronomical depth. The wreck is totally collapsed, well broken up and almost level with the seabed, with the largest sections standing some 2m high around the machinery. Most of the wreck is now no more than a mound of broken debris. Tidal streams are very strong, with overfalls close by to the site. Underwater visibility is usually poor most of the year round.

FANE

Wreck ★★★
Depth 16m
Reference N53 20 525 E000 36 431
Location: 12.05 miles E by S from Mablethorpe

The *Fane,* a steel 1,119-ton Norwegian steamship, was registered at the port of Bergen. She measured 69.62m in length, with a 10.74m beam and a draught of 4.8m. Bergens M.V. built her at Bergen in 1901 and V. Torkildsen of Bergen owned her at the time of loss. A 101hp 3-cylinder triple expansion steam engine that used one boiler powered her single iron screw propeller.

On 6 August 1917, the SS *Fane* foundered and was lost after she detonated a contact mine laid by the Imperial German submarine SM UC 63. The steamship was in ballast under the command of Captain J.S. Pedersen and on passage from Rouen for Sunderland.

Three months later, on 1 November 1917, the U-boat was attacked and sunk by the British submarine HMS E52 near Goodwin Sands, in the English Channel.

Wreck-site

The wreck of the *Fane* is orientated in a north, north-west to south, south-east direction, with her bows to the north, north-west. She lies on a seabed of sand, shells, gravel and mud, in a general depth of 16m, the lowest astronomical depth. The wreck is partially buried, totally collapsed and well broken up, with the largest structures standing just under 3m high around her boiler/engine area. This should make an interesting rummage dive, where a few crustaceans can be found early in the summer months. Tidal streams are fairly brisk and underwater visibility is usually very poor most of the time, however this improves during the summer months.

PACIFIQUE, ex BERKSHIRE

Wreck ★★
Depth 16m
Reference: N53 21 157 E000 34 427
Location: 10.93 miles E from Mablethorpe

The *Pacifique* was an iron 1,526-ton French sailing barque that was registered at the port of Dunkirk. She measured 72.30m in length, with an 11.40m beam and a draught of 7.01m. Barclay Curle & Co. built her as the *Berkshire* at Glasgow in 1867 for G. Marshall & Sons of London. Later, A.D. Bordes & Sons of Paris, who was the owner at the time of loss, purchased her. She had a superstructure consisting of a 17.07m poop deck and a 12.19m forecastle.

The A.D. Bordes & Le Qeuellec shipping company, founded by Antoine Dominique Bordes and Captain Le Quellec in 1847, was one of the largest French sailing ship companies and it was the closest rival to the famous Laeisz 'P' Liners. Captain Le Quellec died in 1867 and Bordes in 1883, but Bordes' three sons, Adolphe, Alexandre and Anonin, became associated with the company a year before he died. In 1882 the company became known as A.D. Bordes & Fils and remained that way until 1917 when it changed to Cie Francaise d'Armement et d'Importation de Nitrate de Soude. Bordes had owned 125 sailing vessels, ten steamers and one tug, the latter stationed at Valparaiso where much of his trade went. Almost all of the vessels were registered at the port of Dunkirk. Amongst his sailing vessels were three that were four-masted and the *France*, which was the very first five-masted barque ever built. In 1935 the company ran into financial difficulties and had to sell off its steamships and eventually it was liquidated.

On 14 October 1895 this large iron barque was on passage from North Shields for Valparaiso when she foundered and was lost following a collision with the German-registered steamship *Emma*. The sailing ship was under the command of Captain Le Bras and carrying an unspecified cargo of coal, a crew of twenty-three and one passenger, of which the passenger (a pilot), her captain and seven crewmen were drowned.

Wreck-site

The wreckage is probably that of the *Pacifique*. She lies on a seabed of sand, shells, gravel and mud, in a general depth of 16m, the lowest astronomical depth. The wreck-site, which is now marked on the chart as 'foul' ground, is partially buried, well broken up and rather dispersed, with the highest structure standing no more than around 1.5m. What there is left should be interesting to explore, it being a very old sailing ship. If her bell is recovered it should probably be inscribed with her previous name 'Berkshire', plus the date she was built, '1867'. Interestingly, the wreck of a similar vessel, the 1,335-ton iron French full-rigged ship *Quillota*, was found off Sunderland in the summer of 2001. She is lying in a depth of 5m and is very close inshore, in position N54 53 153 W001 21 138. The point of the matter is that a great amount of the vessel is still there, including her huge masts etc. and a couple of portholes were recovered into the bargain. Tidal streams are very strong in the vicinity of the *Pacifique* and underwater visibility is rather poor, but she will be well worth a look!

LORD STANHOPE, ex STREPHON
Wreck ★
Depth 15.5m
Reference: N53 20 459 E000 34 386
Location: 10.84 miles E from Mablethorpe

The *Lord Stanhope* (Official No.109820) was a steel 162-ton British steam fishing trawler that was registered at Grimsby. She measured 30.98m in length, with a 6.29m beam and a draught of 3.35m. Cook, Welton & Gemmell built her as Yard No.218 at Hull and launched her as the *Strephon* for the Standard Steam Fishing Co. Ltd at Grimsby on 24 August 1898. She was registered as Grimsby trawler No.GY852 on 4 October 1898. A 45nhp 3-cylinder triple expansion steam engine that used one boiler powered her single iron screw propeller, giving her a maximum speed of 9.5 knots. Charles D. Holmes & Co. built her machinery at Hull. She had one deck, three bulkheads, a 14.33m quarterdeck and a 5.79m forecastle. On 1 March 1912, she was sold to the Port of Blyth Steam Fishing Co. Ltd at Blyth, renamed *Lord Stanhope* and registered as trawler No.BH95. The Beacon Steam Fishing Co. Ltd at Grimsby purchased her on 10 December 1914 and registered her as trawler No.GY401.

On 14 November 1914 she foundered and was lost following a collision with the Inner Dowsing Lightvessel. She was on a return fishing voyage from Grimsby, under the command of Captain J. Wharton.

Wreck-site
The wreck is now totally collapsed, well broken up and quite dispersed. She lies on a seabed of sand, shells, gravel and mud, in a general depth of 15.5m, the lowest astronomical depth. All that remains are some pieces of broken machinery, an anchor, bits of a shaft and a few battered steel plates scattered around the seabed. Tidal streams are extremely strong, with curling white over-falls close by. There is very little of interest and it would be hardly worth the effort of 'kitting up' at this site.

OBEDIENT
Wreck ★★★
Depth 23m
Reference: N53 19 556 E001 01 175
Location: 1.61 miles E from East Dudgeon Shoal and 26.85 miles E from Mablethorpe

The *Obedient* was an iron 994-ton British steamship that was registered at the port of Sunderland. She measured 65.83m in length, with a 9.16m beam and a 5m draught. Short Brothers built her at Sunderland in 1882 and J. Westoll of Sunderland owned her at the time of loss. A 99hp 2-cylinder compound steam engine that used one boiler powered her single iron screw propeller. J. Dickinson built her machinery at Sunderland. She had one deck and a well deck.

On 15 May 1898 the steamer was on passage from Dunston-on-Tyne for London when she foundered and was lost following a collision with the Glasgow-registered sailing barque, *Benavon*. Wind conditions at the time were south-east force two, but there was a thick fog. The steamship was under the command of Captain J. Scarlett, carrying a crew of seventeen and a cargo of coal.

Wreck-site
The wreck, although not positively identified, is probably that of the old steamship *Obedient*. She is orientated in a north, north-west to south, south-east direction, on a seabed of shingle, mud, sandy silt and short weed, in a general depth of 23m, the lowest astronomical depth. She

is intact, partially buried, but totally collapsed and broken up, with the highest section standing 2-3m high amidships around her boiler and engine. Colourful anemones are well established on the highest and most exposed parts of the wreck. Tidal streams are very strong and there are tide rips and over-falls in the immediate vicinity. Underwater visibility is usually excellent during the summer months, but Lion's mane jellyfish can be quite a nuisance between July and August.

ARGO
Wreck ★★★
Depth 18m
Reference: N53 17 905 E000 36 487

Location: 2.26 miles SE from Inner Dowsing buoy/horn and 12.23 miles E by S from Mablethorpe
    The *Argo* was an iron 1,261-ton Norwegian steamship that was registered at the port of Haugesund. She measured 71.55m in length, with a 10.38m beam and a 5.08m draught. Martens, Olsen & Co. built her at Bergen in 1883 and H.M. Wrangll & Co. A/S owned her at the time of loss. Her single iron screw propeller was powered by a 142hp 2-cylinder compound steam engine that used two boilers. The ship's builder also built her machinery.
    On 14 April 1917 the *Argo* was on passage from Hull for Rouen with a 1,650-ton cargo of coal when she detonated a mine laid by the Imperial German submarine SM UC 26, 1.5 miles south-east from the Inner Dowsing Lightship. The crew abandoned ship and the vessel drifted a bit with the tide before going down to the bottom, where her mast was visible 4.5m above the surface. SM UC 26 was lost when the boat was rammed by the destroyer HMS *Milne* on 9 May 1917.

Wreck-site
The wreck was dispersed with heavy explosives in 1939. She is now totally collapsed, well broken up and dispersed, with the highest section standing some 2m high. The wreck lies on a seabed of sand, mud and gravel, in a general depth of 18m, the lowest astronomical depth. Wreckage and debris cover an area of approximately 75m by 15m, with most of it just a mound of debris and almost level to the seabed in many places. Tidal streams are quite severe and underwater visibility usually poor, but the visibility significantly improves during the summer months on neap tides, following a spell of dry settled weather.

ENAR, ex ARLA, ex CELSUS
Wreck ★★★★
Depth 21m
Reference: N53 17 132 E001 13 020
Location: 2.95 miles W from Cromer Knoll and 31.72 miles E by N from St Leonards

The *Enar* (Official No.2629) was an iron 988-ton (745 tons under deck) Swedish schooner-rigged steamship that was registered at the port of Gothenburg and has the signal letters HSVQ. She measured 65.43m in length, with a 9.04m beam and a draught of 5.08m. J.L. Thompson built her at Sunderland as the *Celsus* in 1871 for Ångf. Aktieb. Garm, with F.W. Forsberg as the manager.
    Her single iron screw propeller was powered by a 2-cylinder compound steam engine that developed 107hp using one single-ended boiler. George Clark built her machinery at Sunderland. Her cylinder diameters measured 63.50cm and 127cm with a 76.20cm stroke, (25in and 50in with a 30in stroke). She was classed at Lloyd's as 90 A1 and had one deck, four cemented bulkheads, a 38.10m poop deck and a 6.71m forecastle. She also had a bar-keel of 2,032cm (6in), an area of 17.68m water ballast double bottom aft and 5.79m forward, three

corrugated furnaces, a new boiler delivering 90lbs fitted in 1890 and a new donkey boiler delivering 47lb fitted in 1893. Captain E.O. Lindblom was her master in 1898, but in 1899-1900 Angf. Akttieb. Enar, who was the owner at the time of loss, renamed her *Arla* when the company purchased her. She was later renamed *Enar* by the same owners.

On 9 February 1910 the *Enar* was on passage from Kings Lynn for London when she foundered and was lost following a collision with the London-registered steamer *Armourer*. The *Enar* was under the command of Captain E.A. Nordstrom, carrying an unspecified cargo of coal and a crew of seventeen, none of who were lost. It is understood that the other steamship rescued her crew.

Wreck-site

The wreck lies on a seabed of pebbles, gravel, shells and sand, in a general depth of 21m, the lowest astronomical depth. She is believed to be intact, upright and standing 4m high amidships, but most of the wreck has now collapsed, with her engine and boiler exposed. Lots of marine life can be seen over and all around the wreck, which is covered in a colourful array of soft corals. Tidal streams are very strong, but during the summer mouths the underwater visibility is excellent.

EGRET, ex CYNTHIANA
Wreck ★★
Depth 15m
Reference: N53 16 359 E000 35 499
Location: 9.39 miles NNE from St Leonards

The *Egret* was a steel 4,055-ton Russian steamship that was registered at the port of Petrograd. She measured 106.68m in length, with a 14.04m beam and a draught of 7.16m. William Gray & Co. Ltd built and launched her as the *Cynthiana* at West Hartlepool in 1905 for Sir Christopher Furness MP at West Hartlepool. F.W. Lewis was the manager. Her single iron screw propeller was powered by a 3-cylinder triple expansion steam engine that developed 291hp using two boilers. Central Marine Eng. Works built her machinery at West Hartlepool. She had one deck and a superstructure consisting of an 8.23m poop deck, a 55.47m bridgedeck and a 10.36m forecastle. The vessel was equipped with two pedestal-mounted steering helms, one in the wheelhouse and one aft at the stern. She also had a brass pedestal-mounted-telegraph.

In 1907-1908 she was sold to the British Maritime Trust Ltd at West Hartlepool and renamed *Agnes*. Furness Withy & Co. purchased her in 1910-1911. The West Russian Steamship Co. Ltd at Petrograd, who owned her at the time of loss, bought her in 1916.

On 28 January 1917, the *Egret* was on passage from Archangel for London when she detonated a floating contact mine laid by SM UC 26. The steamer was under the command of Captain R. Joshwich and carrying an unspecified cargo of wood. She was on British government service, under the Russian flag and was insured by the British Government War Risk scheme. SM UC 26 was lost in the Thames estuary when she was rammed by the British destroyer HMS *Milne* on 9 may 1917.

Wreck-site

The wreck is now totally collapsed, well broken up and dispersed over the seabed. She lies on a seabed of mud, sand, gravel and shells, in a general depth of 15m, the lowest astronomical depth. The wreck was dispersed using explosives and very little is left of her, except some scattered steel hull plates and ribs etc., a few bits of broken machinery and part of her engines, which are partially buried. The site is marked on the Admiralty charts as 'foul' ground, because nothing more than 2m high exists. Tidal streams are very brisk and underwater visibility is usually poor most of the year, but this improves significantly during the summer months.

GERTRUDE
Wreck ★★★
Depth 12m
Reference: N53 11 574 E000 53 697
Location: 6.80 miles SE from North Race bell buoy on Race Bank

The *Gertrude* was an iron-hulled 212-ton British steamship that was registered at Middlesbrough. She measured 39.62m in length, with a 6.22m beam and a draught of 3.42m. M. Morse & Co. built her at Stockton in 1873 and J.W. Watson owned her at the time of loss. Her single bronze screw propeller was powered by an aft-positioned 2-cylinder compound steam engine that developed 40hp using one boiler. Blair & Co. Ltd at Stockton-on-Tees built her machinery and she had one deck. On 3 February 1912 the SS *Gertrude* stranded on Race Bank, while on passage from Hull for Weymouth. She was under the command of Captain G. Hunnaford and carrying an unspecified cargo of coal and a crew of seven, all of who were lost with the vessel.

Wreck-site
The wreck lies on an undulating seabed of sand, shells and gravel, in a general depth of 12m, the lowest astronomical depth. She is partially buried, but totally collapsed and well broken up, with her engine and boiler being the highest section at 3m. Very little non-ferrous metal can be seen amongst the mound of iron debris, which often shelters some decent-sized crustaceans. The wreck is exposed to very strong tidal streams that sweep across this area and the best time to visit her is on a low neap tide at slack water. Underwater visibility can be fairly reasonable during the summer months after a spell of settled dry weather.

HEIMLAND I
Wreck ★
Depth 17m
Reference: N53 10 264 E000 39 232
Location: 11.98 miles ESE from St Leonard's

The *Heimland I* was a steel 505-ton Norwegian steamship that was registered at the port of Askeroen. She measured 50.11m in length, with an 8.38m beam and a draught of 3.14m. Fredrikstad M.V. built her at Fredrikstad in 1913 and A/S D/S Heimland of Norway owned her at the time of loss. Her single iron screw propeller was powered by a 3-cylinder triple expansion steam engine that developed 41hp using one boiler. The ship's builders also built her aft-positioned machinery. The vessel had one deck and a small aft bridge structure.

On 28 January 1917, the *Heimland I* was on passage from the Tyne for St Nazaire when she detonated a contact mine laid by the Imperial German submarine SM UC 26. The steamer was under the command of Captain J.B. Johnsen and carrying a 700-ton cargo of coal. She was also insured for war risk to the value of £775,000, which may have included her cargo.

SM UC 26 was lost when the boat was rammed by the destroyer HMS *Milne* on 9 May 1917.

Wreck-site
The wreck of the steamer is now totally collapsed, well broken up and dispersed. She lies on a seabed of fine silty sand and shells, in a general depth of 17m, the lowest astronomical depth. Now, very little remains to be seen, except some battered steel hull plates, sections of ribs and scattered broken machinery. The wreck-site is now no more than a 'foul' ground, with nothing more than 2m high. Tidal streams are very strong and underwater visibility is usually on the poor side, but this improves during the summer months.

The Medal

Pour Le Mérite (The Blue Max)

The Pour Le Mérite, or the Blue Max, was the greatest German war decoration for honour and was given to officers for great military performance and valour. In 1740, Frederich the Great of Prussia, being a great admirer of the French and their customs, created the medal, hence the French name for the medal. However, a higher order was the *Orden Pour le Mérite mit Eichenlaub*, the Order for Mérit with Oakleaf.

The Prussian medal *Orden Pour Le Mérite* however, was not the highest honour for military bravery in the beginning. In 1685 King Friedrich I, then just a young prince, donated a medal, a gold cross with eight points, and on each point a gold ball, which he called the '*Medal de la Generosite*'. In the centre of it was the word 'Generosite' and the cross was hung on blue tape. On the day of his accession to the throne on 31 May 1740, Friedrich der Grosse converted it into the medal '*Pour Le Mérite*'. People who were awarded the medal, formed a knighthood and received a monthly payment. It was always looked on as a medal earned through military services, but some civil servants were also given it for various services. King Friedrich William III decided that on 18 January 1810 the medal could only be earned by extraordinary service on the battlefield. The medal could really only be acquired by officers fighting in a major battle, or by the takeover or successful defence of a fortress, and by 1816 1,000 knights possessed the medal. In the charter of foundation of the Iron Cross, an extension to the *Pour Le Mérite* had been ordered and in extraordinary service or bravery, three gold oak leaves were added to the ring. It was decided later that people who possessed this higher honour for more than fifty years, were allowed to carry a golden crown above the medal's cross. After the campaign 1866, King William I donated the medal, which consisted of a cross double the original size and it carried a portrait of its founder, Friedrich der Grosse, in the centre. With the larger cross, came a four-point gold star, which also had a portrait of Grosse on it, but it was only presented to Emperor Friedrich III, the then Crown Prince, who reigned for ninety-nine days and to General Field Marshal, Prince Friedrich Karl of Prussia. King William I carried the larger cross during his march to Berlin after his victoriously terminated campaign. The tape of the medal was black with one silver edge strip on each side. With the award of the three golden oak pages, a silver centre strip is added to the medal tape. Over the years the medal had a number of variations, until the First World War when it took the form of the one in the photograph.

During the First World War German fighter pilots nicknamed the medal the 'Blauer Max', or Blue Max, because of its blueish colour and in honour of one of Imperial Germany's top air force aces, Max Immelmann.

Out of a total of the 687 medals of *Pour Le Mérite* presented during the conflicts of the First World War, only twenty-seven U-boat commanders received this award, with a further twenty-two going to other officers in the Imperial German Navy.

Imperial German Submarines

SM U-boats (Seiner Majestat U-Boote)
of the Kaiserliche Deutsche Marine, 1914-1918 mentioned in this book

SM U 12

SM U 12 was one of the earlier petrol U-Boats, a type SM U9-U12, built by Kaiserliche Werft at Danzig for the Imperial German Navy, launched on 6 May 1910, but not commissioned for service until 13 August 1911. She had a surface displacement of 493 tons, 611 tons submerged and dimensions measuring: 57.38m by length, by a 5.96m beam and a draught of 3.09m. Two 500hp petrol/paraffin-fuelled engines powered her twin, bronze, screw propellers giving her a surface speed of 14kt. Rows of lead/acid batteries powered her two 580hp electric motors for running submerged and gave her a speed of 8.1kt. She had a range of 3,250 sea miles on the surface at a steady 9kt and carried 52-58 tons of fuel. Running submerged, using battery power, she was capable of eighty sea miles at 5kt. Her maximum diving depth was 50m and it took fifty to ninety seconds to dive. Her armament consisted of two bow and two stern torpedo tubes, she carried six torpedoes and had one reverse facing deck cannon. U 12 was one of the double-hulled boats, capable of being used in the Atlantic Ocean. She had a normal complement of four officers and twenty-five men.

On 9 January 1915, this U-boat was involved in a pioneering experiment off Zeebrugge, when she became the first submarine in naval history to launch an aircraft at sea. Kplt. Walther Forstmann commanded U 12, and the aircraft, a Friedrichshafen FF-29 seaplane No.204, was piloted by Leutnant Fredrich von Arnauld de la Periere, the younger brother of the German submarine ace, Kapitanleutnant Lothar von Arnauld de la Periere, who was awarded the Pour le Merite on 11 October 1916. The seaplane succeeded in taking-off on the submarine's bow section, but with a great deal of difficulty. It was successful due to a very strong headwind and a considerable amount of nerve on behalf of the pilot. The trials were stopped soon after because, although the experiment was a reasonable success, the German High Command was not very impressed by the demonstration.

Kplt. Claus Rücker, born 10 October 18884 commanded U 12 from 13 August 1911 until August 1914. He also commanded U 2, U 34 and U 103. The latter boat was lost in the English Channel, while Rucker was in command. He actually survived the sinking, but died later that day, on 12 May 1918.

Kplt. Walter Forstmann was in command of the U-boat from 6 August 1914 until 10 February 1915.

Kplt. Hans Kratzsch commanded U 12 from 10 February 1915. Kratzach left Heligoland on March 4 1915, with orders to sink Allied shipping off the East Coast of Britain. Arriving off Flamborough Head on 9 March, he sank one vessel, the 3,738-ton steamship *Tangistan*. However the following morning, U 12 had proceeded up the coast as far as Fife Ness, when a group of Royal Navy trawlers sighted her. They gave chase and in an attempt to escape, the U-boat turned south, but unknown to Kratzsch, three Royal Navy destroyers had also been dispatched to intercept her. Within an hour, the trio of warships had found an unidentified submarine on the surface in that vicinity and began shelling it. U 12 began an emergency dive, but one shell scored a direct hit on the conning tower, then one of the destroyers, HMS *Ariel* managed to ram the badly damaged conning tower as she went down. Being in a sinking condition, Kratzsch had to resurface, but a further shell exploded on the conning tower and killed the commander. The crew set the scuttling charges and attempted to abandon ship, but she went down so quickly that, only two officers and ten ratings out of her crew of thirty made it to safety.

SM U 1 was the first submarine built for the Imperial German Navy. She was completed in 1906 and had a displacement of 237 tons. *(Author's Collection)*

SM U 12 sank two vessels during her rather brief service:

AREA	VESSEL'S NAME	FLAG	TONS	D	M	YEAR	LOCATION
E/Channel	HMS *Niger*	GBR	810	11	11	1914	Off Deal.
North Sea	*Tangistan*	GBR	3738	9	3	1915	9m N of Flamborough Head

SM U 13

SM U 13 was an early petrol U-boat, a type SM U13-U15, built by Kaiserliche Werft at Danzig for the Imperial German Navy. She was launched on 16 December 1910 and commissioned for service on 25 April 1912. U 13 was one of the two-hulled boats, capable of operating in the Atlantic Ocean. She had a surface displacement of 516 tons and 644 tons submerged, with dimensions measuring: 57.88m by length and a 6m beam. Two 600hp petrol/paraffin-fuelled engines powered her twin bronze screw propellers, giving her a surface speed of 14.8kt. Rows of lead/acid batteries powered her two 580hp electric motors for running submerged and gave her a speed of 10.7kt. She had a range of 4,000 sea miles on the surface at a steady 9kt and carried 64-74 tons of fuel. Running submerged using battery power she was capable of ninety sea miles at a steady 5kt. Her maximum diving depth was 50m and it took her forty to seventy-eight minutes to dive. Her armament consisted of: two bow and two stern torpedo tubes, six torpedoes and one machine-gun. U 13 normally had a complement of four officers and twenty-five men.

Kplt. Richard Pohle, first commander of SM U 13, served from 25 April 1912 until July 1912. Kplt. Graf A. von Schweinitz was the second and last commander, serving from July 1912 until she was lost on 9 August 1914. Under the command of Schweinitz and carrying a crew of twenty-three, SM U 13 left her base at Heligoland for a war patrol on 6 August 1914 and was never seen, or heard of again. She may have been the victim of an accident arising from a drill failure or mechanical problem, or she may have succumbed to a mine on the German defensive line in the Heligoland Bight. During her twenty-nine months service, SM U 13 failed to sink any Allied vessels.

SM U 15

SM U 15 was one of the early petrol U-Boats, a type SM U13-U15, built at Kaiserliche Werft at Danzig for the Imperial German Navy, launched on 18 September 1911 and commissioned for service on 7 July 1912. The boat had dimensions measuring: 57.88m by length and a beam of 6m. Her surface displacement was 516 tons and 644 tons submerged. Two 600hp petrol/paraffin engines powered her two bronze screw propellers on the surface, giving her a speed of 14.8kt. Rows of lead/acid batteries powered her two 580hp electric motors for running submerged and these gave her a speed of 10.7kt. She had an endurance range of 4,000 *seconds!*

sea miles on the surface at a steady 9kt and carried 64-74 tons of fuel. Running submerged using her battery power, she was capable of ninety sea miles at a steady 5kt. Her maximum diving depth was 50m and it took her forty to seventy-eight minutes to dive. Her armament consisted of: two bow and two stern torpedo tubes, she carried six torpedoes and had one machine-gun. U 15 was a double-hulled boat, capable of operating in the Atlantic Ocean. U 15 had a normal complement of four officers and twenty-five crewmen.

Kplt. Hans Adam, born 5 March 1883 was the first commander of the boat, serving from 7 July 1912 until the end of July 1912. During his service he commanded U 15 and U 82 and died on 23 June 1948.

Kplt. Richard Pohle was her next and final commander, serving from 1 August 1914 until she sank, one week later on 9 August. During her brief service, the SM U 15 sank no Allied vessels.

On 9 August 1914, SM U 15 was on a war patrol off Fair Isle in the North Sea when the British cruiser HMS *Birmingham* sighted her. The submarine, under the command of Kplt. Richard Pohle and carrying a crew of twenty-three, was lying still on the surface in thick fog. It was believed that some kind of maintenance must have been in progress in the submarine, because hammering and clanging was heard coming from her by the crew of the *Birmingham*. Just as the U-boat got under way, the cruiser rammed her at full-speed, almost cutting her in two. Two large pieces of wreckage rose to the surface, but none of her crew survived.

SM U 49

SM U 49 was a Flotten-U-boat, a type SM U 43-U 50, built by Kaiserliche Werft at Danzig for the Imperial German Navy, launched on 26 November 1915 and commissioned for service on 31 May 1916. She had a surface displacement of 725 tons, 940 tons submerged, and measured 65m in length. Two 1,000hp diesel/oil engines powered her two bronze screw propellers, giving her a surface speed of 15.2kt. Rows of lead/acid batteries powered her 600hp electric motors for running submerged gave her a speed of 9.7kt. The SM U 49 had an armament of two bow and two stern torpedo tubes, she carried six torpedoes and had one 88mm (3.46in) deck-gun. She was also a double-hulled boat, capable of operating in the Atlantic Ocean. She had a normal complement of four officers and twenty-five crewmen.

Kplt. R. Hartmann was the first and only commander of SM U 49. Hartmann had been ordered to cut telephone cables in the North Sea, west of the Dogger Bank. However, he had problems and rendezvoused with U 66 to relay his message that his cutting apparatus had broken down. He said he was heading off into the Atlantic for 'Handelskrieg' (this was what the German skippers called 'War on Allied merchant vessels', in other words, to sink as many ships as they could find in the Atlantic). Nothing more was heard from the submarine, but on 11 September 1917, a U-boat surfaced in the Bay of Biscay, in position N46 17 W14 43 and exchanged fire with the steamship *British Transport*. The steamer got away, but later that night her crew sighted the tracks of two torpedoes coming in from ahead. Evasive action was immediately taken, which saved the *British Transport* and she made off ahead at full speed. Soon after the incident, the steamer's crew sighted a long phosphorescent track just below the surface, with a large dark object resembling a submarine at the end of it. Without hesitation, the master ordered his crew to ram the object, in accordance with the British Master's unequivocal instructions: 'if in doubt ram'. The submarine stopped and immediately began to settle by the stern. The steamer then fired a shell from fairly close range, which exploded inside the U-boat's pressure-hull – just as three men had clambered out onto the casing shouting for help. The submarine then sank very quickly and the pitch darkness made any rescue of survivors impossible. Forty-three crewmen, including the Captain went down with her and it was not until sometime later that she was reckoned to be the SM U 49.

During her service, SM U 49 sank thirty-eight Allied vessels totalling 86,433 tons.

Kapitanleutnant Carl-Siegfried Ritter von Georg was awarded Pour Le Merite on 24 April 1918 as Commander on SM U 101. *(From Dutch Collection)*

SM U 57

SM U 57 was a Flotten U-boat of the type SM U 57–U 59, built by A.G. Weser for the Imperial German Navy. She was given her Yard No. on 28 May 1915, launched on 29 April 1916 and commissioned for service on 6 July 1916. The boat had a surface displacement of 786 tons, 945 tons submerged and dimensions of 67m long with a 6.32m beam. Two 900hp diesel/oil engines powered her two bronze screw propellers, giving her a surface speed of 14.7kt. Rows of lead/acid batteries powered her two 600hp motors for running submerged, giving her a speed of 8.4kt. U 57 had an endurance range of 7,730 sea miles at a steady 8kt and carried 78–137 tons of fuel oil. Submerged, she was capable of running fifty-five sea miles at a steady 5kt using her battery power alone. She could dive to a maximum depth of 50m and it took her thirty to forty-nine seconds to dive. The boat's armament consisted of two bow and two stern torpedo tubes. She carried seven torpedoes, one 10.5cm (4.13in) deck-gun from 1916/17 and later one 88mm (3.46in) deck-gun added to it. U 57 was a double-hulled boat, capable of operating in the Atlantic Ocean.

Kplt. Carl-Siegfried Ritter von Georg was her commander from 6 June 1916 until 19 December 1917 and was awarded the *Orden Pour le Mérite* while commanding U 101, though his efforts on U 57 were certainly considered in the award as well.

From late December 1917 until the end of March 1918, U 57 was in the yard for a complete overhaul and repairs to her machinery. On the last patrol, she was towed for twelve hours duration and eventually reached harbour, using the electric motor. During this period in time, the watch officers practised the command, but in January Kplt. Sperling took command, and Kplt. Gühler until March. Oblt.z.S. Walter Stein then commanded SM U 57 from 25 March 1918, until the end of the First World War.

SM U 57 went on to survive the ravages of the First World War and surrendered to the Allies to become French reparation and was broken up at Cherbourg in 1921.

The following is a list of the known vessels sunk or damaged by SM U 57 off the East and North Coast, including a large number of steam fishing-trawlers twenty miles north-east from Scarborough:

VESSEL'S NAME	FLAG	TONS	D	M	YEAR	LOCATION
Sunshine (trawler)	GBR	185	24	9	1916	20m NE of Scarborough
Tarantula (trawler)	GBR	155	24	9	1916	20m NE of Scarborough
St. Hilda (trawler)	GBR	94	25	9	1916	20m NE of Scarborough
Loch Ness (trawler)	GBR	176	25	9	1916	20m NE of Scarborough
Fisher Prince (trawler)	GBR	125	25	9	1916	20m NE of Scarborough
Game Cock (trawler)	GBR	151	25	9	1916	20m NE of Scarborough

Harrier (trawler)	GBR	162	25	9	1916	20m NE of Scarborough
Marquerite (trawler)	GBR	151	24	9	1916	20m NE of Scarborough
Nil Desperandum (trawler)	GBR	148	25	9	1916	20m NE of Scarborough
Otter (trawler)	GBR	123	24	9	1916	20m NE of Scarborough
Otterhound (trawler)	GBR	150	25	9	1916	20m NE of Scarborough
Quebec (trawler)	GBR	133	25	9	1916	26m E by N of Whitby
Seal (trawler)	GBR	135	25	9	1916	33m E by S of Hartlepool
Tiuva	SWE	2270	6	10	1916	In the North Sea
Laila	NOR	807	24	9	1916	10m NE from Flam. Head
Aphelion	GBR	197	24	9	1916	20m E from Flam. Head
Albatross	GBR	158	24	9	1916	20m E from Flam. Head

SM U 63

SM U 63 was a Flotten-U-boat, a type SM U 63-U 65 attack boat, built by Germaniawerft at Kiel for the Imperial German Navy. Her keel was laid on 30 April 1915, she was launched on 8 February 1916 and commissioned for service on 11 March 1916. U 63 had a surface displacement of 810 tons, 927 tons submerged and had dimensions of 68.36m by length and a 6.30m beam. Two 1,100hp diesel/oil engines powered her two bronze screw propellers, giving her a surface speed of 16.8kt, while rows of lead/acid batteries powered her two 600hp electric motors for running submerged, giving her a speed of 9.0kt. U 63 had an endurance range on the surface of 8,100 sea miles at a steady 8kt and carried 78-118 tons of fuel oil. Running submerged using her battery power, she was capable of covering sixty sea miles at a steady 5kt. Her maximum diving depth was 50m and it took her thirty-eight to fifty seconds to dive. She had an armament consisting of two bow and two stern torpedo tubes, she carried eight torpedoes and was equipped with one 105mm (4.13in) deck-gun or one 88mm (3.46in) gun. U 63 was a double-skinned offshore boat, capable of operating in the Atlantic Ocean.

Kplt. Otto Schultz, born 11 May 1884, was her first commander from 11 March 1916 until 14 October 1917. On 18 March 1918, Schultz was awarded the *Pour Le Mérite* for outstanding duty against enemy shipping. He served on two boats: U 4 and U 63, and died in Hamburg on 22 January 1966.

Kplt. Heirich Metzger commanded her from 28 August 1917 until 14 October 1917. Then Otto Schultz returned to the boat from 15 October until 24 December 1917. Kplt. Kurt Hartwig took over command from Christmas Day 1917 until April 1918.

U 63 went on until the end of the First World War and surrendered to the Allies. The boat was broken up at Blyth 1919-1920. Between the three captains, U 63 sank seventy-one Allied vessels, making a total tonnage of 194,208, plus 5,250 tons.

Kapitanleutnant Otto Schutze, awarded Pour Le Merite on 18 March 1918 as commander of SM U 63. *(From Dutch Collection)*

U 63, showing her damaged conning tower after she was involved in an incident. *(From Dutch Collection)*

Known vessels believed sunk by SM U 63 off the East Coast:

VESSEL'S NAME	FLAG	TONS	D	M	YEAR	LOCATION
HMS *Falmouth*	GBR	5250	19	8	1916	7.6m S of Flamborough Head (under tow)

SM U 66

SM U 66 was an UD U-boat, a type SM U 66-U 70 attack boat, built by Germaniawerft at Kiel for the Imperial German Navy. On 1 November 1913 her keel was laid and she was launched on 22 April 1915, then commissioned for service on 23 July 1915. U 66 had a surface displacement of 791 tons, 933 tons submerged, and had dimensions measuring 69.50m by length and a 6.30m beam. Two 1,150hp diesel/oil engines powered her two bronze screw propellers, giving her a surface speed of 16.8kt. Rows of lead/acid batteries powered her two 620hp electric motors running submerged giving her a speed of 10.3kt. The boat had an endurance range at a steady 8kt of some 6,500 sea miles and carried 47-89 tons of fuel. Running submerged, she was capable of 115 sea miles at a steady 5kt. Her armament consisted of four bow and two stern torpedo tubes, she carried twelve torpedoes and had one 88mm (3.46in) deck-gun, with one 105mm (4.13in) added from 1916-17. U 66 was a double-hulled boat, capable of operating in the open ocean.

Kplt. Thorwald Frhr. Von Bother commanded the boat between 23 July 1915 and 19 June 1917. Kplt. Gerhard Muhle took over on 20 June 1917 until his boat disappeared in September 1917. Between them, the two commanders sank twenty-four Allied vessels, with a total tonnage of 69,016.

HMS *Falmouth* was part of the 3rd Light Cruiser Sqn, under the command of Capt. J.D. Edwards RN and carrying a complement of 433, on 19 August 1916. The, warship was a part of the cruiser screen, protecting the British North Sea Battle Fleet. Two German Zeppelin airships were shadowing the Fleet, so *Falmouth* left her position to engage the Zeppelins, but without success, because the two airships, not wishing to confront such a formidable enemy, left the scene. The cruiser turned back at 16.45, to close with her consorts again. Unfortunately, she steamed into a trap when she ran across the line-of-fire of two German submarines, U 66 commanded by Oblt.z.S. Von Bothner and U 49, commanded by Oblt.z.S. Hartmann. U 66 fired two torpedoes at less than 1,000yds (914.4m) range, both of which struck the *Falmouth* and detonated on her starboard side, one at the bow and the other at the stern. The cruiser was left badly damaged, but was kept protected from any more attacks, by use of a six-destroyer screen using a pattern of depth charges. This prevented the submarines from finishing off the *Falmouth* and after two hours the U-boats backed off. The warship was then able to proceed under her own-steam at 6kt throughout the following night. Early the next morning, two tugs from Immingham took her in tow and headed for the relative safety of the Humber. Unfortunately soon after she received two more torpedoes from U 63, commanded by Kplt. Otto Schultz. The vessel stayed afloat for another eight hours before succumbing to the damage. U 66 lasted another two years after the attack on the *Falmouth*.

On a war patrol under the command of Kplt. G. Muhle, she successfully negotiated passage out of the Heligoland Bight, first through the German defensive minefields and then the British minefields. Early on 3 September 1917, she reported her position as being near the Dogger Bank, but the boat was never heard of, or seen again. The submarine disappeared with the loss of her captain and thirty-nine crewmen and may have struck a mine, or had an accident arising from mechanical or drill failure, which was fairly common in the early submarines.

During her service, SM U 66 sank twenty-four Allied vessels totalling 69,016 tons.

SM U 17

SM U 71 was a UE1 Flotten U-boat, a type SM U 71-U 72 mine-laying boat, built by Vulcan A.G. at Hamburg for the Imperial German Navy. She was launched on 31 October 1915 and commissioned for service on 20 December 1915. The boat had a surface displacement of 755 tons, 832 tons submerged, and had dimensions measuring 56.80m by length and a beam of 5.90m. She was an offshore boat, capable of operating in the Atlantic Ocean. Two 450hp diesel/oil engines powered her two bronze screw propellers, giving her a surface speed of 10.6kt, while rows of lead/acid batteries powered her two 450hp electric motors, giving her a speed of 7.9kt. U 71 had a surface endurance distance of 7,880 sea miles at a steady 7kt and carried 103 tons of fuel/oil. Running submerged using her battery power, she was capable of eighty-three sea miles at a steady 4kt. Her maximum diving depth was 50m and it took her forty to fifty seconds to dive. The boat had an armament of one bow torpedo tube offset on the starboard side, and a stern torpedo tube offset to the port side of the boat. She carried four torpedoes, thirty-eight mines using two stern mine-chutes and her artillery consisted of one 88mm (3.46in) deck-gun, with a 105mm (4.13in) gun from 1918.

Kplt. Hugo Schmidt commanded her from 20 December 1915 until 19 April 1917. Kplt. Walter Gude was commander from 20 April 1917 until 25 January 1918. Oblt.z.S. Richard Scheurlen took over from 4 February until 22 July 1918, then Oblt.z.S. Kurt Slevogt from 28 September 1918 until the end of the First World War.

SM U 71 surrendered to the Allies at the end of the First World War and became French reparation. She was broken up at Cherbourg in 1921. Between them the four commanders of SM U 71 sank seventeen Allied vessels, totalling 11,653 tons.

Known vessels believed sunk or damaged by SM U 71 in the North Sea:

VESSEL'S NAME	FLAG	TONS	D	M	YEAR	LOCATION
Trongate	GBR	2553	22	9	1917	5m N of Flamborough Head
HMS *Blackmorevale*	GBR	750	1	5	1918	Mined off Montrose

SM U 84

SM U 84 was a Flotten-U-boat, a type SM U 81-U 86 attack boat, built by Germaniawerft at Kiel for the Imperial German Navy. She was launched on 22 July 1915, but not commissioned for service until 6 June 1916. The boat had a surface displacement of 808 tons, 946 tons submerged, and measured 70.1m by length. Two 1,200hp diesel/oil engines powered her two bronze screw propellers that gave her a surface speed of 16.8kt. Rows of lead/acid batteries powered her two 600hp electric motors for running submerged, giving her a speed of 9.1kt. Her armament consisted of four bow and two stern torpedo tubes, she carried between twelve and sixteen torpedoes and had one 88mm (3.46in) deck-gun. The U-boat was one of the offshore boats, capable of operating in the Atlantic Ocean. The boat's normal complement was four officers and thirty-one crewmen.

Kplt. W. Roehr was the first and only commander of SM U 84. On 26 January 1918, U 84, under the command of Roehr was carrying a crew of forty, when she was rammed and sunk in St George's Channel, in the approximate position of N51 53 W05 44. After sighting U 84, the Royal Navy patrol-boat, PC 62, turned towards her and increased speed to full power. Capt. Roehr saw the patrol-boat approaching and attempted to turn away, but the U-boat was rammed just aft of the conning tower. She sank and was lost with her crew almost immediately, leaving nothing, but a large oil slick on the surface.

During her service, SM U 84 sank twenty-seven Allied vessels totalling 82,946 tons.

SM UB 18

SM UB 18 was one of the smaller U-boats, a UBII class, type SM UB 18–UB 19 attack boat, built by Blohm & Voss at Hamburg. Her keel was laid on 21 May 1915 she was launched on 21 August 1915 and commissioned on 11 December 1915, with Oblt.z.S. Franz Wäger as her First Commanding Officer. UB 18 was a coastal-boat designed with a single hull, making her rather vulnerable if she was ever rammed. The boat had a surface displacement of 263 tons, 292 tons submerged, and had dimensions measuring 36.13m by length, a beam of 4.36m, and a draught of 3.7m. Two 142hp diesel/oil engines that gave her a surface speed of 9.15kt powered her twin bronze screw propellers. She also had an endurance distance of 6,650 miles and carried 25-32 tons of fuel oil. Rows of lead/acid batteries powered her two 140hp electric motors for running submerged, and gave her a speed of 5.81kt. Her armament consisted of two bow torpedo tubes and she carried four to six torpedoes, plus one 88mm (3.46in) deck-gun or one of 5.5cm (2.17in), however from 1917 she had an 88mm gun. Her normal complement was two officers and twenty-one crewmen.

Just before her transfer to Flanders, Oblt.z.S. Otto Steinbrinck assumed command of the boat. Steinbrinck would go on to win the *Orden Pour Le Mérite* for outstanding duty against enemy shipping. He was also the top U-boat commander in English home waters and the fourth highest scoring captain overall. Otto Steinbrinck took UB 18 on the following patrols, (including the transfer to the Flanders base – which should count as a patrol – UB 18 being the first UBII boat in Flanders):

  1 Patrolled off Le Havre from 24-29 February 1916.
  2 Went to Smith Knoll area in support of German surface fleet on 4 March 1916.
  3 Patrolled the area off Boulogne and Le Havre from 7-11 March 1916.
  4 Off Le Havre from 21-24 March 1916.
  5 Off Le Havre from 3-8 April 1916.
  6 Off Lowestoft, in support of German fleet action from 23-26 April 1916.
  7 Patrolled off Haaks Lightvessel from 17-20 May 1916.
  8 Off Terschellig from from 24-27 May 1916.
  9 Patrolled off Terschellig from 30 May-2 June 1916.
 10 Patrolled off the Tyne estuary from 6-18 July 1916.
 11 Went down the English Channel from 31 July-12 August 1916.
 12 Off the English East Coast, to support German fleet action from 19-23 August 1916.
 13 Patrolled the English Channel from 1-16 September 1916.
 14 Patrolled down the English Channel from 19-27 October 1916.

Oblt.z.S. Claus Lafrenz assumed command of UB 18 on 28 October 1916 and Otto Steinbrinck went to Germany to command UC 65. Lafrenz took the boat on the following patrols:

Otto Steinbrinck was born in 1888. He began his career as a sea cadet in 1907. In 1911 he became a Leutnant zur See in the U-boat Waffe and in 1914 he commanded UB 10 and UB 18 at Flanders. In March 1916 he was awarded the *Pour Le Merite* (Order of the Blue Max) and in 1917 he was commander of UC 65, which sunk the British warship HMS *Ariadne*, as Kapitan-leutnant. In 1918 he commanded UB 57 and in April 1918 he became an Admiral-staff-officer in the Staff of the U-boat division at Flanders. He completed twenty-four long voyages and sunk 214 ships totalling 230,000 tons. Steinbrinck was a top ace of the Flanders Division. He ended his naval career in November 1919 and went on to secure a good position in a German heavy industry company around 1937. *(From Dutch Collection)*

15 In the North Sea from 9-15 November 1916.
16 Hunted ships down the English Channel and Bristol Channel area from 22 November-5 December 1916.
17 Hunted around the Scilly Isles from 27 December 1916-9 January 1917.
18 Patrolled western entrance to the English Channel from 30 January-12 February 1917.
19 Off the western entrance to the English Channel from 27 February to 5 March 1917.
20 Patrolled down the English Channel 10-20 March 1917.
21 Down the English Channel from 27 April-3 May 1917.
22 Patrolled down the English Channel from 9-19 May 1917.
23 Hunted down the English Channel from 31 May-14 June 1917.
24 Patrolled down the English Channel from 28 June-7 July 1917.

Oblt.z.S. Ulrich Mayer took over command of UB 18 on 8 July 1917, while Claus Lafrenz assumed command of UC 65 in September 1917. Mayer took UB 18 on these next patrols:

25 Hunted off The Hoofden from 21-29 July 1917.
26 Patrolled off The Hoofden from 14-21 August 1917.
27 Hunted ships down the English Channel from 30 August-4 September 1917.
28 Patrolled the western entrance to the English Channel from 9-21 September 1917.

Oblt.z.S. Georg Niemeyer took over command of UB 18 on 22 September 1917. (Ulrich Mayer is likely to have transferred to a staff position with the Flanders flotillas, because in the Spring, he was there as a Kapitanleutnant.). Georg Niemeyer took UB 18 on the next three patrols which including her final one:

29 Hunted ships off the Flamborough Head area from 6-15 October 1917.
30 Patrolled off the Flamborough Head area from 27 October-10 November 1917.
31 On 1 December 1917, UB 18 left port to hunt ships at the western entrance to the English Channel, under the command of Georg Niemeyer and carrying a crew of twenty-four. She was lost with all hands, presumed in the English Channel, in position N49 17 W05 47, on 9 December 1917. SM UB 18 had been rammed just aft of her conning tower by the Royal Navy trawler HMT *Ben Lawer*, which was escorting a cross-Channel coal convoy. The trawler was so badly damaged in the incident that she was barely able to make it back to port.

Vessels believed damaged or sunk by SM UB 18 in the North Sea:

VESSEL'S NAME	FLAG	TONS	D	M	YEAR	LOCATION
E.22 (HM Submarine)	GBR	725	25	4	1916	Off Yarmouth
Research (fishing-vessel)	GBR	44	17	5	1916	35m E of Cromer
Bertha (sailing vessel)	NOR	203	15	7	1916	60m E of West Hartlepool
Dina (sailing vessel)	NLD	164	15	7	1916	Near Sunderland (40m off the English coast)
Gertrude (fishing-vessel)	GBR	57	17	7	1916	10m NNE of Haisborough Lightvessel
Glance (fishing-vessel)	GBR	60	17	7	1916	10m NNE of Haisborough Lightvessel
Loch Nevis (fishing-vessel)	GBR	58	17	7	1916	Near Smith Knolls
Loch Tay (fishing-vessel)	GBR	44	17	7	1916	10m NNE of Haisborough Lightvessel
V.M.G (fishing-vessel)	GBR	59	17	7	1916	6m NE of Haisborough Lightvessel
Waverley (fishing-vessel)	GBR	59	17	7	1916	10m NNE of Haisborough Lightvessel
Breda	NLD	157	22	7	1917	7m W of Noord Hinder
Nereus (sailing vessel)	NLD	110	22	7	1917	10m S by E of Noord Hinder Lightvessel
Oostzee (tug)	NLD	199	24	7	1917	30m NW of Nieuwe Waterweg
Janna (sailing vessel)	NLD	145	25	7	1917	20m off Nieuwe Waterweg
Spes Mea (sailing vessel)	NLD	75	25	7	1917	Noord Hinder Lightvessel area
Peebles	GBR	4284	13	10	1917	20m SE of Spurn Point

SM U 19

SM UB 19 was one of the small UBII class boats, a type SM UB 18–UB 19 attack boat, built by Blohm & Voss at Hamburg. She was launched on 2 September 1915, commissioned on 17 December 1915 under Oblt.z.S Walter Gustav Becker who was her first CO. UB 19 was a coastal-boat designed with a single hull, which made her extra vulnerable if she was ever rammed. The boat had a surface displacement of 263 tons, 292 tons submerged and had dimensions measuring 36.13m by length, a beam of 4.36m and a draught of 3.7m. Two 142hp diesel/oil engines that gave her a surface speed of 9.15kt powered her twin bronze screw propellers. She also had an endurance distance of 6,650 miles and carried 25–32 tons of fuel oil. Rows of lead/acid batteries powered her two 140hp electric motors for running submerged, gave her a speed of 5.81kt. Her armament consisted of two bow torpedo tubes and she carried four to six torpedoes, plus one 88mm (3.46in) deck-gun or one 5.5cm (2.17in) deck-gun. Her normal complement was two officers and twenty-one crewmen.

Oblt.z.S. Walter Gustav Becker took her on the following patrols:

1. Transferred the boat to Flanders from February 28–1 March 1916.
2. From 9–17 March 1916 patrolled the English Channel.
3. From 16–25 April 1916, went off the Humber.
4. From 13–21 May 1916, patrolled off the Humber.
5. From 24–27 May 1916, went off The Hoofden area.
6. From 30 May–2 June 1916, formed part of a patrol line off Lowestoft.
7. & 8 Patrolled off Terschelling (one of the West Frisian Islands, belonging to Holland. The German U-boat base at Borkum was a few islands over to the east), Lowestoft and the Tyne areas.
9. From 20–26 July 1916, went into the Tyne Estuary.
10. From 5–14 August 1916, went to the Tyne Estuary area and sank the 3,808-ton steamship *San Bernado*, seventeen miles south-east from the Farne Islands.
11. From 18–19 August 1916, she supported the German fleet action against Sunderland.
12. From 26 September–8 October, went to the Humber Estuary and sank four trawlers.
13. From 22 October–3 November 1916, patrolled down the English Channel. Oblt.z.S. Erich Noodt took over command of UB 19. (Oblt.z.S. Walter Gustav Becker was lost in UB 82 with his entire crew, later in the war.) Erich Noodt took the boat on the following patrols:

14. From 10-15 November 1916, off The Hoofden.
15. Noodt left Zeebrugge on 22 November 1916 and patrolled down the English Channel. Eight days later, on 30 November, SM UB 19 encountered the decoy-vessel (or Q-ship) *Penshurst*. She fired a warning shot and closed with her to read the vessel's name for the log. The U-boat commander could see that the crew appeared to be abandoning ship, but he became suspicious when there was no name, and the fact that she was painted 'battleship' grey. Noodt quickly prepared to dive, but *Penshurst* had already brought her gun into place and fired at a 250yd (226.60m) range. The U-boat had no chance of escape from the barrage of shells, but sixteen of her crew, including the commander, did manage to escape. SM UB 19 went down to the bottom with eight of her crew, in position N50 00 02 48W.

During her career, SM UB 19 sank fifteen vessels, totalling 11,558 tons.

Vessels either damaged or sunk by SM UB 19 in the North Sea:

VESSEL'S NAME	FLAG	TONS	D	M	YEAR	LOCATION
Osprey (fishing vessel)	GBR	18	18	5	1916	13m NE from Spurn Head
Mars (sailing vessel)	NOR	106	24	7	1916	Tyne Estuary
San Bernardo	GBR	3803	10	8	1916	17m SE from Longstone
Jennie Bullas (fish vessel)	GBR	26	4	10	1916	14m ENE from Spurn Head LV
Jersey (fishing vessel)	GBR	162	4	10	1916	16m NE by E of Spurn Head LV
Rado (fishing vessel)	GBR	182	4	10	1916	16m NE by E from Spurn Head LV
Rover (fishing vessel)	GBR	42	5	10	1916	10m ENE from Spurn Head LV

SM UB 21

SM UB 21 was one of the smaller boats, a UBII class, type SM UB 20-UB 23 attack boat, built by Blohm & Voss at Hamburg for the Imperial German Navy. She was launched on 20 February 1916, commissioned on 20 February 1916 under Oblt.z.S. Ernst Hashagen and ready for operational service by 14 April 1916. UB 21 was a coastal-boat designed with a single hull and she had a surface displacement of 275 tons, 304 tons submerged. Her dimensions measured: 35.8m by length, a beam of 4.26m and a draught of 3.7m. Two 282hp diesel/oil engines that gave her a surface speed of 9.5kt powered her twin bronze screw propellers. She also had an endurance distance of 6,500 miles and carried 20 tons of fuel/oil. Rows of lead/acid batteries powered her two 140hp electric motors for running submerged, gave her a speed of 5.81kt. Her armament consisted of two bow torpedo tubes and she carried four torpedoes, plus one 5cm (1.97in) deck-gun. Her normal complement was two officers and twenty-one crewmen.

UB 21's first eight patrols under Oblt.z.S. Ernst Hashagen, her first commander, were from German ports, primarily to points along the British East Coast, with the Pentland Firth being a common destination. Hashagen was born on 24 August 1885 and died on 12 June 1947, having also served on U 62. He served on UB 21 from 20 February 1916 until late November 1916, when Oblt.z.S. Franz Walther took over on 27 November. He conducted two patrols using German ports from 4-13 December 1916 and 16-23 January 1917. UB 21 was then transferred to the Flanders Flotilla. Walther would lead the boat on seven more patrols, all to the English East Coast, around the Scarborough area. On 29 July 1917, the boat was interned at Corruna for a while before being released.

On 10 September 1917, UB 21 was transferred to V-U-Flotilla and operated once again out of the German ports of Emden, Heligoland and Brunsburrel. She also got a new commander, Oblt.z.S. Walter Scheffler, who took the boat on five patrols: 15-22 October 1917; 17-28 November 1917; 26 December 1917 to 1 January 1918, 30 January to 19 February 1918; and 14 March to 1 April 1918.

UB 21 was then transferred to 1-U-Flotilla and Oblt.z.S. Bruno Mahn took over as her commander. Mahn took her on four patrols: 1-18 May 1918; 29 June to 14 July 1918; 3-21

August 1918; and 14 September to 3 October 1918. However on 19 July 1918, the boat under Mahn landed two enlisted men on a special operation near Whitby, to sabotage an industrial railroad and munitions factory (source of information, NARS Washington). SM UB 21 then transferred to U-Schule (U-boat school). Following the armistice, she was surrendered to the French and was sunk somewhere along the English East Coast in 1920, en-route to being broken up.

SM UB 21 was one of the most successful of the Kaiser's Imperial U-boat's to operate in the coastal waters of Yorkshire.

Known vessels believed sunk or damaged by SM UB 21 in the North Sea:

VESSEL'S NAME	FLAG	TONS	D	M	YEAR	LOCATION
Harald (sailing vessel)	SWE	275	5	5	1916	In the North Sea
Lekna	SWE	204	20	10	1916	Hartlepool or Pentland Firth
Randi (sailing vessel)	NOR	467	20	10	1916	Hartlepool or Pentland Firth
Svartvik (sailing vessel)	SWE	322	20	10	1916	Hartlepool or Pentland Firth
Grönhaug	NOR	667	21	10	1916	Hartlepool or Pentland Firth
London (sailing vessel)	DEN	184	22	10	1916	Hartlepool or Pentland Firth
Thor	NOR	372	22	10	1916	Hartlepool or Pentland Firth
Fritzöe (Taken as prize)	NOR			10	1916	Hartlepool or Pentland Firth
Pluto (Taken as prize)	NOR	1148		11	1916	Off the north-east coast of England
Lady Ann	GBR	1016	16	2	1917	3m ESE of Scarborough
Excel (trawler)	GBR	157	17	2	1917	Off Scarborough
John Miles	GBR	687	22	2	1917	11m SE of Teesmouth
Bywell	GBR	1522	29	3	1917	3m E of Scarborough
Victoria	GBR	1620	29	4	1917	5m NE by N of Scarborough
Rikard Noordrak	NOR	1123	2	5	1917	4.5m NNE of Scarborough
Edith Cavell (fishing vessel)	GBR	20	5	5	1917	In Robin Hood Bay
Harold	SWE	1563	6	5	1917	Off the English East Coast (Tyne-Göteborg)
Batavier (Taken as prize)	NLD	157	8	5	1917	E of the Doggerbank
S.N.A. 2	FRA	2294	6	6	1917	Off Hornsea area
Sir Francis	GBR	1991	7	6	1917	2m NE of Scarborough
Trelyon	GBR	3099	20	7	1917	3m N of Scarborough
Glow	GBR	1141	22	7	1917	4m ESE of South Cheek, Robin Hood's Bay
Vanland	SWE	1285	24	7	1917	Near Runswick Bay
Springhill	GBR	1507	24	8	1917	4m N of Scarborough
Amsteldam	GBR	1233	18	10	1917	6m N of Flamborough Head
Gemma	GBR	1385	19	10	1917	5m NW of Flamborough Head
Ocean	GBR	1442	23	11	1917	4m ENE of Hartlepool
Inverness	GBR	3734	19	12	1917	Whitby and Sunderland area (only damaged)
Patria	RUS	838	19	12	1917	5m off Teesmouth
Hercules	GBR	1295	30	12	1917	3m ENE of Whitby
Hercules	GBR	1095	25	3	1918	4m NNW of Flamborough Head
Constantia	GBR	772	8	5	1918	2m E of South Cheek, Robin Hood Bay
Anboto Mendi	SPA	2114	10	5	1918	7m off Runswick
Gothia	SWE	1826	11	5	1918	NE of Hartlepool
Haslingden	GBR	1934	12	5	1918	7m E of Seaham Harbour
Mentor (sailing vessel)	NOR	539		7	1918	Off Hartlepool (only damaged)
Paul	BEL	659	26	9	1918	In Robin Hood's Bay

SM UB 22

SM UB 22 was one of the smaller boats, a UBII class, type SM UB 20-UB 23 attack boat, built by Blohm & Voss at Hamburg for the Imperial German Navy. She was launched 9 October 1915 and commissioned for service on 2 March 1916, with Oblt.z.S Bernhard Putzier as her first C.O. UB 22 was a coastal boat designed with a single hull and she had a surface displacement of 275 tons, 304 tons submerged. Her dimensions measured 35.8m by length, a beam of 4.26m and a draught of 3.7m. Two 282hp diesel/oil engines that gave her a surface speed of 9.5kt powered her twin bronze screw propellers. She also had an endurance distance of 6,500 miles and carried 20 tons of fuel/oil. Rows of lead/acid batteries powered her two 140hp electric motors for running submerged and gave her a speed of 5.81kt. Her armament consisted of two bow torpedo tubes and she carried four torpedoes, plus one 5cm (1.97in) deck-gun. Her normal complement was two officers and twenty-one crewmen. The boat served in Germany-based flotillas throughout her career. Bernhard Putzier took her on the following patrols:

1. 16-20 April 1916, guard duty off Horn Reef.
2. 1-5 May 1916, guard duty of Horn Reef again.
3. 21 May-3 June 1916, in support of High Seas Fleet raid, positioned off the River Humber.
4. 10-23 July 1916, went to the Pentland Firth.
5. 4-17 September 1916, patrolled south of the Firth of Forth.
6. 18 October-5 November 1916, along the English East Coast.
7. & 8 Patrolled against Royal Navy submarines in the Heligoland Bight.
9. 15-22 January 1917, along the English East Coast.
10. 1-12 February 1917, along the English East Coast.
11. 8 March-1 April 1917, patrolled off the Flamborough Head and Whitby area.

Oblt.z.S. Karl Wacker assumed command of the boat on 17 April 1917.
12. 26 April-9 May 1917, off the Scottish coast (Peterhead and Moray Forth area).
13. 14-30 June 1917, off the English East Coast.
14. 23 July-14 August 1917, off the English East Coast.
15. 1-21 September 1917, along the English East Coast.
16. 2-11 November 1917, along the English East Coast.
17. 11-18 December 1917, off the English East Coast.
18. On 19 January 1918, Oblt.z.S. Wacker sailed for the English East Coast, He was proceeding through one of the 'safe' channels through the German minefields in the Heligoland Bight when the escort, Torpedo boat S16, detonated an English mine. The boat sank with all hands, north-west of Heligoland. SM UB 22, which was following close behind, also struck a mine and sank with the loss of her crew of twenty-two, in position N54 40-W06 32.

SM UB 27

SM UB 27 was one of the smaller boats, a UBII class, type SM UB 24-UB 29 attack boat, built by A.G. Weser at Bremen for the Imperial German Navy. She was launched on 10 February 1916 and commissioned for service on 23 February 1916. The boat had a surface displacement of 265 tons, 291 tons submerged and had dimensions measuring 36.13m by length, a beam of 4.26m and a draught of 3.7m. Two 135hp diesel/oil engines powered her two bronze screw propellers, giving her a surface speed of 8.9kt. Rows of lead/acid batteries powered her two 140hp electric motors for running submerged, giving her a speed of 5.7kt. Her armament consisted of two bow torpedo tubes, four torpedoes and one 5cm (1.97in) deck-gun. UB 27 had a normal complement of two officers and twenty-one crewmen. She was a single-hulled boat designed for coastal work.

Oblt.z.S. Viktor Dieckmann was the boat's first commander, serving from 23 February 1916.

He took the boat on four patrols: from 23 April to 4 May 1916; 20-30 May 1916; 15-29 August 1916 as part of a U-boat force supporting the German fleet's sortie; and 2-14 October. All left from bases in Germany, with patrols one, two and four taking her to the Firth of Forth and patrol three, to the Pentland Firth.

Oblt.z.S. Hans Georg Lubbe took over command of the boat from 1 November 1916 and he conducted six patrols. The first five were unsuccessful, but on his sixth and the boat's tenth patrol from 5-18 May 1917, Lubbe sank two Norwegian vessels.

SM UB 27 was then transferred to the Baltic, under the command of Oblt.z.S. Heinz Freiherr von Stein (zu Lausnitz) from 24 April 1917. The boat then operated out of Libau, but never made contact with any enemy vessels.

Under Stein on 19 July, UB 27 transferred to Flanders, left on her first patrol on 22 July, but one week later, she was lost. The boat was running submerged at periscope depth on 29 July 1917, when the old torpedo-gunboat HMS Halcyon, on a routine patrol, sighted her off the Smith's Knoll Spar buoy, in the approximate position of N52 47 E02 24. The gunboat immediately increased speed, then turned quickly and rammed UB 27, before dropping two 228.8kg (500lb) depth charges as she passed over the submarine. As Halcyon stood by, a large oil slick and bubbles rose to the surface. Later that day, Royal Navy vessels swept the position with bottom-lines and found a large object lying on the seabed. Divers were sent down to inspect it, but underwater visibility was so poor, they could not find the object. SM UB 27, von Stein and her crew of twenty-two were never seen or heard of again.

Known vessels believed sunk or damaged by UB 27 in the North Sea:

VESSEL'S NAME	FLAG	TONS	D	M	YEAR	LOCATION
Blessing (fishing vessel)	GBR	19	28	4	1916	Near the Tyne Estuary
Christian (sailing vessel)	DEN	180	28	4	1916	Near the Tyne Estuary (refloated)
Teal	GBR	766	29	4	1916	2m E of Seaham Harbour
Wandle	GBR	889	29	4	1916	15m SE of Souter Point (damaged)
Mod	NOR	664	30	4	1916	In the Firth of Forth
Rio Blanco	BRA	2258	1	5	1916	In the Firth of Forth
Mars (lighter)	NOR	777	2	5	1916	N of the Dogger Bank
Memento (sailing vessel)	NOR	654	2	5	1916	N of the Dogger Bank
uperb (lighter)	NOR	721	2	5	1916	N of the Dogger Bank
Duke Of Albany	GBR	1997	25	8	1916	20m E of the Pentland Skerries
Kjaereg	NOR	1019	31	8	1916	In the North Sea
Jupiter	GBR	2124	7	10	1916	In the Firth of Forth (damaged)
Magnus (fishing vessel)	GBR	154	8	10	1916	40m NE of Longstone, Farne Islands
Thode Fagellund	NOR	4352	12	3	1917	In the North Sea
Davanger	NOR	5876	14	3	1917	In the North Sea

SM UB 30

SM UB 30 was one of the smaller UBII class boats, a type SM UB 30-UB 41 attack boat, built by Blohm & Voss at Hamburg for the Imperial German Navy. She was launched on 16 November 1916 and commissioned on 18 March 1916. The boat had a displacement of 274 tons surface weight, 303 tons submerged and with dimensions measuring 36.9m by length, a beam of 4.26m and a draught of 3.7m. Two 135hp diesel engines powered her two bronze screw propellers, giving her a surface speed of 9kt. Rows of lead/acid batteries powered her two 140hp electric motors for running submerged gave her a speed of 5.71kt. Her armament consisted of two bow torpedo tubes and she carried four torpedoes, plus she had one 88mm (3.46in) deck-gun. UB 30 was a single-hulled boat designed more for coastal use and had a normal complement of two officers and twenty-one crewmen.

UB 30 was put into service by 8 May 1916, under the command of her first officer Oblt.z.S.

Kurt Schapler. The boat went on seven patrols in the Baltic Sea, the last of which was under the boat's second C.O., Oblt.z.S. Cassius von Montigny. SM UB 30 then went to Flanders, on 16 February 1917, but she was stranded en route and was interned for a while. On 8 August 1917 the boat was released under a new commander, Oblt.z.S. Wilhelm Rhein. Rhein's took her on the following patrols:

1. The English East Coast, from 26 August-4 September 1917.
2. Off Flamborough Head area from 17-29 September 1917.
3. The English Channel from 7-22 November 1917.
4. The English Channel from 8-18 December 1917.
5. The English Channel from 30 December 1917-14 January 1918.
6. The English Channel, from 31 January-11 February 1918.
7. The English Channel, from 28 February-18 March 1918.
8. On 24 March 1918, the boat was bombed and damaged while in port at Zeebrugge.

Oblt.z.S. Rudolf Stier became UB 30's new commander on 22 April 1918.

9. On 20-31 May 1918, Stier took the boat from the Flamborough Head to Sunderland.
10. 15-30 June 1918, she hunted off the English East Coast.
11. 16-24 July 1918, she returned to the English East Coast.
12. SM UB 30 left her base on 6 August 1918 to hunt Allied vessels off the English East Coast.

However, on 13 August 1918, she was lost with her crew of twenty-six off Whitby. (The boat's normal complement should have been twenty-two.) The armed RN trawler *John Gillman* attempted to ram the submarine, when she sighted UB 30's periscope, but the submarine had observed the trawler's approach and commenced diving. This resulted in HMT *John Gillman* scraping noisily over her casing. Two depth charges were then dropped, which brought an oil slick and wreckage to the surface, so the trawler left a dan-buoy over the spot and waited in anticipation. Two hours later, UB 30 surfaced, but the two RN trawlers, HMT *John Booker* and HMT *Viola*, sighted her. A volley of shells was fired and more depth charges dropped, forcing the boat down to the bottom again. As she went down, the RN crews could clearly see oil pouring out of holes in the submarine's pressure casing. Four more depth charges followed her down and she never moved again. The wreck of SM UB 30 was found that night after wire sweeps and divers inspected her the next day.

Known vessels believed sunk or damaged by SM UB 30 in the North Sea:

VESSEL'S NAME	FLAG	TONS	D	M	YEAR	LOCATION
Vernon	GBR	982	31	8	1917	22m SE by S of Spurn Point
Ragnhild	GBR	1495	3	9	1917	14m S by SSE of Flamborough Head
S.N.A. III	FRA	1709	26	9	1917	7m E of Horsea
Norfolk Coast	GBR	782	18	6	1918	23m SE of Flamborough Head
Madame Renee	GBR	509	10	8	1918	1m NNE of Scarborough

SM UB 32

SM UB 32 was one of the small UBII class boats, a type SM UB 30-UB 41 attack U-boat built by Blohm & Voss in Hamburg for the Imperial German Navy. She was launched on 4 December 1915 and commissioned for service on 11 April 1916. The boat had a displacement of 274 tons surface weight, 303 tons submerged and dimensions measuring 36.9m by length, a beam of 4.26m and a draught of 3.7m. Two 135hp diesel engines powered her two bronze screw propellers giving her a surface speed of 9kt. Two 140hp electric motors powered by rows of lead/acid batteries gave her a submerged speed of some 5.7kt. Her armament consisted of two bow torpedo tubes, one 88mm (3.46in) deck-gun and she carried four torpedoes. UB 32 was a single-hulled craft, designed more for coastal use and had a normal complement of two officers and twenty-one crewmen.

Kplt. Max Viebeg, born on 6 April 1887, commanded UB 32 for a period of time. On 30 January 1917 he was awarded the *Orden Pour Le Mérite* for outstanding duty against enemy shipping. He also served on UB 20, UC 65 and UB 80. Viebeg died on 9 November 1961 at the age of seventy-four.

On 22 September 1917, SM UB 32 was under the command of Kplt. Hans von Ditfurth when she was sunk by an aircraft, near Sunk Light in the English Channel, with the loss of her twenty-three crew members. The U-boat was moving south-east through the English Channel when the crew of an RNAS Curtis H8 Large America flying boat, serial no.8695, sighted her. UB 32 saw the approaching aircraft and began an emergency dive, but the seaplane still managed to drop two 104.33kg (230lb) bombs on their target before she had fully submerged. There were two huge explosions and the submarine was seen to roll over and sink, followed by a massive air bubble and then the emergence of oil and wreckage on the surface. The crew of the flying boat consisted of Flight S-Lt N.A. Magor, Flight S-Lt C.E.S. Lusk, CPO E.A. Boyd and Leading Mechanic R.A. Lucas. (Incidentally, the French *Foucault*, was the first submarine ever to be sunk by an aircraft, She was sunk in the Adriatic on 15 September 1915 when an Austrian aeroplane bombed her.)

Known vessels believed sunk or damaged by SM UB 32 in the North Sea:

VESSEL'S NAME	FLAG	TONS	D	M	YEAR	LOCATION
De Tien Kinders (sailing vessel)	BEL	44	13	3	1917	Off the Smith Knoll Spar buoy
Gold Seeker (fishing vessel)	GBR	62	13	3	1917	Off the Smith Knoll Spar buoy
Feltre	ITA	6455	26	8	1917	4m SSE of Flamborough Head

SM UB 33

SM UB 33 was a UBII class submarine, a type SM UB 30-UB 41 attack boat, built by Blohm & Voss at Hamburg for the Imperial German Navy. She was launched on 4 December 1915 and commissioned on 22 April 1916. The boat had a displacement of 274 tons surface weight, 303 tons submerged and with dimensions measuring 36.9m by length, a 4.26m beam and a 3.7m draught. Two 135hp diesel/oil engines that gave her a surface speed of 9kt powered her two bronze screw propellers. Rows of lead/acid batteries powered her two 140hp electric motors for running submerged and gave her a speed of 5.71kt. She was designed with a single-hull and was used for coast patrols. Her armament consisted of two bow torpedo tubes and she carried four torpedoes, plus one 88mm (3.46in) deck-gun.

UB 33 went into service by 22 June 1916, under the command of her first CO, Oblt.z.S. Herbert Lefholz. Her first nine patrols were in the Baltic Sea and were of no great significance. On 1 February 1917 Oblt.z.S. Waldemar von Fischer took command, and on 21 March 1917, Oblt.z.S. Karl Ruprecht became her commander. While on her 10th patrol, UB 33 searched for merchant vessels in the Skagerrak and Kattegat, during May and June 1917. Oblt.z.S. Fritz Gregor became UB 33's fourth commander on 17 September 1917 and was the only commander when the boat was with the Flanders Flotilla from September 1917 onwards.

The U-boat's eleventh patrol was off the English East Coast from 12-24 October 1917, followed by two short patrols in The Hoofden area. The patrols after this were as follows:

14. From 22 December 1917-4 January 1918, she went to the Hoofden and English East Coast.
15. From 7-23 February 1918, Gregor patrolled the English Channel.
16. From 13-18 March 1918, hunted Allied vessels in Lyme Bay and the Channel area.
17. On 31 March her patrol was aborted because of mechanical problems.
18. From 6 April 1918, UB 33 resumed her patrols and left her base for the English Channel.

Kapitanleutnant Max Viebeg, born 6 April 1887, died 9 November 1961, awarded the *Orden Pour Le Mérite* on 30 January 1917 as Commander of SM UB 80. *(From Dutch Collection)*

However, on 11 April 1918, the boat was returning to her base at Zeebrugge when she detonated a mine and sank in the Strait of Dover, south-west of the Varne sandbank. The Royal Navy drifter *Ocean Roamer* reported the explosion. Later she recovered floating wreckage from the submarine and reported a thick stream of oil rising to the surface. However divers who were sent to investigate the wreck had difficulty locating her because the drifter had not given an accurate position. On 21 May they succeeded in finding her, but divers were unable to enter the boat at first, because the body of her commander, Oblt.z.S. F. Gregor was blocking the hatch on the way down. His body was recovered, along with a waterproof chest containing SM UB 33's confidential books, signals and ciphers. All of the submarine's crew were lost with the boat, but Gregor's body was buried on land.

Known vessels believed sunk or damaged by SM UB 33 in the North Sea:

VESSEL'S NAME	FLAG	TONS	D M	YEAR	LOCATION
Gertie (Taken as prize)	SWE	257	(24/5 to 15/6)	1917	Skagerrak and Kattegat
Gotha (Taken as prize)	SWE	720	(24/5 to 15/6)	1917	Skagerrak and Kattegat
Krager (Taken as prize)	NOR	550	(24/5 to 15/6)	1917	Skagerrak and Kattegat
Genesse	GBR	2830	1 1	1918	Flamborough Head (only damaged)

SM UB 34

SM UB 34 was a UBII class attack boat, of the SM UB 30-UB 41 type, built by Blohm & Voss at Hamburg for the Imperial German Navy. She was launched and commissioned for service on 10 June 1916 and was in service by 27 July 1916. The boat had a surface displacement of 274 tons, 303 tons submerged and had dimensions measuring 36.9m by length, a beam of 4.26m and a draught of 3.7m. Two 135hp diesel/oil engines powered her two bronze screw propellers, giving her a speed of 9kt. Rows of lead/acid batteries powered her two 140hp electric motors for running submerged, giving her a speed of 5.71kt. Her armament consisted of two bow torpedo tubes, four torpedoes and one 88mm (3.46in) deck-gun. UB 34 was a single-hulled boat, designed for use in coastal waters. Her first commander was Oblt.z.S. Theodor Schultz who had six patrols, all from German ports:

1. 7-9 August 1916, supported a Zeppelin raid on England.
2. 11-24 September 1916, off the Firth of Forth.

3. 18 October–1 November 1916, off the East Coast of England.
4. 7-23 December 1916, off the East Coast of England.
5. 16-23 January 1917, patrol in the North Sea.
6. 1-10 February 1917, off the East Coast of England.

Oblt.z.S. Ludwig Schaafhausen assumed command on 17 March 1917 and had four patrols:
7. 16-28 April 1917, off the Scottish East Coast.
8, 9 & 10. Patrols (dates unknown) were off the East Coast of England, but Schaafhausen sank no vessels.

Oblt.z.S. Hellmuth von Ruckteschell took command on 1 September 1917 and conducted seven patrols:

11. 6-10 September 1917, off the East Coast of England.
12. 24-30 September 1917, off the East Coast of England.
13. 21-30 October 1917, off the English East Coast.
14. 8-18 December 1917, off the English East Coast.
15. 21-30 January 1918, off the English East Coast.
16. 16-28 February 1918, left on patrol but returned to base when her escort was mined.
17. 6-20 March 1918, off the English East Coast.

Oblt.z.S. Erich Forste assumed command on 31 March 1918 and took her on three patrols:

18. 16-30 April 1918, off the East Coast of England.
19. 4-20 June 1918, off the East Coast of England.
20. From 17 July-6 August 1918, off the English East Coast.

On 9 September 1918, UB 34 was transferred to the Flanders Flotilla, under the command of Lt Reserve Hans Illing, (Reserve Officer). Illing took her on one patrol:

21. 9-30 September 1918, off the English East Coast. However, the Flanders ports were abandoned, so UB 34 refuelled at Zeebrugge and was then redeployed back to Germany. SM UB 34 surrendered to the Allies at the end of the First World War and became British war reparation. She was scrapped at Canning Town in 1922.

Known vessels believed sunk or damaged by SM UB 34 in the North Sea:

VESSEL'S NAME	FLAG	TONS	D	M	YEAR	LOCATION
Ull	NOR	1139	21	10	1916	Near Rattray Head
Effort (fishing vessel)	GBR	159	22	10	1916	SE of Buchan Ness
Regina (barque)	NOR	823	23	10	1916	SE of Buchan Ness
Titan (fishing vessel)	GBR	171	26	10	1916	SE of Girdleness
Arran (fishing vessel)	GBR	176	18	12	1916	Off the Longstone, Farne Isles
Ansgar (sailing vessel)	NOR	926	19	12	1916	Off the Longstone, Farne Isles
Eva (brigantine)	DAN	109	19	12	1916	Off the Longstone, Farne Isles
Kornmo (barque)	NOR	591	19	12	1916	Off the Longstone, Farne Isles
Mereddio	SWE	1372	19	12	1916	In the North Sea
Nystrand	NOR	1397	19	12	1916	In the North Sea
Hurstwood	GBR	1229	5	2	1917	6m NE of Whitby
Corsican Prince	GBR	2776	7	2	1917	3m E of Whitby
Saint Ninian	GBR	3026	7	2	1917	3m E of Whitby
Este	DAN	1420	26	4	1917	In the North Sea
Grelfryda	GBR	5136	7	9	1917	Flamborough Head area (only damaged)

Aladdin	NOR	3013	8	9	1917	5 miles N by W of Flamborough Head
Greltoria	GBR	5143	27	9	1917	3m NW by N _ N of Flamborough Head
Lady Helen	GBR	811	27	10	1917	0.5m E of South Cheek, Robin Hood Bay
Bangarth	GBR	1872	13	12	1917	13m NNE of the River Tyne
Dafni	GRE	1190	15	12	1917	SE of Sunderland
Desire (HM Tug)	GBR	135	24	1	1918	2.5 miles NE of Filey
Folmina	NLD	1158	25	1	1918	3 miles SE of Sunderland
Humber	GBR	280	25	1	1918	4m E of Souter lighthouse
Hartley	GBR	1150	26	1	1918	2m NE of Skinningrove (Boulogne-Tyne)
Athos	NOR	1708	27	1	1918	1 mile ENE of Kettleness Point
Randelsborg	DAN	1551	9	3	1918	In the Skagerrak
Adine	NOR	2235	13	3	1918	8 miles E of the Heugh, Hartlepool
Quintero (sailing vessel)	DEN	1611	16	3	1918	In the Skagerrak
Lompoc	GBR	7270	21	4	1918	S of Longstone (only damaged)
Lowtyne	GBR	3231	10	6	1918	3.5m ESE of Whitby
Princess Maud	GBR	1566	10	6	1918	2 miles S of Coquet Island
Elise (HMT)	GBR	239	15	9	1918	2 miles SE of Byth

SM UB 35

SM UB 35 was a UBII class attack boat of the SM UB 30-UB 41 type, built by Blohm & Voss at Hamburg for the Imperial German Navy. She was launched on 28 December 1915, but not commissioned until 22 June 1916, going into service on 8 August 1916. The boat had a surface displacement of 274 tons, 303 tons submerged, and had dimensions measuring 36.9m in length, a beam of 4.26m and a draught of 3.7m. Two 135hp diesel/oil engines powered her two bronze screw propellers, giving her a speed of 9kt. Rows of lead/acid batteries powered her two 140hp electric motors for running submerged gave her a speed of 5.71kt. Her armament consisted of two bow torpedo tubes, four torpedoes, and one 88mm (3.46in) deck-gun. UB 35 was one of the single-hulled craft, designed more for inshore waters.

Her first commander was Oblt.z.S. Rudolf Gebeschus, who was lost later with SM UB 63. The boat first operated from German ports. Gebeschus took the boat on five patrols in total:

1. 20-22 August 1916, he operated as part of the High Seas Fleet (HSF) in the North Sea.
2. 24-26 August 1916, Gebeschus covered a Zeppelin airship raid over England.
3,4&5. Patrols took part in the North Sea, but the boat made no contacts with enemy vessels.

Oblt.z.S. Otto von Schrader assumed command of UB 35 and took her on one patrol.

6. From 13 October-2 November 1916, off the Scottish East Coast and down the North Sea.

Oberleutnant Gebeschus returned to command on 6 November 1916, taking her on a further nine patrols:

7-11. Patrols took place in the North Sea, covering possible High Seas Fleet development routes.
12. 16-22 January 1917, in the North Sea.
13. 1-10 February 1917, off the English East Coast.
14. 9-20 March 1917, she went to The Hoofden area to attack Rotterdam to Harwich convoys.
15. From 30 March-12 April 1917, off the Scottish East Coast.

SM UB 35 was then transferred to the Baltic, under the command of Oblt.z.S. Karl Stöter.

18. After two uneventful patrols, the boat was transferred to Flanders.

19. 21-24 July 1917, she patrolled The Hoofden.
20. 7-16 August 1917 again patrolled The Hoofden and sank the 144-ton trawler *Jay* with a torpedo, which was looked on as overkill. Normally they would have used the deck-gun, or scuttling charges to sink a trawler.
21. 1-13 September 1917, patrolled the English Channel.
22. 24 September-8 October 1917, in the English Channel.
23. 28 October-6 November 1917, off the English East Coast.
24. 22 November-6 December 1917, back to the English Channel.
25. 22 December 1917-1 January 1918, patrolled the English Channel.
26. 17 January 1918, UB 35 patrolled the English Channel.

However, on 25 January 1918, carrying a crew of twenty-one, Stoter had just put a scuttling party on board the steamship *Epstatios* in the English Channel when the British patrol boat HMS P34 appeared on the scene. The U-boat was forced to dive, leaving six of her crewmen on board the steamship, all of whom were then taken prisoner. The following day, just to the north of Calais, the destroyer HMS *Leven* immediately attacked UB 35 with depth charges, after sighting her periscope. Wreckage and lots of oil soon bubbled to the surface, along with seven of the submarine's crew. However, only one man could be rescued alive and he died on board the destroyer soon after. The men all probably died from lung damage, after surfacing without any proper escape-apparatus, from very deep water. The luckiest men were the ones taken prisoner by HMS P34. They identified the U-boat later, by items of clothing and letters retrieved from the water by the crew of the destroyer.

Known vessels believed sunk or damaged by SM UB 35 in the North Sea:

VESSEL'S NAME	FLAG	TONS	D	M	YEAR	LOCATION
Sten	NOR	1046	17	10	1916	N of Farne Islands
Cottica (sailing vessel)	NOR	320	19	10	1916	N of Farne Islands
Dido	NOR	333	19	10	1916	N of Farne Islands
Guldaas (sailing vessel)	NOR	636	19	10	1916	N of Farne Islands
Guldborg	DEN	1569	20	10	1916	North Sea
Libra (sailing vessel)	DEN	174	20	10	1916	North Sea
aftsund	NOR	937	21	10	1916	North Sea
Stemshest	NOR	811	27	10	1916	North Sea
Vestra	GBR	1021	5	2	1917	5m NE Hartlepool
Camilla	NOR	2273	1	4	1917	Dogger Bank
Ester	DEN	1210	1	4	1917	Dogger Bank
Lord Scarborough (fishing vessel)	GBR	158	2	4	1917	100m E May Island
Gibraltar (sailing vessel)	GBR	188	4	4	1917	Kinnard Island
Maggie Ross (sailing vessel)	GBR	183	4	4	1917	Kinnard Island
Kongshaug	NOR	380	6	4	1917	NW of Moray Firth
Lord Kitchener (fishing vessel)	GBR	161	6	4	1917	NW of Moray Firth
Recto (fishing vessel)	GBR	177	6	4	1917	NW of Moray Firth
Breda	NLD	157	21/22	7	1917	8m SW Noord Hinder LV (damaged)
Jay (fishing vessel)	GBR	144	11	8	1917	Lowestoft area

Vessels taken as a prize of war by SM UB 35, but were later released:

Paposa	NOR	1067	Skagerrak & Kattegat area 21/5 to 5/6 1917
Rigmor (sailing vessel)	DEN	798	Skagerrak & Kattegat area 21/5 to 5/6 1917
Sara	DEN	1573	Skagerrak & Kattegat area 21/5 to 5/6 1917
Viking (sailing vessel)	DEN	2952	Skagerrak & Kattegat area 21/5 to 5/6 1917

SM UB 38

SM UB 38 was a UBII class attack boat of the SM UB 30–UB 41 type, built by Blohm & Voss at Hamburg for the Imperial German Navy. She was launched on 1 April 1916 and commissioned on 19 July 1916. The boat had a surface displacement of 274 tons, 303 tons submerged and had dimensions measuring 36.9m by length, a beam of 4.26m and a draught of 3.7m. Two 135hp diesel/oil engines powered her two bronze screw propellers giving her a speed of 9kt. Rows of lead/acid batteries powered her two 140hp electric motors for running submerged and gave her a speed of 5.71kt. Her armament consisted of two bow torpedo tubes, one 88mm (3.46in) deck-gun and she carried four torpedoes. UB 38 was one of the single-hulled vessels, designed for coastal patrols and had a normal complement of two officers and twenty-one crewmen.

SM UB 38 was a Flanders-based boat throughout her career and Flanders commanders usually stayed in Belgium, very rarely did they transfer out to command boats based in the German ports. As a result, even the best commanders like Johannes Lohs, Wassner, Hundius, Steinbrinck and Wenniger only ended up commanding UBIII boats and not the larger U-series of boats. Veteran commanders from Flanders were usually sent back to Germany to pick up the newer, bigger and more powerful boats, as they became available. Werner Fürbringer, for example, was the first CO on five different U-boats, a UBI, a UBII, a UCII, and two UBIII. SM UB 38 was in service by 8 September 1916. Her first commander was Kplt. Erwin Wassner, who went on to win the *Orden Pour Le Mérite* for outstanding service against enemy vessels. Kplt. Erwin Wassner took UB 38 on the following patrols:

1. First patrol was the transfer to Flanders.
2. Along the Dutch coast, 15-21 September 1916.
3. Hunted in the English Channel, from 28 September-8 October 1916.
4.& 5. Patrolled off the Flanders coast searching for Allied ships.
6. Along the English Channel, from 2-7 November 1916.
7. Along the English Channel from 12-16 November.

Oblt.z.S. Wilhelm Ambereger assumed command of UB 38 on 19 November 1916. Erwin Wassner took control of the brand new UC 69, while Wilhelm Amsberger was lost, or disappeared, with UB 108 later on in the First World War.

8. Ambereger took the boat to the Hoofden, 20 November–5 December 1916.
9. 11-22 December 1916, patrolled the English Channel.
10. From 11-24 January 1917, hunted in the English Channel.
11. 8-22 February 1917, the English Channel then out as far as the Irish coast.
12. 8-24 April 1917, along the English Channel.
13. 25 April-7 May 1917, hunted in the English Channel.
14. 22-29 May 1917, patrolled the English Channel, but was forced home early with machinery problems when she was damaged in the bombardment of Ostend on 5 June 1917.
15. 4-6 August 1917, started patrolling the English Channel, but was forced to return home with an oil leak.
16. 14-28 August 1917, hunted in the English Channel.
17. 9-23 September 1917, patrol of the English Channel.
18. 11-24 October 1917, patrol in the English Channel, but badly damaged by explosion from unidentified merchant vessel and forced to return home for major repairs.

Oblt.z.S. Waldemar von Fischer took over command of the boat on 6 December 1917.

19. Waldemar patrolled the Hoofden and English East Coast 8-19 December 1917.
Oblt.z.S. Günther Bachmann became the new commander from 25 December 1917.

20. Patrolled the English East Coast, 1-15 January 1918.
21. From 29 January 1918, Bachmann hunted in the English Channel, but on 8 February SM UB 38 disappeared in a minefield in the Strait of Dover. HM Drifter *Gowen II* had sighted the boat on the surface, to the north-east of Le Colbart sandbank and, realising his boat had been sighted, Bachmann immediately submerged. However, *Gowen II* had already radioed for assistance and within twenty minutes, a number of Royal Navy vessels and a destroyer joined her, to hunt for U-boat. Three massive underwater explosions then suddenly rocked the British warships. Nothing more was ever heard from Gunther Bachmann and his crew of twenty-seven again. It was believed that, in trying to escape from the patrol vessels, the U-boat had unknowingly dived into a minefield, in the approximate position of N50 56 E 01 25.

Known vessels believed sunk or damaged by SM UB 38 in the North Sea:

VESSEL'S NAME	FLAG	TONS	D	M	YEAR	LOCATION
Birtley	GBR	1438	5	1	1918	8m N of Flamborough Head
Caledonia	NLD	863	13	1	1918	Whitby area (only damaged)

SM UB 39

SM UB 39 was a UBII class attack boat of the SM UB 30-UB 41 type, designed as a single-hulled vessel for coastal patrol work. She was built by Blohm & Voss at Hamburg for the Imperial German Navy, launched on 29 December 1915 and commissioned for service on 29 April 1916, with Oblt.z.S. Werner Fürbringer as first CO. UB 39 had a surface displacement of 274 tons, 303 tons submerged, and dimensions measuring 36.9m by length, a beam of 4.26m and a draught of 3.7m. Two 135hp diesel/oil engines powered her two bronze screw propellers giving her a speed of 9kt. Rows of lead/acid batteries powered her two 140hp electric motors for running submerged and gave her a speed of 5.71kt. Her armament consisted of two bow torpedo tubes, four torpedoes, and one 88mm (3.46in) deck-gun. Her normal complement was two officers and twenty-one crewmen, but she sometimes carried more on active service.

Werner Furbringer also commanded a number of other Flanders-based U-boats, including: UC 70, UB 58, and UB 110. After the Second World War, Furbringer wrote a best selling book called 'FIPS', which was an account of his time spent in submarines. Werner Furbringer took UB 39 on the following patrols:

1. Transferred the boat to Flanders, 19-21 June 1916.
2. Patrolled off the River Tyne Estuary, 6-17 July 1916.
3. Returned to the River Tyne Estuary, 29 July-7 August 1916.
4. Covered the German fleet action against Sunderland from 18-24 August 1916.
5. Hunted down the west end of English Channel from 2-14 September 1916.
6. Patrolled the west end of English Channel, 18-30 October 1916.

Oblt.z.S. Heinrich Küstner assumed command of the boat on 8 November 1916 and Fürbringer went to Germany take command of the new submarine, UC 70. Kustner took the boat on the following patrols:

7. Off The Hoofden, 12-16 November 1916.
8. Patrolled off The Hoofden, 20-22 November 1916.
9. Down the west end of English Channel, 27 November-11 December 1916.
10. Patrolled the Bay of Biscay, 27 December 1916-11 January 1917.
11. In the Bay of Biscay, 30 January-14 February 1917.
12. Patrolled the English Channel, from 21-24 March 1917.
13. Along the English Channel and Bay of Biscay, from 28 March-10 April 1917.

14. Patrolled the west end of English Channel from 23 April 1917. However, UB 39, Kustner and his crew of twenty-four disappeared in the English Channel between 14/15 May 1917. After she was reported overdue, the CO of UB 12 said that he had observed an underwater explosion close to the British 9A-buoy around position N50 20 E01 20. The buoy was a reference point used by U-boats as they passed through the Strait of Dover. It was then presumed that she had detonated a mine and was lost with all hands. Of course, that explosion could have been something else. Like many more First World War U-boat losses, this one could be confirmed by sport-divers identifying the exact loss site in the future.

Vessels damaged or sunk by SM UB 39 in the North Sea:

VESSEL'S NAME	FLAG	TONS	D	M	YEAR	LOCATION
Staffa	GBR	176	10	7	1916	45m E by N from Tyne
Dalhouse	GBR	89	13	7	1916	10m NNE from Whitby
Florence	GBR	149	13	7	1916	13m N by E from Whitby
Mary Ann	GBR	5	13	7	1916	13m N by E from Whitby
Success	GBR	6	13	7	1916	13m N by E from Whitby
Ben Aden	GBR	176	14	7	1916	15m E from Hartlepool
Bute	GBR	176	14	7	1916	25m SE of the Tyne
Girls Friend	GBR	55	14	7	1916	21m E from Hartlepool
Langley Castle	GBR	93	14	7	1916	18m NE by E of the Tyne
Recorder	GBR	149	14	7	1916	15m NNE by ½ E of the Tyne
Braconash	GBR	192	1	8	1916	36m SE by E of the Tyne
Helvetia	GBR	167	1	8	1916	5m SE of Seaham
King James	GBR	163	1	8	1916	8m E of Seaham
Rhodesia	GBR	110	1	8	1916	14m ESE of the Tyne
Tatiana	GBR	285	1	8	1916	36m SE by E of the Tyne
Zeeland	NLD	1292	1	8	1916	7m E of Sunderland
Prince	GBR	126	2	8	1916	12m SSE of Longstone Light
Smiling Morn	GBR	126	2	8	1916	70m off Coquet Island
Twiddler	GBR	99	2	8	1916	70m E of Coquet Island
Lucania	GBR	92	3	8	1916	4m E by S ½ S of Dunstannrough
Merchant Prince	GBR	130	3	8	1916	9m E by S of Dunstannrough
Olympia	GBR	221	3	8	1916	3m E of off Coquet Island
Egyptian Prince	GBR	129	5	8	1916	8m E by S of Dunstannrough
Jägersborg	GBR	921	4	8	1916	Off Longstone, Farne Islands
St Olive	GBR	202	5	8	1916	11m E of Coquet Island
Stamfordham	GBR	921	4	8	1916	8m S of Longstone

SM UB 40

SM UB 40 was a UBII class attack boat of the SM UB 30-UB 41 type, designed as a single-hulled vessel for coastal patrol work. She was built by Blohm & Voss at Hamburg for the Imperial German Navy, launched on 25 April 1916 and commissioned for service on 17 August 1916. The boat had a surface displacement of 274 tons, 303 tons submerged, and had dimensions measuring 36.9m by length, a beam of 4.26m and a draught of 3.7m. Two 135hp diesel/oil engines powered her two bronze screw propellers giving her a speed of 9kt. Rows of lead/acid batteries powered her two 140hp electric motors for running submerged and gave her a speed of 5.71kt. Her armament consisted of two bow torpedo tubes, one 88mm (3.46in) deck-gun and she carried four torpedoes. Her normal complement was two officers and twenty-one crewmen, but she sometimes carried more on active service.

UB 40 reached her operating base in Flanders on 3 October 1916, under the command of Oblt.z.S. **Karl Neumann**. The boat operated in the English Channel and the North Sea and went on twenty-eight patrols in all. Karl Neumann was in charge for only four of these patrols: from 1-3 October 1916, transit to Flanders; 18-26 October 1916; 5-9 November 1916; and 15-24 November 1916.

Oblt.z.S. Hans Howaldt, born 12 November 1889, was UB 40's second commander. On 28 December 1916, Howaldt was cruising the 'Hoofden' when he stopped the 470-ton Dutch steamship Oldambt, loaded with food supplies for England and took her back to Zeebrugge as a prize of war. On 21 May 1917, UB 40 attacked the British 6,127-ton steamship Karroo with gunfire, but the return gunfire was so heavy that she broke off the attack. UB 40 torpedoed the 4,653-ton steamship Oldfield Grange and the 2,216-ton steamship Mahopac on 7 June 1917. Both vessels were badly damaged, but luckily they were stranded in shallow water. The Oldfield Grange was repaired and put back into service and it is not known what happened to the other ship. On 12 December 1917, Howaldt attacked the British steamer Eros, hitting her with a torpedo, but the missile failed to detonate. On his last patrol, Howaldt was promoted to Kapitanleutnant and was honoured with the Orden Pour Le Mérite on 23 December 1917, for his outstanding success in command of UB 40. Howaldt served on UC 4, UB 40, UB 107 and UB 57, and he died on 6 September 1970.

Oblt.z.S. Karl Dobberstein took over command of the boat on 15 December 1917 and led her on four patrols in the English Channel. On 24 April 1918, Dobberstein hit the SS Agnete with a torpedo, but entered a 'fehschuts' in his diary about the 1,127-ton Agnete, meaning the torpedo did not explode and he did not claim it as a kill. However the 65.41m steamship, owned by the Shipping Controller and managed by R.S. Dagleish, did sink, four miles south by west from Start Point. Her master and eleven crew were killed.

On 18 May 1918, the command passed to Oblt.z.S. Hans Joachim Emsmann, who conducted three patrols along the English East Coast: from 26 May to 7 June 1918; 23 June to 9 July 1918; and 24-31 July 1918. Under the command of Emsmann, on 31 May 1918, UB 40 stopped the 59 ton sailing vessel Alert and sank her with explosives. Many of the vessels Emsmann sank, were unarmed fishing vessels. However, on 2 July 1918, Emsmann fired on and killed the crew of the French sailing lugger Madaleine, as the crew were attempting to escape from the burning lugger in the ship's boat. The Madaleine was under tow by the British tug Admiral, along with the French lighter Nord. On the last patrol, UB 40 was badly damaged, suffering a leak in the machine-room, which shorted the accumulators out. However, she made it safely back to base. Repairs to the U-boat were still not completed, before the Germans, under pressure from the Allies, were forced to abandon their base in Flanders. As a result of this, the boat was taken from the dockyard at Bruges, towed to Ostende and scuttled on 2 October 1918. (Four months later, on the evening of 28/29 October 1918, Emsmann met his end when he went on to command UB 116, which was sunk with all hands in Scapa Flow, just before the war ended.)

SM UB 40 was one of the most successful of the Kaiser's Imperial U-boats, bearing in mind she was a single-hulled coastal-boat that was only equipped to carry a total of four torpedoes per voyage.

Known vessels believed sunk or damaged by SM UB 40 in the North Sea:

VESSEL'S NAME	FLAG	TONS	D	M	YEAR	LOCATION
Dayspring	GBR	57	26	5	1918	Off the Smith's Knoll Spar Buoy
Eclipse	GBR	47	26	5	1918	Off the Smith's Knoll Spar Buoy
Fortuna	GBR	61	26	5	1918	Off the Smith's Knoll Spar Buoy
Antiope	GBR	3004	3	6	1918	Near Tyne Estuary (damaged only)
Beryl	GBR	57	6	6	1918	Off the Smith Knoll Spar Buoy
Dianthus	GBR	51	6	6	1918	Off the Smith Knoll Spar Buoy
Herdis	GBR	1157	29	6	1918	7m SE by S of South Cheek
Grekland	SWE	2744	29	6	1918	In the North Sea
Active	GBR	46	6	6	1918	Off the Smith Knoll Spar Buoy
Charing Cross	GBR	2534	1	7	1918	4m E by N of Flamborough Head

Admiral	GBR	102	2	7	1918	1m N of Flamborough Head
Nord	FRE	550	2	7	1918	1m N Flamborough Head (in tow)
Madaleine	FRE	158	2	7	1918	1m N Flamborough Head (damaged in tow)
Aby	GBR	25	7	7	1918	Off Spurn Point
Albion	GBR	25	7	7	1918	Off Spurn Point
Boy Jack	GBR	57	26	7	1918	Near the Cross Sands Lightvessel
Godesgenage	BEL	40	26	7	1918	Near the Cross Sands Lightvessel
Counsellor	GBR	56	27	7	1918	Near the Haisborough Lightvessel
Fear Not	GBR	59	27	7	1918	Near the Haisborough Lightvessel
I'll Try	GBR	51	27	7	1918	Near the Haisborough Lightvessel
Kirkham Abbey	GBR	1166	27	7	1918	2m NE by E of Winterton
Le Bijou	GBR	46	27	7	1918	Near the Haisborough Lightvessel
Paagon	GBR	56	27	7	1918	Near the Haisborough Lightvessel
Passion Flower	GBR	46	27	7	1918	Near the Haisborough Lightvessel
Success	GBR	54	27	7	1918	Near the Haisborough Lightvessel
Valour	GBR	39	27	7	1918	Near the Haisborough Lightvessel
Francis Robert	GBR	44	28	7	1918	Near the Haisborough Lightvessel

SM UB 41

SM UB 41 was a UBII class attack boat of the SM UB 30-UB 41 type, designed as a single-hulled vessel for coastal patrol work. She was built by Blohm & Voss at Hamburg for the Imperial German Navy, launched on 6 May 1916 and commissioned on 25 August 1916, with Oblt.z.S. Karl Sichart von Sichartshofen as her first CO. The boat had a surface displacement of 274 tons, 303 tons submerged and had dimensions measuring 36.9m by length, a beam of 4.26m and a draught of 3.7m. Two 135hp diesel/oil engines powered her two bronze screw propellers giving her a speed of 9kt. Rows of lead/acid batteries powered her two 140hp electric motors for running submerged and gave her a speed of 5.71kt. Her armament consisted of two bow torpedo tubes, one 88mm (3.46in) deck-gun and she carried four torpedoes. Her normal complement was two officers and twenty-one crewmen, but she sometimes carried more on active service.

Karl Sichart von Sichartshofen took the boat on six patrols from:

1. 5-7 November 1916, Horn Riff anti-English submarine patrol.
2. 12-23 November 1916, off the English East Coast.
3. 26 December 1916-1 January 1917, Horn Riff.
4. 16-22 January 1917, off the Scottish East Coast.
5 & 6. 1-16 February 1917, patrolled along the English East Coast.

Oblt.z.S. Gunther Krause assumed command of the boat on 21 March 1917 and took her on six patrols:

7. 15-23 April 1917, along the English East Coast.
8. 17-27 May 1917, off the English East Coast.
9. 9-21 June 1917, off the Scottish East Coast.
10. 4-16 July 1917, along the English East Coast.
11. 2-12 August 1917, off the English East Coast.
12. 1-13 September 1917, along the English East Coast.

Oblt.z.S. Max Ploen assumed command of UB 41 on 13 September 1917.

13. On her thirteenth patrol, under the command of Max Ploen and carrying a crew of twenty-four, SM UB 41 left her base at Bremerhaven on 30 September 1917. Her patrol

Oberleutnant zur See Hans Howaldt, awarded *Pour Le Merite* on 23 December 1918 as Commander of SM UB 40. *(From Dutch Collection)*

took her to the stretch of coastline between Flamborough Head and Whitby. On 3 October 1917, UB 41 torpedoed and badly damaged the 502-ton steamship *Clydebrae*, some three to five miles north-east from Scarborough. The U-boat was reported as missing on 5 October 1917. However, coastal-watchers at Scarborough reported a massive explosion that same morning in the estimated position of N54 18 W00 21. The explosion was believed to be that of UB 41 detonating a mine. However, it is not really clear what happened to her. She may have been lost in the extensive British minefield laid earlier in September that year, or in the minefield laid by SM UC 55 on 9 July. There is also the possibility that she was lost through a navigational or equipment failure, or perhaps through a drill procedure that had gone fatally wrong.

Known vessels believed sunk or damaged by SM UB 41 in the North Sea:

VESSEL'S NAME	FLAG	TONS	D	M	YEAR	LOCATION
Thyholm	NOR	259	21	11	1916	Near Blyth (captured as prize)
Cetus	GBR	139	18	1	1917	E off Scotland (only damaged)
Ellida	NOR	1124	19	4	1917	2m NW of Whitby
Lanthorn	GBR	2299	22	5	1917	3m E of Whitby
Monarch	NOR	1318	23	5	1917	2m E of Seaham
Alwyn (sailing vessel)	GBR	73	12	6	1917	5m SE of Girdleness
Silverburn	GBR	284	13	6	1917	4m SE of Cove Bay
Angantyr	DAN	1359	14	6	1917	SE Cove Bay
Talisman	GBR	153	6	8	1917	7m ESE of Hartlepool
Harrow	GBR	1777	8	9	1917	4m SE of Whitby
Clydebrae	GBR	502	3	10	1917	3 or 5m NE of Scarborough (only damaged)

SM UB 43

SM UB 43 was a UBII class attack boat of the SM UB 42–UB 47 type, built by Weser A.G. at Bremen for the Imperial German Navy. The boat was one of the single-hulled vessels, designed for coastal patrols and was commissioned on 24 April 1916, with Oblt.z.S. Dietrich Neibuhr as her CO. She had a surface displacement of 272 tons, 305 tons submerged and measured 36.9m by length. Two 142hp diesel/oil engines powered her two bronze screw propellers, giving her a speed of 8.82kt. Rows of lead/acid batteries powered her two electric motors for running submerged, which made her capable of 6.22kt. Her armament consisted of one 88mm

(3.46in) deck-gun and two bow torpedo tubes and she carried four torpedoes. UB 43 had a normal complement of two officers and forty-one crewmen.

The Germans took six of UBII boats (UB 42-UB 47), partially disassembled them and shipped them to Pola (Austria-Hungary) to be assembled later. Four of these, UB 42, UB 44, UB 45 and UB 46 ended up being sent to Constantinople. However, UB 44 disappeared en-route to Turkey, UB 45 and UB 46 were both mined and sunk in the Black Sea, while UB 42 survived the war. (UB 45 and UB 46 have both been at least partially raised since the end of the First World War.)

Oblt.z.S. Dietrich Neibuhr took the boat on two unsuccessful patrols. Because of illness Kplt. Hans von Mellenthin replaced him on 29 August 1916. Mellenthin commanded the boat for six patrols and was fairly consistent by sinking at least two vessels on each patrol. On 25 February 1918, Hans von Mellenthin was awarded the *Pour Le Mérite* (The Order of the Blue Max) for his outstanding duty in sinking Allied vessels. Oblt.z.S Horst Obermuller assumed command of UB 43 on 9 April 1917 and took her on two patrols.

On 15 July 1917, the boat was taken back to her base for a complete overhaul. On completion of the work, she was transferred to Austria on 30 July 1917. Throughout the rest of the First World War, she conducted operations under the Austrian flag, as their U 43. After the surrender, U 43 (UB 43) became French war reparation and was scrapped in 1920.

SM UB 50

SM UB 50 was a UBIII class attack U-boat of the SM UB 48-UB 53 type, built by Blohm & Voss at Hamburg for the Imperial German Navy. She had a surface displacement of 516 tons, 651 tons submerged and measured 55.3m by length. Two 550hp diesel/oil engines powered her two bronze screw propellers, giving her a speed of 13.6kt. Rows of lead/acid batteries powered her two 394hp electric motors running submerged which gave her a speed of 8kt. Her armament consisted of one 88mm (3.46in) deck-gun, four bow and one stern torpedo tubes and she carried ten torpedoes. UB 50 had a normal complement of three officers and thirty-one crewmen and was of the double-hull offshore variety, capable of use in the Atlantic Ocean.

Kplt. Franz Becker was her first commander, serving from 12 July 1917 until 30 June 1918. Oblt.z.S. Heinrich Kukat, born 2 March 1891, took over the boat on 11 July 1918 after first being the CO of UC 20. Kukat served on UB 50 until the end of the First World War and died on 2 April 1920.

UB 50 spent most of her time patrolling in the Mediterranean and was the third most successful UBIII boat at sinking Allied vessels in that region. On 9 November 1918, she was on her way home to Germany when she sank HMS *Britannia*, two days before the end of the First World War ended. She surrendered to the Allies and was broken up at Swansea in 1922.

SM UB 57

SM UB 57 was a UBIII class attack U-boat of the SM UB 54-UB 59 type, built by Weser A.G. at Bremen for the Imperial German Navy. She was launched on 21 June 1917, commissioned for service on 31 July 1917 and was of the offshore double-hulled type, capable of use in the open ocean. The boat had a displacement of 516 tons on the surface and 646 tons submerged and had dimensions measuring 55.85m by length, a 5.73m beam and a draught of 3.6m. Two 530hp diesel/oil engines powered her two bronze screw propellers giving her a surface speed of 13.4kt. Rows of lead/acid batteries powered her two 394hp electric motors, giving her a submerged speed of 7.8kt. The U-boat's armament consisted of one stern and four bow torpedo tubes, one 88mm (3.46in) deck-gun and she carried ten torpedoes. The boat's normal complement was three officers and thirty-one crewmen.

SM UB 57 was a boat in the Flanders Flotilla during 1917. Oblt.z.S. Hans Howaldt, born 12 November 1889, commanded UB 57 on at least one patrol, for which, on 23 December

1917, he was honoured with the *Orden Pour Le Mérite* for his outstanding duty against enemy shipping, while serving with UB 40. Howaldt served on UC 4, UB 40, UB 107 and UB 57. He died on 6 September 1970.

Kplt. Otto Steinbrinck, born 19 December 1888, commanded the boat from 30 July 1917 until April 1918. Steinbrinck served on U 6, UB 10, UB 18, UC 65 and UB 57. During his service, he sank 216 Allied ships, with a total tonnage of 231,614. On 29 March 1916, as an Oblt.zS, he was awarded the *Pour Le Mérite* and was promoted to Kapitanleutnant in 1917.

Oblt.z.S. Johannes Lohs, born 24 June 1889, commanded SM U 75 in 1915, SM UC 75 and finally SM UB 57. Lohs sank seventy-six Allied ships, with a total tonnage of 148,677. On 4 April 1918, he was awarded the *Pour Le Mérite*. He died aged twenty-eight. Under the command of Oblt.z.S. Johannes Lohs, SM UB 57 was believed lost with her crew of thirty-four, in a field of ground magnetic mines in the English Channel off Zeebrugge, on 14 August 1918. The 20th Destroyer Flotilla had laid the mines and if SM UB 57 was lost through these mines, she became the first submarine to be sunk by a magnetic mine. Lohs' last signal came on the 14 August, indicating he was through the Dover defences and that he would be passing through a 'safe-channel' to enter his base at Zeebrugge. Nothing more was ever seen or heard from the boat. Among the vessels that she sank off the Yorkshire Coast in October 1917, was the 4,238-ton *Seistan*, the 1,714-ton *Nitedal*, the 3,764-ton the *Tredegar Hall*, the 2,336-ton *Novillo*, and the *Leander*.

Known vessels believed sunk or damaged by SM UB 57 in the North Sea:

VESSEL'S NAME	FLAG	TONS	D	M	YEAR	LOCATION
Leander	NOR	2968	20	10	1917	3.5m E of Scarborough
Nitedal	NOR	1714	20	10	1917	4.5m ESE of Flamborough Head
Novillo	DAN	2336	22	10	1917	2m NE of Hayburn Wyke, Scarborough
Seistan	GBR	4238	23	10	1917	3.5m N by W ¼ W of Flamborough Head
Tredegar Hall	GBR	3764	23	10	1917	4.5m ESE of Flamborough Head

SM UB 71

SM UB 71 was a UBIII class attack boat of the SM UB 66–UB 71 type, built by Germaniawerft at Kiel for the Imperial German Navy. She was launched on 12 July 1917 and commissioned for service on 23 November 1917. The boat had a surface displacement of 513 tons, 647 tons submerged, and had dimensions measuring 55.83m by length, a 5.73m beam and a draught of 3.6m. She was capable of 13.2kt surface speed and 7.6kt submerged. Two 550hp diesel/oil engines powered her two bronze screw propellers. Rows of lead/acid batteries powered her two 394hp electric motors for running submerged. The submarine had an armament consisting of one 88mm (3.46in) deck-gun, one stern and four bow torpedo tubes, and she carried ten torpedoes. UB 71 was a double-hulled boat, capable of being used in the open ocean. Her normal complement was three officers and thirty-one crewmen.

SM UB 71 left Germany on 4 April 1918, under the command of Kplt. K. Schapler, en route via Pola to reinforce the Mediterranean Flotillas. However on the night of 21 April, the boat was approaching the Strait of Gibraltar, when she ran into a patrol-line of Allied motor-launches that had just been established four days earlier. The noise of the boat's diesel engines were heard by the crew manning HMS ML 413, then the large bow wave, created by the U-boat, was sighted about 10m ahead of the launch. Realising his predicament, Schapler crash-dived, but the RN-launch followed her wake and dropped four depth charges 50m ahead of her estimated position. SM UB 71 and her crew of thirty-two were never seen or heard of again, but oil and wreckage from the submarine was found floating on the surface the following morning. SM UB 71 failed to sink any Allied vessels before being lost herself.

SM UB 75

SM UB 75 was a UBIII attack boat of the SM UB 75-UB 79 type, built by Blohm & Voss at Hamburg for the Imperial German Navy. She was launched on 5 May 1917 and commissioned for service on 11 September 1917, with Oblt.z.S. Franz Walther as her CO. The boat had a surface displacement of 516 tons, 648 tons submerged. Her dimensions measured 55.3m by length, a 5.73m beam and a draught of 3.6m. She was capable of 13.6kt surface speed, 7.8kt submerged. Two 550hp diesel/oil engines powered her two bronze screw propellers. Rows of lead/acid batteries powered her two 384hp electric motors for running submerged. Her armament consisted of one stern and four bow torpedo tubes, one 88mm (3.46in) deck-gun, and she carried ten torpedoes. She was a double-hulled boat, capable of use in the open ocean. UB 75 had two patrols:

1. 2-11 November 1917, she hunted along the English East Coast.
2. On 29 November 1917, UB 75 left the German island base of Borkum, with UB 61 and other U-boats, but UB 61 was lost on her way out from base after detonating a British-laid mine (the wreck of this U-boat has just recently been located and photographed by divers). UB 75 returned to the Yorkshire Coast, under the command of Franz Walther and carrying a crew of thirty-four. In early December 1917, she arrived off Whitby and created mayhem amongst Allied shipping in the first few days, by sinking the 1,780-ton steamship *Highgate* on 7 December, the 2,220-ton *Lampada* on the 9 December. Then, the following day, she sank the large 3,596-ton steamship *Venetia*. From that day, nothing more was ever heard from her again. She failed to answer all signals and when she was due back at her base on 13 December 1917, the boat was listed as missing, presumed lost in an area with extensive British minefields, off Flamborough Head.

Known vessels believed sunk or damaged by SM UB 75 in the North Sea:

VESSEL'S NAME	FLAG	TONS	D	M	YEAR	LOCATION
Lucida	GBR	1477	4	11	1917	2.5m N of Scarborough area (damaged)
Frithjof Eide	NOR	1207	9	11	1917	2.5m ENE of Flamborough Head
Aigburth	GBR	824	5	12	1917	2m NE by E of South Cheek, Robin Hood's Bay
Highgate	GBR	1780	7	12	1917	2.5m E of South Cheek, Robin Hood's Bay
Lampada	GBR	2230	8	12	1917	3m N of Whitby
Venetia	GBR	3596	9	12	1917	3m NNW of Whitby

SM UC 6

SM UC 6 was one of the little 'canoe' boats, a UCI class mine-laying submarine of the SM UC 1-UC 10 type. She was built by Vulcan A.G. at Hamburg for the *Kaiserliche Deutshe Marine* (Imperial German Navy) and was designed with a single hull for use in coastal waters. The boat was launched on 12 June 1916 and commissioned on 16 June 1916, with Oblt.z.S. Mattias Graf von Schmettow as her first CO. She had a surface displacement of 168 tons, 183 tons submerged. Her dimensions measured 33.99m by length with a 3.15m beam. A single 90hp diesel/oil engine powered her single bronze screw propeller, which gave her a surface speed of 6.02kt, while rows of lead/acid batteries powered her single 175hp electric motor giving her a submerged speed of 5.22kt. A distance of 780 sea miles was her endurance on the surface at a steady 5kt and she carried 3.5 tons of fuel/oil. Submerged, UC 6 was capable of covering fifty sea miles at a steady 4kt. It took her between twenty-three and thirty-six seconds to dive, with a maximum depth of 50m. The little boat was equipped with six mine-chutes, carried twelve mines and was armed with one machine-gun. Her normal complement was one officer and thirteen crewmen.

Oblt.z.S. Mattias Graf von Schmettow took UC 6 on the following patrols:

1. The transfer to her base at Zeebrugge from 30-31 July 1915.
2. 4-6 August 1915, she went to the Thames Estuary.

3-13. The pattern of typical mining operations was established over the next twelve patrols. UC 6 would spend two or three days on patrols, mainly to the Thames Estuary, up the English coast to Yarmouth, or points to the north-east, the Downs and occasionally along the French coast, as well.

14. Hunted vessels off the Humber Estuary from 3-10 December 1915.

Oblt.z.S. Otto Ehrentraut assumed command of the boat on 5 May 1916 after her twenty-ninth patrol. (Oblt.z.S. Schmettow went on to commission UC 26 and he was lost when the boat was rammed by HMS *Milne* in May 1917.)

30-43. These patrols were similar to the others, except probably the 40th to Southwold, 24–26 July 1916, when her motor failed. The submarine managed to make 2-3kt per hour under a makeshift sail, until UB 19 discovered her and towed the boat home.

Oblt.z.S. Paul Günther took over command of UC 6 on 6 September 1916. (Otto Ehrentraut would later take UC 39 on her only patrol and was lost with the boat on 8 February 1917.)

46-49. These patrols were similar to the others, but with Oblt.z.S. Paul Günther in command. On 5 November 1916, Oblt.z.See Werner von Zerboni di Sponsetti assumed command of the boat. (Paul Günther went on to command UB 37, but was lost with the boat and her entire crew, when the Q-ship *Penurst* sank her. Divers have just recently located the U-boat's wreck.) (50-68) These patrols were similar to the ones above, but with von Zerboni di Sponsetti in command. The only highlight was another engine failure and being towed into port again, but this time, by a destroyer.

On 1 May 1917 Oblt.z.S. Werner Löwe assumed command of UC 6. (Werner von Zerboni di Sponsetti moved on to bigger and better boats. However, he took command of UC 21 and she was lost with her crew of twenty-seven in September 1917.) Werner Löwe was CO of UC 6 for patrols 69 to 85. He took over the boat from 1 May until 1 September 1917, before moving on to command UC 79. Werner Löwe was eventually lost in March 1918, while in command of UB 58. It seems that she sailed on 9 March and at 4 a.m. the next day she detonated a mine in the Dover Barrage. HMS P 24 recovered documents in the resulting debris field.

On 2nd September 1917 UC 6's last commander Oblt.z.S. Gottfried Reichenbach, took over control and led her on patrols 86 to 89.

(89) Her final patrol. Reichenbach took her into the Thames Estuary, but it appears that she ran into mine-nets near the Kentish Knock Lightvessel. The Royal Navy had swept the area clear of German mines, before laying the nets, just in case any U-boat commander decided to lay more mines. At 2.30 p.m. on 27 September 1917, the noise of the U-boat motors were heard by hydrophone operators on the Kentish Knock lightship, followed by five explosions in the nets at 4.30 p.m. A further three explosions came thirty minutes later. Nothing was done about it at the time, but in January 1918, pieces of wreckage were recovered from the site, which appeared to be of German origin and a German type of mine-sinker, indicating a U-boat had been lost. This seems to account for UC 6 and her crew of sixteen never returning to base.

Vessels damaged or sunk by SM UC 6 in the North Sea:

VESSEL'S NAME	FLAG	TONS	D	M	YEAR	LOCATION
HMT *Worsley*	GBR	309	14	8	1915	Off Aldeburgh
HMT *Japan*	GBR	205	16	8	1915	Mined off the Shipwash Lightvessel
Sir William Stephenson	GBR	1540	29	8	1915	Mined entrance to Yarmouth
Horden	GBR	1434	20	9	1915	Mined 0.5m E of Aldeburgh Napes Buoy
Groningen	GBR	988	23	9	1915	Mined 1.5m N by E Sunk Head Buoy, Thames Estuary
Aleppo	GBR	3870	18	10	1915	Mined 1.5m E of Sunk Head Buoy (damaged)

VESSEL'S NAME	FLAG	TONS	D	M	YEAR	LOCATION
Salerno	NOR	2431	18	10	1915	Mined 2m ESE of Sunk Head Buoy
Monitoria	GBR	1904	21	10	1915	Mined at mouth of River Thames
Friargate	GBR	264	3	11	1915	Mined 4m E of Orfordness
Trignac	FRA	2375	24	2	1916	Mined 7m W of Outer Dowsing Lightvessel
Lavinia Westoll	GBR	3131	28	3	1916	Mined 33m SE by S Spurn Lightvessel
Batavier V	NLD	1569	16	5	1916	Mined 5m E of N Buoy, Inner Gabbard
Volharding (lighter)	BEL	1000	25	5	1916	N of Noord Hinder Lightvessel
Excellenz Mehnert	NOR	646	1	6	1916	Mined 5m SSW of Winterton
HMT Kaphreda	GBR	245	8	6	1916	Mined near Gorton Lightvessel
Otis Tarda	NLD	759	21	6	1916	N52 39. E 02 10
Burma	GBR	706	23	6	1916	15m E Harwich
Waalstroom	NLD	1441	27	6	1916	Mined 4m NE of Shipwash Lightvessel
HMT Hirose	GBR	275	29	6	1916	Mined off Aldeburgh Napes
Gannet	GBR	1127	7	7	1916	Mined 5m ENE of Shipwash Lightvessel
Kara	GBR	2338	10	7	1916	Mined near Pakefield Gate Buoy
Mascotte	GBR	1097	3	9	1916	Mined 6.5m SE of Southwold
Lonada	GBR	1286	29	12	1916	Mined 5m N by SSE Shipwash Lightvessel
HMS Ludlow	GBR	810	29	12	1916	Mined off Shipwash Lightvessel
Roald Amundsen	NOR	4390	16	6	1917	3m W of Tongue Lightvessel (damaged)
Dorte Jensen	DAN	2086	18	6	1917	Mined near Tongue Sand Lightvessel

SM UC 7

SM UC 7 was one of the little UC 1 class mine-laying submarines of the SM UC 1-UC 10 series. She was built by Vulcan A.G. at Hamburg for the Imperial German Navy and was designed with a single hull for use in coastal waters. She was launched on 6 July 1915 and commissioned for service three days later on 18 July. The boat had a surface displacement of 168 tons, 183 tons submerged, and she had dimensions measuring 33.99m by length and a 3.15m-beam. A single 90hp diesel/oil engine powered her single bronze screw propeller, which gave her a surface speed of 6.02kt, while rows of lead/acid batteries powered her single 175hp electric motor for running submerged, giving her a speed of 5.22kt. A distance of 780 sea miles was her endurance range on the surface at a steady 5kt and she carried 3.5 tons of fuel oil. Submerged, UC 7 was capable of covering fifty sea miles at a steady 4kt. It took her between twenty-three and thirty-six seconds to dive, with a maximum depth of 50m. The little boat was equipped with six mine-chutes, carried twelve mines and was armed with one machine-gun. Her normal complement was one officer and thirteen crewmen.

Oblt.z.S Franz Wäger was her first CO, however Wäger was later lost with UB 44 in the Mediterranean when he disappeared between Cattaro and Constantinople. Wager took UC 7 on the patrol in which the boat transferred to Flanders from 11 August 1915. Most of his patrols were to the area north-east of the Thames Estuary and around Lowestoft. UC 7's first operational patrol was from 21-23 August 1915. The patrols were typically only two or three days long.

Following the twelfth patrol on 29 November 1915 (eleven plus the transfer), Oblt.z.S. Georg Haag assumed command of the boat and remained with UC 7 for the rest of her career. Haag commanded UC 7 for twenty-two patrols. On the twentieth overall patrol, Haag's eighth, 9-10 February 1916, UC 7 laid the mine that accounted for the sinking of the light-cruiser HMS Arethusa. Almost all patrols were in the same area. The only exceptions being, the nineteenth which was off the Humber, 24-31 January 1916, and the twenty-fourth patrol off the French Channel coast, 24-25 March 1916. UC 7 was lost on her thirty-fourth patrol. She left Zeebrugge on 3 July 1916 for the north entrance to the Downs. Another U-boat, UB 12 sighted the boat on 5 July, west of Bligh Bank while returning from the Noord Hinder area. UC 7 never reached her base and is presumed to have hit a mine. The bodies of four of her crew were later discovered, two washed up on the Flanders coast, while the body of Haag and another officer were discovered and buried at sea. It has recently been report by divers that two unidentified UCI wrecks have just been found. These are believed to be UC 3 and UC 7, although the wreck most likely to be that of UC 7 is on the Rabsbank, lying in 18m of water. It appears that an outside explosion hit her near her radio–chamber, creating a hole of approximately 75cm. The other wreck is in the area between Thornton and Schoonveld Banks.

Vessels believed damaged or sunk by SM UC 7 in the North Sea:

VESSEL'S NAME	FLAG	TONS	D	M	YEAR	LOCATION
Malta (RN trawler)	GBR	138	1	9	1915	Mined off N Shipwash Buoy
Nadine (RN trawler)	GBR	150	1	9	1915	Mined off N Shipwash Buoy
Savona	GBR	1180	1	9	1915	Mined 0.5m from Shipwash Lightvessel
Churston	GBR	2470	3	9	1915	Mined 2.5m S from Orfordness
Koningin Emma	NLD	9181	22	9	1915	Mined 1m W of Sunk Lightvessel
Vigilant (sailing vessel)	GBR	69	26	9	1915	Mined 3m SE of S Shipwash Buoy
Novocastrian	GBR	1151	5	10	1915	Mined 3.5m SE by E from Lowestoft
Texelstroom	NLD	1601	6	10	1915	Mined off Longsand
HMT William Morrison	GBR	212	28	11	1915	Mined near Sunk Head Buoy
Ignis	GBR	2042	8	12	1915	Mined 5.5m NE from Aldeburgh
Ingstad	NOR	780	10	12	1915	Mined 4m E of N from Aldeburgh Napes Buoy
Knarsdale	GBR	1641	21	12	1915	Mined 2.75m E by S from Orfordness
Speeton (RN trawler)	GBR	205	31	12	1915	Mined off Lowestoft
Balgownie	GBR	1061	6	2	1916	Mined Thames Estuary 1.75m ESE Sunk Head Buoy
Elswick Manor	GBR	3943	8	2	1916	Mined off Southwold (only-damaged)
HMS Arethusa	GBR	3520	11	2	1916	Mined off North Cutler Buoy, Harwich Roads
Dido	GBR	4769	26	2	1916	Mined 4m NNE from Spurn Lightvessel (Hull-Bombay)
Mecklenburg	NLD	2885	27	2	1916	Mined near Galloper Lightvessel
Ameer (RN trawler)	GBR	216	18	3	1916	Mined off Felixstowe
Valpa (RN trawler)	GBR	230	19	3	1916	Mined off Spurn Head
Fulmar	GBR	1270	24	3	1916	Mined 8m SW of Kentish Knock Lightvessel, Thames Estuary
Cerne	GBR	2579	26	3	1916	Mined 4m NE Elbow Buoy, River Thames' mouth
Commandant (RN trawler)	GBR	207	2	4	1916	Mined off Sunk Lightvessel
Avon	GBR	1574	9	4	1916	Mined Thames mouth 2.5m SE by S Tongue Lightvessel
Alberta (RN trawler)	GBR	209	14	4	1916	Mined off Grimsby
Orcades RN trawler)	GBR	270	14	4	1916	Mined off Grimsby
Lena Melling (RN trawler)	GBR	274	21	4	1916	Mined near Elbow Lightvessel
Seaconnet	USA	2294	18	6	1916	Mined in the North Sea

SM UC 10

SM UC 10 was one of the little 'canoe' boats, a UCI class mine-laying submarine of the SM UC 1-UC 10 type. She was built by Vulcan A.G. at Hamburg for the Imperial German Navy and was designed with a single hull for use in coastal waters. She was launched on 15 July 1915 and commissioned for service on 11 May 1916. The boat had a surface displacement of 168 tons, 183 tons submerged, and her dimensions were 33.99m by length and a 3.15m beam. A single 90hp diesel/oil engine powered her single bronze screw propeller, which gave her a surface speed of 6.02kt, while rows of lead/acid batteries powered her single 175hp electric

Reinhold Salzwedel was born in 1889 and became a sea cadet in 1909. He sailed on the SMS *Kaiser* in 1914. From 1915 to 1917, Salzwedel was an Oberleutnant zur See and commander of UB 10, UC 10, UB 17, UC 11, UC 21, UC 71 and UB 81. He was awarded the *Pour Le Merite* in August 1917. On 2 December 1917 Salzwedel was commander of UB 81, which detonated a mine in the English Channel and he was lost along with the boat. *(From Dutch Collection)*

motor for running submerged, giving her a speed of 5.22kt. A distance of 780 sea miles was her endurance range on the surface at a steady 5kt and she carried 3.5 tons of fuel oil. Submerged, UC 10 was capable of covering fifty sea miles at a steady 4kt. It took her between twenty-three and thirty-six seconds to dive and she had a maximum depth of 50m. The little boat was equipped with six mine-chutes, carried twelve mines and was armed with one machine-gun. Her normal complement was one officer and thirteen crewmen.

UC 10 had thirty patrols, each lasting only two or three days, with usual patrol areas being off the Thames Estuary, or the English East Coast as far as Southwold. However one patrol took her to Calais. On 16 August 1915, due to motor problems, there was an unsuccessful attempt to reach Flanders under the command of Oblt.z.S Ernst Rosenow. Oblt.z.S. Max Viebeg became the next CO and finally Oblt.z.S. Alfred Nitzsche. Under Nitzsche, UC 10 finally arrived in Flanders on 19 December 1915. Oblt.z.S. Reinhold Salzwedel took command of her temporarily from 14-26 June 1916 and was the CO for the Patrols twenty-two and twenty-three. Nitzsche then returned to command UC 10 for another four patrols. On her twenty-seventh patrol, on 24 July 1916, the crew shot down a British aircraft, then rescued and captured the crew. After this patrol Oblt.z.S. Werner Albrecht assumed command of the boat and Nitzsche took over command of a brand new U-boat, UC 19, which was lost with her entire crew, on the third patrol. Albrecht commanded UC 10 for patrols twenty-eight to thirty, which proved to be her final one. On the last patrol, UC 10 left her base for the Humber Estuary on 17 August 1916. She exchanged signals with UB 10 on the way back home after having laid her mines off the Humber. On 21 August at 4.35 p.m., a U-boat was sighted by the British submarine HMS E54 off the Schouwen Bank, in the Strait of Dover. The British submarine was on patrol in that area for that very reason. E54 fired two-torpedoes at UC 10 and saw one hit the U-boat before she vanished with her crew of eight, in a cloud of smoke, in position N52 02 E03 54.

Vessels believed sunk or damaged by SM UC 10 in the North Sea:

VESSEL'S NAME	FLAG	TONS	D	M	YEAR	LOCATION
Ellewoutsdijk	NLD	2229	30	12	1915	Mined at N51 42, E01 57
Leto	NLD	3225	4	1	1916	Mined 12m E by N of Galloper Lightvessel
Fridtjof Nansen	NOR	3275	5	1	1916	Mined 1m S by W of Galloper Lightvessel
Apollo	NLD	799	21	1	1916	Mined 1m SSW of the Galloper Lightvessel
Falls City	GBR	4729	22	1	1916	Mined between Elbow Buoy and Kentish Knock (damaged)
Southford	GBR	963	25	2	1916	Mined 4m ESE of Southwold
Birgit	SWE	1117	26	2	1916	Mined 4m outside Kentish Knock Lightvessel

HMS *Coquette*	GBR	335	10	3	1916	Mined at N entrance to Black Deep
NR. 11	GBR	263	10	3	1916	Mined at N entrance to Black Deep. (HM torpedo boat)
Palembang	NLD	6674	18	3	1916	Mined 1 ½m NNE of Galloper Buoy
Malvina	GBR	1244	29	3	1916	Mined and damaged 4.5m ENE of Kentish Knock
Ino	NOR	702	3	4	1916	Mined 10m S of Kentish Knock Lightvessel
Hendonhall	GBR	3994	1	5	1916	Mined 2m SE of Inner Gabbard Buoy (Portland–Rotterdam)
Rochester City	GBR	1239	2	5	1916	Mined 3m off Southwold
Rhenass	GBR	285	22	5	1916	Mined 9m E by N of Orfordness
Lincairn	GBR	3638	27	5	1916	Mined 8m N by E Shipwash Lightvessel
Parkgate	GBR	3232	1	6	1916	Mined and damaged 1.5m ESE of the Sunk Lightvessel
Dragoon (trawler)	GBR	30	20	8	1916	Mined 36m NE by N of Gromeri
Rievaulx Abbey	GBR	1166	3	9	1916	Mined ¾m ENE of Rosse Spit Buoy, Humber
Nora	DAN	772	11	12	1916	Mined 7m S of Withernsea

SM UC 14

SM UC 14 was one of the little UCI class mine-laying boats of the SM UC 11–UC 15 type. She was built by A.G. Weser at Bremen for the Imperial German Navy and was one of the coastal boats, designed with a single hull for use in inshore waters. Her construction commenced on 28 January 1915, she was launched on 13 May 1915 and commissioned for service on 5 June 1915. The boat had a surface displacement of 168 tons, 182 tons submerged, and her dimensions were 33.99m by length and a 3.15m beam. A single 80hp diesel/oil engine powered her single bronze screw propeller, which gave her a surface speed of 6.49kt, while rows of lead/acid batteries powered her single 175hp electric motor for running submerged, giving her a speed of 6.3kt. A distance of 910 sea miles was her endurance range on the surface at a steady 5kt and carried 3.5 tons of fuel oil. Submerged, UC 14 was capable of covering fifty sea miles at a steady 4kt. It took her between twenty-three and forty-five seconds to dive and she had a maximum depth of 50m. The little boat was equipped with six mine-chutes, carried twelve mines and was armed with one machine-gun. Her normal complement was one officer and thirteen crewmen.

Kplt. Caser Bauer was the first commander of UC 14 from 5 June 1915 until 6 January 1916. Kplt. Franz Becker served from 7 January to 30 June 1916. Oblt.z.S. Alfred Klatt followed from 1 July until 22 October 1916. Oblt.z.S. Ulrich Pilzecker became the fourth commander from 11 January until 6 July 1917. Pilzecker went on to command UC 17 from 4 August 1917 and then UB 113 in October 1918. He disappeared with UB 113 and her crew, somewhere in the approaches to Dartmouth on 9 October 1918. He sank eight Allied vessels, totalling 6,888 tons during his service. Oblt.z.S. Helmut Lorenz took over command of UC 14 from 7 July until 13 September 1917. Oblt.z.S. der Reserve Adolf Feddersen commanded from 14 September until the boat went missing off Zeebrugge on 3 October 1917. On this date SM UC 14 was homeward-bound to Zeebrugge when she detonated a mine dropped by a British CMB (coastal motor boat), just off the harbour entrance. UC 14 was carrying a crew of seventeen when watchers on the mole at Zeebrugge witnessed a massive explosion. Feddersen's body was washed ashore some time later, helping to identify UC 14 which lies in the approximate position of N51 19 E02 43.

Vessels believed sunk or damaged by SM UC 14 in the North Sea:

VESSEL'S NAME	FLAG	TONS	D	M	YEAR	LOCATION
HMT *Christopher*	GBR	316	29	3	1917	Off Southwold
Orthos	GBR	218	9	4	1917	Off Lowestoft
HMT *Tettenhall*	GBR	227	23	5	1917	Off Lowestoft
HMT *Loch Ard*	GBR	225	10	9	1917	Off Lowestoft
Willing Boys	GBR	51	2	10	1917	10m NW of Smith Knoll Spar Buoy
Reliance	GBR	60	7	10	1917	Near Smith Knoll Lightvessel

SM UC 16

SM UC 16 was a UCII class mine-laying submarine of the SM UC 16-UC 24 type, built by Blohm & Voss at Hamburg for the Imperial German Navy. She was launched on 1 February 1916 and commissioned on 26 June 1916, with Oblt.z.S Egon von Wener as her first commander. The boat had a displacement of 417 tons on the surface and 509 tons submerged. Her dimensions measured 49.35m by length, by a 5.22m beam and a draught of 3.6m and she was capable of 11.6kt surface speed and 7kt submerged. Her twin bronze screw propellers were powered by two 250hp diesel/oil engines, while rows of lead/acid batteries powered her two 230hp electric motors for running submerged. The boat had an armament consisting of: one stern and two bow torpedo tubes; one 88mm (3.46in) deck-gun; eighteen UC200 mines, which were launched from six vertically inclined mine tubes; and she carried seven torpedoes. SM UC 16 was one of the double-hulled boats, capable of being used in the open ocean.

On 11 September 1916, UC 16 became the first UCII to arrive at the base of Zeebrugge. She conducted the following patrols:

1. Her transfer to Flanders.
2. 21-24 September 1916, along the English East Coast, off Yarmouth.
3. 17-20 October 1916, down the English Channel.
4. 6-19 November 1916, down the English Channel.
5. 20-27 December 1916, down the English Channel.
6. 15 January – 1 February 1917, down the English Channel and into the Bay of Biscay.
7. 25 February – 2 March 1917, down the English Channel and into the Bay of Biscay.
8. 10-16 March 1917, down the English Channel.
9. 14-22 April 1917, down the English Channel. The boat then went into Ostende for an ongoing overhaul, but the work completion date was pushed back until July, when British monitors caused substantial fire damage to the boat.

In the meantime, Oblt.z.S Georg Reichmarus took over as her new commander. Reichmaris took the boat on four patrols:

10. 25-30 July 1917, off the Hoofden.
11. 15-21 August 1917, along the English East Coast.
12. 1-13 September 1917, down the English Channel.
13. On 2 October 1917, UC 16 left her base at Zeebrugge under the command of Reimarus and carrying a crew of twenty-seven. She laid her mines off Boulogne on 3 October 1917, but was never seen or heard of again. The Royal Navy later found her mines and swept the area clear, however on 26 October, a crewman's body from the U-boat was washed ashore at Noordwijk in Holland. UC 14 also disappeared in this same area during that October.

Known vessels believed sunk or damaged by SM UC 16 in the North Sea:

VESSEL'S NAME	FLAG	TONS	D	M	YEAR	LOCATION
Andromeda	GBR	149	23	9	1916	39m SE by E of Spurn Lightvessel
Beechwold	GBR	129	23	9	1916	40m SE by E of Spurn Lightvessel
Britannia III	GBR	138	23	9	1916	42m SE by E of Spurn Lightvessel
Cockatrice	GBR	115	23	9	1916	40m SE by E of Spurn Lightvessel
Mercury	GBR	183	23	9	1916	65m SE by E ½ E of Spurn Lightvessel
Phoenix	GBR	117	23	9	1916	65m SE by E ½ E of Spurn Lightvessel
Refino	GBR	182	23	9	1916	39m SE by E of Spurn Lightvessel
Rego	GBR	176	23	9	1916	40m SE by E of Spurn Lightvessel
Restless	GBR	125	23	9	1916	41m SE ½ E of Spurn Lightvessel
Veilla	GBR	144	23	9	1916	38m SE by E of Spurn Lightvessel
Weelsby	GBR	122	23	9	1916	40m SE by E of Spurn Lightvessel

Dirk	NLD	81	27	7	1917	19m off Zandvoort
Dirk Van Duijnen	NLD	116	27	7	1917	19m WNW of Ymuiden
Jan	NLD	104	27	7	1917	19m WNW of Ymuiden
Mafoor Thomson	NLD	110	27	7	1917	19m off Zandvoort
Pres.Comm.V.D.Bergh	NLD	111	27	7	1917	Off the Dutch coast
Sterna III	NLD	111	27	7	1917	19m WNW of Ymuiden
Neptunus I	NLD	80	28	7	1917	Off Ymuiden
Manchester Engineer	GBR	4465	16	8	1917	4.5m SE of Flamborough Head
Susie	GBR	41	17	8	1917	10m NE by E of Scarborough
Ardens	GBR	1274	18	8	1917	2m E of Filey Brigg (Tyne-London)

SM UC 17

SM UC 17 was a UCII class mine-laying submarine of the SM UC 16-UC 24 type, built with a double hull and capable of being used in the open ocean. Blohm & Voss built her at Hamburg for the Imperial German Navy. She was launched on 19 February 1916 and commissioned for service on 23 July 1916 with Oblt.z.S Ralph Wenniger as her CO. The boat had a surface displacement of 417 tons, 493 tons submerged, and measured 49.35m in length. Two 250hp diesel/oil engines powered her two bronze screw propellers giving her a speed of 11.6kt. Rows of lead/acid batteries powered her two 230hp electric motors for running submerged, and gave her a speed of 7kt. SM UC 17 had an armament consisting of: one stern and two bow torpedo tubes; one 88mm (3.46in) deck-gun; six vertically inclined mine-chutes; and she carried seven torpedoes and eighteen UC200 mines. The boat carried a normal complement of two officers and twenty-three crewmen.

SM UC 17 was a boat of the Flanders Flotilla and operated in the North Sea, English Channel and Bay of Biscay, often covering vast distances on her patrols. She reached Flanders on 30 September 1916 and was credited with the sinking of ninety-four vessels, totalling 143,870 tons. Oblt.z.S. Ralph Wenniger, later promoted to Kapitänleutnant, born 22 April 1890, commanded UC 17 from 23 July 1916 until 25 May 1917 and also served as CO on UB 11, U 37, UB 17 and UB 55. Unfortunately, twenty-three of his crew were lost in the Dover Straights when UB 55 detonated a mine on 22 April 1918, but Wenniger and six crewmen survived. During his service, Wenniger sank sixty-five Allied vessels, totalling 71,242 tons in UC 17 and was awarded the *Pour Le Mérite* for action of outstanding service against enemy shipping.

Oblt.z.S. Erich von Rohrscheidt, later promoted to Kapitanleutnant, took over command of the boat on 26 May until 7 June 1917, but sank no Allied vessels. Oblt.z.S. Werner Fürbringer, later promoted to Kapitänleutnant, born 2 October 1888, commanded UC 17 from 8 June 1916 until 3 August 1917 (his normal boat, UC 70, had been damaged by gunfire at Ostend). Fürbringer had previously served on U1WO, U 20WO, and went on to command UB 2, UB 39, UB 17, UC 70, UB 58 and UB 110. Werner Furbringer sank eight Allied vessels, totalling 20,727 tons on UC 17. He wrote a book about his time in U-boats during the First World War, and died on 8 February 1982.

Oblt.z.S. Ulrich Pilzecker took command of SM UC 17 from 4 August 1917 until 15 January 1918. Before that he commanded UC 14 from 11 January to 6 July 1917 and went on to command UB 113. UB 113 disappeared with Pilzecker and his crew in September or October 1918. He sank eight Allied vessels, totalling 6,888 tons during his service on UC 17.

Oblt.z.S. Erich Stephan was in charge of the boat from 3 February until 4 May 1918 and sank seven Allied vessels totalling 17,214 tons. Oblt.z.S. Nikolaus Freiherr von Lyncker took over from 21 May 1918 until the end of the First World War and sank five Allied vessels totalling 4,965 tons.

UC 17 went on to survive until the end of the First World War and surrendered post-war. She became British war-reparation and was broken up at Preston in 1919-1920.

Some of the vessels believed sunk or damaged by UC 17 in the North Sea:

VESSEL'S NAME	FLAG	TONS	D	M	YEAR	LOCATION
Brema	GBR	1537	19	8	1917	7.5m S ½ E of Flamborough Head
Norhilda	GBR	1175	21	8	1917	5m SE of Scarborough
Thames	GBR	1327	26	5	1918	6m SE by E of Seaham Harbour
Dungeness	GBR	2748	30	5	1918	3m SE of Sunderland (only damaged)
Sunniva	GBR	1913	28	6	1918	4m E of Sunderland
HMS Scott	GBR	1801	15	8	1918	Off the Dutch coast
HMS Ulleswater	GBR	923	15	8	1918	Off the Dutch coast
Thalia	GBR	1308	8	10	1918	4m ESE of Filey Brigg (Rouen-Tyne)

SM UC 26

SM UC 26 was a UCII class mine-laying U-boat of the SM UC 25-UC 33 type, which was built by Vulcan at Hamburg for the Imperial German Navy. She was launched on 22 June 1916 and commissioned for service on 18 July 1916, with Oblt.z.S. Mathias Graf von Schmettow as her CO. She was one of the double-hulled boats capable of being used in the open Atlantic waters. The boat had a surface displacement of 400 tons, 480 tons submerged, and had dimensions measuring 49.45m by length, 5.22m in the beam and a draught of 3.6m. Two 260hp diesel/oil engines powered her two bronze screw propellers, giving her a surface speed of some 11.6kt. Rows of lead/acid batteries powered her two 230hp electric motors for running submerged, and gave her a speed of 6.7kt. The boat had an armament consisting of one stern and two bow torpedo tubes, one 88mm (3.46in) deck-gun, six vertically inclined mine tubes, and she carried eighteen UC200 mines for laying and seven torpedoes. UC 26 had a normal complement of three officers and twenty-three crewmen.

Oblt.z.S Mathias Graf von Schmettow was the boat's only CO and took her on the following patrols:

1. 11-12 September 1916, transferred to the Flanders base.
2. 17-22 September 1916, took her down the English East Coast.
3. 28 September-9 October 1916, along the English Channel.
4. 24 October-1 November 1916, along the English Channel.
5. 13-27 November 1916, along the English Channel.
6. 19-25 January 1917, patrolled off the Humber Estuary.
7. 2-8 February 1917, along the English Channel.
8. 7-20 April 1917, patrolled along the English Channel.
9. On 30 April 1917, SM UC 26 left her base at Flanders to patrol along the English Channel.

Having laid her mines off Le Havre, Ouisterham and Cherbourg she was returning to Zeebrugge, and was off Calais at dawn on the 9 May when the British destroyer HMS Milne sighted her. The destroyer made full speed and rammed the U-boat, which was in the process of diving, and two other destroyers then depth charged her. Eight crewmen did manage to escape from the U-boat, but HMS Milne was only able to pick up two and von Schmettow was not among them. After the encounter the destroyer was left with a badly distorted bow stem and pieces of the submarine's casing embedded in her forecastle. (Johan R. has reported that SM UC 26 was located and dived on in 1999 or 2000.)

Oblt.z.S Mathias Graf von Schmettow had previously commissioned the SM UC 6 on 24 June 1915, which he commanded until 5 May 1916. While SM UC 26 was under repair following a ramming attempt by a steamer on her 7th patrol, von Schmettow, being too valuable to sit around for two months, took command of UB 10 from 13 February to 3 March 1917, for one patrol off the Noord Hinder light-vessel from 23 to 28 February, 1917. However, on 19 February until 20 March 1917, he was given command of UB 23 and went on one patrol off the Hoofden with her from 10 to 11 March 1917 – von Schmettow was actually C.O. of three boats at once over this period, UC 26, UB 10 and UB 23, but the patrols on these three did not produce any 'kills' (note that SM UC 26 was the second UCII boat, by a day to SM UC 16, to arrive in Flanders. Obviously, as the honour suggests, von Schmettow was very highly regarded and a well respected U-boat officer). Von Schmettow's sank something over 100,000 tons of Allied shipping, a total higher than several Flanders-based commanders that were awarded the *Pour Le Mérite*. Had Mathias Graf von Schmettow dived more quickly in the encounter with HMS *Milne* and survived in SM UC 26, he would undoubtedly have won the Order of the Blue Max.

Vessels either sunk or damaged by SM UC 26 in the North Sea:

VESSEL'S NAME	FLAG	TONS	D	M	YEAR	LOCATION
Princsessan Ingeborg	SWE	3670	23	9	1916	Mined 50m SE by E of Spurn Head (damaged)
Argo	NOR	1261	28	1	1917	Mined 1.5m SE of Inner Dowsing Lightvessel
Heimland I	NOR	505	28	1	1917	Mined 2m off Inner Dowsing Lightvessel

SM UC 31

SM UC 31 was a UCII class mine-laying U-boat of the SM UC 25-UC 33 type, built by Vulcan at Hamburg for the Imperial German Navy. She was launched on 7 August 1916 and commissioned for service on 2 September 1916, with Oblt.z.S. Otto von Schrader as her first CO. This type of boat was built with a double hull and was capable of being used in the Atlantic Ocean. UC 31 had a surface displacement of 400 tons, 480 tons submerged, and had dimensions measuring 49.45m by length, a 5.22m beam and a draught of 3.6m. Two 260hp diesel/oil engines powered her two bronze screw propellers, giving her a maximum surface speed of 11.6kt. Rows of lead/acid batteries powered her two 230hp electric motors for running submerged and gave her a maximum speed of 6.7kt. The boat had an armament consisting of one stern and two bow torpedo tubes, one 88mm (3.46in) deck-gun, six vertically inclined mine tubes. She carried eighteen UC200 mines for laying and seven torpedoes. UC 31 had a normal complement of three officers and twenty-three crewmen.

The U-boat was attached originally, to the Germany-based 1 U-Flotilla. Under the command of Oblt.z.S. Otto von Schrader, UC 31 went on the following patrols:

1. 28 December 1916-5 January 1917, along the English East Coast.
2. 25 January-1 February 1917, along the English East Coast.
3. 20-28 February 1917, hunted along the English East Coast.
4. 1-18 April 1917, down the Scottish and English east coasts.
5. 5-20 May 1917, around the Orkney Islands.
6. 20 June-19 July 1917, she went via Dover to the Irish Sea.

On 21 July 1917, Kplt. Kurt Siewert assumed command of UC 31.

7. 31 July-15 August 1917, the boat hunted up the Scottish East Coast and Shetlands Isles.
8. 4-27 September 1917, along the south coast of Ireland, via Dover on the way out and she returned via the northern route.
9. 10-29 November 1917, along the south coast of Ireland, via Dover outward bound.
10. 17 January 10 February 1918, along the south coast of Ireland, via Dover outward.
11. 23 March-14 April 1918, down the North Channel and up the Irish Sea, via the northern route home.
12. 9-14 June 1918, the boat transferred to Flanders base.

Oblt.z.S.d.Res. Willy Stüben assumed command of her in Flanders, however the boat required extensive repairs, which took nearly four months.

13. 1-7 October 1918, SM UC 31 went back to Germany.

Vessels believed sunk or damaged by SM UC 31 in the North Sea:

VESSEL'S NAME	FLAG	TONS	D	M	YEAR	LOCATION
Protector	GBR	200	31	12	1916	Mined off the North Pier (River Tyne)
Lonclara	GBR	1294	4	1	1917	Mined off River Wear
O.B. Suhr	DAN	1482	25	1	1917	150m W of Horns Riff
Alexandra	GBR	179	28	1	1917	60m off Longstone, Farne Islands
Edda	SWE	536	29	1	1917	North Sea
Shamrok	GBR	173	29	1	1917	About 115 NNE of Longstone
Thistle	GBR	167	29	1	1917	140m NE by N ½ N of the mouth of the Tyne
Ravensbourne	GBR	1226	31	1	1917	Mined 8m SE of the River Tyne
Beneficent	GBR	1963	24	2	1917	5m ENE of Hartlepool 5444N 0104W
Kathleen Lily	GBR	521	29	3	1917	Mined 2m E of North Cheek
Harberton	GBR	1443	30	3	1917	Mined North Sea
Helga	DAN	839	4	4	1917	60m off Coquet Island
N.J. Fjord	DAN	1425	5	4	1917	40m N70E of Farne Island
HMT Strathrannoch	GBR	215	6	4	1917	Mined off St Abbs Head 55 55N, 02 07W
VESSEL'S NAME	FLAG	TONS	D	M	YEAR	LOCATION
Quaggy	GBR	993	11	4	1917	Mined 3m E of North Cheek, Robin Hood Bay
Dina Hinderika	NLD	200	12	4	1917	30m ENE of Hartlepool
Neptunus	NLD	209	12	4	1917	20m ENE of Hartlepool
Union	DAN	152	12	4	1917	18-20m E of Souter Point
Voorwaarts	NLD	147	12	4	1917	20m ENE of Hartlepool
Spray	GBR	1072	14	4	1917	3.5m NE of Tyne Pier
Brotheroft	GBR	155	16	4	1917	North Sea
Poseidon I	NLD	98	6	5	1917	9m N of Dogger Bank Lightvessel

SM UC 32

SM UC 32 was a UCII class mine-laying U-boat of the SM UC 25-UC 33 type, built by Vulcan at Hamburg for the Imperial German Navy. She was launched on 12 August 1916 and commissioned for service on 13 September 1916 and was one of the double-hulled boats, capable of being used in the Atlantic waters. She had a surface displacement of 400 tons, 480 tons submerged and had dimensions measuring 49.45m by length, a 5.22m beam and a draught of 3.6m. Two 260hp diesel/oil engines powered her two bronze screw propellers, giving her a surface speed of some 11.6kt. Rows of lead/acid batteries powered her two 230hp electric motors for running submerged, giving her a speed of 6.7kt. The boat had an armament consisting of one stern and two bow torpedo tubes, one 88mm (3.46in) deck-gun, six vertically inclined mine tubes. She carried eighteen UC200 mines for laying and seven torpedoes. UC 32 had a normal complement of three officers and twenty-three crewmen.

UC 32 joined the 1 U-Flotilla on 27 November 1916, under the command of Oblt.z.S Herbert Breyer and conducted a few patrols off Flamborough Head and around the Tyne, Wear and Tee river areas. The boat was credited with the sinking of six Allied vessels under Breyer, two of 2,198 tons in 1916 and four of 4,649 tons at the beginning of 1917, before she was lost on 23 February 1917.

One of the methods used by U-boats to save a torpedo when attacking fishing-boats and other small craft, was to lie submerged until the boats left the harbour. The submarine would then surface and attack the boat with her deck-gun and dive again, before the Royal Navy arrived. Local fishermen at Sunderland were becoming increasingly alarmed with these tactics as the war progressed. The Admiralty, in their wisdom, decided to arm a steam-trawler with a large deck-gun and camouflaged the vessel to look like an ordinary fishing-boat, a 'Q-ship'. On one occasion, UC 32 was caught out by this method when she surfaced, thinking the Q-ship was a normal fishing boat. The armed trawler immediately pulled off her camouflage and let blaze at UC 32, causing Herbert Breyer to crash dive for cover. Unfortunately one submariner who was still on the deck casing, was washed off and drowned – but this time the U-boat escaped.

On 23 February 1917, UC 32 was just beginning to lay her mines in 12m of water, off the mouth of the River Wear, when one of the mines detonated prematurely. It is understood that a plug holding the mine to the sinker had dissolved prematurely, releasing the mine under her stern-end. The vessel blew up and sank killing nineteen of her crew. An examination vessel, which happened to be close to the scene, rescued Cdr Breyer and two of the crewmen. The wreck of this U-boat now lies 0.25 miles east from Roker Lighthouse at Sunderland, in position N54 54 521 W001 19 320.

Author's Comment: Rolf Mitchinson, a diving colleague, tells of his father's recollection as a young boy of nine years old, living in a house that overlooked Sunderland docks at the time. He remembered watching as Herbert Breyer and two of U-boat's sailors were brought ashore under armed guard. He said he could also remember the hatred that many of the local people, who lined the docks, felt for the German sailors, because they jeered and spat at the three men when they stepped onto the quayside to be led away by armed police. However, Breyer did give one of his rescuers a memento from his pocket, in appreciation for helping him and his two crewmen.

Under the command of Breyer, UC 32 was credited with sinking the following four Allied vessels in the North Sea:

VESSEL'S NAME	FLAG	TONS	D	M	YEAR	LOCATION
Burnhope	GBR	1,941	14	12	1916	Off Hartlepool
Appolonia	ITA	2,891	1	3	1917	Mined 1m off Flamborough Head
Jerv	NOR	1,112	1	2	1917	7.25m E of Scarborough
Hildawell	GBR	2,494	20	12	1916	Possibly off English East Coast

SM UC 32 as she looked in January 1917 under the command of Oberleutnant zur See Herbert Breyer. *(Author's Collection)*

The loss of the 2,494-ton British steamship *Hildawell* was attributed to mines laid by UC 32 off Sunderland on 14 December 1916 and this has been uncritically accepted and republished as fact elsewhere. But the problem is, the vessel had a maximum speed of 8.5kt (although Hocking says 10kt) and a Lloyd's internal document accounted for her being off Yarmouth on 19 December. The *Hildawell* disappeared with her captain and crew of twenty-one between 19-20 December. It is most likely that she was a victim of mines, either British or German, but it cannot be ascertained precisely where, or even when she was lost, until evidence is produced by local divers. The *Hildawell* was on passage from Bilbao for Middlesbrough with a cargo of iron ore. E. Gray & Co. built her at Hartlepool in 1892 and T.W. Willis & Co. owned her at the time of loss. There is also the possibility, that carrying a cargo of iron ore, she sank by other means.

SM UC 39

SM UC 39 was a UCII class mine-laying submarine of the SM UC 34–UC 39 type, built by Blohm & Voss at Hamburg. She was launched on 25 June 1916, commissioned for service on 29 October 1916 and was one of the double-hulled boats capable of being used in the Atlantic Ocean. She had a surface displacement of 427 tons, 509 tons submerged, and measured 50.35m by length. Two 300hp diesel/oil engines powered her two bronze screw propellers, giving her a surface speed of 11.9kt. Rows of lead/acid batteries powered her two 230hp electric motors for running submerged, which gave her a speed of 6.8kt. UC 39 had an armament consisting of one 88mm deck-gun, one stern and two bow torpedo tubes and six mine chutes. She also carried seven torpedoes and eighteen UC200 mines. Her normal complement was three officers and twenty-three crewmen.

Kplt. Otto Tornow was the boat's first CO, followed by Oblt.z.S. Otto Ehrentraut, who assumed command on 1 February 1917 and took the boat from Kiel to Flanders that same day, being the boat's first patrol.

On her second patrol, Otto Ehrentraut took UC 39 out into the North Sea and off the English East Coast where he sank three ships. However, on 8 February 1917, the destroyer HMS *Thrasher* sighted UC 39 lying still on the surface and in the process of sinking the British steam collier *Hornsey* with gunfire, (another report says *Ida*) *Thrasher* fired a volley of shells at the U-boat from some distance away, which took Ehrentraut by surprise. With shells exploding all around him and seeing the British warship thundering towards him at full speed, Ehrentraut made an emergency dive, but the U-boat left a large swirl on the surface. The destroyer ran over the position where the boat had submerged and dropped a single depth charge in an estimated position, just ahead of the swirl. The explosion badly damaged the boat and caused volumes of seawater to pour into the control room. She was then forced to surface, whence *Thrasher* immediately commenced a heavy volley of gunfire. The aim was so accurate that the first members of UC 39's crew, including Oblt.z.S. Ehrentraut, who clambered onto the casing, were killed in the barrage. The destroyer's gun-crew finally ceased firing when Capt. J. Souter, master of the Swedish steamship *Hanna Larsen* appeared, bravely waving a white flag. He had been taken prisoner earlier that day after the U-boat sank his ship and emerged from the hatch on the U-boat's conning tower, in an attempt to prevent any more bloodshed. Seven of the U-boat's crew were killed, but HMS *Thrasher* rescued two British prisoners-of-war and seventeen of the boat's crew. Another destroyer, HMS *Itchen* was called in and took UC 39 in tow, but she sank soon afterwards. In May, later that year, another destroyer located the U-boat's wreck. Her divers were sent down to inspect it and found the wreck covered in barnacles after just four months.

Vessels believed sunk or damaged by UC 39 in the North Sea:

VESSEL'S NAME	FLAG	TONS	D	M	YEAR	LOCATION
Hans Kinck	NOR	2667	7	2	1917	5m NW from Nord Hinder Lightvessel
Hanna Larsen	GBR	1311	8	2	1917	20m E ¾ N from Spurn Point
Ida	ITA	1172	8	2	1917	About 15m SE from Flamborough Head

SM UC 43

SM UC 43 was a UCII class mine-laying boat of the SM UC 40-UC 45 type, built by Vulcan at Hamburg for the Imperial German Navy. She was launched on 5 October 1916, commissioned on 25 October, and was one of the double-hulled boats, capable of being used in the open ocean. The boat had a surface displacement of 400 tons, 480 tons submerged, and had dimensions measuring 49.45m by length, a 5.22m beam and a draught of 3.6m. Her two 260hp diesel/oil engines powered two bronze screw propellers, giving her a speed of 11.6kt. Rows of lead/acid batteries powered her two 230hp electric motors for running submerged, giving her a speed of 6.7kt. The UCII type boat had an endurance distance of some 8,500 miles using 46.6 tons of oil-fuel. The boat had an armament consisting of one stern and two bow torpedo tubes, one 88mm (3.46in) deck-gun, and six vertically inclined mine tubes. She carried eighteen UC200 mines for laying and seven torpedoes.

After being put into service, SM UB 43 arrived at the 1 U-Flotilla High Seas Fleet in Germany on Christmas Day December 1916, under the command of Kplt. Erwin Sebelin. Under Sebelin, the boat had a fairly short career, having one patrol off the English East Coast from 1-17 January 1917 and the second from 25 February. On the second patrol under Sebelin, carrying a crew of twenty-six, she was lost on 10 March 1917, north of Muckle Flugga off the Shetland Isles. Two British submarines, HMS E 49 and HMS G 13 were patrolling to the north and east of the Shetlands, to bar the northern route into the Atlantic. However the weather seriously deteriorated and on 10 March, the E 49 signalled to G 13 that she was returning to base. G 13 under the command of Lt-Com. Bradshaw RN, had decided to remain at sea after receiving the signal from E 49. At 4 p.m. on the afternoon of the 10th, Bradshaw sighted a U-boat through the heavy snow squall and rolling Atlantic waves, so he dived. With great difficulty, the coxswain managed to keep the large boat at periscope depth, but found that the U-boat had altered coarse in the opposite direction. G 13 then had to run at maximum speed in order to catch up with the enemy boat. Making little ground on the U-boat, Bradshaw finally decided to fire two torpedoes at 3,000yd, which was in all accounts a very long range. They timed the impact when the torpedoes would detonate, and the navigator was just announcing that the torpedoes had probably missed their target, when there was a huge explosion, which vibrated right through the boat. Bradshaw watched through his periscope as the bows of SM UC 43 rose up into the air and the boat slid down beneath the surface.

Unfortunately, nothing more was ever heard from HMS E 49 again. Speculation was that she had detonated one of the mines laid in that area by UC 43, although some sources list another boat responsible for the mines.

Known vessels believed sunk or damaged by SM UC 43 in the North Sea:

VESSEL'S NAME	FLAG	TONS	D	M	YEAR	LOCATION
Brentwood	GBR	1192	12	1	1917	Mined 4m ENE of Whitby
Brabant	NOR	1492	15	1	1917	3.4m ESE of Bridlington Light
Graafjeld	NOR	728	15	1	1917	3m E of Flamborough Head
Planudes	GBR	542	20	1	1917	Mined off Whitby
Lupus	NOR	539		1	1917	In the North Sea

Some sources credit UC 43's mines with sinking the British steamship *Norwegian* on 13 March 1917. However, Lloyd's attributed this attack to a submarine (torpedo) and not mines.

SM UC 46

SM UC 46 was a UCII class mine-laying boat of the SM UC 46-UC 48 type, built by A.G. Weser at Bremen for the Imperial German Navy. She was launched on 15 July 1916 and commissioned for service on 15 September 1916, with Oblt.z.S. Fritz Moecke as CO, Moecke having previously commanded SM UC 4. She was a double-hulled boat, capable of being used in the open ocean and had a surface displacement of 420 tons, 502 tons submerged. Her dimensions measured 51.85m by length, a 5.22m beam and a draught of 3.6m. Two 300hp diesel/oil engines powered her two bronze screw propellers, giving her a maximum speed of 11.7kt. Rows of lead/acid batteries powered her two 230hp electric motors for running submerged and gave her a maximum speed underwater of 6.9kt. UC 47 had an endurance range of some 7,280 sea miles at a steady 7kt and she carried 47-64 tons of fuel/oil. Submerged, she was capable of covering a distance of some fifty-four sea miles at a steady 4kt using her battery power. Maximum diving depth was 50m and it took her just thirty-three seconds to dive. The boat had an armament consisting of one stern and two bow torpedo tubes, one 88mm (3.46in) deck-gun, and six vertically inclined mine-tubes. She carried eighteen UC200 mines for laying and seven torpedoes. The boat's normal complement was three officers and twenty-three crewmen.

Under the command of Oblt.z.S. Fritz Moecke, UC 46 went on the following patrols:

1. 27 November-19 December 1916, transferred to Flanders base.
2. 4-9 December 1916, hunted along the English East Coast.
3. 19 December 1916-3 January 1917, through the Dover Straits to the Bristol Channel.
4. 25 January-8 February 1917, through the Dover Straits to the Bristol Channel. However, SM UC 46 was rammed by the British destroyer HMS *Liberty* and sunk with all twenty-three hands, south-east of the Goodwin Sands, position N51 07 E01 39, on 8 February 1917.

Vessel believed to have been sunk by SM UC 46 in the North Sea:

VESSEL'S NAME	FLAG	TONS	D	M	YEAR	LOCATION
Modig	NOR	1704	21	12	1916	Mined 15m SE by SSE of Flamborough Head

SM UC 47

SM UC 47 was a UCII class mine-laying boat of the SM UC46-UC48 type, built by A.G. Weser at Bremen and was a double-hulled boat, capable of being used in the open ocean. Her keel was laid on 1 February 1916, she was launched on 30 August 1916, and was commissioned for service on 13 October 1916. The boat had a surface displacement of 420 tons, 502 tons submerged and had dimensions measuring 51.85m by length, a 5.22m beam and a draught of 3.6m. Two 300hp diesel/oil engines powered her two bronze screw propellers, giving her a speed of 11.7kt. Rows of lead/acid batteries powered her two 230hp electric motors for running submerged, giving her a submerged speed of 6.9kt. UC 47 had an endurance range of some 7,280 sea miles at a steady 7kt, using 47-64 tons of oil-fuel. Submerged, she was capable of covering a distance of some fifty-four sea miles at a steady 4kt using her battery power. Maximum diving depth was 50m and it took her just thirty-three seconds to dive. The boat had an armament consisting of one stern and two bow torpedo tubes, one 88mm (3.46in) deck-gun, and six vertically inclined mine tubes. She carried eighteen UC200 mines for laying and seven torpedoes. The boat's normal complement was three officers and twenty-three crewmen.

Kplt. Paul Hindius was her first commander from 13 October 1916 until October 1917. Oblt.z.S. Gunther von Wigankow served from 9 October 1917 until she was lost on 18 November 1917. Between the two commanders, they sank fifty-two Allied vessels, totalling 65,884 tons.

Commanded by Oblt.z.S. Gunther von Wigankow and carrying a crew of twenty-eight, SM UC 47 left her base at Zeebrugge for a war patrol on 17 November 1917, with instructions to sink allied shipping between the Humber and Flamborough Head. The commander of the British patrol-boat, HMS P 57, H.C. Birnie caught UC 47 on the surface after mistaking her for a marker buoy. The officer of the watch, Lt Isdale, and Commander Birnie almost immediately realised, that, what they were looking at just 200 yards away, was the conning tower of a

U-boat. The patrol boat was then immediately swung hard-to-port towards the submarine and her engines put at full speed. It only took about fifteen seconds before the bows of P 57 had ripped into the U-boat, just before the conning tower and almost at a right angle. The force of the impact pushed UC 47 forward and down, but with the submarine still travelling, she began to pass astern of the patrol-boat. Quickly a depth charge was released, then P 57 turned and came racing back to drop another one over the submarine. Commander Birnie turned once again and dropped a marker-buoy where oil and bubbles soon rose to the surface. Another depth charge was then dropped in the middle of the oily slick, along with a second buoy. All day and the following night, P 57 patrolled around the area, but none of the U-boat's crew of twenty-eight came to the surface. Later that day, a minesweeper arrived on the scene, hooked the wreck with an explosive chain-sweep and detonated it. Royal Navy divers in hard-hat gear then went down to the wreck later that day and entered the submarine. They recovered publications and papers, those which identified her as UC 47, but even more important were the valuable charts listing all of the minefields she had laid on her previous missions.

Von Wigankow was a very experienced U-boat commander, having previously been in command of two attack boats, the SM UB12 and the SM UB17, and thus, until recently, it has always been a mystery why he got caught on the surface by a British patrol-boat. The head-quarters of UC 47, being part of the Flanders Flotilla, was at Bruges, and when the boats were operating in the North Sea communication between them and headquarters was always difficult. The wireless/radio mast situated on the low hull of a U-boat only had a range of thirty miles and without use of a telescopic extension, the captain would have had to rely on passing messages via other boats closer to home. The telescope for the mast could be fully extended by use of small electric motors inside of the boat, which increased her wireless/radio range up to about 100 miles. Local divers from Bridlington have reported finding the fully extended mast on the wreck, so it is almost certain now that Von Wigankow was using the fully extended mast to pass a message on, when HMS P 57 caught him on the surface, hence the mystery is finally solved.

Known vessels believed sunk or damaged by SM UC 47 in the North Sea:

VESSEL'S NAME	FLAG	TONS	D	M	YEAR	LOCATION
Modiva	NOR	1276	31	1	1917	Mined 17m of Flamborough Head
Portia	NOR	1127	1	2	1917	Mined off Flamborough Head
Cadmus	GBR	1879	18	10	1917	20m S by SSE of Flamborough Head
Togston	GBR	1057	18	10	1917	20m S by SSE of Flamborough Head
Ballogie	GBR	1207	9	11	1917	1.5m NE of Filey
Isabelle	FRA	2466	9	11	1917	3m NW of Flamborough Head
Dana	SWE	1620	11	11	1917	1m SE from 'R' buoy, War Channel
Huibertje	NLD	68	12	11	1917	25m off the Dutch Coast

SM UC 48

SM UC 48 was a UCII class mine-laying boat of the SM UC 46-UC 48 type, built by A.G. Weser at Bremen for the Imperial German Navy. She was a double-hulled boat, capable of being used in the waters of the open ocean. She was launched on 27 September 1916 and commissioned for service on 6 November 1916, with Kplt. Kurt Ramien as her CO. The boat had a surface displacement of 420 tons, 502 tons submerged and had dimensions measuring 51.85m by length, a 5.22m beam and a draught of 3.6m. Two 300hp diesel/oil engines powered her two bronze screw propellers, giving her a speed of 11.7kt. Rows of lead/acid batteries powered her two 230hp electric motors for running submerged, gave her a submerged speed of 6.9kt. SM UC 48 had an endurance range of some 7,280 sea miles at a steady 7kt, using 47-64 tons of oil-fuel. Submerged, she was capable of covering a distance of some fifty-four sea miles at a steady 4kt using her battery power. Maximum diving depth was 50m and it took her just thirty-three seconds to dive. The boat had an armament consisting of one stern and two bow torpedo tubes, one 88mm (3.46in) deck-gun and six vertically inclined mine tubes. She carried eighteen UC200 mines for laying and seven torpedoes. The boat's normal complement was three officers and twenty-three crewmen.

Kplt. Kurt Ramien took the boat on the following patrols:

1. 1-3 February 1917, the boat transferred to Flanders base.
2. 6-12 February 1917, patrolled off The Hoofden.
3. 12-25 March 1917, along the English Channel and south coast of Ireland.
4. 26 April–10 May 1917, along the English Channel, Bristol Channel and the South Coast of Ireland.
5. 4-20 June 1917, down to the Spanish North Coast.
6. 12-21 July 1917, off the west end of the English Channel.
7. 12-25 August 1917, hunted off the west end of the English Channel.
8. 10-24 September 1917, down the English Channel and South Coast of Ireland.
9. 10-18 October 1917, off the French side of the English Channel.

Oblt.z.S. Hellmut Lorenz assumed command of SM UC 48 on 21 October 1917. Kplt. Kurt Ramien had previously commanded SM UC 1 and took command of the new SM UB 109 boat after Lorenz assumed command of UC 48. Lorenz took UC 48 on the following patrols:

10. 11-21 November 1917, hunted off the English East Coast.
11. 15-27 January 1918, patrolled off the English East Coast.
12. 17-27 February 1918, hunted along the French coast in the English Channel.
13. 17-24 March 1918, patrolled off the French coast side of the Channel. During this patrol on 19 March SM UC 48 was badly damaged by depth charges and was unable to dive. Rather than risk a return via Dover, Hellmut Lorenz sought internment at El Ferrol in Spain. On 15 March 1919, SM UC 48 was supposed to be transferred to Brest, but the crew scuttled the boat instead. Oblt.z.S Hellmut Lorenz was captured when his ship was mined off Dover in August 1918. Lorenz' previous commands were SM UC 14, and SM UB 2 and SM UB 10.

SM UC 48 sank the following vessel in the North Sea:

VESSEL'S NAME	FLAG	TONS	D	M	YEAR	LOCATION
Modemi	NOR	1481	17	11	1917	3m off Whitby

SM UC 49

SM UC 49 was a UCII class mine-laying boat of the SM UC 49-UC 54 type, built by Germaniawerft at Kiel for the Imperial German Navy. She was launched on 7 November 1916 and commissioned for service on 2 December 1916, with Kplt. Karl Petri as her first commander. She was one of the double-hulled boats capable of being used in the open ocean. The boat had a surface displacement of 434 tons, 511 tons submerged, and measured 52.69m in length. Two 300hp diesel/oil engines powered her two bronze screw propellers, giving her a speed of 11.8kt. Rows of lead/acid batteries powered her two 310hp electric motors for running submerged, giving her a speed of 7.2kt underwater. UCII class had an endurance range of around 8,700 miles at a steady five knots and used 46.6 tons of fuel oil. UC 49 had an armament consisting of one 88mm (3.46in) deck-gun, one stern and three bow torpedos tubes, plus six vertically inclined mine-tubes. She carried eighteen UC200 mines and seven torpedoes. Her normal complement was three officers and twenty-three crewmen.

UC 49 began her career based in German ports. Her patrols consisted of:

1. 25 March – 5 April 1917, off the Scottish East Coast.
2. 2-17 May 1917, off the Scottish East Coast and around the Orkney Islands.
3. 6-19 June 1917, off the Orkneys and Shetland Isles.
4. 15 July – 2 August 1917, off the Orkneys, Shetlands and Outer Hebrides.
5. 20 August – 14 September 1917, off the Irish South Coast.
6. 15-29 October 1917, along the English East Coast.

Oblt.z.S. Hans Kukenthal took over as her new commander on 3 November 1917.

7. 28 November – 15 December 1917, off the English and Scottish east coasts.
8. 15-30 January 1918, along the Scottish East Coast.
9. 17 February – 14 March 1918, along the English East Coast.
10. The boat transferred to Flanders.
11. 2-21 June 1918, along the English Channel and into the Bristol Channel.
12. 8-20 July 1918, along the English Channel.
13. On 1 August 1918, UC 49 left her base at Zeebrugge, under the command of Oblt.z.S. Hans Kukenthal, carrying a crew of thirty-one; her mission to lay mines off Plymouth and Falmouth. On the morning of 8 August, she was beginning the process of laying mines off Start Point, when she accidentally fouled and detonated one of her own mines. The boat was badly shaken, but there was no serious damage. However, HMS *Opossum*, an anti-submarine destroyer, which was on a routine patrol in the area, got suspicious when the crew observed a huge column of water thrown into the air, caused by the underwater explosion. Messages went out about the incident and the destroyer was joined by a number of Royal Navy motor launches. Realising his predicament, and hearing the surface vessels running around, Kukenthal decided to go down onto the seabed and lie quiet, with his boat's engines switched off. UC 49 lay there for some hours, before her commander deemed it safe enough to move, then at 3.20 p.m. The U-boat's motors were fired up. The result was a depth charge exploding close to the boat. The British warships had been doing the same as Kukenthal, lying quiet on the surface. At 5.57 p.m., the U-boat commander started his motors again and another depth charge came plummeting down, exploding fairly close to the submarine. Different tactics were then employed by HMS *Opossum* in an attempt to lure the U-boat to the surface. The destroyer retreated to a spot some two and a half miles away, making lots of noise in doing so and there she lay in wait. This tactic paid dividends, because in just over fifteen minutes, the submarine broke the surface and was greeted with a massive volley of gunfire. Within twenty seconds, UC 49 had been destroyed and sent to a watery grave, along with her crew of thirty-one. *Opossum* dropped more depth charges over the spot where she had gone down, then lots of oil and air came bubbling to the surface. To get proof of a 'kill', the following day, *Opossum* returned to drop more depth charges over the doomed submarine. Finally a light bulb bobbed to the surface, bearing the stamp of a Viennese munitions plant, so her hull casing must have broken open, which was satisfactory evidence that the boat was lost.

Known vessels believed sunk or damaged by SM UC 49 in the North Sea:

VESSEL'S NAME	FLAG	TONS	D	M	YEAR	LOCATION
Helge	DAN	162	3	5	1917	140m NW of Horns Riff
Tore Jarl	NOR	1256	7	5	1917	About 95m SSW of Dumburgh Head
Windward Ho	GBR	226	9	5	1917	3m S of Peterhead
Bel Lily)	GBR	168	14	5	1917	1.5m ENE of Peterhead
Bunty	GBR	73	21	10	1917	Mined off Whitby
Leda	NLD	1140	6	12	1917	3m NE of Filey
Maindy Bridge	GBR	3653	8	12	1917	4m ENE of Sunderland
Blackwhale	GBR	237	3	1	1918	Mined off Fife Ness

Fylgia	SWE	1741	24	1	1918	About 10m SE of Bell Rock
Jonkoping 2	SWE	1274	24	1	1918	3m ENE of Bell Rock
Bor	NOR	1149	21	2	1918	5m E of Seaton Point, nr Coquet Island
Reaper	GBR	91	21	2	1918	Mined 2m NE of Tynemouth
Amsterdam	GBR	806	24	2	1918	3m SE by E of Coquet Island
Berwen	GBR	3752	26	2	1918	Mined 3m SW of Shipwash Lightvessel (damaged)
Samso	DAN	324	1	5	1918	Mined 6m ESE of Roker Lighthouse

SM UC 63

SM UC 63 was a UCII class mine-laying boat of the SM UC 61-UC 64 type, built by A.G. Weser at Bremen for the Imperial German Navy. Her keel was laid on 3 April 1916, she was launched on 6 January 1917 and commissioned for service on 30 January 1917. She had a surface displacement of 422 tons, 504 tons submerged and had dimensions measuring 51.85m by length and a 5.22m beam. She was one of the double-hulled boats, capable of working in the open ocean. She had an endurance range of some 8,000 sea miles, at a steady 7kt and used 48-63 tons of fuel-oil. Submerged, she was capable of covering fifty-nine sea miles at a steady 4kt. Two 300hp diesel/oil engines powered her two bronze screw propellers, giving her a speed of 11.9kt. Rows of lead/acid batteries powered her two 310hp electric motors for running submerged, which gave her a speed of 7.2kt. Her maximum diving depth was 50m and it took her thirty to thirty-three seconds to dive. UC 63 had an armament consisting of one stern and two bow torpedo tubes, one 88mm (3.46in) deck-gun, and six vertically inclined mine-tubes. She carried twelve UC200 mines and seven torpedoes. Her normal crew was three officers and twenty-three crewmen.

Oblt.z.S. Karsten von Heydebreck took over the boat the day she was launched and in those nine months, sank thirty-six Allied vessels, totalling 36,404 tons.

On 1 November 1917, under the command of Oblt.z.S. Karsten von Heydebreck, she was returning to her base from a war-patrol when she was attacked and sunk by the British submarine HMS E 52, in the approximate position of N51 23 E02 00. HMS E 52 was positioned off a buoy, north of the Dover Barrage, near the Goodwin Sands in the English Channel, to intercept such U-boats going to and from their bases. UC 63 was carrying twenty-six crew, only one survived.

Vessels believed sunk or damaged by SM UC 63 in the North Sea:

VESSEL'S NAME	FLAG	TONS	D	M	YEAR	LOCATION
Amsteldijk	NLD	186	26	4	1917	Near the Haaks Lightvessel
Gruno	NLD	171	10	5	1917	About 8m SSW of the Noord Hinder Lightvessel
Frigate Bird (mot)	GBR	20	26	6	1917	Off Flamborough Head
Longbenton	GBR	924	27	6	1917	12m S by W of Flamborough Head.
Elsie	GBR	20	28	6	1917	10m NE of Spurn Point
Frances	GBR	20	28	6	1917	10m NE of Spurn Point
Glenelg	GBR	32	28	6	1917	18m off Spurn Point
Harbinger	GBR	39	28	6	1917	18m off Spurn Point
Rose of June	GBR	20	28	6	1917	10m NE of Spurn Point
William and Betsy	GBR	21	28	6	1917	10m NE of Spurn Point
Markersdall	DAN	1640	30	6	1917	About 12m S of Flamborough Head
Advance	GBR	44	1	7	1917	5m SE of the South Ower's Buoy
Gleam	GBR	54	1	7	1917	3.5m ENE of the South Ower's Buoy
Radianc	GBR	57	1	7	1917	3m S by W of the North Lemon Buoy
Empress	GBR	2914	31	7	1917	Mined 4.5m E by ESE of Withernsea Lighthouse
Young Bert	GBR	59	2	8	1917	Off the Humber
Alfred	FRA	107	6	8	1917	Off the Inner Bank, Dunkirk
Fane	NOR	1119	6	8	1917	Mined 2.5m E of the Inner Dowsing Lightvessel
Zamora	GBR	3639	6	8	1917	2m NW of the Inner Dowsing Lightvessel (damaged)

Onesta	ITA	2674	7	8	1917	Near the Inner Dowsing Lightvessel
Marie Jesus Protegez Nous	FRA	46	8	8	1917	Off Lowestoft
Costanza	ITA	2545	14	8	1917	3.5m SE by E ½ E of Inner Dowsing Lightvessel
Luna	NOR	959	14	8	1917	16-18m N of Humber Lightvessel (damaged)
Ethel and Millie	GBR	58	15	8	1917	Off the Humber
G&E	GBR	61	15	8	1917	Off the Humber
G.Y. 541 (mot)	GBR	25	15	8	1917	Off the Humber
Lyra	NOR	1141	4	11	1917	Mined NE of the Humber

SM UC 64

SM UC 64 was a UCII class mine-laying submarine, built by A.G. Weser at Bremen for the Imperial German Navy. Her keel was laid on 3 April 1916. She was launched on 27 January 1917 and then commissioned for service on 22 February 1917. The boat was an SM UC 61-UC 64-type boat and had a surface displacement of 422 tons, 504 tons submerged, and had dimensions measuring 51.85m by length and a beam of 5.22m. This boat was one of the double-hulled boats, capable of working in the open ocean waters. She had an endurance range of some 8,000 sea miles, at a steady 7kt and used 48-63 tons of fuel-oil. Submerged, she was capable of covering fifty-nine sea miles at a steady 4kt. Two 300hp diesel/oil engines powered her two bronze screw propellers, giving her a speed of 11.9kt. Rows of lead/acid batteries powered her two 310hp electric motors for running submerged, which gave her a speed of 7.2kt. Her maximum diving depth was 50m and it took her thirty to thirty-three seconds to dive. UC 64 had an armament consisting of one stern and two bow torpedo tubes, one 88mm (3.46in) deck-gun, and six vertically inclined mine-tubes. She carried eighteen UC200 mines and seven torpedoes. The boat's normal complement was three officers and twenty-three crewmen.

Oblt.z.S. Ernst Muller-Schwartz commanded the boat from 22 February 1917 until 12 September 1917. Oblt.z.S. Erich Hecht took over command of UC 64 on 13 September 1917 until 22 February 1918. Oblt.z.S. Ferdinand Schwartz then took command of the boat from 23 February 1918, until he was lost with the boat on 20 June 1918. Between them, the three commanders sank twenty-five Allied vessels, totalling 24,635 tons.

UC 64 was outward bound from her base in Germany for the Bordeaux-Gironde area when she detonated a mine on 20 June 1918, in the Strait of Dover, between Folkestone and The Varne. The submarine survived and was still moving, but the R.N. drifter *Ocean Roamer* reported the explosion. HM Drifter *Loyal Friend* then joined her and between them they finished off the U-boat with depth charges. Oblt.z.S. F. Schwartz, and her crew of thirty were lost with the boat. The wreck of the boat was found later and identified by RN divers.

Vessels believed sunk or damaged by SM UC 64 in the North Sea:

VESSEL'S NAME	FLAG	TONS	D	M	YEAR	LOCATION
Paraciers	FRA	2542	17	9	1917	8m E of Spurn Head
Ville De Valenciennes	FRA	1734	22	9	1917	About 5m SE of Flamborough Lighthouse
Botha	GBR	17	28	3	1918	3m E of Whitby
Honora	GBR	29	28	3	1918	6m ENE of Whitby
Brotherly Love	GBR	19	28	3	1918	6m NE by E of Whitby
Noel	GBR	21	28	3	1918	6m NE by E of Whitby
Vianna	GBR	401	31	3	1918	4m E of Seaham Harbour
Laurium	GBR	582	23	4	1918	Mined 15m E of Skegness nr Inner Dowsing Lightvessel
Sote	SWE	1379	25	4	1918	3.65m S of Bridlington Harbour
Llwyngwair	GBR	1304	26	4	1918	5m SSE of Seaham Harbour

SM UC 70

SM UC 70 was a UCII class boat of the SM UC 65-UC 73 type, built by Blohm & Voss at Hamburg for the Imperial German Navy. She was one of the double-hulled boats capable of being used in the open ocean. She was launched on 7 August 1916 and commissioned for service on 22 November 1916, with Oblt.z.S. Werner Furbringer as her first CO. The U-boat had a surface displacement of 427 tons, 508 tons submerged and measured 50.35m by length. Two 300hp diesel/oil engines powered her two bronze screw propellers, giving her a speed of some 12kt. Rows of lead/acid batteries powered her two 310hp electric motors for running submerged, gave her a speed of 7.4kt. The boat had a range of around 8,000 miles and carried 46.6 tons of oil/fuel. SM UC 70 had an armament consisting of one stern and two bow torpedo tubes, one 88mm (3.46in) deck-gun, and six vertically inclined mine-chutes. She carried eighteen UC200 mines and seven torpedoes. Her normal complement was three officers and twenty-three crewmen.

Werner Furbringer, born 2 October 1888, was also in command of the U-boat School from March to June 1916 and served on the submarines: U 1WO, U 20WO, UB 2, UB 17, UB 39, UC 17, UB 58 and UB 110. Furbringer sank ten Allied vessels, totalling 27,323 tons, and died on 8 February 1982. He also wrote a book about his time in U-boat service during the First World War. His patrols in UC 70 took him to:

1. 19-22 February 1917, transferred to Flanders.
2. 27 February-2 March 1917, off The Hoofden.
3. 10-22 March 1917, into the Bay of Biscay.
4. 15 April-2 May 1917, into the Bay of Biscay.
5. 16 May-1 June 1917, down the English Channel.

While under repair at Ostende, UC 70 was hit by shellfire from British Monitors off the coast and the boat sank, however she was raised on 22 June 1917. Werner Furbringer and his crew were then assigned to others boats. Furbringer, as a veteran commander, assumed command of UC 17, whose commander was ill, then he was sent back to Germany to take command of a UBIII boat, UB 58.

UC 70 was seaworthy again by April 1918, with Oblt.z.S. Kurt Lock as her new CO. Loch took her on the following patrols:

6. 24 April-6 May 1918, off the English East Coast.
7. 26 May-8 June 1918, off the English East Coast.

Oblt.z.S. Karl Dobberstein assumed command of UC 70 on 9 June 1918 and took her on the following patrols:

8. 9-14 July 1918, off the Hoofden.
9. 16-29 July 1918, off the Hoofden.
11. On 21 July Dobberstein took the boat off the Hoofden and the English East Coast. However, on 28 August 1918, an anti-submarine patrol seaplane, piloted by Lt Waring RAF, spotted an oil slick on the surface, which was coming from a U-boat. Waring dropped a single 113.40kg (250lb) bomb in the vicinity of the vessel, which brought oil and large bubbles of air to the surface. Soon after, the destroyer HMS *Ouse* arrived on the scene and dropped a series of depth charges over the position. Divers were sent down on 14 September and found the destroyed UC 70 and her crew of thirty-one. It is understood that the U-boat had previously been damaged in a new British minefield off Yorkshire and was lying on the bottom effecting repairs when the slick was spotted.

Known vessels believed sunk or damaged by SM UC 70 in the North Sea:

VESSEL'S NAME	FLAG	TONS	D	M	YEAR	LOCATION
Elin	NOR	139	17	7	1917	15m S by E of Flamborough Head (damaged)
Wayside Flower	GBR	21	27	5	1918	20m NE by N of the Humber
Coronation	GBR	19	28	5	1918	13m ESE Flamborough Head
Cento	GBR	3708	4	6	1918	N54 22 30 E0013 (damaged)
Frederika	NLD	91	8	7	1918	20m off Maas Lightvessel
Genesse	GBR	2830	21	7	1918	4m N by W of Flamborough Light (damaged)
Mongolian	GBR	4892	21	7	1918	5m SE of Filey Brigg
Boorara	GBR	6570	23	7	1918	12m S of Tees (damaged)
Kilkis	GRE	4302	24	7	1918	Off Hartlepool
Ango	FRA	7393	26	7	1918	2m E of Flamborough Head (damaged)

SM UC 71

SM UC 71 was a UCII class boat of the SM UC65-UC73 type, built by Blohm & Voss at Hamburg for the Imperial German Navy. She was launched on 12 August 1916 and commissioned with Oblt. z.S. Hans Valentiner, on 28 November 1916. She was one of the double-hulled boats, capable of being used in the open ocean. The boat had a surface displacement of 427 tons, 508 tons submerged and had dimensions measuring: 50.35 metres by length. Two 300hp diesel/oil engines powered her two bronze screw propellers, giving her a speed of 12 knots and a range of around 8,000 miles. She carried 46.6 tons of oil/fuel. Rows of lead/acid batteries powered her two 310hp electric motors for running submerged, gave her a speed of 7.4 knots. UC 71 had an armament consisting of one stern and two bow torpedo tubes, one 88mm (3.46in) deck-gun, six vertically inclined mine-chutes and she carried eighteen UC200 mines and seven torpedoes. Her normal complement was three officers and twenty-three crewmen.

Oberleutnant zur See Hans Valentiner was her first command and served until 25 April 1917. Valentiner was later lost with UB 56 and crew of thirty-seven after detonating a mine in the Dover Straits, on 19th December 1917.

Oblt.z.S. Hugo Thielman served as her C.O. from 26 April until 9 June 1917.

Oblt.z.S. Reinhold Saltzwedel, born 23 November 1889, served as commander of UC 71 from 10 June until 13 September 1917. He was awarded the Pour Le Mérite on 20 August 1917, for outstanding duty against enemy shipping and later promoted to Kapitanleutnant. Saltzwedel later took command of UB 81 and was lost with the boat after she detonated a mine on 2 December 1917, ten miles south-east from Dunose Head off the Isle of White, but six of his crew survived.

Oblt.z. S. Ernst Steindorff commanded UC 71 from 14 September 1917 until 28 January 1918. His next command was UB 74 on which he was lost with his entire crew when the boat was depth charged in Lyme Bay on 26 May 1918.

In 1918 Obtl.z.S. Walter Warzecha took over UC 71 from 29 January-13 August. Obtl.z.S. Eberhard Schmidt took command of the boat from 14 August-14 October. Oberleutnant zur See Werner Lange probably transferred her to Hamburg for repairs on 14-15 October.

SM UC 71 went on to survive the First World War, but sank en-route to being surrendered on 2 February 1919 in position. N54 10' E07 54'. The wreck of this boat was featured on German television, along with the British submarine HMS E16, in recent times and the divers positively identified both vessels.

Known vessels believed sunk or damaged by SM UC 71 off the East Coast:

VESSEL'S NAME	FLAG	TONS	D	M	YEAR	LOCATION
Hornsund	GBR	3646	23	9	1817	2.5m ESE of Scarborough
Atlas	GBR	3090	14	2	1918	10m ESE of Hartlepool
Commonwealth	GBR	3353	19	2	1918	5m NE of Flamborough Head

SM UC 75

SM UC 75 was a UCII class boat of the SM UC 74–UC 79 type, built by Vulcan at Hamburg for the Imperial German Navy. She was launched on 6 November 1916 and commissioned for service on 6 December 1916, with Kplt. Georg Paech as her CO. She was one of the double-hulled boats, capable of being used in the open ocean. The U-boat had a surface displacement of 410 tons, 493 tons submerged and measured 50.54m in length. Two 300hp diesel/oil engines powered her two bronze screw propellers, giving her a speed of some 11.8kt and a range of around 8,000 miles using 46.6 tons of oil-fuel. Rows of lead/acid batteries powered her two 310hp electric motors for running submerged, gave her a speed of 7.3kt. UC 75 had an armament consisting of one stern and two bow torpedo tubes, one 88mm (3.46in) deck-gun, and six vertically inclined mine-chutes. She carried eighteen UC200 mines and seven torpedoes. Her normal complement was three officers and twenty-three crewmen.

Oblt.z.S. Johannes Lohs, born 24 June 1889, took over command of UC 75 on 17 March 1917, having already been in command of SM U 75 in 1915 and finally UB 57. He died at the age of twenty-eight, when UB 57 was lost with its crew, in a minefield off Zeebrugge. Lohs sank seventy-six Allied ships, including the steamship *Gascony* off the Sussex coast, a total tonnage of 148,677. On 4 April 1918, he was awarded the *Pour Le Mérite*, for outstanding service against enemy shipping.

The boat was originally based at Heligoland in Germany and Lohs took the boat on nine patrols:

1. 22 March-4 April 1917, off the English and Scottish east coasts.
2. 28 April-18 May 1917, off the Irish South Coast. On 5 May, UC 75 made herself something of a legend, when she torpedoed and sunk the British warship, HM Sloop *Lavender* in the English Channel.
3. 3-23 June 1917, off the South Coast of Ireland.
4. 22 July-5 August 1917, along the English Channel and into the Irish Sea. After the patrol had ended, Lohs went back to Zeebrugge, instead of Heligoland and became part of the U-Flotilla in Flanders.
5. 20 August-3 September 1917, into the Irish Sea.
6. 30 September-20 October 1917, into the Irish Sea.
7. 28 October-12 November 1917, into the Irish Sea.
8. 30 November-10 December 1917, into the Irish Sea.
9. 22 December 1917-8 January 1918, into the Irish Sea.

On 31 January 1918, Johannes Lohs finally moved on to command a UBIII attack-boat and Oblt.z.S. Walter Schmitz assumed command of UC 75. His patrols were:

10. 20 February-3 September 1918, along the English East Coast.
11. 2-21 March 1918, into the Irish Sea.
12. 11-30 April 1918, down the English Channel.
13. At 7 p.m. on 22 May 1918, UC 75 left her base at Brugge, under the command of Walter Schmitz and carrying a crew of thirty-three. Her mission was to lay mines off the Humber and to attack shipping around the Bridlington Bay area. Having delivered his mines, Schmitz then made his way north and cruised around. By studying the situation, he was able to ascertain that convoys could usually be expected off Flamborough Head about two or three o'clock in the morning. This was the sort of valuable information required for a U-boat commander and usually made his voyage of destruction more worthwhile. On 28 May at 3 a.m., Schmitz succeeded in torpedoing the leading steamship in a southbound convoy, but the British escort destroyer HMS *Ouse* sighted him. The U-boat crash-dived, but HMS *Ouse* dropped a series of depth charges around her, leaving the submarine leaking oil and slightly damaged. UC 75 lost the destroyer and her crew were kept busy for almost

Convoys didn't start until June 1918!

two days repairing what damage they could, before commencing their mission again. On 31 May, Schmitz again spotted a convoy about twelve miles south of Flamborough Head and at 1.55 a.m. was making ready for an attack. She was at periscope depth and without realising his dilemma, Schmitz found himself actually in the middle of the convoy. Suddenly the boat was jolted as the British steamship *Blaydonian* accidentally struck, and ran over her. The U-boat commander had believed he was much further away from the nearest ship and it was a blow to his morale and a severe shock to the crew. Her conning tower had been struck, seriously damaging the hatch cover, which allowed considerable volumes of water to penetrate inside of the conning tower. Schmitz then had no alternative, but to blow all tanks and surface, however, before she had time to rise very far, UC 75 was bumped and rammed by two more steamships, the SS *Tronda* and SS *Peter Pan*. By this time the Royal Navy escort ship HMS *Fairy* had been alerted to the situation. *Fairy* was an old 370-ton destroyer built at Fairfield in 1897 and was the senior officer's ship, commanded by Lt G.H. Barnish. The destroyer was seaward, abaft the beam of the rear vessel in the convoy when the alarm was raised by the *Blaydonian*, which was some 274.32m (300yd) off her port bow. *Fairy* raced over to the incident and challenged the submarine as she broke the surface, but there was no reply and after a second challenge went unanswered, the destroyer rammed the submarine's stern end. This action was meant to frighten the crew into surrender, not sink her, just in case she was British, or there were British personnel on board. The sight of a German U-boat surfacing in the midst of an Allied convoy astounded the crew of *Fairy*. However, there was obvious confusion in the U-boat, as some of her crew scrambled onto the deck casing. Then a voice was heard shouting from the conning tower, 'kamerad', in a tone that sounded as if she was surrendering. Unfortunately, other crewmen had also manned her deck-gun and in that same instant fired a shell at the destroyer. Lt Barnish retaliated immediately by firing forty rapid rounds from her 3.63kg gun (8lb) at the enemy boat. At the same time, the old destroyer steamed at full-speed towards the U-boat causing some of the submariners to jump overboard. With a sickening thud, the destroyer's bows crumpled up to almost her bridge, as she ripped into the submarine's casing. The U-boat was split wide open between the conning tower and the deck-gun, as if a giant can opener had been used and she immediately began to sink. Two German seamen leapt from the deck casing onto the destroyer's forecastle and just stood with their hands held high. Twelve other survivors, who had leapt overboard, including Oblt.z.S. W. Schmitz, were picked up from the sea, but nineteen others perished.

Unfortunately HMS *Fairy*, after sending a much larger adversary to the bottom, also succumbed to her damage and she sank within an hour of the second ramming. The crew from *Fairy* and German crews, who had been rescued earlier, were transferred to a trawler and then an hour later, put aboard another destroyer.

Known vessels believed sunk or damaged by SM UC 75 in the North Sea:

VESSEL'S NAME	FLAG	TONS	D	M	YEAR	LOCATION
Industria	GBR	113	25	3	1917	Off Scotland
Marshall	NOR	1123	25	3	1917	17m E of Peterhead
Median	GBR	214	25	3	1917	30m E by S of Aberdeen
Rosslyn	GBR	113	25	3	1917	54m E ½ S of Girdleness
Schaldis	BEL	1241	29	3	1917	6m N of Whitby
HMT *Dirk*	GBR	181	29	5	1918	Off Flamborough Head
HMS *Fairy*	GBR	355	31	5	1918	SE of Flamborough Head (UC 75 sunk)

Bibliography

Lloyd's Register of Shipping, registers 1914-1918.

The First World War, Lloyd's War Losses.

Allen, Ian, *British Warships 1914-1919* (Dittmar & Colledge, 1972).

Cox, C.B., *The Steam Trawlers & Liners of Grimsby* (Copy Concept).

Credland Arthur G., *The Wilson Line* (Tempus Publishing, 2000).

Fawsett, R.S., *Flamborough Lifeboats,* (RNLI Enthusiast's Society, 1973).

Gill, A., *The Lost Trawlers of Hull* (Hutton Press, 1889).

Godfrey, A., *The Scarborough Lifeboats* (Hendon Publishing Co. Ltd, 1975).

Godfrey, A. and Lassey, P., *Dive Yorkshire* (Underwater World Publications Ltd).

Godfrey, A. and Lassey P., *Shipwrecks of the Yorkshire Coast* (Dalesman Publishing Co. Ltd, 1974).

✳ Gray, E.A., *The Killing Time. German U-boats 1914-1918* (Seeley Services Ltd, 1972).

Hocking, Charles, *Dictionary of Disasters at Sea During the Age of Steam, 1824-1962* (F.L.A.).

Kemp, Paul, *U-boats Destroyed* (Arms & Armour).

Keys, Dick and Smith, Ken, *Steamers at the Staithes* —-.

√ Larn, Richard and Bridget, *Shipwreck Index of the British Isles – The East Coast of England* (Lloyd's Register, London).

Moore, Capt. John, R.N., *Jane's Fighting Ships of World War 1* —-.

Morris, Jeff, *History of the Humber Lifeboats* —-.

Morris, Jeff. *The Closed Lifeboat Stations of Lincolnshire* —-.

Morris, Jeff, *The Story of the Filey Lifeboats* —-.

Smith, Ken, *Turbinia* —-.

Spindler, Rear Admiral, *Der Handelskrieg mit U-Booten, 1914-1918* (Mittler & Sohn, 1932-1966).

√ Tennent, A.J., *British Merchant Ships Sunk by U-boats in the 1914-1918 War* (The Starling Press Ltd).

Thompson, M., Newton, D., Robinson, R. and Lofthouse, T., *Cook, Welton & Gemmell, Shipbuilders of Hull & Beverley 1883-1963* (Hutton Press Ltd).

Young, Ron, *The Comprehensive Guide to Shipwrecks of the North East Coast*, Volume 1 (Tempus Publishing Ltd).

Index